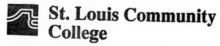

HISTORICAL DICTIONARIES OF RELIGIONS, PHILOSOPHIES, AND MOVEMENTS
Edited by Jon Woronoff

1. *Buddhism,* by Charles S. Prebish, 1993
2. *Mormonism,* by Davis Bitton, 1994
3. *Ecumenical Christianity,* by Ans Joachim van der Bent, 1994
4. *Terrorism,* by Sean Anderson and Stephen Sloan, 1995
5. *Sikhism,* by W.H. McLeod, 1995
6. *Feminism,* by Janet K. Boles and Diane Long Hoeveler, 1995
7. *Olympic Movement,* by Ian Buchanan and Bill Mallon, 1995
8. *Methodism,* by Charles Yrigoyen, Jr. and Susan E. Warrick, 1996
9. *Orthodox Church,* by Michael Prokurat, Alexander Golitzin, and Michael D. Peterson, 1996
10. *Organized Labor,* by James C. Docherty, 1996
11. *Civil Rights Movement,* by Ralph E. Luker, 1997
12. *Catholicism,* by William J. Collinge, 1997

Historical Dictionary of the Civil Rights Movement

Ralph E. Luker

Historical Dictionaries of Religions, Philosophies, and Movements, No. 11

The Scarecrow Press, Inc.
Lanham, Md., & London
1997

SCARECROW PRESS, INC.

Published in the United States of America
by Scarecrow Press, Inc.
4720 Boston Way
Lanham, Maryland 20706

4 Pleydell Gardens, Folkestone
Kent CT20 2DN, England

British Cataloguing-in-Publication Information Available

Library of Congress Cataloging-in-Publication Data

Luker, Ralph.
Historical dictionary of the civil rights movement / Ralph E. Luker.
p. cm.—(Historical dictionaries of religions, philosophies, and movements; no. 11)
Includes bibliographical references.
1. Civil rights movements—United States—History—Dictionaries. 2. Afro-Americans—Civil rights—History—Dictionaries. I. Title. II. Series.
E185.61.L84   1997   323.1'196073—dc20   96-19853   CIP

ISBN 0-8108-3163-5 (cloth : alk.paper)

♾ The paper used in this publication meets the minimum requirements of American National Standard for Information Sciences—Permanence of Paper for Printed Library Materials, ANSI Z39.48–1984.
Manufactured in the United States of America.

Contents

Editor's Foreword

Applying the expression, "movement," as in this case for the civil rights movement, seems to tie up the loose ends and gives us something that is relatively uniform and coherent. That is a mistake in nearly all cases, but particularly here as the author shows. The movement consisted of many individuals of different backgrounds, generations, and views, and many organizations which, while agreeing on some points, disagreed on others. It was also affected by a myriad of social, economic, and political factors and, quite strongly, laws and regulations as well as court decisions. Bringing these variegated aspects together, so that they can be formed into a whole and look more like a movement, was an arduous task.

That task was accomplished with scholarly care but also personal concern in this *Historical Dictionary of the Civil Rights Movement.* It includes entries on many of the leading figures, some of them not adequately acknowledged elsewhere, and also on numerous civil rights organizations. In particular, it provides information on the laws and regulations and the court decisions that formed an essential component of the framework in which the movement had to operate. There is also a helpful chronology showing when various actions occurred in relation to one another and a list of acronyms to more readily recognize the players. The bibliography should prove very useful for newcomers who want to know more or students who wish to research specific aspects or persons.

The author in this case is not just a passive observer; he played his part in the civil rights movement and knows it both from within and without. He has already written extensively on various aspects of the movement and its predecessors, including the book *The Social Gospel in Black and White: American Racial Reform, 1885–1912,* and is known for his work on *The Papers of Martin Luther King.* He has also lectured widely and taught at several colleges. This was an opportunity to pull the many strings together so that there are fewer loose ends in this impressive story.

Jon Woronoff
Series Editor

Preface

I have a friend who lives far from the South now, but who was a student at Duke University with me in the 1960s. When I visit him periodically, there is usually a certain awkwardness in our conversation. Invariably, I feel it when he begins to recollect "our" days together in "the movement." I never point it out to him or his wife, but we spent no time together in the movement, because he never did a thing for it. In retrospect, its cause was so right that one feels obliged to remember having been a part of it, even if you were nowhere to be found at the time. Perhaps that has become the case also with the antiwar movement of the 1960s and the modern feminist movement.

I remember things somewhat differently. During a full year, when we were picketing the segregated movie theaters in Durham, North Carolina, for example, there were many nights when we had scarcely enough people to maintain the picket lines. If all the people who remember having been a part of the movement had only been there at the time, we would have won our point easily. Yet, undoubtedly, some folk were a part of the movement—some of them gave their lives for it—and this book is about such people. There were too many of us to include us all in this book, but there were too few of us to maintain a decent picket line every night.

This book is dedicated to the memory of two men who were my "fathers" in the movement, Floyd B. McKissick and Arthur C. Thomas. I remember Floyd as a fiery young man, who had won a Purple Heart in World War II and returned to North Carolina to fight the battle for racial equality as an attorney in the courts of the land. Art was a charismatic Duke graduate student, who organized the first biracial congregation in Durham and later directed the Delta Ministry for the National Council of Churches. For their courage, which encouraged the rest of us, I am deeply grateful.

Just as more people remember having been a part of the civil rights movement than were there at the time, a look at the bibliography of this book suggests that there are already more books about the movement than it actually generated. The movement captured the nation's attention episodically; it retains it relentlessly. In part, that is because its achievements were both enormous and minimal. De jure racial segregation, an inescapable part of Southern and national life before 1954, is no more; for all too many African Americans, one hardly notices the difference. Conjuring with that apparent incongruity is a task I share with colleagues who study the movement. Among them, I want to thank Phyllis Boanes of Earlham College, whose probing critique helped to sharpen the perspective in my "Introduction."

Many of the problems that we grappled with inadequately in the 1960s remain as a legacy to our children. I am encouraged by the willingness of some of them to take those problems on in good faith. So, just as I thanked my fathers in the movement, Art and Floyd, and my colleague, Phyllis, I must thank my daughter, Amanda, who is now a student at Macalester College. She has been my chief critic and research assistant in developing this book.

Acronyms

ACLU	American Civil Liberties Union
ACMHR	Alabama Christian Movement for Human Rights
ADA	Americans for Democratic Action
AFL-CIO	American Federation of Labor-Congress of Industrial Organizations
BEDC	Black Economic Development Conference
CCCO	Coordinating Council of Community Organizations (Chicago)
CCCV	Chatham County Crusade for Voters (Georgia)
CDGM	Child Development Group of Mississippi
CNAC	Cambridge Nonviolent Action Committee (Maryland)
COFO	Council of Federated Organizations (Mississippi)
CORE	Congress of Racial Equality
CUCRL	Council on United Civil Rights Leadership
DCNA	Durham Committee on Negro Affairs (North Carolina)
DCVL	Dallas County Voters League (Alabama)
DIC	Durham Interim Committee (North Carolina)
EEOC	Equal Employment Opportunity Commission
ESCRU	Episcopal Society for Cultural and Racial Unity
FEPC	Fair Employment Practice Committee
FBI	Federal Bureau of Investigation
FHA	Federal Housing Administration
FOR	Fellowship of Reconciliation
HEW	Department of Health, Education, and Welfare
ICC	Inter-Civic Council (Tallahassee, Florida)
ICC	Interstate Commerce Commission
JCIA	Jefferson County Improvement Association (Alabama)
JDA	Jaybird Democratic Association (Texas)
LCFO	Lowndes County Freedom Organization (Alabama)
LRBW	League of Revolutionary Black Workers
MFDP	Mississippi Freedom Democratic Party

MHDC	Metropolitan Housing Development Corporation
MIA	Montgomery Improvement Association (Alabama)
NAACP	National Association for the Advancement of Colored People
NAACP LDEF	National Association for the Advancement of Colored People Legal Defense and Educational Fund, Inc.
NACW	National Association of Colored Women
NAG	Nonviolent Action Group
NALC	Negro American Labor Council
NCNW	National Council of Negro Women
NWPC	National Women's Political Caucus
PUSH	People United to Save Humanity
RAM	Revolutionary Action Movement
SCEF	Southern Conference Educational Fund
SCLC	Southern Christian Leadership Conference
SCOPE	Summer Community Organization and Political Education
SERS	Southern Educational Reporting Service
SNCC	Student Nonviolent Coordinating Committee
SRC	Southern Regional Council
UNCF	United Negro College Fund
UPAC	Unemployment and Poverty Action Council
VEP	Voter Education Project
WPC	Women's Political Council (Montgomery, Alabama)
YCL	Young Communist League
YMCA	Young Men's Christian Association
YWCA	Young Women's Christian Association

Chronology of the Civil Rights Movement

1941   Lester B. Granger becomes the executive director of the National Urban League.

A. Philip Randolph organizes the March on Washington movement to demand fair employment opportunities for African Americans. (Spring)

In *Mitchell v. United States,* the Supreme Court finds that the segregation laws of Southern states do not apply to interstate transportation. (28 April)

In *Taylor v. Georgia,* the Supreme Court reasserts earlier findings that peonage is unconstitutional.

President Roosevelt signs Executive Order 8802 which establishes the Fair Employment Practice Committee (FEPC). (25 June)

Randolph cancels plans for the March on Washington, which was scheduled for 1 July.

The National Committee to Abolish the Poll Tax is established.

Charles C. Gomillion and others organize the Tuskegee Civic Association in Tuskegee, Alabama.

1942   Members of the Fellowship of Reconciliation in Chicago organize the Congress of Racial Equality (CORE) and hold the first sit-in there.

1943   Race riots in Detroit and Harlem. (June, August)

1944   In *Pollock v. Williams,* the Supreme Court reasserts its position that peonage is unconstitutional.

In *Smith v. Allwright,* the Supreme Court holds that state primary elections are state action, subject to the Fourteenth and

Fifteenth Amendments, and, thus, the "white primary" is unconstitutional. (3 April)

Gunnar Myrdal publishes his massive study of American race relations, *An American Dilemma.*

The Southern Regional Council is organized to address regional issues.

The United Negro College Fund (UNCF) is established.

Adam Clayton Powell is elected to the United States House of Representatives. (November)

1945   In Gary, Indiana, thousands of white students walk out of classes to protest desegregation of city schools.

1946   Malcolm Little (Malcolm X) is arrested and sentenced to prison for burglary in Boston, Massachusetts.

In *Morgan v. Virginia,* the Supreme Court bans segregation in interstate public transportation. (June)

The "Powell Amendment," denying federal funds to any project which discriminates on racial grounds, becomes federal law.

Mary Fair Burks organizes the Women's Political Council in Montgomery, Alabama.

President Harry S Truman's Executive Order 9808 creates the President's Committee on Civil Rights. (5 December)

1947   CORE conducts its Journey of Reconciliation to test compliance with the Supreme Court's *Morgan* decision.

Jackie Robinson joins the Brooklyn Dodgers, breaking the color barrier in major league baseball.

In *Patton v. Mississippi,* the Supreme Court finds the systematic exclusion of African Americans from juries is unconstitutional.

The President's Committee on Civil Rights issues its report, *To Secure These Rights.* (29 October)

1948   In *Sipuel v. Board of Regents of the University of Oklahoma,* the Supreme Court finds that states must provide equal educational opportunity to qualified African American students.

In *Bob-Lo Excursion Company v. Michigan,* the Supreme Court holds that Michigan's antidiscrimination legislation applies to foreign commerce from its shores.

In *Hurd v. Hodge* and *Shelley v. Kraemer*, the Supreme Court finds that the state may not enforce racially restrictive covenants on real estate.

President Truman's Executive Order 9980 establishes a Fair Employment Practice Commission under the Civil Service Commission, which promotes fair hiring and treatment of African Americans in civil service positions. (26 July)

President Truman's Executive Order 9981 directs the armed services to desegregate and appoints the Fahy Committee to monitor equality of opportunity and treatment for service men and women. (26 July)

W. E. B. Du Bois is expelled from the National Association for the Advancement of Colored People (NAACP) for allegedly pro-Communist sympathies.

In a four way contest, President Truman is reelected. (November)

1949   Congressman William Dawson of Illinois becomes the first African American to chair a standing committee of the United States House of Representatives.

WERD, the first radio station owned by African Americans, begins broadcasting in Atlanta, Georgia.

Roy Wilkins assumes much of Walter White's responsibility for the NAACP.

1950   President Truman's Fahy Committee issues its final report, *Freedom to Serve.*

In *Henderson v. U.S. Interstate Commerce Commission and Southern Railway,* the Supreme Court finds that separate dining facilities for African Americans on railroad cars in interstate travel violates equal access requirements of the Interstate Commerce Act. (5 June)

In *McLaurin v. Oklahoma State Regents,* the Supreme Court bars classroom and social segregation at the University of Oklahoma. (5 June)

In *Sweatt v. Painter,* the Supreme Court holds that separate and unequal schools for racial minorities are in violation of the Fourteenth Amendment's equal protection provisions. (5 June)

Gwendolyn Brooks is awarded the Pulitzer Prize for poetry. She is the first African American to receive the award.

Ralph J. Bunche is awarded the Nobel Peace Prize. He is the first African American to receive the award. (11 December)

1951 Governor Adlai Stevenson orders the Illinois National Guard to suppress the rioting of 4,000 white people who protest the effort of a black family to move into Cicero, Illinois.

The Ku Klux Klan is suspected of setting off a bomb in the home of Florida civil rights leaders Harry and Harriette Moore, killing them both. (25 December)

1952 Ralph Ellison publishes *Invisible Man* and wins the National Book Award.

Malcolm Little is paroled from prison and changes his name to Malcolm X.

Tuskegee Institute's Department of Records and Research reports that 1952 is the first year in 71 years of research that there are no lynchings in the United States.

1953 In *Terry v. Adams,* the Supreme Court finds that political parties are not "private clubs" and may not be interpreted as such in order to deny African Americans the right to vote.

In *District of Columbia v. John R. Thompson Company,* the Supreme Court upholds Washington, D.C.'s antidiscrimination statutes and bans segregation in Washington restaurants. (8 June)

African Americans in Baton Rouge, Louisiana, boycott the city's buses and win a less oppressive form of segregation on them. (18–25 June)

Joseph H. Jackson is elected president of the National Baptist Convention. (September)

1954 In *Bolling v. Sharpe, Briggs v. Elliott, Davis v. County School Board of Prince Edward County, Virginia,* and *Brown v. Board of Education,* the Supreme Court finds racially segregated public schools for African Americans are inherently unequal and the practice of public school segregation is, thus, unconstitutional. (17 May)

Malcolm X becomes the minister of New York's Muslim Temple, No. 7. (June)

The white "Citizens Council" is organized at Indianola, Mississippi, to mobilize white opposition to desegregation. (11 July)

Medgar W. Evers becomes NAACP field secretary for Mississippi.

Martin Luther King moves to Montgomery, Alabama, to become the pastor of Dexter Avenue Baptist Church. (1 September)

Baltimore, Maryland, and Washington, D.C., begin massive desegregation of their public schools in a first wave of compliance with the *Brown* decision. (September)

1955   Following the death of Walter White, Roy Wilkins becomes the executive secretary of the NAACP. (April)

In *Brown v. Board of Education, II,* the Supreme Court calls for desegregation of the public schools with "all deliberate speed." (31 May)

In *Flemming v. South Carolina Electric and Gas Company,* the Fourth Circuit Court of Appeals declares segregation in interstate bus transportation is unconstitutional. (15 July)

President Eisenhower nominates John Robert Brown and Elbert P. Tuttle to the Fifth Circuit Court of Appeals.

The Georgia Board of Education adopts a resolution that would revoke the license of any teacher who teaches an integrated class or belongs to the NAACP. (1 August)

Emmett Louis Till, a 14-year-old black youth, is kidnapped and murdered in Mississippi. (28 August)

In *Lucy v. Adams,* the Supreme Court orders the University of Alabama to admit Autherine Lucy to its student body. (10 October)

In *Keys v. Carolina Coach Company* and *NAACP v. St. Louis–San Francisco Railway Company,* the Interstate Commerce Commission finds that racially segregated buses, trains and waiting rooms for interstate passengers violate the Interstate Commerce Act. (November)

In *Holmes v. Atlanta,* the Supreme Court extends the logic of its decision in *Brown v. Board of Education* to prohibit segregation in public recreational facilities. (7 November)

Rosa Parks is arrested for refusing to surrender her seat on a bus in Montgomery, Alabama. The black community organizes the Montgomery Improvement Association to direct its boycott of the buses and chooses Martin Luther King as its president. (1–5 December)

Georgia governor Marvin Griffin bars Georgia Tech from playing in the Sugar Bowl because its opponent, the University of Pittsburgh, has a black player.

1956   Autherine Lucy becomes the first African American student at the University of Alabama, but she is expelled after rioting takes place in the community. (January)

Martin Luther King's home in Montgomery, Alabama, is bombed. (30 January)

The "Southern Manifesto" is signed by 19 United States Senators and 77 Congressmen, who urge resistance to the implementation of the Supreme Court's decision in *Brown v. Board of Education.* (11 March)

South Carolina requires black public employees to sign an oath that they are not members of the NAACP. Students at South Carolina State College in Orangeburg boycott classes in protest. (April)

In *South Carolina Electric and Gas Company v. Fleming,* the Supreme Court finds racial segregation on South Carolina buses is unconstitutional. (23 April)

African Americans in Tallahassee, Florida, boycott the city buses. (27 May–June)

Alabama bans the NAACP from operating in the state; Fred Shuttlesworth and others organize the Alabama Christian Movement for Human Rights. (1–5 June)

Dorothy Height becomes president of the National Council of Negro Women.

In *Gayle v. Browder,* the Supreme Court finds racial segregation on Montgomery, Alabama, buses is unconstitutional and they are desegregated. (13 November–21 December)

Fred Shuttlesworth's home in Birmingham, Alabama, is bombed and he is arrested for defying segregation on the city buses. (25–26 December)

1957 Martin Luther King, Ralph Abernathy, Joseph Lowery, Fred Shuttlesworth, and others organize the Southern Christian Leadership Conference. (10–11 January)

Ralph Bunche, Martin Luther King, Adam Clayton Powell, A. Philip Randolph, and others visit Ghana to attend independence celebration. (March)

Malcolm X leads 2,000 followers to Harlem precinct station to demand medical attention for Johnson Hinton. (April)

The NAACP, SCLC, and other organizations hold the Prayer Pilgrimage to Washington, which draws 25,000 people to the steps of the Lincoln Memorial on the third anniversary of the *Brown* decision. (17 May)

African Americans in Tuskegee, Alabama, begin an economic boycott of white merchants in protest of racial discrimination in the city.

Dorothy Height becomes the president of the National Council of Negro Women.

President Eisenhower nominates John Minor Wisdom to the Fifth Circuit Court of Appeals.

Congress passes and President Eisenhower signs the Civil Rights Act of 1957, which establishes the United States Civil Rights Commission and includes new guarantees of voting rights. (9 September)

President Eisenhower sends federal troops to provide security for African American students who are enrolled in Little Rock, Arkansas's Central High School. (24 September)

1958 Ella Baker organizes SCLC's office in Atlanta, Georgia. (January)

In *NAACP v. Alabama ex rel. Patterson, Attorney General,* the Supreme Court reverses its precedent in *Bryant v. Zimmerman* to find a state law requiring an organization to reveal its membership list is unconstitutional.

James Lawson begins theological studies at Vanderbilt University in Nashville, Tennessee. (March)

Clennon King attempts to desegregate the University of Mississippi and is committed to a state mental institution. (June)

In *Cooper v. Aaron,* the Supreme Court holds that school boards may not avoid desegregation by citing the potential for mob violence. (12 September)

Martin Luther King publishes *Stride toward Freedom.* The Reverend J. H. Jackson blocks its sale at the National Baptist Convention; a deranged black woman stabs King while he is autographing copies of it. (September–October)

About 11,000 people participate in the Youth March for Integrated Schools in Washington, D.C. (25 October)

A bus boycott in Birmingham, Alabama, fails to desegregate the city buses. (November–December)

Louis Lomax and Mike Wallace produce an ABC television documentary, "The Hate that Hate Produced," which is the first national attention to Malcolm X and the Nation of Islam.

1959   Wyatt Tee Walker leads 2,000 marchers on a "Pilgrimage for Integrated Education" in Richmond, Virginia. (1 January)

Martin Luther King visits India and meets with its prime minister, Jawaharlal Nehru. (February–March)

About 26,000 people participate in a Youth March for Integrated Schools in Washington, D.C. (18 April)

Malcolm X visits Ghana, Nigeria, Saudi Arabia, the Sudan, and Egypt, where he meets with its president, Gamal Abdel Nasser.

Tennessee State Police raid Highlander Folk School. (31 July)

Robert F. Williams organizes members of the Monroe, North Carolina, branch of the NAACP into a gun club for self-defense.

1960   Martin Luther King moves to Atlanta to become copastor of Ebenezer Baptist Church and be close to SCLC headquarters in the city. (January)

Greensboro, North Carolina, college students launch the sit-in movement. It spreads through North Carolina to Virginia, Maryland, South Carolina, Tennessee, Georgia, Florida, Louisiana, and Texas. (February–March)

In *Gomillion v. Lightfoot,* the Supreme Court rejects the redrawing of Tuskegee, Alabama, city lines to exclude black voters.

James Lawson is expelled from Vanderbilt University for his role in sit-in demonstrations in Nashville, Tennessee. (3 March)

San Antonio, Texas, is the first major Southern city to desegregate its lunch counters. (19 March)

The Student Nonviolent Coordinating Committee (SNCC) is organized at Shaw University in Raleigh, North Carolina. Marion Barry is its first chairman. (15–17 April)

Congress passes and President Eisenhower signs the Civil Rights Act of 1960. (21 April)

The home of NAACP attorney Z. Alexander Looby in Nashville, Tennessee, is bombed. Several people are injured and nearby buildings are damaged. (April)

Federal district judge J. Skelly Wright orders New Orleans' public schools to desegregate in September. (May)

A. Philip Randolph organizes the Negro American Labor Council. (May)

Aaron Henry becomes president of the Mississippi conference of branches of the NAACP.

Wyatt Tee Walker becomes the executive director of SCLC. (August)

Charles McDew replaces Marion Barry as chairman of SNCC. (October)

Martin Luther King and others are arrested in a sit-in at Rich's Department Store in Atlanta. King is sent to the Reidsville, Georgia, State Prison. Robert Kennedy intercedes to win his release. (October)

Martin Luther King, Sr., endorses John F. Kennedy for president and Kennedy defeats Richard M. Nixon in a very close race. (November)

In *Boynton v. Virginia,* the Supreme Court finds segregation in bus and railroad terminals violates the Interstate Commerce Act. (5 December)

1961 The University of Georgia admits Hamilton Holt and Charlayne Hunter, its first African American students. (January)

In *Burton v. Wilmington Parking Authority,* the Supreme Court holds that businesses that rent facilities from the state must not discriminate against its citizens.

Adam Clayton Powell becomes chairman of the House of Representatives' Education and Labor Committee.

James Forman becomes SNCC's first executive secretary.

Tougaloo College students launch nonviolent civil rights demonstrations in Jackson, Mississippi. (March)

President Kennedy signs Executive Order 10925 establishing the Equal Employment Opportunity Commission. (6 March)

The Freedom Riders test the compliance of interstate buses and terminal facilities with the Supreme Court's *Boynton* decision. (May)

Charged with kidnapping a white couple in Monroe, North Carolina, Robert F. Williams flees from the United States to Cuba.

Whitney M. Young, Jr., succeeds Lester B. Granger as executive secretary of the Urban League. (August)

Four Atlanta, Georgia, high schools are desegregated. (September)

President Kennedy appoints Thurgood Marshall to the Second Circuit Court of Appeals. (23 September)

Herbert Lee is murdered by state representative E. H. Hurst in Amite County, Mississippi. (28 September)

The Interstate Commerce Commission rules that racial segregation in interstate bus terminals is illegal. (1 November)

The Albany, Georgia, Movement is organized and launches a broadscale attack on racial discrimination in the city. (November–December)

1962   Backed by the Kennedy administration and Northern founda-
        tions, the Voter Education Project begins to finance the voter
        registration efforts of major civil rights organizations. (January)

        Aaron Henry, Robert Moses, and others reorganize the Council
        of Federated Organizations (COFO) in Mississippi. (February)

        The Federal Bureau of Investigation begins surveillance of
        SCLC for Communist influence. (March)

        In *Baker v. Carr*, the Supreme Court finds that states must
        reapportion legislative districts equitably, so that no citizen's
        vote weighs more heavily than that of another.

        CORE's "Freedom Highways" campaign in North Carolina
        aims at desegregation of hotels, motels and restaurants. (Sum-
        mer 1962–Summer 1963)

        The Supreme Court orders the admission of James Meredith
        to the University of Mississippi, leading to the most violent
        campus riot of the decade. (October)

        Leroy Johnson is elected to the Georgia state senate, becoming
        the state's first black legislator in the twentieth century. (Nov-
        ember)

        Edward Brooke is elected attorney general of Massachusetts.
        (November)

        President Kennedy issues Executive Order 11063, which struck
        at racial discrimination in housing. (20 November)

1963   In *Edwards v. South Carolina*, the Supreme Court sustains the
        civil rights of demonstrators to peaceful assembly, free speech
        and petition.

        In *Goss v. Board of Education of Knoxville*, the Supreme Court
        finds a system of "voluntary student transfers," allowing white
        students to transfer out of desegregated schools, is uncon-
        stitutional.

        In *Johnson v. Virginia*, the Supreme Court reverses the contempt
        of court conviction of an African American who disobeyed a
        judge's order to sit in a black section of the courtroom. (April)

        John Lewis replaces Charles McDew as SNCC's chairman.

In Birmingham, Alabama, sit-ins, civil rights marches, protests, arrests, bombings, and riots focus the nation's attention on racial discrimination in the South. Martin Luther King publishes his "Letter from Birmingham Jail." (April–May)

In Cambridge, Maryland, civil rights demonstrations lead to riot and martial law. (April–July)

An economic boycott and nonviolent civil rights demonstrations begin in Jackson, Mississippi. (28 May)

In Greensboro, North Carolina, Jesse Jackson is among 278 CORE demonstrators who are arrested in civil rights demonstrations. (June)

Hosea Williams's Chatham County Crusade for Voters mounts massive demonstrations in Savannah, Georgia. (June–July)

Governor George Wallace unsuccessfully tries to block the admission of two African Americans, James Hood and Vivian Malone, to the University of Alabama. (11 June)

Medgar W. Evers is assassinated in Jackson, Mississippi. (12 June)

President Kennedy and Attorney General Robert Kennedy pressure Martin Luther King to dismiss Jack O'Dell from the SCLC staff. After stalling, he does so. (22 June–3 July)

President Kennedy signs Executive Order 11114, which extends guarantees against employment discrimination to federally assisted construction contracts. (23 June)

Fannie Lou Hamer and others are arrested, jailed and beaten in Winona, Mississippi. (August)

The March on Washington for Jobs and Freedom draws 250,000 people to the Lincoln Memorial in Washington, D.C., where Martin Luther King delivers his "I Have a Dream" speech. (28 August)

Four Sunday school children die in the bombing of Sixteenth Street Baptist Church in Birmingham, Alabama. (15 September)

James Baldwin publishes *The Fire Next Time.*

President Kennedy is assassinated. (22 November)

Malcolm X refers to the assassination as an example of "chickens coming home to roost"; Elijah Muhammad suspends him as minister of the Harlem Mosque and silences him.

1964 President Johnson declares a War on Poverty and wins congressional approval of the Economic Opportunity Act, which establishes the Head Start program for preschool children, Upward Bound for high school students, and the college work-study financial aid program.

Malcolm X resigns from the Nation of Islam. (12 March)

SCLC organizes demonstrations in St. Augustine, Florida. (March–June)

In *Griffin v. Prince Edward County School Board,* the Supreme Court holds that school boards may not close public schools to avoid desegregation.

The Twenty-Fourth Amendment to the Constitution, barring the poll tax, is ratified.

Alabama governor George Wallace enters Democratic presidential primaries in Maryland, Wisconsin and Indiana. (Spring)

Malcolm X makes a pilgrimage to Mecca, takes the name El Hajj Malik El-Shabazz, founds the Organization of Afro-American Unity, and warns that a growing black nationalism will no longer accept white patronage. (April–June)

At the beginning of Freedom Summer in Mississippi, three young civil rights workers, James Earl Chaney, Andrew Goodman, and Michael Schwerner, are murdered near Philadelphia, Mississippi. (21 June)

Andrew Young replaces Wyatt Walker as executive director of SCLC. (July)

President Johnson wins congressional approval of and signs the Civil Rights Act of 1964, which bars racial discrimination in public accommodations, strengthens guarantees of the right to vote, and establishes the Equal Employment Opportunity Commission. (2 July)

Race riots occur in Harlem and Brooklyn. (18–26 July)

The Democratic National Convention refuses to seat the Mississippi Freedom Democratic Party delegation. (22–27 July)

Constance Baker Motley is the first African American woman elected to the New York state senate. (November)

The Federal Bureau of Investigation escalates its campaign to destroy the credibility of Martin Luther King. (November)

Martin Luther King receives the Nobel Peace Prize. (10 December)

In *Heart of Atlanta Motel v. United States,* the Supreme Court finds that the federal government may require hotels to admit African Americans under the public accommodations clause of the Civil Rights Act of 1964. (14 December)

1965 Faced with a court order to do so, Lester Maddox closes his Atlanta restaurant, The Pickrick, rather than serve African American customers. (February)

The home of Malcolm X is firebombed in New York. (14 February)

Malcolm X is assassinated in a New York hotel. (21 February)

SCLC's campaign for voting rights culminates in the Selma to Montgomery March. The campaign is marred by the murders of Jimmy Lee Jackson, Viola Liuzzo and the Reverend James Reeb. (February–March)

President Johnson nominates Thurgood Marshall to be solicitor general of the United States. (June)

SCLC's Summer Community Organization and Political Education Program (SCOPE) attempts to register black voters in 50 counties in the Deep South. (June–August)

Race riots occur in Chicago and Los Angeles, where rioting in Watts is more destructive than any previous race riot. (July–August)

President Johnson wins congressional approval of and signs the Voting Rights Act of 1965. (6 August)

Jonathan Daniels is murdered at Hayneville, Lowndes County, Alabama. (20 August)

President Johnson signs Executive Order 11246 authorizing federal agencies to enforce the Civil Rights Act of 1964. (24 September)

Alex Haley publishes *The Autobiography of Malcolm X.*

Constance Baker Motley is elected president of the Borough of Manhattan. (November)

1966 Martin Luther King and the Southern Christian Leadership Conference join the Chicago, Illinois, Movement. (January)

Floyd McKissick succeeds James Farmer as the national chairman of CORE and moves it in a nationalist direction. (3 January)

Sammy Younge, Jr., is murdered in Tuskegee, Alabama. (3 January)

SNCC becomes the first major civil rights organization to oppose the United States' role in the Vietnam War. (6 January)

Because of his opposition to the war, the Georgia legislature bars Julian Bond from taking a seat in the body; the decision is later overturned by the courts. (10 January)

Vernon Dahmer is murdered in his home by Klansmen in Vicksburg, Mississippi. (10 January)

As secretary of housing and urban development, Robert C. Weaver becomes the first African American to serve in a presidential cabinet.

In *Miranda v. Arizona,* the Supreme Court holds that statements obtained by police interrogation from suspects uninformed of their rights to counsel or to be silent or of the possible use of their statements as evidence are inadmissible as evidence.

Stokely Carmichael succeeds John Lewis as chairman of SNCC and popularizes the call for "Black Power." Ruby Doris Smith-Robinson succeeds James Forman as executive secretary of SNCC. (May)

The White House Conference "To Fulfill These Rights" meets in Washington, D.C. (1–2 June)

James Meredith is shot on his march from Memphis, Tennessee, to Jackson, Mississippi. Carmichael, King, McKissick, and others continue the march to Jackson. (5–26 June)

Martin Luther King leads civil rights demonstrations in Chicago. (July–August)

Race riots occur in Chicago, Cleveland, New York, and elsewhere. (July)

Lester Maddox wins the Democratic Party's nomination for and is subsequently elected governor of Georgia. (27 September–November)

Huey Newton and Bobby Seale organize the Black Panther Party in Oakland, California. (October)

The Lowndes County, Alabama, Freedom Organization mounts campaigns for local offices. (November)

Dorothy Brown, Grace Hamilton, and Barbara Jordan are elected to the Tennessee, Georgia, and Texas state legislatures. (November)

Edward W. Brooke of Massachusetts is the first African American elected to the United States Senate since the end of Reconstruction. (November)

1967   Martin Luther King announces his opposition to the war in Vietnam. (25 February)

The House of Representatives refuses to seat Adam Clayton Powell because of allegations of the misuse of government funds, but he is reelected by his constituents. (March–April)

Eldridge Cleaver becomes the editor of *The Black Panther.* (April)

H. Rap Brown succeeds Stokely Carmichael as chairman of the SNCC. (May)

Mississippi National Guardsmen fire on African American college students at Jackson State College, killing Ben Brown. (11 May)

In *Reitman v. Mulkey,* the Supreme Court finds a California constitutional amendment preventing the state from interfering with private discrimination in real estate is unconstitutional. (29 May)

In *Loving v. Virginia,* the Supreme Court finds state laws against interracial marriages are unconstitutional. (12 June)

President Johnson nominates Thurgood Marshall to the United States Supreme Court. When confirmed, he becomes the first African American to serve on the Court. (July)

Race riots occur in Cambridge, Maryland, Chicago, Detroit, Newark and elsewhere. (July)

President Johnson appoints the National Commission on Civil Disorders (the Kerner Commission). (27 July)

Roy Innis succeeds Floyd McKissick as national director of CORE. (September)

Huey Newton is arrested for the murder of a policeman in Oakland, California. (October)

Floyd McCree, Richard G. Hatcher, and Carl B. Stokes are elected mayors of Flint, Michigan, Gary, Indiana, and Cleveland, Ohio. (November)

Walter Washington is appointed mayor of Washington, D.C.

1968   In *Green v. New Kent County School Board, Virginia,* the Supreme Court rejects "freedom of choice" school attendance plans as unconstitutional.

In *Jones v. Alfred H. Mayer Co.,* the Supreme Court bars private discrimination in the sale or rent of housing.

The Black Panther Party and SNCC announce their merger. (February)

In a confrontation with South Carolina state police, three South Carolina State College students are killed and dozens are injured at Orangeburg. (8 February)

The National Commission on Civil Disorders publishes its final report, which concludes that the nation "is moving toward two separate societies, one black, one white—separate and unequal." (1 March)

Martin Luther King is assassinated in Memphis, Tennessee. (4 April)

After King's assassination, there are 39 deaths and 14,000 arrests in race riots in Baltimore, Chicago, Kansas City, Washington, and other cities. (5–9 April)

President Johnson wins congressional approval of and signs the Civil Rights Act of 1968, with its open housing provisions. (11 April)

As King's successor as president of SCLC, Ralph Abernathy leads the Poor People's March on Washington. (May–June)

Huey Newton is convicted of manslaughter and sent to prison for the killing of a policeman. (July)

A biracial delegation led by Aaron Henry unseats the regular Mississippi delegation to the Democratic National Convention. The names of the Reverend Channing Phillips and Julian Bond are submitted for the Democratic Party's nominations for president and vice president.

In a three way contest, Republican Richard Nixon defeats Democrat Hubert Humphrey and the American Independent Party's George Wallace for president. (November)

Shirley Chisholm defeats James Farmer in a congressional race and becomes the first African American woman elected to the United States Congress. (November)

Adam Clayton Powell is reelected by his Harlem constituents. The House of Representatives agrees to allow him to take his seat, but he refuses to do so when he is stripped of 22 years of seniority. (November)

1969   In Chicago, police kill Black Panthers Mark Clark and Fred Hampton. In New Haven, Black Panther Alex Rackley is burned to death, allegedly for disloyalty. Bobby Seale is arrested for his murder. In California, Black Panthers and members of Ron Karenga's US organization have armed confrontations.

President Richard Nixon establishes the Office of Minority Business Enterprise.

James Farmer is appointed assistant secretary of health, welfare and education in the Nixon administration.

James Forman leads his followers from SNCC into a merger with the League of Revolutionary Black Workers to form the Black Economic Development Conference. (April)

President Nixon signs Executive Order 11478 which requires equal opportunity and affirmative action programs of all federal agencies. (8 August)

In *Alexander v. Holmes,* the Supreme Court modifies its 1955

Brown decision by ordering public school systems to desegregate "at once." (29 October)

Charles Evers and Howard Lee are elected mayors of Fayetteville, Mississippi, and Chapel Hill, North Carolina.

1970   Jesse Jackson leaves the Southern Christian Leadership Conference to found People United to Save Humanity (PUSH).

Coretta Scott King founds the Martin Luther King Center in Atlanta.

Sought on charges of conspiracy, kidnapping, and murder, Angela Davis is placed on the FBI's Ten Most Wanted List, captured, and put in prison without bail.

Police fire on students who were protesting at Jackson State University in Mississippi; two students are killed and twelve are wounded.

C. B. King is the first African American to run for governor of Georgia in the twentieth century.

Kenneth Gibson is elected mayor of Newark, New Jersey, becoming the first black mayor of a major American city.

Charles Rangel, George W. Collins, Ralph H. Metcalfe, and Ronald V. Dellums are elected to the House of Representatives from New York, Illinois and California. (November)

1971   The Congressional Black Caucus is organized. Charles C. Diggs of Detroit is its first chairman. (January)

In *Griggs v. Duke Power Company,* the Supreme Court finds that tests that discriminate on a racial basis when given to workers are unconstitutional. (8 March)

In *Griffin v. Prince Edward School Board,* the Supreme Court finds the school board's action to close its public schools is unconstitutional.

In three cases, *Moore v. Charlotte-Mecklenburg Board of Education, North Carolina State Board of Education v. Swann,* and *Swann v. Charlotte-Mecklenburg Board of Education,* the Supreme Court finds that school busing to achieve desegregation is constitutional. (20 April)

Jesse Jackson runs against Richard J. Daley for mayor of Chicago.

Shirley Chisholm, Fannie Lou Hamer, and Dorothy Height are among the founding members of the National Women's Political Caucus. (July)

Parren J. Mitchell is elected to the House of Representatives from Baltimore; Walter Fauntroy is elected as a nonvoting delegate from the District of Columbia. (November)

1972   Congress passes and President Nixon signs the Equal Employment Opportunity Act. (8 March)

President Nixon appoints Benjamin Hooks to the Federal Communications Commission.

Vernon Jordan becomes executive director of the Urban League.

Shirley Chisholm is a candidate for the Democratic presidential nomination.

Charles Evers is a candidate for governor of Mississippi.

While campaigning for president, Alabama governor George Wallace is shot and wounded in Laurel, Maryland.

The Negro American Labor Council is reorganized as the Coalition of Black Trade Unionists. (23–24 September)

Yvonne Braithwaite Burke, Barbara Jordan, and Andrew Young are elected to Congress from California, Texas and Georgia. (November)

1973   In *Keyes v. School District No. 1, Denver, Colorado,* the Supreme Court finds that school boards complying with desegregation orders are not obliged to abolish segregation based on housing patterns or other factors.

Marian Wright Edelman organizes the Children's Defense Fund. (June)

Bernice Johnson Reagon organizes Sweet Honey in the Rock, an a cappella singing group of African American women.

Bobby Seale wins 43,000 votes in a race for mayor of Oakland, California.

Thomas Bradley and Maynard Jackson are the first African Americans elected mayors of Los Angeles and Atlanta.

1974   In *Milliken v. Bradley, I,* the Supreme Court holds that unless schools had been segregated by law, courts could not require them to abolish de facto segregation.

1975   William T. Coleman is appointed secretary of transportation.

Wallace D. Muhammad succeeds his father, Elijah Muhammad, as leader of the Nation of Islam, reshapes it in the direction of traditional Islam, and renames it the World Community of Islam.

Mervyn Dymally becomes the lieutenant governor of California.

1976   Alex Haley's *Roots: The Saga of an American Family* is published, becomes a best-seller and wins a Pulitzer Prize.

Pauli Murray, the first black female priest in the Episcopal Church, is ordained.

Unita Blackwell, who first sought to register to vote during Freedom Summer and was a Freedom Democratic Party delegate to the Democratic National Convention in 1964, is elected mayor of Mayersville, Mississippi.

Barbara Jordan is the keynote speaker at the Democratic National Convention.

With ninety percent of the African American vote, Jimmy Carter is elected president of the United States. (November)

1977   Alex Haley's *Roots* is seen by an audience estimated at 130,000,000 as a television miniseries in eight installments. (23–30 January)

In the Carter administration, Clifford Alexander serves as secretary of the army, Mary Francis Berry as assistant secretary of education, Patricia Roberts Harris as secretary of housing and urban development, Louis Martin as special assistant to the president, Andrew Young as ambassador to the United Nations, and Eleanor Holmes Norton chairs the Equal Employment Opportunity Commission.

Benjamin Hooks succeeds Roy Wilkins as executive director of the NAACP. (August)

Louis Farrakhan defects from Wallace D. Muhammad's World Community of Islam to lead a group of members of the Nation of Islam in the tradition of Elijah Muhammad.

When Ralph Abernathy resigns as president of SCLC to run for Congress, Joseph E. Lowery becomes his successor.

Ernest N. Morial is the first African American elected mayor of New Orleans.

1978   In *University of California Regents v. Bakke,* the Supreme Court narrowly rejects the use of racial quotas in educational institutions as reverse discrimination.

The House Select Committee on Assassinations reopens the investigation of Martin Luther King's assassination.

After 148 years, the Church of Jesus Christ of Latter-Day Saints (Mormons) reverses a policy that excludes black men from the priesthood. (9 June)

1979   In *United Steelworkers of America v. Weber,* the Supreme Court finds that racial quotas and timetables are constitutional.

Franklin A. Thomas becomes president of the Ford Foundation.

William H. Gray III is elected to the House of Representatives from Philadelphia. (November)

1980   In *Fullilove v. Klutznick,* the Supreme Court finds that Congress may enact laws requiring racial quotas to correct past discrimination.

In *City of Mobile v. Bolden,* the Supreme Court holds that, without proof of intentional racial discrimination, municipal at-large elections are constitutional. (22 April)

Vernon Jordan is near-fatally wounded by a gunshot fired by a white supremacist in Fort Wayne, Indiana. (29 May)

Ralph D. Abernathy and Hosea Williams endorse Republican Ronald Reagan who is elected president of the United States. (November)

Angela Davis runs for vice president of the United States on the Communist Party ticket. (November)

1981   Clarence Pendleton serves as chairman of the United States Civil Rights Commission and Samuel Pierce, Jr., serves as secretary of housing and urban development in the Reagan administration.

Morehouse School of Medicine is founded in Atlanta, Georgia.

Jewell Jackson McCabe founds the National Council of 100 Black Women.

Andrew Young is elected mayor of Atlanta, Georgia.

1982   John Jacob succeeds Vernon Jordan as executive director of the Urban League.

The Voting Rights Act of 1965 is renewed for another twenty-five years.

T. J. Jemison succeeds Joseph H. Jackson as president of the National Baptist Convention. (September)

1983   In *Bob Jones University v. United States,* the Supreme Court holds that the Internal Revenue Service may withhold tax-exempt status from a private, sectarian institution that racially discriminates.

Alice Walker wins the Pulitzer Prize for *The Color Purple*.

Harold Washington is the first African American elected mayor of Chicago.

1984   Robert N. C. Nix, Jr., is inaugurated as chief justice of the Pennsylvania supreme court, the first African American to be chief justice of a state supreme court.

Leontine T. C. Kelly is elected a bishop of the United Methodist Church, the first African American woman to become a bishop of a major religious denomination.

W. Wilson Goode becomes the first African American mayor of Philadelphia.

Jesse Jackson seeks the Democratic Party's nomination for president.

Mary Francis Berry, Walter Fauntroy, and Randall Robinson launch a sit-in protest movement at the South African embassy in Washington, D.C.

1985   Philadelphia mayor W. Wilson Goode authorizes police assault on the residence of members of a black radical group, MOVE. When police bomb the house, 11 of its members, including four children, are killed.

William H. Gray III becomes chairman of the House Budget Committee.

Reuben V. Anderson becomes the first African American appointed to the Mississippi supreme court.

L. Douglas Wilder is elected lieutenant governor of Virginia. (November)

1986   The birthday of Martin Luther King, Jr., becomes a national holiday.

One black man is killed and two are injured by a mob of white youths in Howard Beach, a white section of Queens, New York.

Criticized for her plans to meet with President P. W. Botha and Zulu Chief Mangosuthu Buthelezi in South Africa, Coretta Scott King cancels the meeting and meets with Winnie Mandela of the African National Congress instead.

After defeating Julian Bond in a Democratic primary for the House of Representatives, John Lewis is elected to Congress from Atlanta. (November)

Sidney Barthelemy succeeds Ernest Morial as mayor of New Orleans.

1987   Johnetta B. Cole and Niara Sadarkasa become the first black women presidents of Spelman College and Lincoln University.

Carrie Saxon Perry and Kurt Schmoke are elected mayors of New Haven, Connecticut, and Baltimore, Maryland.

Mike Espy and Kweisi Mfume are elected to Congress from Mississippi and Maryland. (November)

1988   Eugene Marino becomes archbishop of Atlanta, the first black archbishop of the Roman Catholic Church in the United States.

Jesse Jackson seeks the Democratic Party's nomination for president.

Toni Morrison wins the Pulitzer Prize for *Beloved.*

Mississippi Burning, a film about the civil rights movement in Mississippi, is criticized for celebrating FBI agents, rather than local African Americans.

James Bevel is nominated for vice president by Lyndon La Rouche's U.S. Labor Party. (November)

1989   Barbara Harris becomes the first woman consecrated a bishop in the Episcopal Church.

President George Bush names General Colin Powell as chairman of the Joint Chiefs of Staff and Louis Sullivan as secretary of health and human services.

William H. Gray III becomes Democratic majority whip in the House of Representatives.

James Meredith joins the staff of Senator Jesse Helms of North Carolina.

Ronald H. Brown, former campaign manager for Jesse Jackson, becomes the first African American to chair the Democratic National Committee.

L. Douglas Wilder is elected governor of Virginia, the first African American to serve as governor of a state by popular vote. (November)

David Dinkins is the first African American elected mayor of New York City. (November)

1990   South Africa's Nelson Mandela is released from prison and makes a five-day tour of the United States, meeting with President Bush, Jacqueline Kennedy Onassis, and Randall Robinson.

President Bush names Arthur Fletcher as chair of the United States Civil Rights Commission.

Mayor Marion Barry of Washington, D.C., is arrested, convicted, and sentenced to prison for purchasing and smoking crack cocaine. Sharon Pratt Kelly is elected as his successor.

Ralph Abernathy's autobiography, *And the Walls Came Tumbling Down,* draws severe criticism from black leaders for its allegations of Martin Luther King's marital infidelity.

Harvey Gantt and Theo Mitchell win the Democratic Party's nominations for senator from North Carolina and governor of South Carolina, but lose the general elections to Republicans Jesse Helms and Carroll Campbell. (November)

Maxine Waters and Gary Franks are elected to Congress from California and Connecticut. Franks is the first black Republican in the House of Representatives in 56 years and the first African

American to be elected from a predominantly white district. Eleanor Holmes Norton is elected as the delegate from the District of Columbia. (November)

1991   Thurgood Marshall announces his retirement from the Supreme Court. (27 June)

President Bush nominates Clarence Thomas to succeed Thurgood Marshall on the Supreme Court.

William H. Gray III becomes president of the United Negro College Fund.

Emmanuel Cleaver and Wellington Webb are elected mayors of Kansas City, Missouri, and Denver, Colorado.

The Civil Rights Act of 1991 is passed and signed by President Bush. (21 November)

1992   The acquittal of Los Angeles police officers charged in the beating of Rodney King leads to a massive riot in which there is $1 billion in property loss or damage.

Bobby Rush, a former Black Panther, is elected to Congress from Illinois. (November)

Carol Moseley Braun of Illinois is the first African American woman elected to the United States Senate. (November)

1993   Benjamin Chavis succeeds Benjamin Hooks as executive secretary of the NAACP. (9 April)

In *Shaw v. Reno, Attorney General,* the Supreme Court holds that race may not be the exclusive criteria for drawing congressional district lines. (28 June)

1994   Benjamin Chavis is forced to resign as executive secretary of the NAACP.

Henry J. Lyons succeeds T. J. Jemison as president of the National Baptist Convention. (September)

Marion Barry is elected mayor of Washington, D.C. (November)

1995   James Lawson is elected chairman of the national council of the Fellowship of Reconciliation.

Myrlie Evers is elected chairman of the board of directors of the NAACP.

Benjamin Chavis and Louis Farrakhan lead the Million Man March on Washington. (16 October)

Kweisi Mfume is chosen as president and chief executive officer of the NAACP. (9 December)

Introduction

Within the expanding body of secondary literature on the civil rights movement, there are reference books on the subject already.[1] Why, then, another reference work in a growing field of books? For the same reasons that lead to multiple reference works on other subjects: a different point of view and better information.

The *Historical Dictionary of the Civil Rights Movement* assumes a particular understanding of the framework of African American history since emancipation and that the movement is best understood in that framework. African American history from 1865 to 1910 was largely dominated by adjustments throughout the nation, but primarily in the South, to the consequences of emancipation. The promise of emancipation and reconstruction gave way to the disappointment of reaction and a turning inward to build the institutions of freedom. African American history from 1910 to 1945 was largely dominated by the great migration, which led to large African American communities outside the South as resources in the long struggle for freedom. From large Northern communities which claimed renewed political influence to urban churches of unprecedented size and to a cultural renaissance which probably could have taken place only at a remove from the South, the great migration contributed immeasurably to that struggle. African American history after 1945 has been largely dominated by the struggle and its continuing legacy. While it built on accomplishments in the first two periods, the modern civil rights movement is unquestionably an achievement of the post–World War II era. Unlike other works in the field, the *Historical Dictionary of the Civil Rights Movement* focusses exclusively on that period and, wherever possible, it corrects misinformation in earlier works.

Emphasis on the post–World War II era points to one key to tracing the origins of the modern civil rights movement. As a struggle against racism and colonialism abroad, the war was a formative experience for many of its leaders. Some of them (Edward Brooke, Medgar Evers, Aaron Henry,

1

Benjamin Hooks, C. B. King, Floyd McKissick, Amzie Moore, Hosea Williams, and others) had been called to arms or quasi-military duty (Jack O'Dell) in it. For others (James Farmer and Bayard Rustin), the war was a severe test of their pacifism. For younger men, the crucible of military experience (James Forman and James Meredith) and pacifist dissent (James Lawson) came in the years immediately after World War II. All of them knew that there was a battle to be fought against racism at home. An interesting group of participants in the movement in the 1950s and 1960s (Virginia Foster Durr, George Houser, Coretta Scott King, Floyd McKissick, Samuel Williams, and others) supported Henry Wallace's Progressive Party campaign in 1948, but emphasis on prior military or political experience can also be misleading clues to the breadth of the movement in subsequent decades.

The *Historical Dictionary of the Civil Rights Movement* seeks a balanced acknowledgment of the contributions of both genders and at least four generations of people. Only recently have the roles of women in the movement begun to receive the attention they deserve.[2] Men commonly dominated leadership positions in the major civil rights organizations, but women may have outnumbered men by two to one in the movement's mass meetings. It would be interesting to know if twice as many women went to jail in freedom's cause. In recognition of women's contribution to the movement, I have included biographical sketches of Ella Jo Baker, Daisy Bates, Mary Francis Berry, Amelia Boynton, Shirley Chisholm, Septima Clark, Dorothy Cotton, Angela Davis, Marian Wright Edelman, Fannie Lou Hamer, Dorothy Height, Ruby Hurley, Barbara Jordan, Viola Liuzzo, Constance Baker Motley, Diane Nash, Eleanor Holmes Norton, Rosa Parks, Jo Anne Robinson, and Ruby Doris Robinson. Remarkably, many of them have gone unnoticed in earlier reference works on the movement.

A generation born between 1880 and 1900, here represented by Septima Clark, Roscoe Dunjee, Lester B. Granger, Charles H. Houston, Vernon Johns, Charles S. Johnson, Carl Murphy, E. D. Nixon, A. Philip Randolph, Paul Robeson, A. P. Tureaud, A. T. Walden, Walter White and P. B. Young, was the leadership of the movement in 1945. Some of them had yet to make their greatest contributions in the postwar era and a few of them would continue to be active for another thirty years. A second generation, born between 1900 and 1920, was on the cusp of leadership at the end of World War II. Its members here include: Ella Jo Baker, Daisy Bates, Amelia Boynton, Ralph J. Bunche, Kenneth B. Clark, Vernon Dahmer, William Allison Davis, Fannie Lou Hamer, William H. Hastie, Dorothy Height, Ruby Hurley, T. J. Jemison, Herbert Lee, Thurgood Marshall, Amzie Moore,

Harry Tyson Moore, Rosa Parks, Adam Clayton Powell, Jr., Jo Ann Robinson, Bayard Rustin, C. K. Steele, and Roy Wilkins. An interesting generation, noteworthy for the number of women among them, it includes both long-established leaders of the movement by 1955 and people unknown until then or thereafter.

The generation born between 1920 and 1940, however, gave leadership to the movement in numbers too large to list them all here. A few names—James Baldwin, James Bevel, Charles and Medgar Evers, James Farmer, James Forman, Alex Haley, Aaron Henry, Benjamin Hooks, LeRoi Jones, Vernon Jordan, Martin Luther King, Jr., James Lawson, Malcolm X, Floyd McKissick, Robert Moses, Constance Baker Motley, Diane Nash, Fred Shuttlesworth, Wyatt Tee Walker, L. Douglas Wilder, Andrew Young, and Whitney M. Young—represent the quality of the generation's contribution. Largely educated by 1960, in many cases, very well educated, they made their careers with the movement and carried the burden of responsibility for it. Yet, there is a fourth generation of participants in the movement, born since 1940. We are represented here by Julian Bond, H. "Rap" Brown, Stokely Carmichael, James Earle Chaney, Angela Davis, Andrew Goodman, Jesse Jackson, Maulana Karenga, John Lewis, Huey P. Newton, Ruby Doris Robinson, Emmett Till, and Sammy Younge. We were the children of the movement. Not yet admitted to segregated public schools in 1945, we heard about the *Brown* decision a decade later from our parents, from newspapers, radio, or television and wondered what it meant. We were the first generation to attend desegregated public schools in the South. We came to self-consciousness in the movement; its history was our formative experience. Our generation was disproportionately represented among its martyrs. Those of us who survived argued passionately and often fought with each other about its meaning. The embers still burn among us.

If one looks at the civil rights movement at the national or regional level, it appears to have been led by a coalition of five major civil rights organizations. Ranged vaguely to the right were the National Association for the Advancement of Colored People (NAACP) and the National Urban League. Older, more firmly based in the black middle class and committed to social change by legislation and litigation, lobbying and public relations, they had borne the brunt of the struggle through the first half of the century. Ranged vaguely to the left were the Congress of Racial Equality (CORE) and the Student Nonviolent Coordinating Committee (SNCC). Younger and more volatile, they were committed to nonviolent direct action from their origins and burned themselves out in the cause. At the movement's center was Martin Luther King's Southern Christian Leadership

Conference (SCLC). Based in the charismatic ministerial leadership of the Southern black church, SCLC employed both the bureaucratic skills of its more conservative allies, though it never perfected them, and the nonviolent direct action of its more radical allies, though it never abandoned it. On state and local levels, these generalizations do not necessarily prevail.[3]

At the time, Southern white opponents of the movement would have scoffed at the notion that the NAACP was among the more "conservative" civil rights organizations. In some local areas, such as Durham, North Carolina, NAACP youth councils spearheaded nonviolent direct action campaigns about which the organization's national office was at least skeptical. In time, the commitment of CORE and SNCC to nonviolence gave way to internal and external criticism of the impotence of not forcefully defending the community. Leaders of some local NAACP chapters, such as Dr. Robert Hayling in St. Augustine, Florida, and Robert Williams in Monroe, North Carolina, however, were advocates of armed self-defense. The NAACP's national office disciplined both of them by removing them from office. Despite the eloquent commitment of SCLC's national leadership to nonviolence, Hayling then became its local agent in St. Augustine. In other places, demographic variances and issues of social class in the African American community gave local color to the civil rights movement. The lack of a large urban black middle class and the dispersion of its large black population in rural areas and small towns gave the movement in Mississippi a quality quite different from that in Atlanta or Nashville, for example. Such local differences suggested the need to include brief sketches of the movement in several different localities.

I believe that the chief accomplishment of the postwar civil rights movement was the abolition of de jure segregation and legal barriers to the full participation of African American citizens in American life. The *Historical Dictionary of the Civil Rights Movement* therefore includes a generous number of the executive orders, judicial decisions, and legislative acts that were significant steps in that direction. Internal references to prior and to subsequent judicial decisions, for example, allow the reader to trace a history of court action on particular issues, such as voting rights or the desegregation of public higher education. Lest anyone think that this was done without major opposition, I have also included significant opponents of the movement (Citizens' Council, Theophilus Eugene Connor, and George Wallace) and their position as articulated in the Southern Manifesto.

Some historians, interpreting the movement through the prism of the Mississippi Delta perhaps, might argue that it was not primarily about desegregation and would have produced a somewhat different reference work. It might have been called the *Historical Dictionary of the Modern African-American Freedom Struggle* and, for example, might not have included the Supreme Court's crucial civil rights decision in *Miranda v. Arizona* because the case did not involve an African American. Surely, they would be correct in at least two senses: 1) that African Americans made up the primary constituency of the movement and 2) that one of its results was an enhanced sense of racial identity within the African American community. Some of those who contributed to that end were civil rights activists such as H. "Rap" Brown, Stokely Carmichael, and Floyd McKissick, who fought the battle for desegregation and moved to a more nationalist or separatist position in the mid-1960s.

There were African Americans who stood at a critical distance from the movement in the South, but who made major contributions to the enhanced sense of racial identity in the African American community. In deference to those contributions, I have included in the *Historical Dictionary of the Civil Rights Movement* such figures as Eldridge Cleaver, LeRoi Jones, Maulana Karenga, Malcolm X, Huey Newton, and Bobby Seale, who had little or no personal experience with the movement in the South and often differed radically with its leaders and among themselves. The movement was larger than any one of us and the issues that they raised are as relevant today as they were thirty years ago.

Notes

1. Charles D. Lowery and John F. Marszalek, *Encyclopedia of African-American Civil Rights: From Emancipation to the Present* (Westport, Connecticut: Greenwood Press, 1992); and Mark Grossman, *The ABC-CLIO Companion to The Civil Rights Movements* (Santa Barbara, California: ABC-CLIO, 1993).

2. See: Daisy Bates, *The Long Shadow of Little Rock: A Memoir* (New York: David McKay Co., 1962); Septima Clark, *Echo in My Soul* (New York: E. P. Dutton & Co., 1962); Vickie L. Crawford, et al., eds., *Women in the Civil Rights Movement: Trailblazers and Torchbearers, 1941–1965* (Brooklyn, New York: Carlson, 1990); Virginia Foster Durr, *Outside the Magic Circle* (University: University of Alabama Press, 1985); Sara Evans, *Personal Politics* (New York: Alfred A. Knopf, 1979); Gayle J. Hardy, *American Women Civil Rights Activists* (Jefferson, North Carolina: McFarland & Company, 1993); Coretta Scott King, *My Life with Martin Luther King, Jr.* (New York: Holt, Rinehart and Winston, 1969); Mary King, *Freedom Song: A Personal Story of the 1960s Civil Rights Movement* (New York: William Morrow, 1987);

Kay Mills, *This Little Light of Mine: The Life of Fannie Lou Hamer* (New York: Dutton, 1993); Anne Moody, *Coming of Age in Mississippi* (New York: Dial Press, 1968); Amelia Boynton Robinson, *Bridge across Jordan* (Washington, D.C.: Schiller Institute, 1991); and Jo Anne Gibson Robinson, *The Montgomery Bus Boycott and the Women Who Started It* (Knoxville: University of Tennessee Press, 1987).

3. Among the excellent state and local studies, see: William H. Chafe, *Civilities and Civil Rights: Greensboro, North Carolina and the Black Struggle for Freedom* (New York: Oxford University Press, 1980); David Colborn, *Racial Change and Community Crisis: St. Augustine, Florida, 1877–1980* (New York: Columbia University Press, 1985); John Dittmer, *Local People: The Struggle for Civil Rights in Mississippi* (Urbana: University of Illinois Press, 1994); Adam Fairclough, *Race and Democracy: The Civil Rights Struggle in Louisiana, 1915–1972* (Athens: University of Georgia Press, 1995); Robert J. Norrell, *Reaping the Whirlwind: The Civil Rights Movement in Tuskegee* (New York: Alfred A. Knopf, 1985); and Charles M. Payne, *I've Got the Light of Freedom: The Organizing Tradition and the Mississippi Freedom Struggle* (Berkeley: University of California Press, 1995).

The Dictionary

A

ABERNATHY, RALPH DAVID (1926–90). Civil rights activist and pastor.

Ralph D. Abernathy was born on 11 March 1926 in Linden, Alabama. One of twelve children, he studied in Marengo County's public schools for African American students. Abernathy graduated from Alabama State College in Montgomery (B.S., 1950) and did graduate study in sociology at Atlanta University. In 1951, he became the pastor of Montgomery's First Baptist Church and dean of students and instructor in sociology at Alabama State College. Abernathy was an active member of the local branch of the National Association for the Advancement of Colored People (NAACP; q.v.). When Rosa Parks (q.v.) was arrested for disobeying a bus driver's order to yield her seat to a boarding white passenger in December 1955, Abernathy, Martin Luther King (q.v.), and others organized the Montgomery Improvement Association (MIA; q.v.) to support the Montgomery bus boycott (q.v.).

In 1957, after the desegregation of Montgomery's buses, Abernathy, King, Theodore J. Jemison (q.v.), Joseph Lowery (q.v.), Fred Shuttlesworth (q.v.), C. K. Steele (q.v.), and other African American pastors organized the Southern Christian Leadership Conference (SCLC; q.v.) to coordinate efforts for racial justice throughout the South. King's closest personal friend in the movement, Abernathy was arrested with King in the cause of civil rights nineteen times between 1955 and 1968. In 1960, when King moved to Atlanta, Abernathy succeeded him as president of the MIA. In March of that year, apparently without their knowledge or consent, the names of Abernathy, Lowery, Shuttlesworth, and S. S. Seay, Sr., of Montgomery were signed to a controversial full-page advertisement, headlined "Heed Their Rising Voices," in the *New York Times* to raise money to defend King. In response to charges in the ad, Montgomery, Alabama, police commissioner L. B. Sullivan sued the four preachers and the *Times* for libel in the case of *Sullivan v. New York Times* (q.v.). A Montgomery trial court jury awarded Sullivan $500,000 in damages. Montgomery mayor Earl James won another suit for $500,000 in damages and Governor John Patterson won a third for a larger amount. Total damage awards approached $3,000,000. The case dragged on for four years, ending in the United States Supreme Court. By 1962, however, Alabama had begun seizing the personal property of the four clergymen.

In part to avoid the continued seizure of his property, Abernathy joined King in Atlanta to become pastor of West Hunter Street Baptist Church and serve as secretary/treasurer of SCLC. Together, King and Abernathy planned and executed SCLC's most critical campaigns, from Albany, Georgia, to Memphis, Tennessee. Abernathy was named King's heir apparent in 1965 and, after King's death in 1968, he succeeded his friend as president of SCLC at a time when the movement was in disarray. Abernathy sought to maintain an agenda for racial justice by leading the Poor People's March on Washington (q.v.), a demonstration at the Republican National Convention, and an Atlanta sanitation workers' strike in 1968. In succeeding years, he was jailed in a successful Charleston, South Carolina, hospital workers' strike and planned a march from Perry, Georgia, to Atlanta. In 1977, Abernathy resigned as president of SCLC for an unsuccessful race for a congressional seat vacated by Andrew Young (q.v.). Three years later, he joined Hosea Williams (q.v.) in endorsing Ronald Reagan's bid for the presidency. In poor health after a stroke in 1983, Abernathy incurred the wrath of many African American leaders in 1989, when his autobiography, *And the Walls Came Tumbling Down,* alleged that King was sexually promiscuous. He died on 17 April 1990.

ADDERLY v. FLORIDA, 385 U.S. 39 (1966). A case in which the Supreme Court gave state property rights priority over civil rights.

In a case growing out of the Tallahassee, Florida, Movement (q.v.), 107 students from Florida Agricultural and Mechanical University were arrested in September 1963 for demonstrating outside Tallahassee's Leon County Jail. Convicted of "trespass with a malicious and mischievous intent," Harriet Adderly and 31 others appealed the decision. After losing in a Florida district court and a district court of appeals, on 18 October 1966 attorneys Richard Felder and Tobias Simon argued before the Supreme Court that the students had been denied their "rights of free speech, assembly, petition, due process of law and equal protection of the laws under the 14th Amendment." Justice Hugo Black, speaking for the Court majority, held that "the state, no less than a private owner of property, has power to preserve the property under its control for the use to which it is lawfully dedicated." In dissent, Justice William O. Douglas argued that the Court's decision did "violence to the First Amendment" by allowing "this 'petition for redress of grievances' to be turned into a trespass action."

ADICKES v. S. H. KRESS AND CO., 398 U.S. 144 (1970). A case in which the Supreme Court held that private businesses are not liable for damages from racial discrimination, even if it violates state policy.

The plaintiff, Sandra Adickes, a New York school teacher, was refused service and arrested at an S. H. Kress lunch counter in Hattiesburg, Mississippi. Under provisions of the United States Code which prohibited discrimination "under the color of the law," Adickes sued S. H. Kress and Co. for civil damages. Her case was dismissed in a Mississippi district court, which held that Adickes had not proved that the state acted in cooperation with the chain store management. After losing in the court of appeals, Adickes appealed to the Supreme Court. Speaking for the Court majority, Justice John Marshall Harlan held that, since Kress was not under state order to maintain segregation, it was not liable for damages. Justices William Brennan and William O. Douglas dissented from the Court's opinion.

AFFIRMATIVE ACTION. Positive efforts to eliminate discrimination against women and minority groups in education and employment.

The legal bases for affirmative action lie in the Equal Protection Clause of the Fourteenth Amendment, President John Kennedy's Executive Order 10925 (q.v.), Title VII of the Civil Rights Act of 1964 (q.v.), and President Lyndon Johnson's Executive Order 11246 (q.v.). Affirmative action has been the rationale for reserving some government contracts for minority businesses, ethnic quotas in college admissions, and preferred status in hiring practices. Support for affirmative action as a remedy for past discrimination peaked in the late 1960s, but it came under severe attack as "reverse discrimination." Within a decade, in dramatic contrast to the Supreme Court's unity in *Brown v. Board of Education* (q.v.), which directed legal and moral authority to desegregation, sharply divided Court decisions in *University of California Regents v. Bakke* (q.v.) and *United Steelworkers v. Weber* (q.v.) merely reflected severely divided public opinion about affirmative action.

ALABAMA CHRISTIAN MOVEMENT FOR HUMAN RIGHTS (ACMHR). An African American organization which spearheaded the Birmingham, Alabama, Movement (q.v.).

In June 1956, Alabama's attorney general, John Patterson, sued to prevent the NAACP (q.v.), as an unregistered out-of-state corporation, from operating in Alabama. That led to a series of four suits, *NAACP v. Alabama* (q.v.), which inhibited effective work by the major national civil rights organization in the state from 1956 to 1964. As an alternative, parallel to the Montgomery Improvement Association (q.v.), Birmingham pastors Fred L. Shuttlesworth (q.v.), R. L. Alford, Edward Gardner, and Nelson H. Smith organized the Alabama Christian Movement for Human Rights. Founded at a mass meeting on 5 June 1956 at the city's Sardis Baptist Church, the ACMHR chose Shuttlesworth as its first president, adopted nonviolent direct action as its primary vehicle for social change and, in 1957, became the Birmingham affiliate of the SCLC (q.v.).

When the Supreme Court found Montgomery's segregated public transportation unconstitutional in December 1956, ACMHR notified Birmingham authorities that it would attempt to desegregate the city's buses. Shuttlesworth survived the bombing of his house on Christmas night to lead 200 ACMHR activists in the effort to desegregate Birmingham buses on 26 December 1956. Police arrested 21 demonstrators, who were then convicted of trespass. ACMHR sought the desegregation of the city's public schools and its train station in 1957, led a boycott of its still segregated buses in 1958, and supported the sit-in movement (q.v.) in 1960 and the Freedom Rides (q.v.) in 1961. Nonetheless, Birmingham maintained its reputation as the South's most rigidly segregated city in 1963, when ACMHR invited Martin Luther King and SCLC to mount a dramatic assault on racial segregation there. After that confrontation, Edward Gardner replaced Shuttlesworth in 1969 as ACMHR's president. ACMHR helped elect Richard Arrington to Birmingham's city council in 1971 and as the city's first African American mayor in 1979.

AL-AMIN, JAMIL ABDULLAH. *See* **Brown, Hubert Gerold.**

ALBANY, GEORGIA, MOVEMENT. A coalition of African American organizations, including the Ministerial Alliance, the NAACP (q.v.), and the Student Nonviolent Coordinating Committee (SNCC; q.v.), which made the southwest Georgia city of 56,000 people the site of a major test of nonviolent direct action against segregation.

Responding to the Freedom Rides (q.v.), the Interstate Commerce Commission (ICC) ordered the desegregation of interstate travel facilities effective on 1 November 1961. Students associated with SNCC tested Albany's Trailways Bus Station on that day and found it not in compliance with the ICC order. Within three weeks, as students continued to test the city's racial segregation, Albany's African American community organized the Albany Movement to coordinate a broadscale assault on racial injustice and chose Dr. William Anderson, a local osteopath, as its leader. Seeking to bridge differences among its members, Anderson invited Martin Luther King (q.v.) and SCLC (q.v.) to assist in the local struggle. From December 1961 through August 1962, King, SCLC, and national media attention focused on Albany. Despite thousands of arrests and unfulfilled promises of concessions from the city's white leaders, King left Albany in defeat. Yet, Albany was a testing ground for SCLC's more dramatic confrontation in the Birmingham Movement (q.v.) and for SNCC's broader attack in Mississippi's Freedom Summer (q.v.). With King's departure, national attention turned from Albany, and the local movement refocussed its attention on voter registration. Among its leaders, C. B. King (q.v.) would make unsuccessful races for congress and governor and Charles Sherrod would win election to Albany's city council.

ALEXANDER v. HOLMES COUNTY BOARD OF EDUCATION, 396 U.S. 1218 (1969). A case in which the Supreme Court held that public schools had moved with "all deliberate speed" to end segregation long enough and that school boards were to act immediately to create "unitary" schools.

The Holmes County, Mississippi, Board of Education argued that midterm integration would be disruptive of public education. On 28 August 1969, the Fifth Circuit Court of Appeals (q.v.) ruled that the school board's schedule for desegregation was in compliance with the Supreme Court's decision in *Brown v. Board of Education* (q.v.) that public school systems must desegregate with "all deliberate speed." On appeal to the Supreme Court, attorneys for the Justice and Health, Education and Welfare departments argued the school board's position against attorneys from the NAACP Legal Defense and Educational Fund (q.v.). Yet, on 29 October 1969, a unanimous Supreme Court rejected the appeals court's ruling. It ordered Holmes County to desegregate its schools immediately and create a single public school system for all of its children under the appeals court's supervision. As a precedent, the *Alexander* decision ended 15 years of school desegregation with "all deliberate speed" and ensured widespread southern school desegregation within the next year. Paired with the Court's decision in *Green v. County School Board of New Kent County* (q.v.), *Alexander* implied that the Court had moved from desegregation, allowing white and black students to attend schools together, to integration, requiring white and black students to attend the same schools, as the model of public school policy.

ALLEN v. STATE BOARD OF ELECTIONS, 393 U.S. 544 (1968). A case in which the Supreme Court disallowed state legislation that effectively diminished the impact of votes cast by African Americans.

Although the Voting Rights Act of 1965 (q.v.) guaranteed African Americans' right to vote throughout the South, some laws or electoral practices effectively diluted their influence. Multiseat electoral districts or the election of officials at large could reduce the impact of black voters on election results. Some Southern white politicians believed that, so long as they did not impede black citizens from voting, the Voting Rights Act did not prevent manipulating the results. In *Allen v. State Board of Elections,* attorneys for the NAACP Legal Defense and Educational Fund (q.v.) challenged a Mississippi statute which permitted a change from district to at-large elections of some county officials. The Court found the Mississippi law violated the Voting Rights Act because its effect diminished the right of African American voters to equal representation.

AN AMERICAN DILEMMA. Gunnar Myrdal's classic sociological study of American race relations, one of the most influential works of its kind published in the first half of the twentieth century.

In 1938, the Carnegie Foundation awarded $250,000 to the distinguished Swedish political economist, Gunnar Myrdal (6 December 1898–17 May 1987), to direct a study of American race relations. His team of African American and white scholars, including Ralph J. Bunche (q.v.), Kenneth B. Clarke (q.v.), and Charles S. Johnson (q.v.), produced a series of monographs on aspects of race relations that laid the foundations for Myrdal's capstone study, *An American Dilemma: The Negro Problem and Modern Democracy* (1944). Myrdal argued that racism kept African Americans from full participation in American life and that this denial of their freedom and equality was in conflict with American democratic values. Yet, he believed that Americans would resolve their dilemma by dismantling racial segregation and rooting out the vestiges of racism thereafter.

Welcomed by black and white racial liberals and condemned by many white Southerners when it was published, *An American Dilemma* was widely regarded as the authoritative study of race relations within a decade. Attorneys who attacked segregation in the courts cited its findings and, in a classic instance of sociological jurisprudence, Chief Justice Earl Warren cited its evidence in the Supreme Court's decision in *Brown v. Board of Education* (q.v.). By the mid-1960s, however, when American urban ghettoes were exploding in race riots, many scholars became skeptical of Myrdal's optimism about the end of racism in the near future, many African Americans rejected his racial assimilationism, and Myrdal himself speculated that poverty was a greater barrier than segregation to African Americans' full participation in American life.

ANTHONY v. MARSHALL COUNTY BOARD OF EDUCATION, 409 F.2d 1287 (5th Cir., 1969).
A case in which the Fifth Circuit Court of Appeals (q.v.) rejected two Mississippi school boards' "freedom of choice" plans for desegregation in favor of plans for full integration.

The parents of African American students brought a class action suit against the Holly Springs and Marshall County, Mississippi, school boards. When the U. S. District Court for Northern Mississippi affirmed the school boards' "freedom of choice" plans for desegregation, the plaintiffs turned to the Fifth Circuit Court of Appeals (q.v.). Citing evidence that no white students had attended a predominantly black school and that only 21 of 1,868 black students in one district and 22 of 3,606 black students in the other district had attended a predominantly white school in the 1967–68 school year, the appeals court ruled that Holly Springs and Marshall County were maintaining dual school systems. Following the Supreme Court's logic in *Alexander v. Holmes County Board of Education* (q.v.) and *Green v. County School Board of New Kent County* (q.v.), the Appeals Court ruled that "freedom of choice" was ineffective in dismantling segregation and that the school boards must create racially integrated school systems.

ARLINGTON HEIGHTS v. METROPOLITAN HOUSING DEVELOPMENT CORPORATION, 429 U.S. 252 (1977).
A case in which the Supreme Court avoided a decision on whether a municipality could refuse to rezone an area for building low-cost, racially integrated public housing.

The Metropolitan Housing Development Corporation (MHDC) in Illinois bought acreage within Arlington Heights and asked the town to rezone it from single family residences to public housing. When the town refused to rezone the property, MHDC sued the town. Reasoning that the town acted to preserve property values in the area, the district court found for Arlington Heights and MHDC turned to the Seventh Circuit Court of Appeals, which reversed the district court's ruling. Arlington Heights appealed to the United States Supreme Court. On 11 January 1977, the Court returned the case to lower courts because there had been no hearing on whether the town's refusal to rezone constituted a violation of fair housing provisions of the Civil Rights Act of 1968 (q.v.). The Court's action left the central issue of the case in doubt.

ARNOLD v. NORTH CAROLINA, 376 U.S. 733 (1964). A case in which the Supreme Court held that evidence of African Americans' exclusion from a grand jury that indicted a black defendant was sufficient grounds for his claim of the denial of equal protection.

Found guilty of murder in a North Carolina state court, two black men, Jesse James Arnold and George Dixon, appealed to the state supreme court. There, they claimed that their convictions should be thrown out because African Americans were routinely excluded from grand juries. They presented evidence that over one-fourth of local taxpayers were African Americans and the clerk of the state trial court admitted that he could recall only one black person serving on a grand jury in his 24 years of experience. The state supreme court held that this was insufficient evidence to prove that black people were systematically excluded from grand jury service. On appeal, the United States Supreme Court reversed the North Carolina court's decision, holding that the evidence and testimony had made a prima facie case for the denial of equal protection.

THE AUTOBIOGRAPHY OF MALCOLM X. *See* **Haley, Alexander Palmer** and **Malcolm X.**

AVERY v. GEORGIA, 345 U.S. 559 (1953). A case in which the Supreme Court decision helped to define the issue of racial discrimination in the selection of juries as a violation of the Fourteenth Amendment's equal protection clause.

James Avery, a black man, was convicted of rape in a Fulton County, Georgia, court in 1952. Claiming that racial discrimination in the selection of his jury had denied him the equal protection of the law, Avery appealed his conviction. The Supreme Court upheld his appeal on 25 May 1953. Avery might be unable to prove discrete acts of discrimination, the Court reasoned, but the process of selecting jurors, in which white prospects were given white tickets and black prospects were given yellow tickets, was so prone to the alleged abuse as to be *"prima facie* evidence of discrimination." Without evidence of black people serving on juries, said the Court, such racial distinctions must be considered evidence of the denial of equal protection.

B

BAKER, ELLA JOSEPHINE (1903–86). Civil rights activist and organizer.

Ella Jo Baker was born 7 December 1903 in Norfolk, Virginia. She grew up and went to school in Littleton, North Carolina. Hoping to be a medical missionary, Baker studied and graduated as valedictorian at Shaw University in Raleigh. Financial considerations precluded her pursuit of medicine, so after graduation from Shaw in 1927 she moved to New York City. In her early years there, Baker helped to organize the Young Negroes Cooperative League, an organization for black consumers, and through the depression years she lectured and wrote on civil rights and consumer affairs. Baker joined the staff of the National Association for the Advancement of Colored People (NAACP; q.v.) in 1938 as an assistant field secretary. As national director of branches from 1943 to 1946, Baker traveled throughout the country to organize NAACP branches. Leaving that position to care for a niece, she helped to gather information for the case of the NAACP Legal Defense and Educational Fund (LDEF; q.v.) against public school segregation on its negative effects on African American children and was active in the New York City branch of the NAACP, serving as its president from 1954 to 1958.

In 1957, Ella Baker helped to organize the Southern Christian Leadership Conference (SCLC; q.v.). Between 1958 and 1960, she was its acting director and its associate director. As a woman, however, Baker knew that SCLC's ministerial inner circle would not accept her authority and she became critical of its charismatic style of leadership. On 15 April 1960, at the end of her career with SCLC, Baker convened a meeting of student activists at Shaw University, her alma mater, to organize the Student Nonviolent Coordinating Committee (SNCC; q.v.). They acted on her advice to remain independent of any existing civil rights organization and seemed to share her vision of a grassroots movement in which decisions flowed from the bottom up rather than from the top down. Baker's vision was later embodied in the Mississippi Freedom Democratic

Party (q.v.), to whose state convention she gave the keynote address in 1964. She helped to spearhead its challenge to the all-white Mississippi delegation to the Democratic National Convention in Atlantic City that year and shared the disenchantment of its defeat. Ella Baker died in New York on 18 December 1986.

BAKER v. CARR, 369 U.S. 186 (1962). A case in which the Supreme Court affirmed the courts' jurisdiction over state apportionment plans for representation.

Tennessee's 1901 law established a formula for periodic reapportionment, but it did not allow for changing demographic conditions. By 1960, urban growth had produced significant underrepresentation of the state's urban voters in the General Assembly. Arguing that the reapportionment formula denied them due process under the Fourteenth Amendment, Baker and others sued Tennessee state officials. A federal district court rejected Baker's argument on the grounds that relief must come from the state legislature, not the courts. When Baker appealed to the Supreme Court, Justice William J. Brennan spoke for the majority in reversing the district court opinion and asserting the courts' jurisdiction. "An unbroken line of our precedents sustains the federal courts' jurisdiction of the subject matter of federal constitutional claims of this nature," Brennan wrote. Justices Felix Frankfurter and John Marshall Harlan dissented from the majority opinion. Two years later, in *Reynolds, a Judge, et al. v. Simms et al.* (q.v.), the Supreme Court took up the issue of apportionment more directly.

BALDWIN, JAMES ARTHUR (1924–87). Author.

On 2 August 1924, James Baldwin was born in New York City to Emma Berdis Jones, an impoverished, unwed mother, who later married an evangelical preacher. Young James Baldwin attended Frederick Douglass Junior High School. At 14, he became youth minister at Fireside Pentecostal Assembly, a Harlem storefront church. At DeWitt Clinton High School, Baldwin edited the school magazine. After graduating from high school, he earned a living as a dishwasher, handyman, office boy, and waiter. At the same time, Baldwin was writing essays and book reviews. After the death of his stepfather in 1946, he determined to make his living as a writer. In 1948, Baldwin won a Rosenwald fellowship that allowed him to go abroad. Thereafter, Baldwin spent most of his life in France and in Turkey, returning to the United States for only an occasional visit. His first novel, the semiautobiographical *Go Tell It on the Mountain,* was published in 1953 to popular critical acclaim. His play, *The Amen Corner,* was first performed in 1954. *Notes of a Native Son,* a collection of essays, and a second novel, *Giovanni's Room,* followed quickly in 1955 and 1956. In 1961 and 1962, he published *Nobody Knows My Name,* a second collection of essays, and *Another Country,* his third novel. That body of work made Baldwin a major voice in American literature.

When the sit-in movement (q.v.) in 1960 and the Freedom Rides (q.v.) in 1961 fixed the nation's attention on the crisis in race relations, Baldwin published "Letter from a Region in My Mind" in the *New Yorker.* Widely thought to be the most brilliant contemporary description of what it meant to be black in white America, the essay became a part of his best-selling *The Fire Next Time* in 1963. For the next few years, Baldwin was hailed in lectures and the press and was much in demand for appearances on radio and television across the nation. His plays, *The Amen Corner* and *Blues for Mr. Charlie,* went into production and were modest successes in New York. The latter won the Foreign Press Association's drama award for 1963–64. Yet, Baldwin's literary reputation was strangely intertwined with the success of the civil rights movement and, as it disintegrated in the late 1960s, his reputation slumped. Baldwin regarded his 1968 novel, *Tell Me How Long the Train's Been Gone,* as his first "grown-up" work of fiction. Few critics were enthusiastic about it, however, and some thought the novel "a disaster." At the same time, Baldwin was attacked by Eldridge Cleaver (q.v.), LeRoi Jones (q.v.), and other spokesmen for the Black Arts Movement both for the insistence on racial reconciliation and the openly gay themes in his work.

Baldwin seemed to retreat. He had become deeply angry, despairing and pessimistic about race relations. Despite the appearance of another book of essays, *No Name in the Street,* some people believed that he was no longer writing. In 1971, Baldwin and Margaret Mead published *A Rap on Race* and, three years later, he published another novel, *If Beale Street Could Talk.* Yet, his work seemed to lack the fiery polemical power of a decade earlier. Baldwin continued to publish through the mid-1980s, but his later work did not capture the literary world's attention as his early work had done. In all, Baldwin wrote 16 books and coauthored three others. In 1984, he was named a Five College professor in the W. E. B. Du Bois Department of Afro-American Studies at the University of Massachusetts at Amherst. Two years later, the French government made him a commander of the Legion of Honor, France's highest civilian award. James Baldwin died in France on 1 December 1987. The winter 1987 issue of *The Massachusetts Review* was devoted to him.

BARAKA, IMAMU AMIRI. *See* Jones, LeRoi.

BARROWS v. JACKSON, 346 U.S. 249 (1953). A case in which the Supreme Court barred property owners from recovering damages when a court enjoined the enforcement of a racially restrictive covenant.

In *Shelley v. Kraemer* (q.v.), the Court ruled unanimously that racial covenants on property could be voluntarily maintained, but that state enforcement of them violated private "rights to acquire, enjoy, own and dispose of property." When Barrows and Jackson purchased a residential property in Los Angeles, both parties agreed not to sell or rent his or her part of the property to nonwhite persons. Later, however, Jackson leased her part of the property to an African American couple and Barrows sued for damages. A lower court rejected his claim on the grounds that the restrictive covenant violated the equal protection clause of the constitution and an appeals court sustained that judgment. Writing for a majority of the Supreme Court, Justice Sherman Minton quoted from *Shelley v. Kraemer:* "The Constitution confers upon no individual the right to demand action by the State which results in the denial of equal protection of the laws to other individuals."

BARRY, MARION S. (1936–   ). Civil rights activist and politician.

Marion S. Barry was born on 6 March 1936 in Itta Bena, Mississippi, and educated in local public schools for African American students. He graduated from Le Moyne College (B.S., 1958) in Memphis, Tennessee, and was working on an M.S. at Fisk University when he became active in the Nashville, Tennessee, Movement (q.v.). In April 1960, at the founding meeting of SNCC (q.v.) at Shaw University in Raleigh, North Carolina, Barry was chosen as its first national chairman. In August, he helped to organize SNCC's direct action efforts in Jackson and McComb, Mississippi. After six months as SNCC's national chairman, however, Barry resigned to pursue doctoral studies in chemistry at the University of Kansas and the University of Tennessee. Informally, he continued to participate in movement activities, conducting workshops on nonviolence, fund raising, and registering voters.

In 1964, Marion Barry left graduate school to return to full-time work in the civil rights movement. After opening an office for SNCC in New York, he moved to Washington, D.C., to direct its work in the nation's capital. As SNCC began to disintegrate thereafter, Barry struck out on his own, organizing nonviolent direct action campaigns against housing discrimination and police brutality. After his election to Washington's city council in the early 1970s, Barry was elected mayor of the city in 1978. Inaugurated in 1979, he won two additional four-year terms before being forced out of office in 1990 after being convicted and sentenced to six months in prison on charges of drug possession and use. Upon his release from prison, Barry began his campaign for restoration. In 1992, he was elected to Washington's city council and, two years later, he was returned to the mayor's office.

BATES, DAISY LEE GATSON (1920–   ). Journalist and civil rights activist.

Daisy Lee Gatson was born about 1920 in Huttig, Arkansas, a small town in the southeastern lumbering region of the state. At an early age, she learned that her mother had been raped and murdered, allegedly by three white men, and that her father had placed her with childless adoptive parents, Orlee and Susie Smith, before he disappeared in fear of further retribution. Daisy Lee Gatson was doted on by her adoptive parents who sheltered her from white prejudice, but she saw the effects of discrimination in Huttig's inadequate public schools for African American children. In the mid-1930s, Orlee Smith introduced Daisy Lee Gatson to his friend, Lucius Christopher Bates, a former journalist and successful insurance salesman. Smith died in 1941 and, soon thereafter, Daisy Lee Gatson and L. C. Bates, who was many years her senior, were married. They settled in Little Rock, used their savings to lease a newspaper plant and launched the *Arkansas State Press*. Daisy Bates studied at Shorter and Philander Smith colleges in Little Rock to prepare for a career in journalism.

During World War II, black recruits from nearby Camp Robinson filled Little Rock streets on the weekends. In March 1942, when the *State Press* told the story of the brutal murder of a black soldier by a white policeman, powerful advertisers withdrew their accounts from the paper. L. C. and Daisy Bates struggled to continue publishing and slowly their advocacy for the interests of black people won a large following for the paper across the state. By 1952, when Daisy Bates was elected president of the Arkansas conference of branches of the NAACP (q.v.), she was confident that Little Rock was a "liberal southern city" in a state with many problems. When the Supreme Court held that segregation in public schools was unconstitutional in *Brown v. Board of Education* (q.v.), the Bateses and the *State Press* urged Little Rock's school board to implement its plan for gradual desegregation of its schools. Counterpressure by Little Rock segregationists sought to force Daisy Bates to divulge the names of NAACP contributors and members, leading to *Bates v. Little Rock* (q.v.), a case that went to the Supreme Court.

Daisy Bates was a tower of strength for the nine black students who were to desegregate Little Rock's Central High School in September 1957. Arkansas governor Orval Faubus ordered up the Arkansas national guardsmen and white mobs gathered around the school to prevent their admission. Three weeks later, President Eisenhower federalized the Arkansas national guardsmen and sent paratroopers to Little Rock to protect the black students who were then admitted to Central High School. Daisy Bates continued to intervene on their behalf as they faced harassment during Little Rock's early experience with school desegregation. Financial pressures forced the Bateses to discontinue the *State Press* in 1959, but Daisy Bates continued to be active in the civil rights movement. In 1959, she joined Martin Luther King and 26,000 students in the second Youth March for Integrated Schools.

Daisy Bates resigned as president of the Arkansas conference of branches of the NAACP in 1961, but she later became a member of its national board of directors. In 1962, Bates published her autobiography, *The Long Shadow of Little Rock.* During the 1960s and 1970s, she worked with the Democratic Party and antipoverty programs. L. C. Bates died in 1980, but Daisy Bates resumed publication of the *Arkansas State Press* in 1984 in his honor. Slowed by illness, she sold the newspaper in 1988. Daisy Bates has been honored by national, state, and local organizations in the last two decades, but none was more appropriate than the opening of Little Rock's Daisy Bates Elementary School in 1987.

BATES v. LITTLE ROCK, 361 U.S. 516 (1960). A case in which the Supreme Court held that the state may not require disclosure of membership lists because that might infringe on citizens' due process rights to freedom of association.

In the mid-1950s, some Southern states, including Alabama and Louisiana, and some localities, such as Little Rock, Arkansas, adopted laws requiring organizations to register their membership lists and other information with local or state authorities. In 1928, the United States Supreme Court sustained a New York state law which required that the Ku Klux Klan make its membership list available to the public in *Bryant v. Zimmerman.* Thirty years later, similar laws in the South led to a series of cases, including *Bates v. Little Rock; Louisiana, Ex Rel. Gremillion. Attorney General v. NAACP* (q.v.); and *NAACP v. Alabama* (q.v.), in which the Court reversed itself.

A 1957 Little Rock, Arkansas, ordinance required that, on request, any organization in the city must give the city clerk its official name, headquarters or meeting place, names of its officers and staff, its purpose, a record of its finances, and a statement about its subordination to any parent organization. Citing a hostile political climate, the records keeper of the local branch of the NAACP (q.v.), Daisy Bates (q.v.), withheld the names of its members and contributors. She supplied all the other required information, but Bates was convicted of violating the ordinance. In upholding her conviction, the Arkansas supreme court said that "compulsory disclosure of the membership list was not an unconstitutional invasion of the freedoms guaranteed." The United States Supreme Court reversed the state court. Coerced disclosure of lists of members and supporters, reasoned the Court, might hinder citizens' rights to freedom of association.

BATON ROUGE, LOUISIANA, MOVEMENT. The civil rights movement in Louisiana's state capital.

African Americans boycotted public transportation in the urban South when it was segregated in the late nineteenth and early twentieth centuries, but the effort failed to prevent its expansion. In 1953, four years after the Reverend Theodore J. Jemison (q.v.) became pastor of Baton Rouge's Mt. Zion Baptist Church, the city's black leaders persuaded the city council to pass an ordinance that allowed passengers to be seated on a first come, first served basis. Black passengers would occupy seats from the back of the bus forward and white passengers from the front of the bus backward, but no seats would be strictly reserved for either race. When the city's bus drivers ignored the ordinance, black passengers held a one-day boycott of the busses. Louisiana's attorney general ruled that the new city ordinance was unconstitutional. From 18 to 25 June 1953, Jemison led a boycott of the city busses. Against the wishes of the bus company, the city council agreed to reinstate the ordinance, which maintained racial segregation under conditions less offensive to black passengers. The little-known Baton Rouge bus boycott became a model for the later, more famous and protracted Montgomery bus boycott (q.v.), as well as those of the Birmingham, Alabama, Movement (q.v.) and the Tallahassee, Florida, Movement (q.v.). Jemison became the leader of the Baton Rouge affiliate of SCLC (q.v.), the Baton Rouge Christian Movement.

The sit-in movement (q.v.) reached Baton Rouge in March 1960, when African American students from Southern University, including H. Rap Brown (q.v.), sat in at segregated lunch counters at the bus terminal, Kress department store, and Sitman's drugstore. They asked to be served, but otherwise made no disturbance. The management did not ask them to leave, but the police were called and, when the students refused a police order to leave, they were arrested and convicted in trial court of "disturbing the peace." The students' appeal to the state supreme court was denied. Their appeal to the United States Supreme Court was the first sit-in movement (q.v.) case it would hear. On 11 December 1961, the Court unanimously overturned the convictions in *Garner v. Louisiana* (q.v.). Louisiana's law against disturbing the peace did not apply to the students' peaceful demonstration, wrote Chief Justice Earl Warren. They had violated racial customs in the state, not its law. Their conviction, said Warren, was "so totally devoid of evidentiary support as to violate the Due Process Clause of the Fourteenth Amendment."

Later in the decade, CORE organizer B. Elton Cox led civil rights demonstrations in Baton Rouge. Arrested during the protest action for violating a state law barring demonstrations near courthouses, he was convicted in an East Baton Rouge district court and the conviction was sustained by Louisiana's supreme court. The United States Supreme Court reversed his conviction on appeal in *Cox v. Louisiana* (q.v.). It noted that city officials had granted Cox permission to demonstrate in an area near the courthouse. Application of the state law in this case amounted to entrapment and violated his First Amendment rights to freedom of assembly, petition and speech, and his Fourteenth Amendment due process rights. The state's right to regulate demonstrations, said the Court, could not be used to suppress elemental human rights.

BATSON v. KENTUCKY, 471 U.S. 1052 (1986). A case in which the Supreme Court ruled that a prosecutor's peremptory challenges to a perspective juror may not be based on race.

When James Kirkland Batson, an African American, faced an all-white jury in Louisville, Kentucky, on charges of second degree burglary and receiving stolen goods, his attorney moved for the dismissal of the jury on the grounds that Batson's right to equal protection of the law was about to be violated. The prosecuting attorney had removed four potential African American jurors by peremptory challenge, those which are allowed without explanation. The judge rejected the defense attorney's motion and Batson was convicted. Both a circuit court and the state supreme court confirmed Batson's conviction, arguing that there was no obligation to explain peremptory challenges. A divided Supreme Court, with Chief Justice Warren Burger and Justice William Rehnquist in dissent, held that when peremptory challenges remove all African American jurors the prosecutor is obliged to explain them on grounds other than race.

BELL, GRIFFIN BOYETTE (1918–   ). A member of the Fifth Circuit Court of Appeals (q.v.) and Attorney General of the United States.

Born on 31 October 1918 and raised in Americus, Georgia, Griffin Bell attended public schools and Georgia Southwestern College there. He worked in his father's appliance store and gas station before joining the Army Transportation Corps in World War II. After the war, Bell studied law at Mercer University's law school in Macon, graduating in 1948. He was associated with private legal firms in Savannah, Rome, and Atlanta until 1961. In 1958, Bell joined the gubernatorial campaign of Ernest Vandiver and, from 1959 to 1961, served as Governor Vandiver's chief of staff. During that time, he also cochaired John F. Kennedy's presidential campaign in Georgia. In 1961, Bell was Kennedy's first appointee to the Fifth Circuit Court of Appeals. At 42, he was the youngest person ever named to that court.

In 15 years on the Court of Appeals, Bell joined in over 3,000 decisions, including 141 desegregation cases. He concurred in many desegregation decisions, but Bell's association with the staunchly segregationist Vandiver and his opposition to busing (q.v.) gave him a reputation as a judicial conservative. On a three-judge panel which tried *Bond v. Floyd,* Bell was one of two judges who found that Georgia's state legislature had legitimately refused to seat Julian Bond (q.v.) because of his opposition to the Vietnam War. The Supreme Court reversed the appellate court's decision. In 1976, Bell resigned from the court of appeals to practice law and join Jimmy Carter's presidential campaign. When Carter was elected, Bell was named his attorney general. Confirmed despite doubts about his commitment to civil rights, Bell served as attorney general from 1977 to 1979, when he returned to private legal practice in Atlanta. Later, Bell served as President George Bush's personal attorney in the Iran-Contra arms case.

BELL v. MARYLAND, 378 U.S. 226 (1964). The last of four cases adjudicated by the Supreme Court in 1964 before the public accommodations provisions of the Civil Rights Act of 1964 (q.v.) were implemented.

For their roles in a sit-in (q.v.) at Hooper's Restaurant in Baltimore, Maryland, 12 African American students were convicted of criminal trespass. Because Baltimore passed a public accommodations law after the sit-ins, the Supreme Court reversed the convictions and returned the case to a Maryland court for clarification. In doing so, the court avoided deciding whether the Constitution's Fourteenth Amendment protected the right of service in public accommodations. In supporting opinions, however, six justices split evenly on the issue. Justice Arthur J. Goldberg, joined by Chief Justice Earl Warren and Justice William O. Douglas, held that the Fourteenth Amendment intended to prohibit racial discrimination in public accommodations. Justice Hugo L. Black, joined by Justices John Marshall Harlan and Byron R. White, argued that racial segregation in public accommodations was not prohibited by the Fourteenth Amendment and that if it were there would be no reason for Congress to pass prohibitive legislation.

BERRY, MARY FRANCES (1938–). Civil rights activist, attorney, and historian.

Mary Frances Berry was born on 17 February 1938 to Frances Southall Berry and George Ford Berry in Nashville, Tennessee. She lived for a time in an orphanage and studied in local public schools, graduating from Nashville's Pearl High School. Berry entered Fisk University, but transferred to Howard University, where she received her B.A. in 1961 and an M.A. in history the following year. Moving to the University of Michigan, Berry earned a Ph.D. in American constitutional history in 1966 and a J.D. from the university's law school in 1970. After early faculty appointments at Central Michigan University, Eastern Michigan University, and the University of Michigan, Berry directed Afro-American Studies and chaired the Behavioral and Social Sciences at the University of Maryland between 1970 and 1976.

In 1976, Berry became chancellor and professor of history and law at the University of Colorado at Boulder, but she took a leave of absence the following year to serve as assistant secretary of education in the Carter administration. In 1980, Berry left the University of Colorado and the Department of Health, Education, and Welfare to become professor of history at Howard University and a member of the United States Civil Rights Commission. Three years later, President Reagan sought to remove

Berry from her position on the commission. She was arrested for sitting in at the South African embassy in Washington a year later. In 1986, Berry became Geraldine Segal Professor of Social Thought and professor of history at the University of Pennsylvania. Her most important publications include: *Black Resistance/White Law* (1974); *Military Necessity and Civil Rights Policy* (1977); *Why ERA Failed* (1986); *The Politics of Parenthood* (1993); and, with John Blassingame, *Long Memory* (1982). In 1990, Berry became the first African American woman to serve as president of the Organization of American Historians. President Clinton appointed her as chairperson of the United States Civil Rights Commission in 1993.

BEVEL, DIANE NASH. *See* **Nash, Diane.**

BEVEL, JAMES LUTHER (1936–   ). Civil rights activist and pastor.
Born on 19 October 1936 at Itta Bena, Mississippi, James Bevel was educated in public schools for African American children there and in Cleveland, Ohio, where he worked in a steel mill as a teenager. After serving in the United States Naval Reserve in 1954 and 1955, Bevel entered American Baptist Theological Seminary in Nashville, Tennessee, and was ordained as a Baptist minister in 1959. While in seminary, Bevel worked with other students, such as Fisk's Marion Barry (q.v.) and Diane Nash (q.v.), Vanderbilt's James Lawson (q.v.), and fellow seminarian John Lewis, in the Nashville, Tennessee, Movement (q.v.). On 12 February 1960, they launched the local sit-in movement (q.v.). Later in the spring, Bevel and the Nashville students met sit-in movement leaders from other parts of the South at Tennessee's Highlander Folk School (q.v.) and North Carolina's Shaw University, where they organized SNCC (q.v.). In May 1961, when it appeared that the Freedom Rides (q.v.) might collapse, Bevel led a group of Nashville student activists who continued the Freedom Rides (q.v.) from Montgomery, Alabama, to Jackson, Mississippi, and served time in Mississippi's Parchman Prison. Later in 1961, when he married fellow Nashville activist Diane Nash, Bevel left SNCC, became a youth organizer for SCLC (q.v.), and began its work in Jackson, Mississippi.

In 1963, as SCLC looked toward its major struggle in the Birmingham, Alabama, Movement (q.v.), the Bevels moved to Alabama. As the primary organizer of marches by the city's school children, James Bevel played a catalytic role in the Birmingham confrontation. He and Diane Nash Bevel primed SCLC's more cautious, older leaders for the Alabama voting rights campaign that led to the Selma to Montgomery March (q.v.) and the Voting Rights Act of 1965 (q.v.). In 1966, Bevel moved to Chicago and played a leading role in SCLC's Chicago and Memphis campaigns. Early in 1967 he became the national director of the Spring Mobilization Committee to End the War in Vietnam and helped to persuade Martin Luther King (q.v.) to speak forcefully against the war. At King's side in Memphis when he was assassinated in 1968, James Bevel was less visible in later years. In the 1980s, he was pastor of Chicago's South Shore Community Church and promoted Students for Education and Development, a program for African American youth. In 1988, Bevel was the nominee of Lyndon La Rouche's U.S. Labor Party for vice president of the United States.

BIRMINGHAM, ALABAMA, MOVEMENT. A group of African American organizations, including the Alabama Christian Movement for Human Rights (q.v.) and the Jefferson County Improvement Association, which made Birmingham the site of nonviolent direct action's most dramatic confrontation with segregation.

In 1955, Birmingham, Alabama, was the urban citadel of racial segregation in the Deep South. A racist white power structure maintained a segregated regimen so thoroughly that opposition was almost unthinkable. When the Supreme Court attacked segregation in *Brown v. Board of Education* (q.v.), Alabama's attorney general countered with a series of law suits, *NAACP v. Alabama* (q.v.), which immobilized Birmingham's NAACP branch from 1956 to 1964. Inspired by the Montgomery Improvement Association (q.v.) and the Montgomery Bus Boycott (q.v.), however, the Reverend Fred Shuttlesworth (q.v.) and others organized the Alabama Christian Movement for Human Rights on 5 June 1956. Choosing Shuttlesworth as its president, the ACMHR adopted nonviolent direct action as its method for social change and became the Birmingham affiliate of SCLC (q.v.) in 1957. Others, offended by Shuttlesworth's style, looked to the Reverend J. L. Ware's Baptist Ministers' Conference and his Jefferson County Improvement Association for more prudent leadership in civil rights.

In December 1956, when the Supreme Court settled the case in *Browder v. Gayle* (q.v.), Shuttlesworth warned Birmingham authorities that segregation on city buses was unconstitutional. He survived the dynamiting of his parsonage on Christmas evening to lead an attempt to desegregate Birmingham's buses on the following day. Shuttlesworth and 20 other demonstrators were arrested and convicted of trespass. The ACMHR sought the desegregation of the city's public schools and its railroad station in 1957. On 31 October 1958, the ACMHR and Ware's Jefferson County Improvement Association began a boycott of Birmingham's still-segregated buses. The boycott failed within two months, however, because of divisions within the African American community, police intimidation, and the failure to win press coverage. Birmingham's buses were officially desegregated by a federal court order on 14 December 1959. ACMHR and Shuttlesworth gave local support for the Freedom Rides (q.v.) in 1961, but Birmingham remained a largely segregated city in 1963, when Martin Luther King (q.v.) and SCLC fixed the nation's attention on its brutal racism.

The confrontation began on 3 April 1963, when two dozen black college students began sit-ins at four Birmingham stores. Four days later, Public Safety Commissioner T. Eugene "Bull" Connor (q.v.) loosed police dogs on civil rights marchers, unintentionally drawing dramatic media attention to the Birmingham story. On Good Friday, 12 April, King, Shuttlesworth and Ralph Abernathy (q.v.) were arrested and jailed with other marchers for violating a state court injunction against additional demonstrations. From his cell, King wrote "A Letter from Birmingham Jail" (q.v.), his famous apologia for nonviolent direct action. Two weeks later, King and others were convicted of criminal contempt and released on appeal, leading to the case of *Walker v. City of Birmingham* (q.v.). Birmingham demonstrations recaptured the nation's attention when SCLC's James Bevel (q.v.) organized school children to march against segregation on 2 May. When "Bull" Connor's police and fire departments used powerful water hoses against the young people the following day, black spectators retaliated by throwing bricks and bottles. After the intervention of the Kennedy administration, a settlement was announced on 10 May 1963.

On 11 May, however, Klansmen bombed the A. G. Gaston Motel and the home of Martin Luther King's brother, A. D. King, a leader of the Birmingham Movement. African Americans reacted in the first urban race riot of the decade by burning automobiles and buildings. Alabama state troopers under Colonel Al Lingo intervened to suppress the rioting. Four months later, a bomb destroyed Birmingham's Sixteenth Street Baptist Church and killed four Sunday School children: Addie Mae Collins, Denise McNair, Carol Robertson and Cynthia Wesley. Again, black residents of Birmingham vented their anger in rioting. No one was arrested for the crime immediately, but a Ku Klux Klan member, Robert Edward Chambliss, was convicted of the murder of Denise McNair in 1977 and died in prison eight years later. For all of its terrifying violence, the events of the Birmingham Movement won national support for many of the Civil Rights Movement's goals and led to the passage of the Civil Rights Act of 1964 (q.v.).

BLACK PANTHER PARTY. A militant African American organization committed to the liberation of black communities.

In 1962, Huey P. Newton (q.v.) and Bobby Seale (q.v.) met at Merritt Junior College in Oakland, California. There, they organized "The Soul Students Advisory Council." By early October 1966, it had evolved into the "Black Panther Party for Self-Defense." It was inspired by Malcolm X's (q.v.) militant black nationalism and the anti-imperialism of the Algerian writer, Frantz Fanon. The Black Panthers issued a Ten Point Program, which assumed that African Americans lived in a black colony within an imperialist white nation. Committed to liberating the African American colony by any means, the Black Panthers combined militant rhetoric with ameliorating social programs and a readiness to use force if necessary to free black America. They demanded freedom from white power structures, autonomy of black communities to determine their own destiny, exemption from the draft, better education and housing, and social justice. Their social service programs in African American communities included free health clinics and free breakfasts for black children. When Huey Newton was arrested for the death of a police officer in October 1967, Black Panther influence spread from the West Coast in "Free Huey Newton" campaigns in urban radical circles across the Midwest and Northeast. By 1968, with about 2,000 members, the Black Panther Party was led by Seale, its chairman; Newton, its minister of defense; Stokely Carmichael (q.v.), its prime minister; James Forman, its minister of foreign affairs; Bobby Hutton, its minister of finance; and Eldridge Cleaver (q.v.), its minister of information.

The Black Panthers' militant rhetoric and open display of weapons, as they monitored the treatment of African Americans by Oakland police, captured media attention. In turn, the Federal Bureau of Investigation (q.v.) and police agencies fixed the Panthers in their sights. In August 1967, J. Edgar Hoover's FBI created COINTELPRO (Counter Intelligence Program) to infiltrate, monitor, and give disinformation to radical black organizations and to exploit differences among them, sometimes with deadly results. In July 1968, Newton was convicted of the murder of an Oakland policeman and remained in prison until 1970, when the California Supreme Court overturned the decision and released him. By then, however, police repression and violence had halved the Panthers' membership. Mark Clark, Fred Hampton, and Bobby Hutton had been killed by police. Ideological conflict with Maulana Ron Karenga's (q.v.) US Organization in Los Angeles had led to several gun battles. The remaining members were further divided when Cleaver and Newton-led factions expelled each other from the party.

As Huey Newton shifted the Black Panthers' emphasis to free health clinics and voter registration, the party drew less publicity and its leaders went in different directions. Later charged with diverting public funds to his personal use and murdering a teenage prostitute, Newton was in and out of jail until 1989, when he was killed, allegedly by a crack cocaine dealer, whom he had attempted to rob. Bobby Seale was acquitted by a hung jury of murdering Black Panther Alex Rackley for disloyalty in New Haven, Connecticut; he returned to Oakland and, in 1973, won 43,000 votes in a run-off election against the incumbent mayor. Thereafter, he left the Black Panther Party and moved his family to a comfortable Denver suburb. Eldridge Cleaver returned from exile abroad in 1975 to negotiate a settlement of assault charges with community service on probation. Subsequently, he became a spokesman for American patriotism and evangelical Christianity. In 1992, former Panther Bobby Rush was elected to Congress from Illinois.

BOB JONES UNIVERSITY v. UNITED STATES, 461 U.S. 574 (1983). A case in which the Supreme Court affirmed the federal government's right to withhold tax-exempt status from private institutions with racially discriminatory policies.

The Internal Revenue Service (IRS) gave tax-exempt status to private schools regardless of their racial policies until 1971, when a federal district court ruled in *Green v. Connally* that private schools with racially discriminatory policies were not entitled to tax exemption. Greenville, South Carolina's Bob Jones University did not admit African American students until then. From 1971 to 1975, it admitted only African Americans who were married to African Americans. Thereafter, it accepted single African Americans, but banned interracial dating or marriage. On those grounds, in January 1976, the IRS revoked Bob Jones University's tax-exempt status retroactive to 1970. The university and the IRS sued each other over unemployment taxes. South Carolina's federal district court found in favor of the university, claiming that the IRS did not have the authority to revoke the tax exemption. On appeal to the Fourth Circuit Court of Appeals, the lower court's ruling was reversed. The Supreme Court reaffirmed the appellate court's decision against Bob

Jones University. "There can no longer be any doubt," wrote Chief Justice Warren Burger for the Court, "that racial discrimination in education violates deeply and widely accepted views of elementary justice."

BOB-LO EXCURSION CO. v. MICHIGAN, 333 U.S. 28 (1948). A case in which the Supreme Court held that the application of a state's antidiscrimination statute in foreign commerce did not violate the constitutional right of Congress to regulate foreign trade.

In June 1945, 13 young women bought tickets and boarded the ferry from Detroit, Michigan, to Bois Blanc Island, Canada. The one African American among them, Sarah Elizabeth Ray, was ordered to leave the ship before its departure. Ray left the ship, but then filed a grievance against the company under state antidiscrimination law. The state filed charges against the company and a state court levied a fine against it. The state supreme court upheld the lower court's decision and the company appealed to the Supreme Court. Had the Court invoked its own precedent in *Morgan v. Virginia* (q.v.), it would have found state regulation of racial policy in interstate or foreign commerce violated the constitutional authority of Congress to regulate such trade. The effect in this case would have been to bar the application of state antidiscriminatory legislation from interstate or foreign trade. Instead, the Court noted that the only access from the United States to the Canadian island was from Detroit and that most of the company's customers lived there. Invoking the state's antidiscrimination law was, therefore, basically a local matter which did not violate congressional authority to regulate interstate or foreign commerce.

BOLLING v. SHARPE, 347 U.S. 497 (1954). A case in which the Supreme Court decision held that segregation in the District of Columbia's public schools was unconstitutional.

Spottswood Bolling, Jr., a 12-year-old African American, and his attorney, James M. Nabrit, Jr., sued the president of the District of Columbia's Board of Education, C. Melvin Sharpe, for relief from the racial segregation policies in its public schools. The case was grouped with those encompassed in *Brown v. Board of Education* (q.v.), because it dealt with the same fundamental issues. It was distinguished from the *Brown* cases, however, because while the Fourteenth Amendment, which was decisive in them, prohibited states from denying its citizens the equal protection of the law, it did not refer to territory under the direct authority of the federal government. In *Bolling,* the Court ruled unanimously that racial discrimination in the District of Columbia's public schools was "so unjustifiable" as to violate the Fifth Amendment's guarantee of due process. "In view of our decision that the Constitution prohibits the states from maintaining racially segregated public schools," argued the Court, "it would be unthinkable that the same Constitution would impose a lesser duty on the Federal Government." As though summoning citizens of the nation's capital to set an example for the rest of the nation, only in *Bolling* among the *Brown* cases did the Court rule that desegregation must begin immediately.

BOND, HORACE JULIAN (1940–). Civil rights activist, politician and lecturer.

Julian Bond was born in Nashville, Tennessee, on 14 January 1940, the son of Horace Mann and Julia Bond, who were members of a distinguished family of African American educators. Young Julian Bond grew up in the Pennsylvania countryside around Lincoln University, where his father was the first African American president of the historic African American college. Julian Bond attended a private Quaker school in Bucks County, Pennsylvania, where he coedited the high school newspaper. The family moved to Atlanta in 1957, when Horace Mann Bond became dean of the School of Education at Atlanta University. In 1958, Julian Bond entered Morehouse College in Atlanta. There, he and Lonnie King organized the Committee on Appeal for Human Rights, the student organization which coordinated early nonviolent student protests against segregation in Atlanta. In April 1960, Bond represented the Atlanta student movement at the Raleigh, North Carolina, conference which organized SNCC (q.v.). By mid-1961, he had married, left Morehouse without a degree, and combined his passions for civil rights and journalism by helping to found the *Atlanta Inquirer,* a paper more sympathetic to the movement than the *Atlanta World.* Within months, SNCC's executive director, James Forman (q.v.), persuaded Bond to join its staff as director of public relations. His role in the organization was not on the picket lines of nonviolent demonstrations or the country roads of voter registration drives, but in the Atlanta office interpreting the work of his colleagues for the public's edification.

In 1965, Julian Bond resigned from SNCC and won election to Georgia's house of representatives with 82 percent of the vote in his district. Because of his opposition to the war in Vietnam, however, members of the legislature refused to seat him and called a special election to fill the vacancy. Voters in his district reelected Bond to the seat, but the legislature still refused to allow him to be sworn in. His appeal to the courts for relief in *Bond v. Floyd* was lost in the Fifth Circuit Court of Appeals (q.v.). In 1966 the United States Supreme Court reversed the appeals court's decision, holding that denying a seat to a duly elected representative on the grounds of his political beliefs was unconstitutional. He was then seated in the legislature.

In 1967, Julian Bond helped to organize the Conference on New Politics, which sought to form a coalition of the antipoverty, antiwar, civil rights, and student movements on the Democratic left. A year later, after he led a successful challenge to Governor Lester Maddox's regular delegation to the Democratic National Convention, a coalition of civil rights and anti-Vietnam war delegates sought to place Bond in nomination for the vice presidency, only to withdraw his name because, at 28, he did not meet the constitutional requirement for the office. In 1974, Bond moved from the state house of representatives to a seat in the state senate, where he served until 1986. In that year, he was defeated in a bitter congressional race by his former SNCC ally, John Lewis (q.v.). Later, following a divorce, Bond left elective politics, moved to Washington, D.C., and teaches at American University and the University of Virginia.

BOYNTON, AMELIA (Amelia Platts Boynton Billups Robinson; 1911–). Civil rights activist.

Amelia Platts was born on 18 August 1911 in Savannah, Georgia, to George G. and Anna Eliza Platts. Her father was a carpenter and wood yard operator. Amelia Platts graduated from Savannah public schools for African American children and, in 1927, from Tuskegee Institute. In 1930, she moved to Selma, Alabama, as the Department of Agriculture's black home demonstration agent for Dallas County. There, she worked with the county's black agricultural agent, Samuel W. Boynton. In 1936, they were married. In the next two decades, they became influential voices in the Dallas County branch of the NAACP (q.v.) and the Dallas County Voters League. Amelia Boynton operated an employment agency until 1952, when her husband retired from government service and they launched an insurance and real estate business. Segregationists tried to intimidate the Boyntons, but they testified before the U. S. Civil Rights Commission (q.v.) in 1958 and their son, Bruce, a law student at Howard University, filed suit to force the desegregation of interstate public transportation in *Boynton v. Virginia* (q.v.). From 1961 until his death in 1963, S. W. Boynton was hospitalized with a heart condition.

By 1961, Amelia Boynton was the most influential local leader of the civil rights movement in Alabama's western black belt. She made unsuccessful races for the United States House of Representatives in 1964, for Dallas County probate judge in 1972, and for state senator in 1974. After her first husband's death, Amelia Boynton was married to Robert W. Billups from 1970 until his death in 1975. In 1976, she married James Robinson and moved to his home in Tuskegee. There, she published her autobiography, *Bridge across Jordan,* in 1979. James Robinson died in 1988. In recent years, Amelia Boynton Robinson has been a loyal follower of Lyndon La Rouche. In 1991, his Schiller Institute published a second, revised and expanded edition of her autobiography. Her son, Bruce, has served as county attorney for Dallas County.

BOYNTON v. VIRGINIA, 364 U.S. 454 (1960). A case in which the Supreme Court extended its prohibition of racial segregation in interstate commerce from seating in buses to service in bus terminals.

In 1946, the Supreme Court barred racially segregated seating on interstate buses in *Morgan v. Virginia* (q.v.). The Congress of Racial Equality (CORE; q.v.) tested the *Morgan* decision in the Journey of Reconciliation (q.v.) and found it was not enforced in the South. It would be two decades before it was fully implemented. Bruce Boynton, a Howard University law student, bought a Trailways Bus ticket from Washington, D.C., to Montgomery, Alabama. At Richmond, he asked for service in the white section of the terminal's privately owned restaurant. When ordered to move to the section reserved for black customers, Boynton refused, was arrested, and found guilty of trespass. Lower courts rejected his argument that as an interstate passenger he had a right to nondiscriminatory service in bus terminals. On 5 December 1960, by a seven to two vote, Justices Tom Clark and Charles E. Whittaker dissenting, the Supreme Court reversed the lower courts and extended its ruling in *Morgan* to include accommodations in bus terminals. Justice Hugo Black wrote for the Court majority that terminal facilities serving interstate passengers must not discriminate among them. Because the *Morgan* decision had gone unenforced in the South, CORE decided to test the *Boynton* decision in the Freedom Rides (q.v.).

BRIGGS v. ELLIOT, 132 F. Supp. 776 (E.D. S.C., 1955). A case, originating in South Carolina and grouped with *Brown v. Board of Education* (q.v.), in which the Court found racial segregation in public schools unconstitutional.

In 1951, Harry Briggs, an African American parent, sued R. W. Elliot, chairman of the Clarendon County, South Carolina, school board, for relief from the state requirement that Briggs's children must attend the county's inferior schools for African Americans. Briggs's attorneys from the NAACP Legal Defense and Educational Fund (LDEF; q.v.) were led by Thurgood Marshall (q.v.). Resting heavily on the testimony of Kenneth Clark (q.v.), they argued that Clarendon County's separate black schools were "inherently inferior," in violation of the *Plessy v. Ferguson* edict of "separate and equal," and that racial segregation was both harmful to black students and unconstitutional. Finding for the state, within the logic of *Plessy,* the federal district court refused to order the desegregation of Clarendon County's schools, but it did order the state to bring the black schools to a level of equality with the white schools. The NAACP LDEF attorneys appealed the decision to the Supreme Court, where this case was grouped with *Brown v. Board of Education* (q.v.) and a unanimous Court ruled that even "separate but equal" schools were unconstitutional.

BROOKE, EDWARD WILLIAM (1919–   ). The first African American to serve in the United States Senate since Reconstruction.

Edward William Brooke was born in Washington, D.C., on 26 October 1919. He was educated at Howard University (B.S., 1941). During World War II, Brooke served with the 366th Infantry. After the war, he studied law at Boston University (LL.B., 1948; LL.M., 1949). In 1960, Brooke was the Republican nominee for secretary of the Commonwealth of Massachusetts. He was defeated in that race, but Brooke was successful in a race for attorney general of Massachusetts in 1962 and was reelected in 1964. As attorney general, he won national attention as an intelligent spokesman for the progressive wing of the Republican Party. In 1966, Brooke was elected to the United States Senate from Massachusetts, defeating former governor Endicott Peabody. President Lyndon Johnson named Brooke to the Kerner Commission (q.v.) the following year. The first African American to serve in the Senate since Reconstruction, Brooke won reelection to the Senate in 1972. In the Senate, Brooke became an expert on housing legislation. As a member of the Senate Banking, Housing, and Urban Affairs Committee, he supported desegregated private housing and low to moderate income public housing projects. When he was defeated for reelection to the Senate by Representative Paul E. Tsongas in 1978, Brooke returned to private legal practice.

BROOKS v. BOARD OF EDUCATION OF THE CITY OF MOBERLY, MISSOURI, 3 R.R.L.R. 660 (E.D. Mo., 1958). A case in which a federal district court held that an all-white faculty of a desegregated school was not proof that its officials had wrongly discriminated against African American teachers.

When the school board of Moberly, Missouri, desegregated its schools in compliance with the Supreme Court's decision in *Brown v. Board of Education* (q.v.), it hired only white teachers to staff the desegregated school. African Americans taught only in schools with an African American student body. Naomi Brooks and seven other African American teachers sued, arguing that they had been discriminated against. The school board countered that qualifications and talent, not race, were the criteria in its hiring policies. Although the federal court acknowledged that the school board's criteria were subjective, the board was not guilty of racial discrimination. Later, NAACP LDEF (q.v.) attorneys would argue that a segregated faculty was evidence of a segregated school.

BROWDER v. GAYLE, 352 U.S. 903 (1956). A case in which the Supreme Court sustained a federal district court finding that state and local laws which required racial segregation in public transportation violated the due process and equal protection requirements of the Fourteenth Amendment.

The case grew out of the protest of the Montgomery Improvement Association (MIA; q.v.) against racial segregation on the city's buses. MIA attorneys filed the case in February 1956 on behalf of five African American women in federal district court. They argued that laws requiring racial segregation in public transportation should be found unconstitutional. On a three-judge federal panel, Judges Frank Minis Johnson (q.v.) and Richard Taylor Rives (q.v.) concurred with the plaintiffs. Precedents based on *Plessy v. Ferguson,* wrote Judge Rives, had been reversed in recent Supreme Court rulings and there was "no rational basis upon which the separate-but-equal doctrine can be validly applied to public transportation." Montgomery and Alabama state officials appealed the decision to the Supreme Court in *Gayle v. Browder,* but on 17 December the higher court unanimously sustained the lower court's ruling. The decision in *Gayle v. Browder* ended the Montgomery Bus Boycott (q.v.) and led to the desegregation of the city's buses.

BROWN, HUBERT GEROLD (H. Rap Brown; Jamil Abdullah al-Amin; 1943–   ). Civil rights activist.

H. Rap Brown was born on 4 October 1943 in Baton Rouge, Louisiana. His father was a World War II veteran who worked for Esso Oil Company and his mother was a maid and teacher at an orphanage. Young Brown attended segregated public schools for African American youth until his mother transferred him from Baton Rouge's all-black McKinley High School to the newly desegregated Southern High School. From 1960 to 1962, Brown studied at Southern University in Baton Rouge, where he played football. His early participation in a voter registration drive and protests of segregation at Baton Rouge's Greyhound Bus Terminal led to increased political activity when Brown participated in the March on Washington (q.v.) and transferred to Howard University there, in 1963. At Howard, he was active in the Nonviolent Action Group (NAG). In 1964, he attended the Democratic National Convention to support the challenge of Mississippi's Freedom Democratic Party (q.v.) to the state's all-white delegation. Brown became the director of NAG and joined SNCC (q.v.) in 1965. As director of its direct action and voter registration project in 1966, Brown was arrested for carrying a gun. In 1967, he succeeded Stokely Carmichael (q.v.) as the national director of SNCC. As SNCC's national director, Brown escalated Carmichael's separatist "black power" rhetoric and abandoned SNCC's commitment to nonviolence in favor of armed self-defense.

Like Carmichael, Brown became an officer in the Black Panther Party (q.v.). His celebration of violence—"as American as cherry pie"— alienated SNCC's white supporters long before it was repeated in his book, *Die Nigger Die!* (1969). By then, however, SNCC itself was dead. Internal disintegration was signalled as the early departures of James Bevel (q.v.) and Diane Nash (q.v.) were followed by those of Robert Moses (q.v.), John Lewis (q.v.), Julian Bond (q.v.), Fannie Lou Hamer (q.v.), and white organizers, as SNCC shed its commitment to integration and nonviolence. Externally, Brown was sought by the police. In August 1967, he urged black youth in the Cambridge, Maryland, Movement (q.v.) to "burn this town down." That evening, as black people rioted in Cambridge, Brown was wounded by a gunshot. After the shooting, two blocks in black Cambridge burned to the ground. Arrested and released on bail in Washington, Brown was then sought by police in Dayton, Ohio, where another riot followed one of his appearances. Later, he was arrested for carrying a registered rifle aboard an airplane flight to Louisiana. He was on a 40-day fast in a Louisiana prison cell when

Martin Luther King (q.v.) was shot in April 1968. Released from prison a month later, Brown married Lynne Doswell, a New York City school teacher.

In his absence, much of SNCC's remaining adherents replaced him with a "collective leadership." Brown still claimed to be in control of it in the summer of 1968, however, when he sought to change its name to Student National Coordinating Committee. By then, Brown was excommunicating one-time allies—Carmichael, Cleveland Sellers, and Willie Ricks—on ideological grounds. In March 1970, he was to be tried in a Bel Air, Maryland, courthouse on charges stemming from the incidents in Cambridge. When a car bomb killed two of his closest SNCC allies, Ralph Featherstone and William H. Payne, in front of the courthouse, Rap Brown went underground. Placed on the Federal Bureau of Investigation's Ten Most Wanted List, he was charged with arson, riot, violations of the Federal Firearms Act, and flight to avoid prosecution. In 1971, Manhattan police shot and captured Brown in a gun battle when he allegedly tried to rob some black crapshooters in a New York bar. His attorney, William Kunstler, sought to portray him as a political victim of police harassment, but Brown was sentenced to five to fifteen years in prison. From 1971 to 1976, he was moved within the New York State prison system about every six months, serving time in Attica, Sing Sing, and elsewhere. While in prison, Brown converted to Islam and adopted Jamil Abdullah al-Amin as his name. He was paroled on 21 October 1976. Since then, he has lived in Atlanta's West End near Atlanta University, where he operates a grocery store and serves as the Imam to a small group of Muslims.

BROWN, JOHN ROBERT (1909–   ). A member of the Fifth Circuit Court of Appeals (q.v.).

John Robert Brown was born on 10 December 1909 in Funk, Nebraska. He studied at the University of Nebraska (A.B., 1932) and attended law school at the University of Michigan (J.D., 1933; LL.D., 1939). In 1932, Brown was admitted to the Texas bar and joined a law firm with offices in Galveston and Houston, which specialized in maritime law. During World War II, he served as a port commander in the Philippines. Brown became active in Texas Republican politics after the war. He served on the Eisenhower delegation from Texas which was seated at the Republican National Convention in 1952 and became Harris County (Houston) party chairman the following year. Brown was something of an enigma. He was at once a hard-drinking brilliant attorney with a flamboyant flair and a devout Presbyterian layman, who believed strongly in brotherhood, human equality, and minority rights in the law. In 1955, Brown was appointed by President Eisenhower to the Fifth Circuit Court of Appeals. On the Fifth Circuit Court, with fellow judges Richard Taylor Rives (q.v.), Elbert Parr Tuttle (q.v.), and John Minor Wisdom (q.v.), he took up a heavy caseload on the South's major judicial battleground to implement the Supreme Court's desegregation decisions. Beyond desegregation of the South's public school systems, Brown participated in decisions to bar racial discrimination in employment, jury selection, and voting rights. He succeeded Tuttle as chief judge of the Fifth Circuit Court in 1967 and continued in that capacity until 1979.

BROWN v. BOARD OF EDUCATION, TOPEKA, KS 347 U.S. 483 (1954). A case in which the Supreme Court found racial segregation in public schools unconstitutional.

On 17 May 1954, a unanimous Supreme Court reversed the "separate but equal" logic of its *Plessy v. Ferguson* decision in 1896 to find that racially segregated public school systems were inherently discriminatory and, thus, unconstitutional. Building on a series of Court decisions since the 1930s, the NAACP Legal Defense and Educational Fund (LDEF; q.v.) launched a broad assault on public school segregation after World War II. In *Brown*, it took up the case of Linda Brown, the daughter of an African American pastor in Topeka, Kansas, who was barred by law from attending a white school. Brown's case was lost in lower courts. Her appeal reached the Supreme Court in December 1952 and was grouped with similar NAACP LDEF cases from Delaware, South Carolina, Virginia, and the District of Columbia. Among the five cases, only in Delaware had a lower court, still under *Plessy* logic, found separate black schools inferior and therefore ordered the admission of African American students to white schools.

Given the equal protection requirements of the Fourteenth Amendment and the *Plessy* precedent, the Supreme Court was badly divided on how to treat the issue of racially segregated public schools until Earl Warren succeeded Chief Justice Fred M. Vinson in 1953. Under Chief Justice Warren's careful nurture, the Court heard the consolidated cases in 1954. The District of Columbia case, *Bolling v. Sharpe* (q.v.), involved questions of federal jurisdiction and the Court treated it in a separate decision. On 17 May, Warren spoke for a unanimous Supreme Court in ruling that "in the field of public education the doctrine of 'separate but equal' has no place. Separate educational facilities are inherently unequal."

"Separate but equal," the Court now argued, violated the equal protection guarantees of the Fourteenth Amendment. In dignified legal language, the Supreme Court had issued a mandate for sweeping social change.

BROWN v. BOARD OF EDUCATION, 349 U.S. 294 (1955). A case in which the Supreme Court ordered that racially segregated public school systems should begin desegregation "with all deliberate speed."

A year after its sweeping decision in *Brown v. Board of Education,* commonly known as *Brown I,* which found racial segregation in public schools unconstitutional, the Supreme Court heard attorneys' arguments and issued an opinion, commonly known as *Brown II,* about how its earlier decision would be implemented. *Brown I* held that children in racially segregated public schools were deprived of "the equal protection of the laws guaranteed by the Fourteenth Amendment." In recognizing that constitutional rights are always "personal and present" and ordering the immediate desegregation of the District of Columbia's public schools in *Bolling v. Sharpe* (q.v.), the Court seemed to imply that petitioners for school desegregation might expect immediate relief. *Brown II* disappointed such expectations, for the Court noted that implementation of its sweeping decision would be gradual and determined by local conditions. School desegregation cases would be returned to federal district courts where they had been tried. There, judges more familiar with local conditions were to apply the Supreme Court's mandate that school boards must begin to desegregate their schools "with all deliberate speed." Given that latitude, some school boards would delay school desegregation for another dozen years.

BUNCHE, RALPH JOHNSON (1904–71). Prominent African American scholar, diplomat and Nobel Prize winner.

Ralph J. Bunche was born in Detroit, Michigan, on 7 August 1904. He was orphaned at the age of eleven and raised thereafter by his grandfather, a former slave. Bunche attended the University of California at Los Angeles on an athletic scholarship and graduated summa cum laude in 1927. His graduate work in political science, government and international relations was at Harvard University (M.A., 1928; Ph.D., 1934). Bunche taught political science from 1928 to 1934 at Howard University, where he chaired the department. He helped to organize the National Negro Congress in 1936. By then a recognized authority on the roots and effects of race discrimination, Bunche became a member of Gunnar Myrdal's research team which produced *An American Dilemma* (q.v.).

In 1941, Ralph Bunche joined the federal government, serving the Office of Strategic Services and the State Department as an intelligence officer. He was an advisor to the United States delegation to the San Francisco conference which wrote the United Nations' charter. Already regarded as an expert mediator and authority on peoples of the third world, Bunche joined the UN staff in 1948. Widely admired for his work as acting mediator of the UN's Special Committee on Palestine and negotiating an armistice between Israel and Egypt, Bunche received the Spingarn Medal from the NAACP (q.v.) in 1949 and the Nobel Peace Prize in 1950. Named under secretary general of the United Nations in 1954, Bunche participated in negotiations on the Congo, Kashmir and Yemen. In 1965, he joined Martin Luther King (q.v.) on the Selma to Montgomery March (q.v.). He published more than 40 monographs and articles and was awarded 69 honorary degrees. Ralph Bunche died on 9 December 1971.

BURTON v. WILMINGTON PARKING AUTHORITY, 365 U.S. 715 (1961). A case in which the Supreme Court held that states were accountable for the policies of private businesses that are tenants of the state.

Burton, an African American, was denied service in the Eagle Coffee Shoppe, a private business located in a parking garage owned by the Wilmington, Delaware, Parking Authority. Rather than charging Eagle's management, Burton sued the Wilmington Parking Authority, a state agency. His attorney argued that the state became a party to discrimination by leasing to a tenant who discriminated. Delaware's supreme court rejected Burton's case, holding that the restaurant was not required by law to serve all customers, that it was a separate agency from the state and that its policies were not dictated by the state. By a six-to-three decision, with Justices Felix Frankfurter, John Marshall Harlan, and Charles Whittaker dissenting, the United States Supreme Court reversed the Delaware court decision. As landlord and tenant, said Justice Tom Clarke for the Court, the state and the restaurant had an interdependent relationship and the restaurant's discrimination violated the state's obligation to equal protection of all its citizens. Together with *Derrington v. Plummer* (q.v.) and *Coke v. City of Atlanta* (q.v.), *Burton v. Wilmington Parking Authority* helped to define state and private discriminatory action and legal requirements of tenants of state property.

BUSH v. ORLEANS PARISH SCHOOL BOARD, 364 U.S. 500 (1960). A case in which the Supreme Court affirmed a federal district judge's injunction against Louisiana officials to prevent them from enforcing recently adopted state legislation to prevent school desegregation.

When Judge J. Skelly Wright (q.v.) of Louisiana's Eastern District tried to implement the Supreme Court's decision in *Brown v. Board of Education*, Governor Jimmie Davis encouraged the state legislature to pass many legal obstructions, including an "Interposition Act," in which the state interposed its authority between the federal court and the people of Louisiana. Judge Wright found this obstructive legislation unconstitutional and enjoined state officials from acting on it. In this case, the Supreme Court refused Louisiana's request for a stay of Wright's injunction pending an appeal. On hearing the appeal in *Orleans Parish School Board v. Bush*, the Supreme Court issued an opinion that sustained Wright's injunction.

BUSING. A controversial means, sometimes mandated by the courts, of desegregating public school systems.

In 1971, the United States Supreme Court in *Swann v. Charlotte-Mecklenburg Board of Education* (q.v.) endorsed the use of public school buses to move large numbers of students to integrate previously segregated public schools. The Court held that busing—even mandatory, massive crosstown busing or the redrawing of school district lines—violated no one's constitutional rights, but that it should not impose an undue burden on students. A student's bus ride should not, for example, be for more than several miles or take more than 35 minutes. Court-ordered busing contributed to "white flight" from urban areas, school boards generally resisted it, and the Nixon administration sought congressional legislation limiting school busing. By 1974, when Northern cities such as Boston, Denver, Detroit, and Pontiac, Michigan, faced busing orders, opponents of school busing promoted a constitutional amendment banning court-ordered busing.

In *Milliken v. Bradley* (q.v.), a severely divided Supreme Court seemed to signal a retreat from *Swann*. School systems that had maintained de jure segregation, or written segregation into its law, might be subject to court-ordered busing, the court reasoned; but in systems where segregation derived from other factors, de facto segregation, the Court majority reasoned, there were no constitutional grounds for court-ordered busing. Many African American parents were unhappy with mandated busing of their children and school boards experimented with other means of desegregating schools, such as magnet schools and transfer plans. Busing remains a means of desegregating schools, but it is widely viewed as a crude tool of social engineering and many urban schools continue to be segregated de facto.

C

CALHOUN v. LATIMER, 377 U.S. 263 (1964). A case in which the Supreme Court approved a plan by the Atlanta, Georgia, school board to integrate its public schools by 1968.

Vivian Calhoun sued to force Atlanta's public schools to comply with the Supreme Court's rulings in *Brown v. Board of Education* (q.v.). Atlanta school officials had delayed integration with a variety of tactics, including a plan to desegregate its schools one year at a time from the twelfth grade to the first grade. This plan would have taken more than ten years to integrate the city's first-grade classes. Urged by officials of the National Association for the Advancement of Colored People (NAACP; q.v.) and the NAACP Legal Defense and Educational Fund (LDEF; q.v.), black Atlantans challenged this plan. It deferred desegregation so long, they argued, as to be noncompliant with *Brown.* NAACP attorneys also asked the Court to require the Atlanta school board to integrate public school faculties more quickly and thoroughly. In its decision, the Supreme Court approved another plan that aimed to achieve integration of Atlanta's public schools by 1968 and granted the plaintiffs little relief in desegregating faculties.

CAMBRIDGE, MARYLAND, MOVEMENT. A local movement in a community on Chesapeake Bay, which was noted for a high degree of racial tension.

In 1963, Cambridge, Maryland, was a community of 11,000 people. Desegregation, however, had made few inroads in its way of life. Poverty and unemployment were widespread among the one-third of Cambridge residents who were African Americans. In 1962, Gloria Richardson (q.v.) and others organized the Cambridge Nonviolent Action Committee (CNAC) and won outside support from the Student Nonviolent Coordinating Committee (SNCC; q.v.). On 25 March 1963, Richardson and CNAC demanded that the city council desegregate the city. Days later, student demonstrators from Baltimore, Philadelphia, and New York joined residents of black Cambridge in an economic boycott, marches, picket lines, and sit-ins. Richardson was among the 80 demonstrators who were arrested in the next seven weeks. Early in May 1963, they were tried, convicted, given suspended sentences, and fined a penny each. After her release, Richardson renewed the demonstrations. On 14 May,

62 demonstrators were arrested in Cambridge. White authorities agreed to release them and establish a human relations committee to prepare to implement the demonstrators' demands.

Richardson vowed to continue the demonstrations until the demands were met. She believed that white authorities in Cambridge were violating constitutional rights of local activists and asked Attorney General Robert Kennedy to intercede. Three days after the windows of white-owned stores were broken and shooting began on 11 June, the governor declared martial law in Cambridge and national guardsmen surrounded black neighborhoods. The guardsmen were withdrawn a month later, demonstrations were renewed, and violence broke out again. The guardsmen returned to Cambridge, negotiations with state officials broke down, and Richardson was arrested again. On 22 July, Attorney General Robert Kennedy interceded to negotiate commitments to desegregate public accommodations and schools, a public housing project, and a biracial commission to deal with issues of jobs and poverty. Desegregation of public accommodations in Cambridge was delayed until July 1964, when President Lyndon Johnson signed the Civil Rights Act of 1964 (q.v.) into law. Two months later, Gloria Richardson left Cambridge to live in New York.

The state militia continued to patrol Cambridge streets until 1965. A public rally of the racist National States Rights Party again inflamed Cambridge race relations in July 1967. On 24 July, Hubert Gerold (H. Rap) Brown (q.v.) of SNCC (q.v.) called on Cambridge's African Americans to seize the moment. "It's time for Cambridge to explode," he cried. After Brown was wounded by gunshots, black people rioted. Fire burned over two blocks of black Cambridge and white firemen refused to extinguish it without protection. Maryland's governor, Spiro T. Agnew, sent national guardsmen back into the city to quell the rioting.

CARMICHAEL, STOKELY (Kwame Toure; 1941–   ). Civil rights activist.

Stokely Carmichael was born in Port-of-Spain, Trinidad, on 29 June 1941. At eleven, he immigrated to the United States. Carmichael attended Bronx High School of Science and received a bachelor's degree from Howard University in Washington, D.C., in 1964. While he was a student at Howard, Carmichael joined the Congress of Racial Equality (q.v.) and, during 1960, participated in its demonstrations, picketing, and sit-ins in the Washington area. In 1961, Carmichael joined the Freedom Rides (q.v.), was arrested in Jackson, Mississippi, and served forty-nine days in Mississippi's Parchman Prison. After his release from prison, he joined SNCC (q.v.), participating in both its nonviolent social action and its voter registration work in the Deep South. As early as 1963, Carmichael began questioning SNCC's commitment to nonviolence. He was an effective coordinator of its voter registration project in Mississippi's Second Congressional District during Freedom Summer (q.v.) in 1964. Increasingly, however, he doubted the effectiveness of nonviolence, arguing that African Americans must defend themselves against white violence and use political processes to secure control of their own lives.

Believing now that only black people could work effectively with black people for their liberation, Carmichael called for the exclusion of white people from SNCC. In March 1965, as the Southern Christian Leadership Conference (SCLC; q.v.) was developing its voting rights campaign in nearby Selma, Carmichael moved into rural Lowndes County, Alabama, to launch SNCC's voter registration project there. Of Lowndes County's 15,000 people, 80 percent were black, but less than 100 of them were registered to vote when he arrived. Citing the apparent failure of the biracial Mississippi Freedom Democratic Party (q.v.), Carmichael hoped to make Lowndes County a model for the empowerment of black people through the political process to control their own communities. By 1966, Carmichael and his fellow workers increased black voter registration in Lowndes County to over 2,600 and created a separate black political party, the Lowndes County Freedom Organization (LCFO; q.v.). In 1965 and 1966, it unsuccessfully challenged the Democratic Party for local offices. In May 1966, John Lewis (q.v.) sought reelection as SNCC's chairman. Challenged by Carmichael, Lewis initially won over-whelming reelection. Then, in a defining moment for SNCC, the decision was reconsidered in a long night of debate. In the early morning hours, Carmichael narrowly defeated Lewis in a second vote.

When James Meredith (q.v.) was shot on a march from Memphis to Jackson, Mississippi, in June 1966, Carmichael, as SNCC's new leader, and other civil rights leaders moved in to continue his pilgrimage. During the march, his intonation of its new "black power" theme alienated such traditional civil rights veterans as the NAACP's Roy Wilkins (q.v.) and Whitney Young (q.v.) of the National Urban League (q.v.). In May 1967, Hubert Gerold (H. Rap) Brown (q.v.) replaced Carmichael as SNCC's national chairman. As SNCC and the Black Panther Party (q.v.) moved into closer cooperation, Carmichael and Brown joined the Panther organi-zation. In February 1968, the two organizations announced their merger and Stokely Carmichael became the Panthers' prime minister. Already under severe pressure from the Federal Bureau of Investigation's counter-intelligence programs and police surveillance, however, the announcement came as both organizations were disintegrating. In August, Brown expelled Carmichael from SNCC for refusing to clear his speeches with its leadership. In 1973, after changing his name to Kwame Toure, Stokely Carmichael left the United States for the African country of Guinea. There, he was briefly under house arrest for advocating the overthrow of the Guinean government.

CASSELL v. TEXAS, 339 U.S. 282 (1950). A case in which the Supreme Court found the systematic exclusion of African Americans unconstitutional.

Cassell, an African American, was indicted for murder by a Dallas County, Texas, grand jury. Local practice was for grand jurors to be selected from among the friends of the jury commissioners, all of whom were white. The effect was to exclude African Americans from grand jury service. Cassell sought to have his murder indictment thrown out because of this violation of his Fourteenth Amendment equal protection rights, but his case was lost in Texas courts. He appealed to the Supreme Court. On 24 April 1950, it reversed the lower courts' decision by a vote of eight to one, with Justice Robert H. Jackson in dissent. Writing for the majority, Justice Stanley Reed argued that the systematic exclusion of African Americans from grand juries violated Cassell's equal protection rights.

CHANEY, JAMES EARL (1943–64). Civil rights activist.

James Earl Chaney was born on 30 May 1943 at Meridian, Mississippi. His parents were farmers. After attending public schools for African American students, Chaney enrolled in Harris Junior College. There, he was suspended from school for wearing a piece of paper with the initials "NAACP" pinned on his shirt. A year later, Chaney was expelled from the junior college for African American students. Rejected for service in the army because of his asthma, Chaney left home for Wichita Falls, Texas, where he worked at odd jobs. Shortly thereafter, however, Chaney returned to Meridian where he worked with his father as a plasterer.

In October 1963, Chaney met a Hispanic civil rights organizer for the Congress of Racial Equality (CORE; q.v.) in Meridian and became increasingly active with it and the Council of Federated Organizations (COFO; q.v.), organizing freedom schools, recruiting workers for the movement and promoting voter registration. In 1964, he joined the staff of the Meridian Community Center, which a white CORE organizer from New York, Michael Henry Schwerner (q.v.), had helped to establish. On 20 June 1964, Chaney and Schwerner were joined by a third CORE organizer, Andrew Goodman (q.v.). On the next day, they went to the Longdale community outside Philadelphia, in nearby Neshoba County, to investigate the burning of Mount Zion Methodist Church. Arrested by local authorities, they were apparently released and then taken captive, beaten, and shot. National authorities were notified and FBI agents searched until 4 August when they found the bodies of Chaney, Schwerner, and Goodman buried in an earthen dam. James Chaney had been shot three times. He was reburied in Meridian's Memorial Park Cemetery on 7 August 1964.

CHARLOTTE, NORTH CAROLINA, SIT-IN MOVEMENT. The sit-in movement (q.v.) in North Carolina's largest city.

On 9 February 1960, eight days after the movement began in Greensboro, North Carolina, about 100 African American students, mostly from Johnson C. Smith University, began sitting in at the segregated lunch counters of five downtown Charlotte locations. As if spontaneously, the movement had spread across the upper South and produced visible social change. Four of the five Charlotte lunch counters were closed and business suffered at the fifth. Demonstrations at the lunch counters continued intermittently for several months thereafter. As in Greensboro, behind-the-scenes negotiations eventually led to the desegregation of Charlotte lunch counters. Nearly 100 African Americans were served at desegregated lunch counters in the city on 9 July 1960.

CHICAGO, ILLINOIS, MOVEMENT. A coalition of African American, civil rights, neighborhood, and religious organizations in the nation's second largest city.

The great migration from the South created huge black ghettoes in Chicago by the end of World War II. They had strong African American institutions and traditional civil rights organizations, such as the National Urban League (q.v.) and the NAACP (q.v.), had been active there for decades. African Americans were represented in the city's political structures, but, in return for modest shares of power, many of their leaders had made peace with the city's white economic and political establishment. By the 1960s, two generations of black Chicagoans were caught in a familiar web of problems: inadequate and de facto segregated housing and schools, poverty, and unemployment mediated by a bureaucratic welfare system.

In 1962, complaints about the schools led to the formation of the Coordinating Council of Community Organizations (CCCO), a coalition of neighborhood groups led by community activist Al Raby. In 1963, CORE (q.v.) picketed the Board of Education to protest segregated schools and 200,000 students boycotted them in October 1963 and January 1964. By July 1965, SCLC (q.v.) organizers James Bevel (q.v.), Jesse Jackson (q.v.), and Bernard LaFayette planned to bring it to Chicago. Despite opposition from many of Chicago's white and traditional black leaders, by January 1966 CCCO and SCLC formed a coalition to attack education, employment, and housing problems in the ghetto. With support from the black middle class, young people, and black slum dwellers, demonstrations would focus on specific targets and build to climactic mass action uniting the forces of good will and the underprivileged against "the power of the existing social order."

When Jesse Jackson organized Operation Breadbasket to win jobs for black Chicagoans, boycotts persuaded several dairy store chains to hire black workers. SCLC-CCCO focused its nonviolent action at the housing issue. Martin Luther King (q.v.) and his aides seized a cold tenement building, cleaned, heated, and rewired it, and called a renters' strike, vowing to use the rent to pay for more improvements. They demanded an end to discrimination in real estate listings, showings, and bank loans, improved low income public housing, and tenant protection legislation. They also wanted a civilian review board of the police, school desegregation, and a federal guaranteed income. SCLC-CCCO began its direct action on 10 July 1966, when 25,000 to 50,000 people met at Soldier Field and marched on City Hall to present the demands. They got a cold reception from Mayor Richard Daley's administration, which blamed the movement when youth gangs rioted across the city in the next three days. As SCLC-CCCO began demonstrations at real estate offices in the city's white neighborhoods, King worried that white authorities would reenforce tendencies to violence in black Chicago by responding more directly to riot than to nonviolence. On 29–31 July, civil rights demonstrators at white real estate firms in Gage and Marquette Parks were outnumbered by angry white mobs who showered them with rocks, bottles, bricks, and debris. The mob overturned and burned 15 automobiles in Marquette Park before the police secured the area. King led demonstrators back to Marquette Park on 5 August and was felled by a flying rock. He said that he had never seen such hostility as he witnessed that day in Chicago.

Mayor Daley urged white community leaders to ignore civil rights demonstrations in their neighborhoods and began quiet negotiations to end them. A summit conference of several dozen of Chicago's black and white business, civil rights, political, and religious leaders began on 17 August. Under threat of continued demonstrations and a march into Cicero, even in violation of a court order against them, the Chicago summit negotiators unanimously agreed to a ten-point settlement, which included stronger enforcement of the city's fair-housing ordinance, endorsement by the city's real estate board of stronger state open occupancy legislation, and the location of public housing in scattered sites rather than concentrated in the ghettoes. When the agreement was announced, some black Chicagoans, including supporters of CORE and SNCC (q.v.), accused King, Raby, SCLC, and CCCO of "selling out." By September 1966, it was clear that implementation of the agreement would be a slow process. Many observers believed that SCLC's first campaign in a major Northern city was, at best, a limited failure.

CHISHOLM, SHIRLEY ANITA ST. HILL (1924–   ). The first African American woman to serve in the United States Congress.

Shirley Anita St. Hill Chisholm was born on 30 November 1924 in the Bedford-Stuyvesant section of Brooklyn, New York. Her father was a Guyanese factory worker, who was a follower of Marcus Garvey, and her mother was a Barbadian seamstress. For much of her childhood, Chisholm lived with her maternal grandmother in Barbados and went to school there. At ten, she returned to Brooklyn and attended public schools there. After graduating from high school, she attended Brooklyn College. There, she earned a bachelor's degree in sociology in 1946. Later, she received a master's degree in education from Columbia University. In 1949, she married Conrad Chisholm. Shirley Chisholm worked as a teacher, directed a nursery school, and was an education consultant with the Day Care Division of New York's public schools. She was active in community service and worked her way up from the precinct ranks of the Democratic Party.

In 1964, Chisholm was elected from Bedford-Stuyvesant to New York's state assembly, only the second African American woman to serve there. Reelected in 1966, she focused her attention on college scholarship, day care, and unemployment compensation legislation. In 1968, Chisholm became the Democratic nominee for the United States House of Representatives from New York's Twelfth District and defeated Republican-Liberal Party nominee James Farmer (q.v.), the former national director of CORE (q.v.). The first black woman elected to the House of Representatives, serving from 1969 to 1983, she specialized in education, labor, veterans' affairs, and women's issues. In 1972, Chisholm campaigned for the Democratic nomination for president, becoming the first African American and the first woman to run within the two-party framework. She retired from Congress in 1983 to her home in Williamsville, New York. Thereafter, Chisholm taught courses in politics briefly at Mount Holyoke and Spelman Colleges and lectured widely on college and university campuses. In 1993, she was offered the position of ambassador to Jamaica by the Clinton administration, but Chisholm was unable to accept the appointment for reasons of health.

CITIZENS' COUNCIL. An organization of white Southerners who were determined to preserve racial segregation.

On 11 July 1954, two months after the Supreme Court's ruling in *Brown v. Board of Education* (q.v.), Robert "Tut" Patterson organized a "Citizens' Council" at Indianola, Sunflower County, Mississippi, to mobilize white opposition to desegregation. A 32-year-old former captain of the Mississippi State University football team and former paratrooper, Patterson was a plantation manager who gathered the town's business and civic elite to discuss nonviolent means of maintaining segregation. They held a public rally and recruited 75 white members of the council's first chapter. Patterson spread the movement across the Delta and then across the state.

By October 1954, when the Citizens' Council claimed 25,000 members in Mississippi, including Senator James Eastland and scores of local public officials, it organized its first chapter outside the state at Selma, Alabama. The Citizens' Council played a significant role in mobilizing local white opposition to the Montgomery Bus Boycott (q.v.). By 1956, Citizens' Councils claimed 56,000 members in Mississippi and Alabama, with thousands of others from Virginia to Florida and Texas. They shunned identification with the Ku Klux Klan and officially denounced violence, but the council advocated every legal means to maintain segregation: economic pressure, intimidation, litigation, and mobilizing white voters. Under Governor Ross Barnett's administration from 1960 to 1964, it controlled Mississippi state government. As the civil rights movement in Mississippi grew and federal courts forced the desegregation of some public schools in the state, the Citizens' Council was discredited for its failure to preserve segregation.

CITY OF MOBILE v. BOLDEN, 446 U.S. 55 (1980). A case in which the Supreme Court held that, in order to challenge electoral practices, intent to discriminate must be proved; it could not merely be inferred from results.

Rather than electing city commissioners from single-member districts, the city of Mobile, Alabama, used an at-large method of electing commissioners. One result was that, although 35 percent of Mobile's population was black, no African American had been elected to the city commission 15 years after the passage of the Voting Rights Act of 1965 (q.v.). Attorneys for the plaintiff charged that, particularly in a racially polarized electorate, the at-large method of electing commissioners thus reduced the voting strength of black people in violation of the Fourteen and Fifteenth Amendments. Following the logic of the Supreme Court's decision in *Baker v. Carr* (q.v.), federal district and appellate courts agreed and ordered Mobile to abandon at-large elections in favor of electing commissioners from single-member districts.

On 22 April 1980, with Justices William J. Brennan, Thurgood Marshall, and Byron R. White in dissent, the Supreme Court reversed the lower federal courts' decisions and accepted Mobile's at-large election of commissioners. Speaking for a majority of six justices, Potter Stewart said that official bias could not be inferred from the effects of official acts. In order to challenge an official act successfully, a plaintiff must be able to prove intent to discriminate. When the case was retried in a federal district court, however, attorneys for the plaintiff were able to meet this strict standard of evidence and won their case. In 1982, the Voting Rights Act was amended to allow proof of the effects of an act, not just the intentions of the actor, to be a sufficient standard of evidence.

CITY OF RICHMOND v. UNITED STATES, 422 U.S. 358 (1975). A case in which the Supreme Court held that the dilution of minority representation by the addition of voting population is not unconstitutional.

When the city of Richmond, Virginia, attempted to annex a section of Chesterfield County, members of the city's African American community complained that the annexation would reduce it from 52 percent to 42 percent of the city's population. Although it would continue to have the same number of members of Richmond's city council, their strength would be reduced by the addition of new members to the council to represent the annexed area. Backed by the Justice Department, Richmond African Americans asked the courts to vacate the annexation because it was intended to dilute their political influence. By a vote of five to three, with Justices William J. Brennan, William O. Douglas, and Thurgood Marshall in dissent, the Supreme Court held that the annexation did not deny or abridge the right of African Americans to vote and be represented. The expansion of the city's boundaries by annexation might dilute black electoral influence, said Justice Byron White for the Court majority, but it was not unconstitutional.

CIVIL RIGHTS ACT OF 1957. Federal legislation that strengthened federal authority in voting rights.

On 9 September 1957, President Dwight Eisenhower signed the Civil Rights Act of 1957. The first major federal legislation to protect civil rights since the end of Reconstruction, it was aimed primarily at protecting voting rights. The act made it a federal crime to conspire to deny citizens their right to vote, authorized federal prosecutors to get court injunctions against interference with voting rights, and provided for jury trials of persons indicted of conspiracy to deny citizens their right to vote. It established the Civil Rights Division within the Justice Department and the United States Civil Rights Commission to investigate the denial of civil rights and make recommendations to correct them.

CIVIL RIGHTS ACT OF 1960. Federal legislation that strengthened federal authority in civil rights.

After mounting evidence of the denial of African American voting rights in large parts of the South and local incidents of violent resistance to school desegregation in Cleveland, Tennessee, Little Rock, Arkansas, and elsewhere, Congress passed and President Eisenhower signed the Civil Rights Act of 1960. The Act authorized federal judges to appoint referees to hear testimony that state officials were interfering with the right to register or vote. It also made flight to avoid arrest and prosecution for incendiary acts and interfering with court ordered desegregation a federal offense.

CIVIL RIGHTS ACT OF 1964. Comprehensive federal legislation that expanded federal guarantees of civil rights in public accommodations, employment, and voting.

After the Birmingham, Alabama, Movement (q.v.) confronted the city's virulent white racism, and the March on Washington (q.v.) stirred the national conscience, President Lyndon Johnson called for passage of civil rights legislation with widespread dimension. Its passage was delayed for three-and-a-half months in the United States Senate by a Southern filibuster, during which Southern senators focused their opposition on its required desegregation of public accommodations and public facilities throughout the nation. Ultimately, however, Congress passed and Johnson signed the most comprehensive civil rights legislation in the nation's history.

The Civil Rights Act of 1964 banned racial discrimination in public accommodations (bars, entertainment parks, gas stations, hotels, motels, restaurants, and theaters) and authorized the attorney general to sue states that tolerated segregation of public facilities (libraries, parks, playgrounds, schools, and swimming pools). It further protected African Americans' voting rights in federal elections by barring the unequal application of registration requirements and severely restricting the use of literacy tests. It authorized federal agencies to withhold federal money from programs that tolerated racial discrimination. It authorized the Justice Department to sue education systems that continued to discriminate and called for financial aid to schools seeking to end segregation. It barred racial discrimination by employers and labor unions and created the Equal Employment Opportunity Commission (EEOC) to investigate complaints of such discrimination. Finally, it created a Community Relations Service to help local communities resolve racial difficulties.

CIVIL RIGHTS ACT OF 1968. Federal legislation which made housing discrimination a federal offense and listed criminal penalties for violating specific civil rights or inciting to riot.

Originally sent to Congress by President Johnson in 1966, this legislation was stalled for two years by the opposition of Southern Democrats and Senate Republican minority leader Everett Dirksen because it barred discrimination in the rental or sale of housing. Congress had not passed any legislation on this issue in a century. In 1968, the House of Representatives passed a measure to provide federal protection for civil rights workers in the South. The assassination of Martin Luther King (q.v.) produced increased racial tension and widespread urban rioting. In the Senate, the bill was amended to include the open housing legislation. When Dirksen joined supporters of the legislation, a filibuster by Southern Democrats was halted by a cloture vote and the Senate approved it. President Johnson signed the legislation into law on 11 April, a week after King's assassination. In addition to banning racial discrimination in 80 percent of the rental and housing sales markets, it provided criminal penalties for interfering with a person's right to attend school, serve on a jury, vote, or use public accommodations and facilities. The Act also had antiriot provisions that offered criminal penalties for using interstate communications (the mail, radio, telephone, or television) to incite, organize, or participate in a riot and for manufacturing or teaching the use of explosives or weapons in a civil disturbance or riot.

CIVIL RIGHTS ACT OF 1991. Federal legislation that strengthened protection against employment discrimination.

During the 1980s, Reagan and Bush administration appointees to the Supreme Court formed court majorities that seemed to threaten gains in civil rights protection for women and minorities. In *Wards Cove Packing Company Inc. v. Frank Atonio* (q.v.), for example, the Court had ruled by a vote of five to four that gender or ethnic imbalances in employment were not in themselves evidence that an employer was discriminating and that the burden of proof of discrimination lay with the employee, not the employer. In October 1990, Congress passed a bill sponsored by Senator Edward Kennedy and Representative Augustus Hawkins, which strengthened guarantees in the Civil Rights Act of 1964 against discrimination in hiring and promotion. President George Bush vetoed the bill, however, and the Senate failed by two votes to override Bush's veto. In February 1991, the legislation was revived. After passing both houses of Congress, it was signed by President Bush on 21 November 1991. It placed the burden of proof of nondiscrimination on the employer and provided for damage awards in cases of intentional discrimination.

CIVIL RIGHTS COMMISSION. *See* **United States Civil Rights Commission.**

CLARK, KENNETH BANCROFT (1914–   ). African American educator, psychologist, and sociologist.

Kenneth B. Clark was born on 24 July 1914 in the Panama Canal Zone. Against the wishes of his father who worked for the United Fruit Company, Clark's mother moved with him to New York five years later. His parents were later divorced. Young Clark studied in New York public schools before earning bachelor's and master's degrees from Howard University. In 1940, he received a doctorate in experimental psychology from Columbia University. By then, he was an expert on the effects of racism and segregation on black self-esteem. As part of Swedish sociologist Gunnar Myrdal's team that studied racism in the United States and published *An American Dilemma* (q.v.), Clark and his wife developed a "doll test." They asked African American children to choose among black and white dolls. When they commonly rejected black dolls as "bad," the Clarks held that a racist environment contributed to black self-contempt.

Clark summarized these findings in a report, "Effects of Prejudice and Discrimination on Personality Development," for the White House Mid-Century Conference on Youth in 1950 and a book, *Prejudice and Your Child,* in 1955. The Supreme Court's use of Clark's evidence in *Brown v. Board of Education* (q.v.) to justify its decision that racial segregation in public schools was unconstitutional is a classic example of "sociological jurisprudence" that remains controversial. In *Dark Ghetto* (1965), Clark studied the effects of de facto segregation in Northern neighborhoods and schools, which he found as debilitating as the South's de jure segregation. In 1967, he established the Metropolitan Applied Research Center, a center for social research. Clark served as visiting professor at Harvard and Columbia Universities before launching the Joint Center for Political Studies in Washington, D.C. It provided research and technical assistance to the increasing numbers of black public officials.

CLARK, SEPTIMA POINSETTE (1898–1987). Civil rights activist and educator.

Septima Poinsette Clark was born on 3 May 1898 in Charleston, South Carolina. She was the daughter of a Haitian woman and Peter Poinsette, a former slave whose master, Joel Poinsette, had imported a plant from Mexico to South Carolina that was given the family name, poinsettia. South Carolina offered inadequate public education for African Americans, so young Septima Poinsette received her formal education in private normal schools, taught by missionaries from the North. In 1916, Septima Poinsette moved to Johns Island, a heavily black sea island off the South Carolina coast, to teach literacy. While teaching on Johns Island, she married Nerie Clark, a sailor. They became the parents of two children, only one of whom survived, before Nerie Clark died in 1924. Never remarried, Septima Clark taught on Johns Island until 1927, when she moved to Columbia, South Carolina, where she earned a B.A. at Benedict College in 1942. After she received an M.A. from Hampton Institute in 1945, Clark taught in Columbia and worked with the NAACP on a class action law suit to win pay equity for African American teachers.

Southern lawmakers tried to cripple the NAACP's attack on segregation in a variety of ways in the mid-1950s. South Carolina required that African American teachers swear that they did not belong to it. The law was repealed in 1957; but, by then, Septima Clark had left South Carolina rather than resign from the NAACP. She became the director of education at Tennessee's Highlander Folk School (q.v.). A labor education center in the 1930s and 1940s, Highlander became a training center for the civil rights movement in the 1950s and a frequent target of state and federal police harassment, FBI surveillance, Internal Revenue Service audits, and state investigations. State police raided Highlander on 31 July 1959 and later used a bathtub, which was used to cool drinks for guests, as evidence that Clark, who abstained from alcoholic drinks, was guilty of illegal liquor sales. At trial, prosecutors accused her of engaging in subversive activities.

By December 1961, when Highlander was closed, Septima Clark had moved her Citizenship Education Program to SCLC (q.v.) sponsorship at Dorchester Center in McIntosh, Georgia. For another decade, Clark taught reading, writing, civics, and arithmetic to illiterate black people, in the hope that they, in turn, would teach others. When she retired in 1970, Clark returned to Charleston. In her last years, she received pay due to her from losing her teaching position in South Carolina and served a term on Charleston's public school board. When she died on 15 December 1987, Septima Poinsette Clark was hailed as "queen mother of the civil rights movement."

CLEAVER, ELDRIDGE (1935–   ). Black Panther activist.

Eldridge Cleaver was born on 31 August 1935 in Wabbaseka, near Pine Bluff, Arkansas. He moved to the Watts section of Los Angeles as a child and went to public school there. Cleaver's trouble with the law began in his early teens, when he served time in a California Youth Authority institution. There, he was converted to Roman Catholicism. At 18, he was caught with what he called "a shopping bag full of love"—marijuana—and entered San Quentin Prison about a month after the Supreme Court decision in *Brown v. Board of Education.* A conviction on rape charges followed his release and Cleaver spent nine of the next twelve years in Folsom and San Quentin, where he received most of his education. He was converted to the Nation of Islam in 1960 and remained active in the Nation until Elijah Muhammad sent Malcolm X (q.v.) into exile. Cleaver was paroled in December 1966, wrote for *Ramparts,* San Francisco's radical antiwar magazine, and began editing his own prison writings for publication. On a speaking tour of black colleges, he met and married Kathleen Neal at Fisk University.

Returning to San Francisco, Cleaver met Huey Newton (q.v.) and Bobby Seale (q.v.) who persuaded him to become the Black Panther's minister of information and launch *The Black Panther* as its editor in April 1967. In 1968, Cleaver published *Soul on Ice*, a best-selling expression of black radicalism in the late 1960s. His autobiographical characterization of the rape of a white woman as an insurrectionary act influenced subsequent discussions of race and gender. Yet, Cleaver recognized that the rage that led to rape was self-destructive and he sought healing in written self-expression. His campaign for president in 1968 was a case of theatrical politics. If sent to the White House, he said, "I'll burn the mother fucker down." Convinced that he would lose a parole revocation hearing, Cleaver fled the United States late in the year. He traveled in Cuba, North Korea, the Soviet Union, and North Vietnam before settling on Algeria's Mediterranean coast, where he called for the formation of a North American Liberation Front, patterned on insurrectionary movements in Cuba and Vietnam. By March 1971, Cleaver's celebration of murder, race warfare, and terrorism diverged so dramatically from Huey Newton's new emphasis on the Black Panthers' community social service that their factions expelled each other from the Black Panther Party.

By 1976, Eldridge Cleaver had returned from exile abroad to negotiate a settlement of assault and weapons violations charges in Oakland with community service on probation. He supported Jimmy Carter for president that year, joined the Mormon Church, and became a voice for American patriotism and conservative Christianity. His autobiographical *Soul on Fire*, published in 1978, criticized government action on behalf of workers and emphasized the importance of constitutional liberties and religious values. Divorced from his wife, Kathleen, who attended Yale Law School and became a professor of law at Emory University, Eldridge Cleaver settled in Berkeley and earned a living on the conservative lecture circuit, in sales, and a recycling business. He failed to get conservative Republican backing for a race for the United States Senate, but he attended the 1984 Republican National Convention to support the renomination of Ronald Reagan. In March 1994, Cleaver suffered a brain hemorrhage and was subsequently arrested on a charge of cocaine possession.

COFFEE v. RICE UNIVERSITY, 408 S.W. 2d 269 (1966). A case in which a federal district court authorized Rice University to depart from the terms of its endowment to admit qualified students regardless of race.

In 1964, the Board of Trustees of Rice University in Houston, Texas, sought and received authorization from the Harris County, Texas, state district court to deviate from the terms of its endowment to admit qualified students, regardless of their ethnic background, and to charge tuition of its students. Some Rice University alumni challenged the district court's judgment in the Texas court of appeals. The appeals court reaffirmed the district court's judgment on 27 October 1966. The appeals court noted that the primary purpose of the endowment by William Marsh Rice in 1891 was to endow a premier institution of higher education. This purpose was jeopardized, however, by subsidiary purposes that it was to contribute to the "instruction of the white inhabitants of the City of Houston and the state of Texas" and that its benefits be "free and open to all." The primary purpose of the endowment prevailed in such conflicts, argued the court, because its tuition-free and racially restrictive admissions policies would cripple its purpose of being a premier institution.

COKE v. CITY OF ATLANTA, 184 F. Supp. 579 (N.D. Ga., 1960). A case in which a federal district court held that racial discrimination by a private business operating in a public facility was "state action" and, therefore, violated Fourteenth Amendment rights.

A black insurance executive from Birmingham, Alabama, D. H. Coke, sued the city of Atlanta because of racial segregation in a restaurant at Atlanta's Municipal Airport. Atlanta leased space in the airport to Dobbs House Inc., which served African American diners in a section of its restaurant separated from white diners by a screen. The question before the court was whether Dobbs House policy constituted private or state action. Precedents held that the Fourteenth Amendment barred only discrimination by the state. Attorneys for the city and for Dobbs House contended that the restaurant's policy was private action, not dictated by the city, and, therefore, not in violation of the Fourteenth Amendment. The court found to the contrary, however. Segregation in a state-owned facility was "state action" and, therefore, violated the Fourteenth Amendment. Together with *Burton v. Wilmington Parking Authority* (q.v.) and *Derrington v. Plummer* (q.v.), *Coke v. City of Atlanta* helped to define state and private discriminatory action and legal requirements of tenants of state property.

COLLINS, THOMAS LEROY (1909–91). Florida politician and civil rights mediator.

Thomas Leroy Collins was born on 10 March 1909 in Tallahassee, Florida. The great-grandson of a Confederate army chaplain, Collins graduated from a Tallahassee high school in 1927 and earned a law degree in 1931 from Cumberland University in Williamsburg, Kentucky. A year later, he was married and defeated in his first race for public office. Collins was elected to Florida's house of representatives in 1935 and served there until his election to the state senate in 1940. He continued to serve there until he was elected Governor of Florida in 1954. In his inaugural address, Collins pledged to maintain segregation in Florida's public schools, but his racial moderation was evident in his eight years as governor. He refused to allow the execution of an African American who he thought was condemned to death by mob rule; he rejected legislation intended to nullify school desegregation or allowed school boards to close white schools if black students were admitted to them; he promoted redistricting to give equitable representation to urban voters; and he urged white store owners to serve black customers during the sit-ins. After leaving the governor's office, Collins was asked by President Johnson to mediate the crisis at Selma, Alabama, in 1965. His work there helped to prevent bloodshed. Republican Edward Gurney used Collins's racial moderation to defeat him in a race for the United States Senate in 1968. Collins retired from public life after this defeat and died on 12 March 1991.

COLLINS v. WALKER, 339 F.2d 100 (5th Cir., 1964). A case in which a federal circuit court of appeals remanded the case of a black man, indicted, convicted, and sentenced to death for rape, to a new grand jury because black people were intentionally included in the grand jury that indicted him.

From the 1930s through the 1950s, the convictions of many African American defendants were appealed and, in many cases, set aside because of the exclusion of African Americans from jury service. In a strange reversal on that theme, *Collins v. Walker* was the case of a defendant who claimed discrimination, not because black people had been excluded from his jury, but because they were intentionally included in his jury. Woodman J. Collins was an African American who was indicted, convicted and sentenced to death for the aggravated rape of a white woman. In 1962, Louisiana's supreme court sustained this decision. In appealing the decision to the federal court of appeals, Collins's attorneys claimed that he was mentally incompetent, unable to stand trial, that his confession had been coerced, and that he had been discriminated against because the grand jury that indicted him, which included five black people among twelve jurors, included black people placed on the jury only for his trial hearing. Agreeing that the five jurors were on the case only because the defendant was black, the court of appeals agreed that Collins was discriminated against and ordered that the case be heard by a new grand jury.

COLORADO ANTI-DISCRIMINATION COMMISSION v. CONTI-NENTAL AIRLINES, 372 U.S. 714 (1963). A case in which the Supreme Court helped to define federal commerce power and the rights of states to defend their citizens from discrimination.

When Continental Airlines refused to give pilot training to an African American, Marlon D. Green, on racial grounds, the Colorado Anti-Discrimination Commission found the company in violation of the Colorado Anti-Discrimination Act. A district court in Denver sided with Continental Airlines, but the Commission appealed to the Supreme Court. The Court reinstated the Anti-Discrimination Commission's ruling. State antidiscrimination legislation did not unconstitutionally impinge upon federal authority to regulate interstate commerce, the Court reasoned. The legislation was neither an undue burden on interstate commerce nor was it in conflict with less comprehensive federal antidiscrimination legislation.

COLUMBUS BOARD OF EDUCATION v. PENICK, 439 U.S. 1348 (1979). A case in which the Supreme Court ordered the Columbus, Ohio, school board to comply with a federal district court desegregation order.

In 1976, Penick and others sued the Columbus school board for "pursuing a course of conduct having the purpose and effect of causing and perpetuating racial segregation in the public schools, contrary to the Fourteenth Amendment." Finding that the school board had avoided desegregation in many ways, a district court agreed with Penick and ordered Columbus school authorities to desegregate their schools immediately. Following the Supreme Court's ruling in *Dayton Board of Education v. Brinkman* (q.v.) in 1977, however, the Columbus school board appealed for modification of the district court's desegregation order. The petition was denied in appellate court and the school board appealed to the Supreme Court. In a seven-to-two decision, with Justices William Rehnquist and Lewis Powell in dissent, the Court ruled that the Columbus school board must comply with the original district court order.

COMMONWEALTH OF PENNSYLVANIA v. BROWN, 270 F. Supp. 782 (E.D. Pa., 1967). A case in which a federal district court ordered the desegregation of a private school.

In 1848, a wealthy Philadelphia banker and businessman, Stephen Girard, founded Girard College, a secondary school for "poor, white, male orphans." Philadelphia authorities, who were to execute Girard's wishes, appointed a board of trustees that followed the terms of his will closely. Earlier, the Supreme Court had ruled that the board of trustees' refusal to admit black students amounted to racial discrimination by the city. Philadelphia authorities then dissolved the board of trustees and put private individuals in charge of the school. Girard College remained all-white in 1967, when seven black male orphans, the city of Philadelphia, the Commonwealth of Pennsylvania, and its attorney general brought a class action suit against Girard's private trustees in federal district court to end their racial policy.

Citing a 1966 Supreme Court decision in *Evans v. Newton* (q.v.), which involved a privately endowed park, the federal district court held that the school's relation to the state implied public authorities' approval of its restrictive policies. Admission to Girard was not open to the general public, said the court, but it was always "available to any needy, fatherless boy—as long as he is white." The college was, thus, like a segregated public boarding school or orphanage. Pennsylvania had supervised the nurture and teaching of Girard students by requiring the trustees to make periodic reports. The school's restrictive admissions policy was thus "so afflicted with State action," said the court, that it violated the equal protection rights of African American youth.

CONGRESS OF RACIAL EQUALITY (CORE). One of five major organizations at the heart of the civil rights movement.

The Congress of Racial Equality was founded in Chicago by members of the pacifist Fellowship of Reconciliation (q.v.) in 1942. Primarily seminarians and graduate students at the University of Chicago, the founding members of CORE included James Farmer (q.v.), Bernice Fisher, Joseph Guinn, George Houser, Homer Jack, and James R. Robinson. This biracial group of young idealists, originally known as the Chicago Committee of Racial Equality, intended to use nonviolent direct action to achieve social change and racial justice. As pioneers in nonviolent direct action, early members of CORE took part in both the first sit-in movement (q.v.), in Chicago in 1942, and the first Freedom Ride (q.v.), the Journey of Reconciliation (q.v.), in 1947. As field secretaries for the Fellowship of Reconciliation, Farmer and Bayard Rustin (q.v.) promoted its pacifist agenda and encouraged the formation of other CORE action groups in major cities across the North.

Yet, CORE was still a small, marginal organization as late as 1961, when it called James Farmer from the staff of the NAACP (q.v.) to become its new national director. Inspired by the courage of Southern black college students who launched the sit-in movement in 1960, CORE mounted sympathetic boycotts and picket lines of Northern outlets of chain stores that practiced segregation in the South. Seeking to test rulings by the Interstate Commerce Commission and the Supreme Court, Farmer and other members of CORE organized the Freedom Rides in the spring of 1961 to promote desegregation of interstate bus transportation throughout the South. Burning buses and Freedom Riders beaten viciously by segregationists offered dramatic visual evidence of fierce Southern white resistance to desegregation. Within six months, however, the Kennedy administration was persuaded of the necessity of federal authority to protect interstate passengers in the free exercise of their civil rights.

The Freedom Rides took many CORE activists to Mississippi, where dozens of them spent the summer of 1961 in its notorious Parchman penitentiary. Upon their release, some of them remained in the state to organize black Mississippians for direct action and voter registration. Its mission in the Deep South would begin to transform CORE itself. Previously a largely Northern, biracial group of idealistic pacifists, in February 1962 CORE became a key factor in Mississippi's Council of Federated Organizations (COFO; q.v.). It helped to organize Mississippi's Freedom Summer (q.v.) and the Mississippi Freedom Democratic Party (q.v.) and its challenge to the all-white regular Democratic Party's delegation to the Democratic National Convention in 1964. Both the disillusionment that followed that dramatic confrontation with mainstream Democratic liberalism and the experience of Northern CORE workers combatting poverty and racism in urban ghettoes offered fertile soil for the appeal of "black power," with its nationalist connotations. When James Farmer resigned as CORE's national director in 1966, he was replaced by Floyd McKissick (q.v.), who became, with Stokely Carmichael (q.v.), the foremost spokesmen for black power among the nation's major civil rights leaders. Two years later, McKissick was replaced by Roy Innis and CORE's transformation into a black separatist organization was complete.

CONNOR, THEOPHILUS EUGENE ("Bull"; 1898–1973). Politician.
Eugene Connor earned his nickname during his youth, when a megaphone broadcast his deep voice to relay telegraphic reports of baseball

games to crowds in the pool halls of downtown Birmingham, Alabama. When radio became common in the homes of the city, Eugene "Bull" Connor became a sportscaster for a local radio station. His radio celebrity helped to win his election to the Alabama state legislature in the 1920s. In 1936, he was elected police commissioner, a position which he held for 16 years. When he was convicted of sharing a hotel room with his secretary in 1952, Connor chose not to run for reelection. After being exonerated of the charge, he won reelection as Birmingham's police commissioner in 1956 and held the office until 1963, when a change in the city's form of government terminated the position. During his long years in Birmingham public office, he was the dominant voice in local government. One of three commissioners, he had greater longevity in office than the others and the authority to appoint temporary judges. He had a reputation for controlling Birmingham's court system by using that authority, in one case at least, to appoint the same judge once a week for several years.

By the end of World War II, Connor had become a symbol of Birmingham's racial oppression and an ardent enemy of black or white resistance to it. His police squelched the city's first attempt to desegregate its buses and its first sit-in movement (q.v.) by arresting the demonstrators. When, however, Fred Shuttlesworth (q.v.) of the Alabama Christian Movement for Human Rights (q.v.) and Martin Luther King (q.v.) of SCLC (q.v.) mounted the major assault of the Birmingham, Alabama, Movement (q.v.) on racial segregation in April 1963, "Bull" Connor became the perfect foil for their tactics. His use of powerful water hoses and police dogs on children and nonviolent demonstrators dramatized for a shocked nation the character of his racist regime. At the same time, he was being forced out of power by a change from a commissioner to a mayor-council form of governing Birmingham. Despite a stroke that confined him to a wheelchair in 1966, "Bull" Connor was elected to two terms as president of the Alabama Public Service Commission. Defeated for reelection in 1972, he was left unconscious by a second stroke on 26 February and died on 10 March 1973.

COOPER v. AARON, 358 U.S. 1 (1958). A case in which the Supreme Court held that the threat of mob violence was not to be used to delay desegregation.

When the Supreme Court issued its verdict in *Brown v. Board of Education* (q.v.) that segregation in public schools was unconstitutional, the school board in Little Rock, Arkansas, drew up a plan to desegregate its schools. Several African American parents challenged the plan in court, contending that its gradual phasing was a denial of *Brown*'s intent. A federal district court approved the board's desegregation plan and ordered the board to implement it. Governor Orval Faubus precipitated a crisis, however, by declaring Little Rock's Central High School off-limits to black students and ordering the Arkansas National Guard to turn them away. The school board petitioned the court to delay implementing its plan, but the petition was denied and the court issued an injunction to prevent the governor and the guardsmen from blocking the black students' admission to Central High. Faubus withdrew the National Guard.

On 23 September 1957, the first black students entered Little Rock's previously all-white high school. A rioting mob of white segregationists surrounded the school, authorities secreted the students out of the school, and Little Rock's mayor appealed to President Dwight Eisenhower to preserve order. Eisenhower nationalized the guardsmen and sent 1,000 armed federal troops to restore order in Little Rock and escort the students into the school. A federal district court granted a school board petition to delay desegregation of Little Rock's schools until 1961. African American parents counterpetitioned to the Eighth Circuit Court of Appeals to reverse the district court's decision and won their case in the appeals court. In special session, on 12 September 1958, the Supreme Court unanimously sustained the appellate court decision. "The constitutional rights of respondents are not to be sacrificed or yielded to the violence and disorder which have followed upon the actions of the governor and legislature," said the Court, "and law and order are not here to be preserved by depriving the Negro children of their constitutional rights."

COTTON, DOROTHY FOREMAN (1931–   ). Civil rights activist. Dorothy Cotton was born in 1931 in Goldsboro, North Carolina. After his wife's death in 1934, Claude Daniel Foreman, a tobacco factory worker, raised his four daughters in Goldsboro, where they attended public schools for African American youth. Dorothy Foreman left Goldsboro to attend Shaw University in Raleigh, North Carolina, where she worked as a housekeeper for the president of the university. When he became the president of Virginia State University in Petersburg, she transferred to that institution and graduated with a degree in English and library science. Shortly thereafter, she married a college friend, George Cotton. Dorothy Cotton then entered graduate school at Boston University, where she earned a degree in speech therapy in 1960. While finishing her degree, she joined Petersburg's historic Gillfield Baptist Church and became a protégé of its pastor, Wyatt Tee Walker (q.v.), who was president of the local branch of the NAACP (q.v.) and led the Petersburg Improvement Association, an SCLC (q.v.) affiliate.

When Walker became the executive director of SCLC in 1960, Cotton followed him to Atlanta to join its staff. In 1963, she became a director of SCLC's Citizenship Education Program, which taught literacy, encouraged voter registration and promoted nonviolent means of social action. As an SCLC staff member, Cotton became a close confidant of Martin Luther King (q.v.). After his death, she remained on the SCLC staff until 1972, when she left to become the director of a federal child development Head Start program in Birmingham, Alabama. From 1975 to 1978, she worked for Atlanta's Bureau of Human Services and, from 1978 to 1981, she was southeastern regional director for ACTION, a federal agency for volunteer programs. After service on the staff of the Martin Luther King, Jr., Center for Nonviolent Social Change in Atlanta, Cotton became director of student activities at Cornell University in Ithaca, New York. She left that position in May 1991 to lead seminars on leadership development and social change.

COUNCIL OF FEDERATED ORGANIZATIONS (COFO). A coalition of civil rights organizations in Mississippi.

The Council of Federated Organizations was founded in May 1961 by Aaron Henry (q.v.) of the NAACP (q.v.) and others to negotiate with Mississippi's governor Ross Barnett. Encouraged by the promise of grants from the Voter Education Project (q.v.), it was reorganized by Henry, Medgar Evers (q.v.), and Amzie Moore (q.v.) of the NAACP, James Forman (q.v.) and Robert Moses (q.v.) of SNCC (q.v.), and David Dennis and Tom Gaither of CORE (q.v.) in February 1962 as a coalition of all the major civil rights groups in Mississippi, including SCLC and local groups unaffiliated with the national organizations. Intended to give black Mississippians a sense of ownership in their own organization, COFO allowed participants to retain their other affiliations, served as a conduit of funds to sustain the movement in Mississippi and presented a united front to the state's hostile white power structure. Its most influential leaders were its president, Aaron Henry, its program director, Robert Moses, and its assistant program director, David Dennis.

Through 1962 and 1963, COFO conducted a statewide voter registration effort, which was meagerly sustained by funds from the Southern Regional Council's Voter Education Project (q.v.). Faced with white harassment and violence, however, COFO field workers could show only limited results by August 1963, when they persuaded over 700 black Mississippians to present petitions at the Democratic primary that they had been illegally denied the right to register to vote. Pursuing a different tactic for the run-off primary for governor three weeks later, COFO members nominated Aaron Henry and the Reverend Edwin King (q.v.), the white chaplain at Tougaloo College, for governor and lieutenant governor. With the help of about a hundred Northern white college students, COFO offered black Mississippians alternate polling places in black churches, as well as alternate candidates, and 83,000 black Mississippians took part in this unofficial "freedom election."

Convinced now that the only way to draw national attention to the Mississippi movement was to draw Northern white college students, COFO leaders made plans for "Freedom Summer" (q.v.) in 1964. Students from Stanford and Berkeley to Harvard and Yale converged on Miami University in Oxford, Ohio, for their orientation sessions. Before leaving Ohio for Mississippi, they knew that James Chaney (q.v.), Andrew Goodman (q.v.), and Michael Schwerner (q.v.), who had gone before them, were missing near Philadelphia, Mississippi, and were most likely dead. Despite arrests, beatings, church burnings, and home bombings, the Northern student volunteers promoted voter registration and set up "freedom schools" to teach literacy. They participated in the organization of the Mississippi Freedom Democratic Party (q.v.), which challenged the seating of Mississippi's all-white regular delegation to the Democratic National Convention in 1964. Disaffected with mainstream political liberalism by the convention, Robert Moses left Mississippi in the fall and, by mid-1965, COFO was dissolved.

COX v. LOUISIANA, 379 U.S. 559 (1965). A case in which the Supreme Court limited state regulation of First Amendment rights.

B. Elton Cox, an organizer for CORE (q.v.), had a permit to lead a civil rights demonstration in Baton Rouge, Louisiana, but he was arrested during the protest action for violating a state law barring demonstrations near courthouses. He was convicted in an East Baton Rouge district court and the conviction was sustained by Louisiana's supreme court. The United States Supreme Court reversed Cox's conviction on appeal. The Court held that the Louisiana statute was constitutional, because the state has a right to regulate protests to prevent disruption of the processes of government. City officials, however, had granted Cox permission to demonstrate in an area near the courthouse. Application of the state law in this case amounted to entrapment and violated his First Amendment rights to freedom of assembly, petition and speech, and his Fourteenth Amendment due process rights. The state's right to regulate demonstrations, said the Court, could not be used to suppress elemental human rights.

D

DAHMER, VERNON FERDINAND (1908–66). A businessman and civil rights activist in Hattiesburg, Mississippi.

Vernon Dahmer was born on 10 March 1908. Although he attended public schools for African American youth only through the tenth grade, Dahmer became the owner of a 220-acre cotton farm, a grocery store, and a sawmill in Hattiesburg, Mississippi. He and his wife, Ellie, a school teacher, were the parents of six boys and one girl. Prominent in Hattiesburg's African American community by the 1950s, Dahmer was active in the National Association for the Advancement of Colored People (NAACP; q.v.), but became impatient with the inactivity of its local branch by the early 1960s. He supported Clyde Kennard, a young African American who tried unsuccessfully to be admitted to Mississippi Southern College. In 1962, he invited the Student Nonviolent Coordinating Committee (SNCC; q.v.) to launch a voter registration campaign in Hatties-burg. After the passage of the Voting Rights Act of 1965 (q.v.), voter registration efforts increased in Hattiesburg. This activity brought Dahmer to the attention of the Mississippi Sovereignty Commission, its secret police, and the Ku Klux Klan. There were drive-by shootings at Dahmer's grocery and his hay-filled barn was burned.

Before dawn on 10 January 1966, two cars of Klansmen pulled in front of Dahmer's ranch-style house and grocery store. While one group set fire to the store, the other fired shotguns and threw firebombs through a picture window in the house. Dahmer ordered his wife and children out of the house, made his way through smoke and flames to the front door, and fired his shotgun to cover their escape. He was caught in the draft of the open front door and enveloped in flames. Suffering from facial burns, smoke inhalation, and a seared respiratory tract, Vernon Dahmer was hospitalized and died the following afternoon. Of thirteen people who were arrested and charged with the crime, only six went to trial. Four of them were convicted and sent to prison. A fifth, Ku Klux Klan Imperial Wizard Sam Bowers, who would serve a three-year sentence for his role in the deaths of James Chaney (q.v.), Michael Schwerner (q.v.), and Andrew Goodman (q.v.), was tried twice and twice acquitted for his role in the Dahmer case by hung juries of eleven to one. In the mid-1990s, there have been efforts to reopen the case.

DANIEL AND KYLES v. PAUL, 395 U.S. 298 (1969). A case in which the Supreme Court helped to define "public accommodations" under Title II of the Civil Rights Act of 1964 (q.v.) and expanded federal authority to restrict private discrimination.

In the Civil Rights Act of 1964, Congress banned racial discrimination in public accommodations under its authority to regulate interstate commerce. After the act's adoption, many facilities which catered to white people in the South sought exemption from its open access requirements by claiming that they were private clubs. The Lake Nixon Club, near Little Rock, Arkansas, was a privately owned recreation center with facilities for boating, dancing, eating, and swimming. It routinely advertised its facilities, distributed membership cards, admitted all white customers and excluded all African Americans. The plaintiffs, Daniel and Kyles, sued, maintaining that the Lake Nixon Club was a "public accommodation" in the terms of the act's jurisdiction. The district court and the appellate court agreed that the recreation complex was not a private club and that the plaintiffs had been excluded because of their race, but they found for the club's owners who held that it was not a "public accommodation" in the eyes of the law. On appeal, the Supreme Court sided with the plaintiffs. The club's snack bar catered to interstate travelers and the act covered all places of entertainment, said the Court, not just "spectator entertainment," as attorneys for the Lake Nixon Club maintained.

DANIELS, JONATHAN MYRICK (1939–65). Episcopal seminarian and civil rights activist.

Jonathan Myrick Daniels was born on 20 March 1939 in Keene, New Hampshire, the son of a medical doctor and his wife. As a young man, Daniels left his family's Congregational Church to become an Episcopalian. Studying at Virginia Military Institute, Daniels was a sufficiently serious student of literature to win a Danforth Fellowship for graduate study in English at Harvard. After a year, however, he entered Cambridge's Episcopal Theological School to study for the priesthood. After the bloody confrontation of civil rights demonstrators with Alabama state police in March 1965 at Selma's Edmund Pettis Bridge, Jonathan Daniels responded to a summons by Martin Luther King (q.v.) to ministers of all faiths to the city. Daniels extended his participation in the

Selma to Montgomery March (q.v.) by representing the Episcopal Society for Cultural and Racial Unity (ESCRU) in Selma and Lowndes County. He lived with a black family in Selma's George Washington Carver Homes, supported civil rights organizing and voter registration in the city, and sought to communicate with white moderates.

In August 1965, Daniels moved into nearby rural Lowndes County to work with SNCC. Lowndes County was deeply impoverished and perhaps even more hostile to the civil rights movement than Selma. On 14 August, he was jailed in Hayneville for his role in demonstrations at Port Deposit. Six days later, Daniels was released on his own recognizance pending trial on misdemeanor charges. When the Reverend Richard Morrisroe, a Catholic priest from Chicago, two black women, and Daniels went to a store to buy soft drinks, Daniels opened the door of the country grocery and was ordered out by Tom L. Coleman. When he questioned the white grocer, Daniels was shot and killed in the doorway. He died on 20 August 1965. Six weeks later, a local white jury acquitted Coleman on grounds of self-defense.

DAVIS, ANGELA (1944–   ). Radical black Marxist intellectual.

Angela Davis was born on 26 January 1944 in Birmingham, Alabama. Her parents, Sallye E. and B. Frank Davis, were teachers, but Angela spent her first four years in public housing. Her parents had belonged to the Southern Negro Youth Congress in the late 1930s and, later, to the NAACP (q.v.) and the Alabama Christian Movement for Human Rights (q.v.). In 1948, they were the first African Americans to buy a house on Center Street. A year later, the house of a black neighbor was bombed. Ultimately, the neighborhood became known as "Dynamite Hill" for all the bombings there. Angela Davis attended public schools for African American children until she was 14, when her parents sent her to New York City. There, she lived with the Reverend William Howard Melish and his wife and attended the Elizabeth Irwin private high school in Greenwich Village. There, too, she met Herbert Aptheker, a Marxist historian, and his daughter, Bettina, and was introduced to ADVANCE, a Marxist-Leninist youth organization. When Davis graduated from high school, she entered Brandeis University, thinking of herself as a Communist.

While she studied at Brandeis, Davis attended the Communist-sponsored Eighth World Youth Festival in Helsinki, Finland, and spent her third year at the Sorbonne in Paris, where she became interested in political philosophy. She returned to Brandeis, audited a course with

Herbert Marcuse and graduated magna cum laude and Phi Beta Kappa in 1965. After two years of study with Theodore Adorno in Frankfurt, Germany, Davis returned to the United States to complete her doctoral studies with Marcuse at the University of California, San Diego. There, she was arrested in protests against the war in Vietnam and was active with both the Black Panthers (q.v.) and the Student Nonviolent Coordinating Committee (SNCC; q.v.). In 1968, she joined the Communist Party. A year later, she spent a month in Cuba and joined the philosophy department at the University of California, Los Angeles. Despite harassment and the efforts of Governor Ronald Reagan to have her fired, Angela Davis continued to teach at UCLA.

In 1970, Davis was fired when she declared solidarity with the Soledad Brothers, who were accused of murdering a prison guard. Tension escalated when the 17-year-old brother of one of the accused took a judge, a district attorney, and several prisoners hostage. In a shoot-out with police, the youth, the judge, and a prisoner were killed and others were wounded. Angela Davis went underground and was added to the FBI's Ten Most Wanted List. Arrested by the FBI in October 1970, she was charged with unlawful flight to avoid arrest, murder, kidnapping, and conspiracy. After 16 months in prison, she was tried in San Jose, California, and acquitted on all charges in 1972. Thereafter, she toured the United States and the Soviet Union. In 1974, Davis published her autobiography. Four years later, she was hired by San Francisco State University to teach women's and ethnic studies. In 1979, the Soviet Union awarded Davis the Lenin Peace Prize and, in 1980 and 1984, she was the Communist Party's candidate for vice president of the United States. Davis's most important publications include *Women, Race and Class* (1981) and *Women, Culture and Politics* (1989). By 1990, she had resigned her membership in the Communist Party. She teaches now at San Francisco State University, at the University of California, Santa Cruz, and in the San Francisco County Jail Education Program.

DAVIS v. COUNTY SCHOOL BOARD OF PRINCE EDWARD COUNTY, VIRGINIA, 344 U.S. 1 (1954). A case, grouped with *Brown v. Board of Education* (q.v.), in which the Supreme Court ruled segregation in public schools was unconstitutional.

Plaintiffs from Prince Edward County, Virginia, sued in Federal District Court for the Eastern District of Virginia for relief from sections of the state's constitution that required separate schools for black and for white children. The district court found that schools for black children in Prince Edward County were inferior, both academically and physically, to white schools, but it held that, under the *Plessy v. Ferguson* doctrine, the sections of the state constitution requiring separate schools were constitutional. The plaintiffs appealed to the Supreme Court, where this case was grouped with *Brown*. With the *Brown* decision, the Court found that in all related cases school segregation was unconstitutional and ordered subsequent hearings to decide how the decision was to be implemented.

DAVIS v. SCHNELL, 81 F. Supp. 872 (S.D. Ala., 1949). A case in which a federal district court barred voter registrars from arbitrary racial discrimination under the cover of a literacy requirement.

In 1944, the Supreme Court banned the "white primary" in *Smith v. Allwright* (q.v.). Alabama's conservative white Democrats then sought other means to keep black people from registering and voting. In 1946, State Representative E. C. Boswell sponsored an amendment to the state constitution that required that voter registration applicants be able to read and interpret any article of the United States Constitution to the satisfaction of a board of registrars. Hunter Davis and other African Americans in Mobile who had been denied the right to register filed this case in federal court against Milton Schnell and others of the Mobile County Board of Registrars. During testimony, E. J. Gonzales, one of the county registrars, admitted that Mobile registrars ordinarily rejected black applicants who could not meet the Boswell requirement, but that the same test was not administered to most white applicants. Evidence from Democratic Party literature and newspaper editorials also showed that it was generally understood that the purpose of the Boswell amendment was to restrict black voting. In his decision, Federal District Judge Clarence Mullins held that the Boswell amendment to the state constitution gave boards of registrars "arbitrary power to accept or reject any prospective elector," in violation of the Fifteenth Amendment to the United States Constitution. The Supreme Court sustained the federal district court's decision.

DAVIS, WILLIAM ALLISON (1902–83). Educator and social anthropologist.

Allison Davis was born on 14 October 1902 in Washington, D.C. He was educated at Williams College in Williamstown, Massachusetts, and Harvard University. From Harvard, Davis went to the University of Chicago, where he joined the Department of Education faculty in 1939 and was awarded his doctorate in 1942. Following publication of John Dollard's *Caste and Class in a Southern Town* (1937), Davis published his own most important work, *Deep South* (1941), which was also a study of caste, race, and social class in a Southern town. Davis and Dollard coauthored a critique of the effects of segregation and the use of I.Q. tests on low-income black youth, *The Children of Bondage* (1940). One of the first tenured African American professors at the University of Chicago, Allison Davis served on the United States Civil Rights Commission (q.v.) in 1966–67 and was named John Dewey Distinguished Service Professor at the University of Chicago in 1970. Shortly before his death on 21 November 1983, Davis published a work summarizing years of reflection, *Leadership, Love, and Aggression* (1983).

DAYTON BOARD OF EDUCATION v. BRINKMAN, 433 U.S. 406 (1977). A case in which the Supreme Court ruled against optional school attendance zones if they maintained segregated public schools.

African American plaintiffs filed suit in the Federal District Court of Southern Ohio in 1972 to end "attendance zones" in Dayton's public school system, which allowed white children to transfer out of biracial school districts to white schools. The district court found that this policy violated the Fourteenth Amendment's requirements of equal protection and ordered the school board to offer options throughout the school system. The Dayton School Board appealed the decision to the Supreme Court, which heard the case in 1977. Justice William Rehnquist wrote for a unanimous Court in overturning the district court's ruling. A systemwide remedy, he argued, was not necessary in order to "eliminate all vestiges of the state-imposed school segregation."

DEFUNIS v. ODEGAARD, 416 U.S. 312 (1974). A case prior to *University of California Regents v. Bakke* (q.v.), in which the Supreme Court avoided a decision on the constitutionality of ethnic quotas in school admissions policies.

In 1970 and 1971, the University of Washington Law School turned down the application of Marco DeFunis, a Sephardic Jew, for admission despite the fact that his test scores were higher than those of some ethnic minority students who were admitted to the school. DeFunis sued the school for admission. A trial court ruled in his favor and DeFunis enrolled in the school; but the law school appealed to the state supreme court, which reversed the trial court's ruling. When DeFunis appealed to the United States Supreme Court, it agreed to hear the case. Yet, the Court ultimately avoided a decision on the merits of the case. Since the trial court had ordered DeFunis's admission to the school and he had been attending it for two years, ruled the Court majority, the question of whether he had earlier been discriminated against was now immaterial. Justices William Brennan, Thurgood Marshall and Byron White chastised their colleagues for avoiding the critical issues raised by the case and Justice William O. Douglas registered an opinion about why he would have sustained the trial judge's decision.

DELTA MINISTRY. A National Council of Churches program in Mississippi.

In preparation for Freedom Summer (q.v.) of 1964, the Commission on Religion and Race of the National Council of Churches sponsored the training of young volunteers at Oxford, Ohio, sent many ministers into Mississippi during the summer, and asked the Lawyers' Committee for Civil Rights under Law to defend them if they were arrested for civil rights activity. The National Council's Delta Ministry was founded in September 1964 and led by the Reverend Arthur C. Thomas, who had been active in the Durham, North Carolina, Movement (q.v.). Its headquarters were at Greenville and Mt. Beulah Academy in Edwards, midway between Jackson and Vicksburg, but it also was active in Hattiesburg, McComb, Natchez, and elsewhere. The Delta Ministry had two purposes: to improve economic, health, and social conditions among black Mississippians and seek reconciliation of the state's black and white communities in justice.

The Delta Ministry organized community centers that offered day care, education, and recreation for children and classes in literacy, liberal arts, public health, and vocational education for older people. The ministry developed workshops in citizenship education for potential voters and political skills for potential candidates for public office. Despite opposition from the state government, the Delta Ministry organized government surplus food distribution and community Head Start programs. It cosponsored the proposal for the Child Development Group of Mississippi, a major antipoverty program in Mississippi, which was controversial because of the large appropriation of federal funds that were put at the disposal of civil rights activists in the state. As an activist agency itself, the Delta Ministry organized demonstrations against corporations guilty of racial discrimination, filed discrimination charges against plants that had government contracts, and supported plantation workers who went out on strike. Controversial throughout its existence, between 1964 and 1974 the Delta Ministry stepped into a crucial gap as SNCC (q.v.) left Mississippi and first the Council of Federated Organizations (COFO; q.v.) and then the Mississippi Freedom Democratic Party (MFDP; q.v.) were dissolved. Its creative energies largely spent in its first decade, the ministry continued in attenuated form for another decade before finally being dissolved itself.

DERRINGTON v. PLUMMER, 240 F.2d 922 (5th Cir., 1957). A case in which a federal appeals court expanded the application of the Fourteenth Amendment's equal protection requirements to cases where public and private interests cooperated in racial discrimination.

Harris County, Texas, leased the basement cafeteria in its courthouse to Derrington who was its proprietor. The terms of Derrington's lease required that the cafeteria keep courthouse hours, that the county receive a percentage of its gross sales, and that county employees would be served at a discount. Derrington did not serve African Americans in the cafeteria. Some of them sued, arguing that his action denied them equal protection of the law. Derrington and the county countered that the Fourteenth Amendment banned only discrimination by the state and that discrimination in the cafeteria was acceptable individual action. The Fifth Circuit Court of Appeals found for the plaintiffs, reasoning that the facility was built with public funds and served official county interests. Under those conditions, said the court, the lessee stands "in the place of the County" and his discrimination is "as much state action as would be the conduct of the County itself." Together with *Burton v. Wilmington Parking Authority* (q.v.) and *Coke v. City of Atlanta* (q.v.), *Derrington v. Plummer* helped to define state and private discriminatory action and legal requirements of tenants of state property.

DETROIT RACE RIOT (1967). Of 59 urban race riots in the United States in 1967, this was the most severe.

On 23 July 1967, 11 days after the Newark, New Jersey, race riot (q.v.) began, Detroit police raided an after-hours night club in the heart of the city's black ghetto. As the police arrested the club's patrons, bystanders jeered, began throwing bottles, and broke the windows of the police vehicle. That spark touched off rioting that raged across Detroit's west side for the next 5 days. Because they followed President Lyndon Johnson's legislative victories for civil rights and against poverty, the fury of the Newark and Detroit riots puzzled white liberals. White politicians retained power in these two deteriorating industrial cities with large concentrations of impoverished African Americans. Detroit mayor Jerome P. Cavanagh had organized model antipoverty and urban renewal programs, but there was severe tension between the city's police department and its African American community.

Without clear direction, Mayor Cavanagh's 600 policemen failed to quell the rioting. Governor George Romney's 200 state policemen and 700 national guardsmen acted more aggressively, but by Tuesday they too failed to end the riot. President Johnson responded to appeals from Cavanagh and Romney by sending 4700 federal troops from the 82nd and 101st Airborne Divisions into the city. By 27 July, the federal troops had ended the Detroit rioting. By then, however, 43 people had been killed, hundreds of others injured, 1300 buildings destroyed, 5,000 people were left homeless, and $10,000,000 worth of property was destroyed. It was the most destructive and violent American race riot in more than a century. The Newark and Detroit race riots contributed to the tone of the subsequent political dialogue, as conservative politicians called for "law and order" and liberals, speaking through the Kerner Commission (q.v.), warned that the United States was moving toward becoming "two societies, one black, one white—separate and unequal."

DISTRICT OF COLUMBIA v. JOHN R. THOMPSON COMPANY, 346 U.S. 100 (1953). A case in which the Supreme Court upheld the validity of Washington, D.C.'s antidiscrimination statutes.

During Reconstruction, Washington, D.C., had adopted two ordinances that compelled bars, restaurants, and similar places to serve all "respectable, well-behaved" people and to serve them "at their usual prices." The laws had gone unenforced for years, however, when the district board of commissioners sued a segregated restaurant owned and operated by the John R. Thompson Company. A municipal judge held that the lack of enforcement for decades had repealed the laws "by implication." A local court of appeals sustained the lower court's decision about service, but reversed the decision about prices. The federal appeals court reversed the local court of appeals' decision and affirmed the municipal judge's decision. Until the case was appealed to the Supreme Court, the Truman administration's Justice Department had declined to become involved in it. The Eisenhower administration's Justice Department supported the District of Columbia's commissioners' appeal and Attorney General Herbert Brownell personally presented an amicus curiae brief in favor of the district's old ordinances. The Supreme Court unanimously affirmed the validity of Washington's laws requiring public accommodations not to discriminate on racial grounds.

DOWELL v. SCHOOL BOARD OF OKLAHOMA CITY PUBLIC SCHOOLS, 244 F. Supp. 971 (W.D. Okla., 1965). A case in which a federal district court found that a school attendance plan that allowed white students to transfer from predominantly black to predominantly white schools was unconstitutional.

In 1963, A. L. Dowell of Oklahoma City filed a class action suit on behalf of his son and other African American students against the city's public school board. Dowell challenged a board policy that allowed white students to transfer from predominantly black public schools to predominantly white public schools. The federal district court for western Oklahoma ruled that the board policy was unconstitutional and ordered the board to present a plan for school desegregation within three months. A review of the new plan by a panel of experts found that its neighborhood school attendance policy would perpetuate segregation. The court rejected the board's new plan and ordered the board to submit a second revised plan by 30 October 1965. That plan, said the court, must merge racially segregated schools, transfer teachers to achieve faculty desegregation, and allow black students to transfer from predominantly black to predominantly white schools. The court also reserved the right to review the operation of the new policy and issue new orders to achieve full desegregation of Oklahoma City's public schools.

DUNJEE, ROSCOE (1883–1965). Newspaper editor and civil rights activist.

Roscoe Dunjee was born on 21 June 1883 in Harpers Ferry, West Virginia, the son of a Baptist minister who was the financial officer of Storer College and publisher of a local newspaper. The family moved to the Oklahoma Territory, where his father was employed by the American Baptist Missionary Society to organize new churches. After the founding of Langston University at Langston, Oklahoma, in 1897, young Roscoe Dunjee received most of his formal education there. The death of his father left him with a family to support, a farm to maintain, and a library of 1500 books to study. From 1915, when Roscoe Dunjee began publishing the *Black Dispatch,* Oklahoma's leading African American newspaper, until 1955, Dunjee was the foremost African American civil rights leader in the state. Believing that civil rights could be secured within the framework of American law, he led Oklahoma's struggle for

African American voting rights in the 1920s and 1930s. During that period, he helped to organize the Oklahoma Commission on Interracial Cooperation and founded the Oklahoma Conference of Branches of the NAACP (q.v.). He served as president of both the Oklahoma State Negro Business League and the state's conference of NAACP branches.

Dunjee's support of litigation on the exclusion of African Americans from juries and residential segregation won an NAACP Award of Merit in 1935. By 1940, Dunjee had a national presence as a national director of the NAACP and a keynote speaker for the NAACP, the National Negro Democratic Association and the Negro land-grant college presidents. In 1941, his work as a vice chairman of the Southern Conference for Human Welfare and organizer of the Oklahoma Federation for Human Rights led to an accusation and investigation by the state legislature's Little Dies Committee of Dunjee's "subversive activities." Yet, his patriotism was unquestioned when he chaired the Oklahoma County Council of Defense, Negro Division, throughout World War II. Thereafter, as president of the state branches of the NAACP, Dunjee spearheaded the legal struggle in *Sipuel v. Board of Regents of the University of Oklahoma* (q.v.) that led to desegregation of the state university law school. From 1951 to 1954, he was president of the National Negro Business League. Dunjee retired in 1955 and his activities were severely curtailed after 1961 by poor health.

DURHAM, NORTH CAROLINA, MOVEMENT. A local coalition of black academic, business, and religious leaders, NAACP (q.v.) branches, and a CORE (q.v.) chapter.

Located in the North Carolina piedmont, Durham had strong African American leaders based in businesses such as North Carolina Mutual Life Insurance Company, churches such as White Rock Baptist Church, and educational institutions such as North Carolina College. They cooperated in the Durham Committee on Negro Affairs (DCNA), the traditional voice of the city's African American community. Espousing methods of self-help, political organizing, lobbying, and litigation, the DCNA had won a voice in city affairs for African Americans by the mid-1950s even though the city remained thoroughly segregated. Two younger men, Floyd McKissick (q.v.) and the Reverend Douglas E. Moore, worked with the DCNA, but they expanded the Durham movement's range of tactics to include nonviolent social action. McKissick participated in CORE's Journey of Reconciliation (q.v.) in 1947 and was the first black graduate of the University of North Carolina Law School in 1951. After his admission to the state bar, he practiced law in Durham and became advisor of NAACP youth branches in North Carolina. Douglas E. Moore was a graduate of Boston University School of Theology, became the pastor of Durham's Asbury Temple Methodist Church, and was active with SCLC (q.v.).

In August 1957, Moore and students from North Carolina College sat down in the white section of Durham's Royal Ice Cream Store, asked for service, and were arrested for trespass. Like others that occurred between 1957 and 1960 from North Carolina to Florida and Oklahoma, their sit-in did not spread, but Moore and McKissick were weaving networks that caught fire after 1 February 1960, when black students began the Greensboro, North Carolina, sit-in (q.v.) at Woolworth's Department Store. A week later, students from North Carolina College's NAACP youth branch, led by Callis Brown and Lacy Streeter, launched Durham's sit-in movement. They were joined by students from Bull City Barber College, DeShazor's Beauty College, Duke University, Durham Business College, and Hillside High School in sit-ins at lunch counters and the bus station. Moore's plan to form a coordinating council among student activists eventually led to the formation of SNCC (q.v.). In January 1961, Durham's student activists moved on segregated movie theaters. Despite encouragement by the visits of Martin Luther King (q.v.), Roy Wilkins (q.v.), and Ralph Abernathy (q.v.), Durham's students achieved only limited desegregation of public accommodations by 1962, when a local chapter of CORE was organized by Floyd McKissick.

CORE's James Farmer (q.v.) and James Peck visited Durham and approved plans to make it the center of CORE's "Freedom Highways" campaign in North Carolina. Demonstrations continued through 1962 and 1963. On 12 August 1962, for example, 700 of 4,000 demonstrators were arrested. Nine months later, on the evening of Wense Grabarek's election as Durham's mayor, civil rights demonstrators marched through the city and sat in at six restaurants. CORE and the NAACP announced that thirty days of demonstrations would begin two days later. Grabarek met with civil rights activists and white restaurant owners repeatedly in the following weeks and organized the Durham Interim Committee (DIC). The DIC and its successor, the Committee on Community Relations, negotiated the desegregation of the public accommodations that remained segregated in 1963 and 1964, when the passage of the Civil Rights Act of 1964 (q.v.) put the authority of federal law behind it.

DURR, CLIFFORD JUDKINS (1899–1975). Civil libertarian and attorney.

Clifford J. Durr was born on 2 March 1899 in Montgomery, Alabama. He was educated in Montgomery public schools and at the University of Alabama. His study at the University of Alabama was interrupted by a year in the armed forces during World War I. Winning a Rhodes Scholarship upon his graduation from the university, Durr went to Oxford University, where he earned a law degree in 1922. Durr returned to Montgomery, was admitted to the bar, practiced law and, in 1925, married Virginia Foster of Montgomery. In 1933, the Durrs went to Washington, where he served in the government for 18 years as assistant general counsel of the Reconstruction Finance Corporation, general counsel to and director of the Defense Plant Corporation, and finally as a member of the Federal Communications Commission. Related by marriage to Supreme Court Justice Hugo Black, Durr became a devout civil libertarian and declined reappointment to the Federal Communications Commission in 1948 because of his objection to President Truman's loyalty program. His defense of some of its victims, including J. Robert Oppenheimer, and his wife's active, public support of Henry Wallace's campaign for president during the post–World War II "red scare" alienated the Durrs from Cold War liberals. They returned to Montgomery in 1951.

Durr resumed private legal practice in Montgomery, but the Durrs were ostracized by white people there because of Clifford Durr's defense of the city's black citizens. In December 1955, he accompanied Edgar Daniel Nixon (q.v.) to bail Rosa Parks (q.v.) out of jail when she was arrested for refusing to give up her seat on a Montgomery bus to a boarding white passenger. The Durrs supported the Montgomery Bus Boycott (q.v.) and Durr worked with black attorney Fred Gray in preparing the legal briefs in *Browder v. Gayle* (q.v.), which led to the desegregation of Montgomery's buses in 1956. Despite the loss of most of his white clients, Clifford and Virginia Foster Durr were among the few white liberals in Alabama who supported the civil rights movement. They sheltered Freedom Riders (q.v.) in their home in the early 1960s. In 1966, Clifford Durr was given the Civil Liberties Award of the New York Civil Liberties Union. He died on 12 May 1975.

E

EDELMAN, MARIAN WRIGHT (1939–   ). Children's and civil rights activist.

Marian Wright was born on 6 June 1939 in Bennettsville, South Carolina. She studied in local public schools for African American children and earned her B.A. at Spelman College in 1960. From Spelman,

Wright entered Yale Law School, where she earned an LL.B. in 1963. Wright joined the New York staff of the NAACP Legal Defense and Educational Fund (LDEF; q.v.) for a year, before becoming director of its work in Jackson, Mississippi. There, she worked with the Council of Federated Organizations (COFO; q.v.) and the Child Development Group of Mississippi. She succeeded in bringing influential lawmakers from Washington to the Mississippi Delta to see the living conditions of America's poorest citizens for themselves. Wright left Mississippi to serve during the summer of 1968 as the congressional and federal agency liaison person for the Poor People's March on Washington (q.v.).

After marrying fellow attorney Peter Benjamin Edelman, Marian Wright Edelman became a fellow of the Field Foundation and a partner in the Washington Research Project of the Southern Center for Public Policy, a public interest law firm that became the parent organization of the Children's Defense Fund. From 1971 to 1973, Marian Wright Edelman was director of Harvard's Center for Law and Education. Since June 1973, she has been the president of the Children's Defense Fund. In that capacity, Edelman has become known as the nation's foremost advocate for children's rights and interests. The author of *Children Out of School in America* (1974), *Portrait of Inequality: Black and White Children in America* (1980), and *Families in Peril: An Agenda for Social Change* (1987), Edelman has received over 45 honorary degrees and many other honors for her advocacy of children's rights.

EDWARDS v. SOUTH CAROLINA, 372 U.S. 229 (1963). A case in which the Supreme Court affirmed the rights of peaceful civil rights demonstrators to freedom of assembly, petition, and speech.

During the spring of 1961, James Edwards, Jr., and nearly 200 African American college and high school students marched on the South Carolina State House in Columbia in protest of racial discrimination and segregation. As they marched on public sidewalks around the capital building, they carried signs publicizing their grievances. Police ordered the demonstrators to disperse when a crowd of bystanders gathered to watch. When the demonstrators responded to the police order by singing freedom songs, they were arrested and convicted of violating South Carolina breach-of-peace laws. The Supreme Court overturned their conviction, finding that state breach-of-peace laws could not be used to subvert citizens' constitutional rights to free assembly, free speech, and petition the government freely.

EL-SHABAZZ, EL HAJJ MALIK. *See* Malcolm X.

EQUAL EMPLOYMENT OPPORTUNITY ACT OF 1972. Legislation that authorized the Equal Employment Opportunity Commission (EEOC; q.v.) to file suit against noncompliant employers and extended its jurisdiction to state and local governments and educational institutions.

From 1961 to 1972, the Equal Employment Opportunity Commission lacked enforcement authority, either directly in cease and desist orders or indirectly in suits through the courts. The chief contribution of the Nixon administration to civil rights legislation was passage of the Equal Employment Opportunity Act of 1972. It authorized the EEOC to file suit against discriminating employers and extended its jurisdiction to state and local governments and educational institutions. Subsequently, the EEOC filed class action suits that won significant awards for ethnic minorities and women in promotions and back pay and damages for past discrimination.

EQUAL EMPLOYMENT OPPORTUNITY COMMISSION (EEOC). A presidential committee established in 1961, which the Civil Rights Act of 1964 (q.v.) made a federal agency.

On 6 March 1961, twenty years after Franklin D. Roosevelt established the Fair Employment Practice Committee (FEPC; q.v.), President John F. Kennedy signed Executive Order 10925 (q.v.), establishing the president's Equal Employment Opportunity Commission. Chaired by Vice President Lyndon B. Johnson, it was essentially a committee of the president's cabinet which was responsible for eliminating discrimination based on color, national origin, race, or religion in union membership and employment by the government or government contractors. It was authorized to publicize the names of noncompliant contractors or unions and recommend that the Justice Department file suits to compel compliance. Title VII of the Civil Rights Act of 1964 made the EEOC an agency of the federal government. It was a commission of five members appointed by the president to staggered five-year terms of office. As of July 1965, the EEOC was required to supervise the act's provisions against hiring discrimination based on color, national origin, race, or religion by employment agencies, private employers, and unions. Until 1972, congressional reservations about the agency's work limited its powers to investigation and mediation. Unlike similar agencies created in most states outside the South after World War II, it had no authority to issue cease and desist orders or initiate legal action to compel employers to conform to antidiscrimination legislation.

Between 1972 and 1990, the Nixon, Ford, Carter, and Bush administrations expanded Equal Employment Opportunity Commission responsibility. The Equal Employment Opportunity Act of 1972 gave EEOC authority and jurisdiction to cover educational institutions and state and local governments and to bring class action suits to end discrimination. The Fair Labor Standards Act Amendments (1974), the Age Discrimination in Employment Act and Amendments (1974, 1978), and the Americans with Disabilities Act (1990) extended EEOC's jurisdiction to monitor age, gender, and physical handicap discrimination. The EEOC's most noteworthy chairpersons have included: Clifford L. Alexander (1968–69), the first African American to chair the commission; Eleanor Holmes Norton (q.v.; 1979–81), the commission's first chairwoman, who reorganized the agency for greater efficiency; and Clarence Thomas (1983–89), who chaired the EEOC during the Reagan administration. Thomas was noted for his restraint in enforcing its authority and was later appointed by President Bush to succeed Thurgood Marshall (q.v.) on the Supreme Court.

EVANS v. NEWTON, 382 U.S. 296 (1966). A case in which the Supreme Court decided that a privately owned park managed by the city must not discriminate on racial grounds.

The 1911 will of Senator Augustus O. Bacon appointed the city of Macon as trustee of land reserved as a park for white people in perpetuity. When the Civil Rights Act of 1964 made clear that the city could no longer exclude black people from its parks, members of Bacon Park's board of managers and some of Bacon's heirs sued to remove trusteeship from the city and put it under private trustees who would enforce the terms of Senator Bacon's will. The city relinquished its trusteeship to three private trustees and members of Macon's black community sued, claiming that the city's action and their continued exclusion from the park was an unconstitutional violation of their rights. The trial court and Georgia's supreme court held that the terms of Senator Bacon's will had priority over other considerations and that both the city's action and the private trustees' exclusion of African Americans were legal. Macon's African Americans appealed to the Supreme Court. In an eight-to-one decision, with Justice John Marshall Harlan in dissent, the Supreme Court reversed the lower courts' decision. The park was privately owned, conceded the Court, but its operation by the city was state action and brought the equal protection clause of the Fourteenth Amendment into play. Racial discrimination by the city was unconstitutional and action by the city to avoid compliance with the Fourteenth Amendment was equally unconstitutional.

EVERETT, RONALD MCKINLEY. *See* **Karenga, Maulana.**

EVERS, JAMES CHARLES (1922–   ). Civil rights activist, businessman and politician.

Charles Evers was born on 11 September 1922 in Decatur, Mississippi, to James and Jessie Evers. His father operated a small farm and worked at a sawmill. His mother was a domestic worker. Evers and his younger brother, Medgar, studied at a one-room public school for African American children. When members of the Evers family attempted to register to vote in 1946, they were threatened. Charles Evers graduated from Alcorn A & M College in 1951 and moved to Philadelphia, Mississippi. For the next five years, he worked as a cab driver, disk jockey, mortician, and teacher. As state chairman of a black voter registration drive, Evers antagonized white people in Philadelphia. Driven bankrupt and the target of an attempted killing, he left Mississippi in 1956 for Chicago. According to Evers, he prospered there as a teacher, as well as a tavern owner, bootlegger, numbers runner, and petty thief. He kept in touch with the movement in Mississippi through his brother; Medgar's assassination in 1963 prompted Charles Evers's return to Mississippi.

At his brother's funeral, Evers stunned Roy Wilkins (q.v.) with the announcement that he would become Mississippi field secretary for the National Association for the Advancement of Colored People (NAACP; q.v.). The NAACP's Gloster Current and Medgar Evers's widow, Myrlie, shared Wilkins's reservations about Charles Evers, and Wilkins later regretted allowing Charles Evers to take the position, but he accepted it to avoid a divisive public fight with the brother of the civil rights martyr. As Mississippi's NAACP field secretary, Charles Evers challenged the racism of white Mississippians. He also played on his own team, however, often alienating the NAACP national office, members of Mississippi's black middle class and the Council of Federated Organizations (COFO; q.v.), the state's civil rights umbrella organization, which included CORE (q.v.), SCLC (q.v.), SNCC (q.v.), and other local groups.

Nonetheless, Charles Evers dominated the movement in southwestern Mississippi, including Natchez, where a black economic boycott won modest commitments to desegregation from the city's white leaders, and his home base in nearby rural counties, where black voters organized by Evers outvoted their white neighbors. Other civil rights forces in Mississippi were so hostile to him, however, that they would not allow Evers to address the Jackson mass meeting that marked the end of the Meredith March in June 1966. By 1968, rival factions in the Mississippi movement overcame their differences to unite behind Evers's unsuccessful race for a congressional seat and he won election as a loyalist member of the Democratic National Committee. In 1969, he was elected mayor of Fayette, Mississippi, and he won three subsequent elections for that office between 1973 and 1981. He also ran unsuccessful races for governor and for the United State Senate from Mississippi. A far more controversial person in Mississippi's civil rights movement than his martyred younger brother, Charles Evers nevertheless is a major figure in its history.

EVERS, MEDGAR WILEY (1925–63). Civil rights activist.

Medgar W. Evers was born on 2 July 1925 in Decatur, Mississippi, to James and Jessie Evers. His father operated a small farm and worked in a sawmill. His mother was a domestic worker. Young Evers and his older brother, Charles, studied at a one-room public school for African American children at Newton, Mississippi. Medgar Evers joined the army in 1943 and was stationed in France during World War II. When he returned from the war, Evers studied at Alcorn A & M College. In 1951, he married Myrlie Beasley. After graduation from Alcorn in 1952, he sold insurance in the Mississippi Delta and joined the NAACP (q.v.). In 1954, he became a full-time state field secretary for the NAACP in Mississippi. In that capacity, Evers gathered and publicized information about racial injustice in the state, organized and revitalized NAACP branches across the state, and led voter registration drives and direct-action programs. Becoming the symbol of the African American challenge to discrimination and segregation in Mississippi, he was beaten, jailed, and faced with death threats. In June 1963, Medgar Evers was leading a campaign to desegregate and improve black economic opportunity in Jackson, Mississippi. After a late-night meeting with other civil rights leaders about strategy for the effort, he returned home early in the morning of 12 June. Evers parked his car in the driveway and, as he stepped out of it, a sniper fired a rifle bullet that hit him below his right shoulder.

Driven to a nearby hospital by a neighbor, Medgar Evers died from his wounds shortly after his admission. His assassination, while Martin Luther King (q.v.) led the Birmingham, Alabama, Movement (q.v.), a week before President Kennedy called for new comprehensive civil rights legislation, two months before the March on Washington (q.v.), and five months before President Kennedy's assassination, electrified the nation and set off massive demonstrations in Jackson. The fingerprints of Ku Klux Klansman Byron de la Beckwith were found on the murder weapon and his alibi was dubious, but two all-white juries failed to convict him of the murder. In May 1964, Medgar Evers was reburied in Arlington National Cemetery. Thirty years after the assassination, with the testimony of witnesses who placed him at the scene of the crime, Mississippi prosecutors won a conviction of Beckwith. In death, Medgar Evers became an even more powerful symbol of black resistance to oppression. His brother, Charles, became the NAACP's field secretary for Mississippi, and the state's civil rights movement drew strength from the witness of its fallen leader.

EXECUTIVE ORDER 8802. President Franklin D. Roosevelt's executive order establishing the Fair Employment Practice Committee (FEPC; q.v.) and barring racial discrimination in departments of the federal government, the armed forces, and defense industries.

Mobilization for the United States' entry into World War II pumped billions of dollars into a sluggish American economy and created a boom for white Americans. Racial discrimination kept most African Americans from full participation in the renewal of the economy, however. A. Philip Randolph (q.v.), president of the Brotherhood of Sleeping Car Porters and Maids, summoned 100,000 African Americans to march on Washington in protest. The march was scheduled for 1 July 1941. On 25 June, a week before the protest march was to take place, President Roosevelt's executive order established the Fair Employment Practice Committee and barred racial discrimination in departments of the federal government, the armed forces, and defense industries. The armed forces remained segregated and the enforcement of Roosevelt's order was not consistent, but it significantly improved black access to the benefits of the wartime economy.

EXECUTIVE ORDER 9808. President Harry S Truman's executive order establishing the President's Committee on Civil Rights.

As World War II's end refocused national attention on domestic issues, Walter F. White (q.v.) of the NAACP (q.v.) persuaded President Truman to establish the President's Committee on Civil Rights. He did so in Executive Order 9808, which was signed on 5 December 1946. The committee's 15 members were asked to make recommendations about how federal, state, and local governments could strengthen protections of the people's civil rights. Their report, *To Secure These Rights* (q.v.), was published on 29 October 1947. It called for establishing a permanent federal Civil Rights Commission (q.v.), a Congressional Committee on Civil Rights, and a Civil Rights Division of the Justice Department, for strengthening existing civil rights laws, for making lynching a federal crime, for abolishing the poll tax and strengthening protections of the right to vote, for ending segregation in the armed forces, and for establishing a Fair Employment Practices Commission. The Committee's report led to President Truman's Executive Order 9981 (q.v.), which ordered the desegregation of the armed services, and it focussed national attention on civil rights issues, but it did not lead to significant federal civil rights legislation.

EXECUTIVE ORDER 9980. President Truman's executive order establishing a Fair Employment Board under the Civil Service Commission to promote fair hiring and treatment of African Americans in civil service positions.

After the release of the report of the President's Committee on Civil Rights, *To Secure These Rights* (q.v.), on 29 October 1947, President Truman made some of its recommendations a part of his address to Congress on 2 February 1948 and promised to act on several of them. On 26 July 1948, he signed Executive Orders 9980 and 9981 (q.v.). Executive Order 9980 established a Fair Employment Board under the Civil Service Commission to promote fair hiring and treatment of African Americans in civil service positions. President Eisenhower abolished the Fair Employment Board in his Executive Order 10590 (q.v.), which he signed on 18 January 1955. By the terms of Eisenhower's order, the Fair Employment Board's responsibilities were turned over to the president's Committee on Government Employment Policy.

EXECUTIVE ORDER 9981. President Truman's executive order desegregating the armed services and establishing the president's Committee on Equality of Treatment and Opportunity in the Armed Forces (the Fahy Committee).

Following the release of the president's Committee on Civil Rights' report, *To Secure These Rights* (q.v.), on 29 October 1947, President Truman made its recommendations a part of his address to Congress on 2 February 1948 and promised to act on some of them. On 26 July 1948, he signed

Executive Orders 9980 (q.v.) and 9981. Executive Order 9981 called for the desegregation of the armed forces and established the president's Committee on Equality of Treatment and Opportunity in the Armed Forces (the Fahy Committee). In 1949, the Air Force and the Navy began desegregation. With far more black enlistees, the Army adopted a more gradual approach in 1950. The Fahy Committee, informally named for its chairman, Charles Fahy, monitored the desegregation process and made recommendations for further progress in its final report, *Freedom to Serve*, in 1950. Desegregation of the armed forces was hastened by the Korean War and was nearly complete by 1954. By then, the armed forces were the most thoroughly integrated element of American society and that was probably President Truman's most important achievement in civil rights.

EXECUTIVE ORDER 10577. President Dwight D. Eisenhower's executive order clarifying nondiscrimination orders to federal government contractors and subcontractors.

On 3 September 1954, President Eisenhower signed Executive Order 10577 to clarify existing nondiscrimination orders to government contractors and subcontractors. They were not to discriminate against job applicants or employees on the grounds of their color, national origin, race, or religion. Nondiscrimination applied to recruitment, hiring, job training, apprenticeship, compensation, promotion, demotion, transfer, layoff, and termination. Employers were to post nondiscrimination notices in prominent places. Eisenhower's executive order did not apply to emergency contracts, contracts to meet special requirements, or contracts outside the United States that did not recruit American workers.

EXECUTIVE ORDER 10590. President Eisenhower's executive order establishing the president's Committee on Government Employment Policy.

On 18 January 1955, President Eisenhower signed Executive Order 10590 which abolished the Fair Employment Board of the Civil Service Commission and established the president's Committee on Government Employment Policy. In addition to two presidential appointees, it included representatives of the Civil Service Commission, the Labor Department and the Office of Defense Mobilization. It was charged with maintaining nondiscrimination policies in hiring for and employment with the federal government. Without power to act on its own, the Committee on Government Employment Policy was authorized only to conduct inquiries and make recommendations to the president and federal agencies.

EXECUTIVE ORDER 10925. President John F. Kennedy's executive order establishing the Equal Employment Opportunity Commission (EEOC).

On 6 March 1961, President John F. Kennedy signed Executive Order 10925, which established the president's Equal Employment Opportunity Commission. It was chaired by Vice President Lyndon B. Johnson. Essentially a committee of the president's cabinet, it was responsible for eliminating discrimination based on color, national origin, race, or religion in union membership and employment by the government or government contractors. It had authority to publicize the names of noncompliant contractors or unions and recommend that the Justice Department file suits to compel compliance. This is the first executive order to use the term "affirmative action" (q.v.), though the term was not given definition for another eight years.

EXECUTIVE ORDER 11063. President Kennedy's executive order banning racial discrimination in federally assisted housing.

In the presidential campaign of 1960, John F. Kennedy had promised to bar racial discrimination in federally assisted housing. Yet, protecting other domestic initiatives and Democratic prospects in the mid-term congressional elections, he delayed acting on that promise for the first 22 months of his presidency. On 20 November 1962, Kennedy signed Executive Order 11063, which established a presidential Committee on Equal Opportunity in Housing and banned racial discrimination in federally owned or operated housing, federally assisted public housing, and new private housing built with loans from the Federal Housing Authority or the Veterans Administration. It did not cover housing built with commercial loans from banks or savings and loan associations, about 75 percent of the new housing market, and had limited impact on racial patterns in housing. Six years later, Kennedy's executive order was replaced by the Civil Rights Act of 1968 (q.v.), which made racial discrimination in housing a violation of federal law. On 31 December 1980, President Jimmy Carter signed Executive Order 12259, disbanding the president's Committee on Equal Opportunity in Housing.

EXECUTIVE ORDER 11114. President Kennedy's executive order extending the coverage of Executive Order 10925 (q.v.) to federally assisted construction contracts.

On 23 June 1963, immediately after the crisis in the Birmingham, Alabama, Movement (q.v.), President Kennedy signed Executive Order 11114, which extended the coverage of his Executive Order 10925 to federally assisted construction contracts. This coverage had been delayed because it struck at the interests of two different constituencies of Kennedy's administration: white construction unions and black workers. The Birmingham crisis had created an atmosphere, however, in which the Kennedy administration felt that it could both send strong civil rights legislation to the Congress, which would become the Civil Rights Act of 1964 (q.v.), and issue this executive order. Subsequent developments, including conflict over the "Philadelphia Plan" during the Nixon administration, reflected the difficulty of implementing Kennedy's executive order.

EXECUTIVE ORDER 11246. President Lyndon B. Johnson's executive order authorizing federal agencies to enforce the Civil Rights Act of 1964.

On 24 September 1965, President Johnson signed Executive Order 11246, which authorized federal agencies to enforce the Civil Rights Act of 1964. It required procuring agencies to include an equal employment opportunity clause in every federal contract with contractors and subcontractors. The clause barred employment discrimination on grounds of color, national origin, race, or religion. Gender discrimination would be added later by President Johnson's Executive Order 11375 in 1967. Executive Order 11246 required contractors and subcontractors to undertake "affirmative action" (q.v.) to employ and promote people without regard to color, national origin, race, or religion. President Johnson's executive order authorized the secretary of labor to enforce this requirement through the Office of Federal Contract Compliance Programs.

EXECUTIVE ORDER 11478. President Richard M. Nixon's executive order requiring equal employment opportunity and affirmative action (q.v.) programs of all federal agencies.

On 8 August 1969, President Nixon signed Executive Order 11478, which required equal employment opportunity and affirmative action programs of all federal agencies. Nixon's executive order superseded President Johnson's 1965 Executive Order 11246 (q.v.) and Johnson's 1967 Executive Order 11375, which barred gender discrimination. Thus, even as conservatives attacked the Labor Department for trying to enforce hiring quotas, Nixon issued an executive order that became the source of authority for "affirmative action" and equal employment opportunity programs in federal agencies.

F

THE FAHY COMMITTEE. *See* **Executive Order 9981.**

FAIR EMPLOYMENT PRACTICE COMMITTEE (FEPC). A presidential committee established by Franklin D. Roosevelt's Executive Order 8802 (q.v.) on 25 June 1941 to monitor racial discrimination in departments of the federal government, the armed forces, and defense industries.

When Franklin D. Roosevelt declared racial discrimination in employment in the government, the armed forces, and defense industries violated federal policy, he created a Fair Employment Practice Committee for the duration of the war to hold inquiries into alleged violations of the policy. The FEPC had mediatorial and advisory authority, but no powers of enforcement. Between 1941 and 1943, it held hearings around the country to hear complaints and make recommendations. Between mid-1943 and mid-1944, Roosevelt subordinated it to the War Manpower Commission, which justified the suspension of FEPC hearings on the grounds of national security. Urged by civil rights leaders, Roosevelt then reaffirmed its independence.

During FEPC's five-year existence, it held 15 national public hearings and helped to resolve 40 race-related labor strikes, involving some 5,000 claims of discrimination. Yet, the armed forces remained segregated and FEPC's lack of enforcement authority made application of Roosevelt's order inconsistent. By 1946, when its mandate lapsed and FEPC issued its report to President Truman, many states outside the South had begun to establish state agencies to monitor race discrimination in employment. When civil rights leaders urged Congress to establish a permanent FEPC to enforce nondiscrimination in industries with government contracts, Southern legislators were able to kill the legislation. Only in the Civil Rights Act of 1964 (q.v.) did many of FEPC's goals become national law.

FAIR HOUSING ACT OF 1968. *See* **Civil Rights Act of 1968.**

FARMER, JAMES LEONARD, JR. (1920–   ). Civil rights activist and lecturer.

James Farmer was born on 12 January 1920 in Marshall, Texas. His father, the son of impoverished former slaves, was the first black Texan with a doctorate. His mother, Pearl Houston, was a teacher. Dr. J. Leonard Farmer taught religion at black colleges and seminaries in Marshall, Holly Springs, Mississippi, and Atlanta, Georgia, where his three children studied in public schools for African American youth. James Farmer graduated from Wiley College in 1938. As vice president of the National Council of Methodist Youth, he grew interested in pacifism and opposed American entry into World War II. Farmer graduated from Howard University's theological seminary in 1941, but he chose not to become an ordained minister. He moved to Chicago and became race relations secretary for the pacifist Fellowship of Reconciliation (FOR; q.v.).

As one of the founders of the Congress of Racial Equality (CORE; q.v.) in 1942, Farmer and Bernice Fisher, Joseph Guinn, George Houser, Homer Jack, and James R. Robinson used Gandhian nonviolent direct action for social change and racial justice. CORE organized the first sit-in (q.v.), at Chicago's Jack Spratt Coffee House in 1942, and the first Freedom Ride (q.v.), the Journey of Reconciliation (q.v.), in 1947. As FOR field secretaries, Farmer and Bayard Rustin (q.v.) promoted its pacifist agenda and encouraged the formation of CORE action groups in major cities across the North. Farmer left FOR's staff in 1945 because of disagreements with its leader, A. J. Muste. From 1946 to 1950, he worked with the Upholsterers' International Union; from 1950 to 1955, he worked for the League for Industrial Democracy; and from 1955 to 1959, he worked for the State, County, and Municipal Employees Union.

In 1959, James Farmer joined the staff of the National Association for the Advancement of Colored People (NAACP; q.v.) as its program director. CORE was still a little-known organization in 1961, when Farmer left the NAACP to become its national director. That spring, seeking to test desegregation rulings by the Interstate Commerce Commission (ICC) and the Supreme Court of interstate bus transportation in the South, Farmer and CORE organized the Freedom Rides. The pictures of burning buses and Freedom Riders viciously beaten by segregationists offered dramatic visual evidence of fierce Southern white resistance to desegregation. Six months later, the Kennedy administration was persuaded that federal authority must protect the civil rights of interstate passengers.

Until 1966, Farmer led the expansion of CORE's activities across the nation. He was himself arrested and served time in prison in Mississippi and Louisiana as part of his leadership of its direct-action protest. In Mississippi, CORE was a major force in the Council of Federated Organizations (COFO; q.v.) and the Mississippi Freedom Democratic Party (MFDP; q.v.). In North Carolina, its "Freedom Highways" campaign led to the desegregation of hotels, motels, and restaurants. Outside the South, CORE's direct action campaigns focused on living conditions in urban ghettoes. Many of these activities were carried on by active local chapters, but Farmer led a CORE demonstration at the New York World's Fair to protest conditions for black people in the city.

Farmer's position as national director of CORE was repeatedly threatened throughout his tenure and in 1966 he resigned to become director of a national adult literacy project. Two years later, as the nominee of the Republican and Liberal Parties, he was defeated by Shirley Chisholm (q.v.) in a race for Congress. From 1969 to 1971, Farmer was an assistant secretary of health, education and welfare in the Nixon administration. Despite criticism for serving in a relatively conservative administration, he was able to expand black employment opportunities in government. From 1971 to 1981, Farmer was the executive director of the Coalition of American Public Employees and directed the Council on Minority Planning and Strategy, a black think tank, in Washington. In 1981, he joined the faculty of Mary Washington College in Fredericksburg, Virginia, where he teaches the history of the civil rights movement. He began losing his eyesight and is now blind, but Farmer continues to lecture widely on the civil rights movement and its legacy.

FELLOWSHIP OF RECONCILIATION (FOR). An organization of Christian pacifists.

The Fellowship of Reconciliation had its origin among English and American Christian pacifist opponents of World War I. Beyond their opposition to war, they espoused a sense of human unity that transcended divisions of nationality, race, or social class. Among its early members, Will Winton Alexander, James Weldon Johnson, and L. Hollingsworth Wood devoted more of their attention to issues of racial justice than to pacifism. By the 1930s, FOR field secretaries Howard A. Kester (q.v.) and Claude Nelson were touring the South, lecturing about its economic, racial, and social ills and organizing interracial conferences to discuss these issues. In 1942, FOR members in Chicago organized the Congress of Racial Equality (CORE; q.v.) to use the methods of Gandhian nonviolent direct action for racial justice and social change. With the approval of FOR's executive secretary, Abraham John (A. J.) Muste, FOR fund raising, membership, and staffing overlapped with CORE's for the next decade.

James Farmer (q.v.), George Houser, and Bayard Rustin (q.v.) were three key links between CORE and FOR. As CORE's parent organization, FOR has a claim to sponsoring both the 1942 sit-ins in Chicago and the first Freedom Ride, the Journey of Reconciliation (q.v.), in 1947. Early in 1956, Rustin and FOR secretary Glenn Smiley brought its resources to support Martin Luther King (q.v.) and the Montgomery Bus Boycott (q.v.). FOR remained a significant network for rallying liberal Northern support for the civil rights movement thereafter. By the early 1960s, FOR members from Farmer, Houser, and Rustin to King, James Lawson (q.v.), Fred Shuttlesworth (q.v.), and Smiley were scattered throughout the center/left leadership of the civil rights movement, in CORE, the Southern Christian Leadership Conference (SCLC; q.v.), and the Student Nonviolent Coordinating Committee (SNCC; q.v.).

FIFTH CIRCUIT COURT OF APPEALS, United States. The intermediary federal court for six states in the Deep South.

In 1951, when President Truman appointed Alabama's Richard Taylor Rives (q.v.) to the Fifth Judicial Circuit Court of Appeals, it was about to become the major legal battleground for the civil rights movement because it covered Alabama, Florida, Georgia, Louisiana, Mississippi, and Texas. In 1952, John Robert Brown (q.v.), Elbert Parr Tuttle (q.v.), and John Minor Wisdom (q.v.) led insurgent Eisenhower delegations from Texas, Georgia, and Louisiana to the Republican National Convention. Their seating confirmed his nomination; his election brought their reward in nominations to the Fifth Circuit Court of Appeals. Brown and Tuttle were nominated by President Eisenhower in 1955; Wisdom joined them in 1957. The Supreme Court's decisions in *Brown v. Board of Education* (q.v.) handed responsibility for interpreting and implementing its intentions to lower federal courts. Over the next decade, these four civil rights-minded judges dominated three judge panels of the Fifth Circuit Court, which handled a flood tide of civil rights litigation from Alabama, Florida, Georgia, Louisiana, Mississippi, and Texas. They assumed an activist posture, taking responsibility for dismantling public school segregation within their jurisdiction.

Beyond school desegregation, the Fifth Circuit Court decisions hit at racial discrimination in employment, jury selection, and voting rights. Thus, during the high tide of the civil rights movement from 1960 to 1965, its leaders regarded the Fifth Circuit Court of Appeals as a reliable ally in destroying overt racial discrimination in the Deep South. Already, however, the swell of liberal court decisions was beginning to moderate. President Kennedy appointed moderate Georgia Democrat Griffin Bell (q.v.) to the court in 1961 and President Johnson nominated the much more conservative former governor of Mississippi, James P. Coleman, to the court in 1965. During the Nixon administration, conservative appointees moved the court more strongly in that direction. In 1979,

President Carter nominated two staunch judicial friends of civil rights to the Fifth Circuit bench: Alabama's Frank Minis Johnson (q.v.) and Florida's Joseph W. Hatchett, the first African American to serve on a federal appeals court. In 1981, when the court's senior activist leaders, Brown, Rives, Tuttle, and Wisdom, had all retired, the Fifth Circuit Court of Appeals was divided. Alabama, Florida, and Georgia are now the Eleventh Circuit, headquartered in Atlanta. Louisiana, Mississippi, and Texas are now the Fifth Circuit, headquartered in New Orleans.

FIKES v. ALABAMA, 352 U.S. 191 (1957). A case in which the Supreme Court barred the use of confessions obtained under coercive circumstances.

William Earl Fikes was a black Alabaman of limited mental ability. In 1953, he was convicted and sentenced to death in Alabama for burglary with the intent to rape. His conviction rested on a confession obtained under circumstances that were the basis for his attorney's appeal to the Supreme Court. When he was arrested, Fikes was jailed in a distant county and held in isolation there. Except for periods of interrogation, which lasted for hours, he was isolated in the distant jail cell for five days. During that time, he was denied the right to visits with both his father and an attorney who had come to talk with him. Near the end of his isolation and interrogation, Fikes confessed to the crime for which he was sentenced to death. The Supreme Court ruled that his confession was obtained under coercive circumstances and its use to convict Fikes violated his Fourteenth Amendment rights to due process. In this case, the Court acknowledged, there had been no physical coercion, but the circumstances under which Fikes's confession was elicited were psychologically coercive. Neither physical nor psychological coercion could be used in winning confessions, said the Court; Fourteenth Amendment due process required that confessions must be voluntary.

THE FIRE NEXT TIME. *See* **Baldwin, James.**

FIREFIGHTERS v. STOTTS, 467 U.S. 561 (1984). A case in which the Supreme Court found that courts could not set aside employment seniority systems unless they were intended to discriminate.

In *Firefighters v. Stotts,* a federal district court held that layoffs in a fire department based on seniority would be discriminatory since until recently the department had not hired African Americans. Dismissing firemen with little or no seniority would only reaffirm the department's discriminatory hiring policy, reasoned the court, so it ordered the department to develop a work-force reduction plan that would not reduce the proportion of African American employees, even if that meant dismissing white employees with greater seniority than African Americans who retained their positions. Aggrieved white firemen sought to reverse the federal district court judgment modifying their seniority rights by appealing to the Supreme Court. The Reagan administration Justice Department entered the case as a friend of the court on the firemen's side. The Court reversed the district court's ruling. Seniority systems could not be set aside under federal civil rights law, the Court ruled, unless the intention in their adoption was to discriminate. The Supreme Court's ruling was narrowly drawn, but the Reagan administration interpreted it more broadly to mean that courts had no authority under Title VII of the Civil Rights Act of 1964 (q.v.) to establish racial quotas in employment.

FISHER v. HURST, 333 U.S. 147 (1948). A case in which the Supreme Court ruled that states must offer equal educational opportunities for qualified African American students.

In *Sipuel v. Board of Regents of the University of Oklahoma* (q.v.), the Supreme Court ruled that Oklahoma's tuition grants to African American law students at schools outside the state did not meet the constitutional requirement that the state must offer educational opportunities for African American students within its boundaries equal to those offered white students. Oklahoma responded by opening a law school for African American students, which operated in three rooms in the state capitol, had only three white attorneys on its faculty, offered access to the state law library, and could not begin the academic year when the University of Oklahoma Law School did. Ada Louise Sipuel Fisher, who had brought original legal challenge before she married, refused to apply to the new law school.

In *Fisher v. Hurst,* Fisher's attorney returned to Oklahoma courts, arguing that, even when the new law school opened, it would not meet the Fourteenth Amendment's due process requirement of equal educational opportunity and asking the court to order Fisher's admission to the University of Oklahoma Law School. State courts held that the university law school could either admit Fisher or suspend the enrollment of white students until the new African American law school was open and prepared to meet the test of equality. With Justices Frank Murphy and Wiley Rutledge in dissent, the Supreme Court held that the state court decision met the requirements of its ruling in *Sipuel.* Recognizing that the state was unlikely to be able to give a racially separate new law school the appearance of equality, Oklahoma authorities reversed course. In 1949, Fisher was admitted to and, in 1951, she graduated from the University of Oklahoma Law School.

FLORIDA ex rel. HAWKINS v. BOARD OF CONTROL OF FLOR-IDA, 347 U.S. 971 (1954); 350 U.S. 413 (1956). A case in which the Supreme Court ordered the desegregation of the University of Florida's law school.

When the University of Florida's law school refused admission to an African American applicant, Virgil D. Hawkins, in 1949, he sued for relief. Three years later, Florida's supreme court dismissed Hawkins's case, reasoning that he could study law at Florida Agricultural and Mechanical University. Hawkins appealed the case to the United States Supreme Court. On 24 May 1954, a week after its decision in *Brown v. Board of Education* (q.v.), the Supreme Court remanded the *Hawkins* case to Florida's supreme court and ordered it to reconsider its decision in light of the decision in *Brown*. Failing to get relief there, two years later Hawkins returned to the Supreme Court, which ordered his admission to the University of Florida's law school without delay. Still, the state court offered opportunity for the university to stall Hawkins's admission. In 1957, he appealed to the Supreme Court a third time. It refused to hear Hawkins's appeal, but referred the case to a federal district court. On 18 June 1958, federal district judge Dozier De Vane ordered graduate and professional schools at the University of Florida to admit qualified African American students. In the fall of 1958, the University of Florida's law school admitted George H. Starke, an African American, to its student body.

FORMAN, JAMES (1928–   ). Civil rights activist and writer.

Born on 4 October 1928, James Forman went to public schools in a working-class district of southside Chicago, Illinois. After graduating from high school, he joined the United States Air Force and served in the Korean War. After the war, Forman attended Roosevelt University in Chicago, earning a B.A. in 1957. He became a reporter for the city's leading African American newspaper, the *Chicago Defender*. He was introduced to the civil rights movement on an assignment to cover the desegregation of schools in Little Rock, Arkansas. By 1959, Forman was involved in the plight of African Americans in Tennessee's Fayette and Haywood Counties. When they registered to vote, their white neighbors retaliated by forcing black agricultural workers off of farms into tent cities and refusing to sell them basic necessities. Forman joined the Student Nonviolent Coordinating Committee (SNCC; q.v.) when it was organized in 1960. Ten years older than most of SNCC's student activists and with military experience behind him, he became its executive secretary in 1961. Forman held that position until 1966 and was active in SNCC for several years thereafter.

As the movement took its toll among student activists, Forman published his tribute to Sammy Younge, Jr. (q.v.) in 1968. Forman had moved from a nonviolent, integrationist posture in the early 1960s to a separatist position contemplating the necessity of armed struggle. Briefly, from February to July 1968, he was the Black Panther Party's minister of foreign affairs. Following a conference in April 1969, Forman led SNCC activists into a union with the League of Revolutionary Black Workers (LRBW), an organization of black members of the United Automobile Workers in Detroit, to form the Black Economic Development Conference (BEDC). As its spokesman, Forman called for a Black Workers Congress and demanded reparations from white America. He stormed into New York City's Riverside Church to demand $500 million in reparations for the nation's history of racial exploitation. The reparations demand, articulated again in Forman's "Black Manifesto" in 1969, generated considerable national debate and perhaps $500,000 in actual contributions.

In the early 1970s, Forman lectured around the nation and published *The Political Thought of James Forman* (1970) and *The Making of Black Revolutionaries* (1972). Since the mid-1970s, he has directed the Unemployment and Poverty Action Council (UPAC). Forman returned to school, earning an M.A. at Cornell in 1980 and a Ph.D. at Union Institute in 1982. He published *Self-Determination and the African-American People* in 1981. He rejected Stokely Carmichael's social analysis, which fixed on race as the exclusive category of identity politics. As a women's liberation advocate, who embraced Frantz Fanon's critique of the exploitation of black masses by bourgeois African nationalists, Forman insisted that any adequate social analysis must conjure with categories of race, gender, and social class. In 1990, the National Conference of Black Mayors awarded James Forman its Fannie Lou Hamer Freedom Award.

FRASIER v. BOARD OF TRUSTEES OF THE UNIVERSITY OF NORTH CAROLINA, 134 F. Supp. 589 (M.D. N.C., 1955). A case in which a federal district court ordered the desegregation of the undergraduate school at the University of North Carolina.

Although the University of North Carolina admitted African American students to its graduate and professional schools by 1955, its undergraduate program continued to be segregated. In the spring of 1955, Leroy Benjamin Frasier and two other African American students challenged this policy by applying for admission. When rejected by the admissions office on racial grounds, they appealed to the university's board of trustees. The board rejected the applicants' appeal and reaffirmed its segregationist admissions policy. Frasier and the other applicants then filed a class action suit against the university trustees in the federal district court for the middle district of North Carolina. Their attorney argued that the exclusion of Frasier and the others violated their Fourteenth Amendment equal protection rights. The federal judge agreed and, in the fall of 1955, the university's entering class included three African American students.

FREEDOM RIDES. Tests of Supreme Court and Interstate Commerce Commission (ICC) rulings that called for the desegregation of interstate public transportation.

In June 1946, the United States Supreme Court ruled against segregation in interstate public transportation in *Morgan v. Virginia* (q.v.). In 1947, 16 black and white male members of the Congress of Racial Equality (CORE; q.v.), the Fellowship of Reconciliation (FOR; q.v.), and the Workers Defense League traveled by bus through the Upper South to test compliance with the Court's decision. Outside the bus station at Chapel Hill, North Carolina, four of them—Joe Felmet, Andrew Johnson, Igal Rodenko, and Bayard Rustin (q.v.)—were arrested. They were convicted and sentenced to serve 30 days on a North Carolina road gang. Except for Johnson, they served 22 days of their sentences. In 1955, the ICC ruled in *Keys v. Carolina Coach Company* (q.v.) that separate but equal seating on interstate public transportation violated the Interstate Commerce Act. Despite the *Morgan* and the *Keys* rulings, interstate public transportation in the South continued to be segregated. In 1960, the Supreme Court found in *Boynton v. Virginia* (q.v.) that segregated public transportation facilities violated the Interstate Commerce Act.

Led by James Farmer (q.v.) and remembering the example of the Journey of Reconciliation (q.v.), members of CORE determined to test compliance with the Supreme Court and Interstate Commerce Commission decisions early in 1961. On 4 May 1961, thirteen black and white male representatives of CORE left Washington, D.C., by bus. Intending to reach New Orleans in time to celebrate the anniversary of the Supreme Court's decision in *Brown v. Board of Education* (q.v.) on 17 May, they traveled largely without incident to Atlanta. At Anniston, Birmingham, and Montgomery, Alabama, however, the Freedom Riders met violent opposition. A bus was burned at Anniston. Freedom Riders on another bus were viciously beaten at Birmingham. In Montgomery, they were trapped at a mass meeting at First Baptist Church by a rioting mob of white segregationists. Yet, members of CORE and other civil rights organizations continued the Freedom Ride. Now, protected by federal marshals and state police, they went on to Jackson, Mississippi, where they were arrested and jailed. Despite the opposition of the Kennedy administration, during the summer of 1961 over a thousand Freedom Riders tested implementation of the Supreme Court's decisions in interstate air, bus, and rail transportation throughout the South. The Freedom Rides came to an end only in November 1961 when, under pressure from the Kennedy administration, the ICC implemented its ban on segregated interstate transportation.

FREEDOM SUMMER. The summer of 1964, when hundreds of Northern college students went to Mississippi to participate in the African American freedom struggle there.

Encouraged by political activist Allard Lowenstein and Robert Moses (q.v.) of the Student Nonviolent Coordinating Committee (q.v.), hundreds of Northern, mostly white, college students were prepared to spend the summer of 1964 in Mississippi's freedom struggle. Under the sponsorship of the Council of Federated Organizations (COFO; q.v.), they were oriented in workshops on Mississippi race relations, nonviolent direct action, self-protection, and voter registration at Miami University in Oxford, Ohio. Before leaving Ohio, they learned that Mississippi civil rights workers James Chaney (q.v.), Andrew Goodman (q.v.), and Michael Schwerner (q.v.) were missing and feared dead. The threat of racial violence hung over them throughout the summer. Before it was over, they experienced 67 incidents of arson and bombings, 80 beatings, and 1,000 arrests.

During the summer of 1964, however, the Northern college students joined local organizers to establish community centers and health clinics, to organize freedom schools for children, and to encourage thousands of black Mississippians to register to vote. They helped to organize the

Mississippi Freedom Democratic Party (MFDP; q.v.) and its challenge to the all-white regular delegation to the Democratic National Convention that summer. There was considerable internal tension between black civil rights workers and the idealistic Northern college students. The continued racial violence and the frustration of MFDP hopes at the Democratic National Convention signaled a new disillusionment with mainstream liberal politics. Yet, Freedom Summer contributed to pressures for the Voting Rights Act of 1965, the development of significant antipoverty, education, and public health programs in Mississippi, and a dramatically increased black presence in state politics.

FREEMAN v. PITTS, 503 U.S. (1992). A case in which the Supreme Court ruled that school districts that attempted to desegregate in good faith, but were still hampered by segregated housing patterns, were not required to continue busing to overcome de facto segregation.

In 1969, the DeKalb County, Georgia, school system was ordered to destroy the vestiges of its segregated history and establish a unitary school system. In order to implement the court order, the school system attempted to create local school student bodies and faculties that reflected the makeup of the district as a whole and to distribute resources equitably throughout the system. In the subsequent two decades, however, there were massive demographic shifts in the school district's population, as white residents, particularly in the southern part of the district, moved out and black people moved into their places. The system attempted to meet this challenge by the creation of "magnet schools" to attract students to particular academic emphases and a "majority to minority" school transfer policy. That policy allowed students to transfer from one school to another if the move took them from a school in which they were of the majority group to a school in which they were a minority group. Still, the demographic shifts left some schools in the district with racial imbalances. The Eleventh Circuit Court of Appeals ordered DeKalb County school authorities to bus its students to overcome the imbalances. The Supreme Court unanimously reversed the appeals court, with Justice Clarence Thomas not participating in the decision. If a school district that has made a good-faith effort to remedy segregation, including busing, continues to be frustrated by segregated housing patterns, said the Court, it is no longer obliged to continue massive busing of students to overcome the problem.

FULLILOVE v. KLUTZNICK, 448 U.S. 448 (1980). A case in which the Supreme Court found that Congress had authority to pass laws making limited use of racial quotas to overcome past discrimination.

In the Public Works Employment Act of 1977, Congress required state and local governments receiving construction grants from the program it established to reserve 10 percent of those funds to purchase goods or services from minority business enterprises. Fullilove, a New York contractor, sued for relief from the act's requirement, claiming that it was "reverse discrimination." He lost in two lower courts, which held that the congressional act's requirement was constitutional. On appeal to the Supreme Court, Fullilove lost again, by a vote of six to three. Yet, the controversial character of minority set-aside programs was reflected in the inability of the six justices to agree on a majority position. Three of them held that class-based remedies were justified to overcome class-based discrimination. Three of them argued that several of Congress's powers enabled it to act constitutionally in establishing minority set-aside programs. The other three justices held that such programs were unconstitutional. In 1989, in *City of Richmond v. J. A. Cronin Co.*, a Supreme Court with additional Reagan-appointed justices held that a Richmond, Virginia, minority set-aside program similar to one approved by the Court in *Fullilove* was unconstitutional.

G

GARNER v. LOUISIANA, 368 U.S. 157 (1961). A case in which the Supreme Court overturned the conviction of Louisiana sit-in demonstrators for "disturbing the peace."

The sit-in movement (q.v.) reached Baton Rouge, Louisiana, in March 1960, when African American college students sat in at segregated lunch counters at the bus terminal, the Kress department store, and the Sitman drugstore. They asked to be served, but otherwise made no disturbance. The management did not ask them to leave, but the police were called and, when the students refused a police order to leave, they were arrested. They were convicted in trial court of disturbing the peace, which state law defined as "the doing of specified violent, boisterous or disruptive acts and any other act in such a manner as to unreasonably disturb or alarm the public." The students' appeal to the state supreme court was denied. They appealed to the United States Supreme Court, which heard three cases—*Briscoe v. Louisiana, Garner v. Louisiana* and *Houston v. Louisiana*—combined as one. On 11 December 1961, the Supreme Court unanimously overturned the convictions. Louisiana's law against disturbing the peace did not apply to the students' peaceful demonstration, wrote Chief Justice Earl Warren, noting that, after their arrest, the state legislature had tried to modify the law to cover their actions. They had violated racial customs in the state, but not its law. The conviction of the students, Warren argued, was "so totally devoid of evidentiary support as to violate the Due Process Clause of the Fourteenth Amendment."

GASTON COUNTY v. UNITED STATES, 395 U.S. 285 (1969). A case in which the Supreme Court confirmed a federal district court's suspension of a literacy test for voter registration in Gaston County, North Carolina.

When Gaston County, North Carolina, came under provisions of the Voting Rights Act of 1965 (q.v.), its literacy test for voter registration, which was used in some places to deny African Americans the right to vote, was suspended. County authorities petitioned the federal district court to reinstate the literacy test by issuing a judgment that no such device had been used in Gaston County to disfranchise anyone on racial grounds. District Judge J. Skelly Wright (q.v.) denied Gaston County's petition on the grounds that the majority of the county's black citizens had attended inferior, segregated schools. Even a fairly administered test, therefore, would have a discriminatory effect. When the county authorities appealed to the Supreme Court, the Court reaffirmed the district court's decision for "substantially the reasons given by the majority of the District Court." The Supreme Court's decision meant that any literacy test for voter registration would remain suspended in other areas of the country that had segregated schools and were covered by the Voting Rights Act of 1965.

GAYLE v. BROWDER, 352 U.S. 903 (1956). *See* **Browder v. Gayle.**

GIBSON v. FLORIDA LEGISLATIVE INVESTIGATION COMMIT-TEE, 372 U.S. 539 (1963). A case in which the Supreme Court overturned a Florida supreme court's order to a local NAACP (q.v.) official to consult his files in responding to a state legislative investigating committee.

After the *Brown v. Board of Education* (q.v.) decision, state authorities in many parts of the South sought ways to cripple the NAACP. In Florida, the state legislature's Investigation Committee launched an inquiry into Communist influence in race relations. In March 1958, it ordered Father Theodore R. Gibson, president of the Miami NAACP branch, to turn over its membership list. Fearing the possibility of retaliation against its members, Gibson refused to do so. In *Bates v. Little Rock* (q.v.), the

United States Supreme Court had already sustained the refusal of Daisy Bates (q.v.), president of the Little Rock, Arkansas, NAACP branch, to turn over its membership list. When the Gibson case went to Florida's supreme court, it did not order him to surrender the branch's membership list. Rather, it ordered him to consult his files in responding to the investigating committee's questions about Communist influence in the branch. Again, Gibson refused to comply with the state supreme court's order, pending an appeal to the United States Supreme Court. In a closely contested decision, a five-judge majority of the Court rejected the Florida supreme court ruling. The investigating committee had not established any prior link between the NAACP and subversive activity, the Court held, and had no right to threaten its members' rights of free association and privacy. The Court's decisions in *Bates v. Little Rock*, *Gibson v. Florida Legislative Investigation Committee* and *NAACP v. Alabama* (q.v.) limited state legal threats to the civil rights movement.

GOMILLION, CHARLES G. (1900–1995). Civil rights activist and sociology professor at Tuskegee Institute.

Charles G. Gomillion was born on 1 April 1900 in Johnston, South Carolina. He studied in local schools for African American students and at Paine College in Augusta, Georgia. When Gomillion graduated from Paine in 1928, he was hired to teach history at Tuskegee Institute. On a leave of absence from Tuskegee's faculty in 1933–34, Gomillion studied sociology at Fisk University with E. Franklin Frazier. He returned to Tuskegee and taught sociology there for the rest of his career. Increasingly, Gomillion became interested in civic improvement in Tuskegee. Finding the local government of white men unresponsive to African Americans' need of adequate public services, Gomillion believed the answer lay in the security of African American voting rights. After years of trying, he succeeded in registering to vote and encouraged others to register.

In 1941, Gomillion and other black professional men at Tuskegee Institute and the town's Veterans Hospital organized the Tuskegee Civic Association (q.v.) to seek better public services for the African American community, equal educational opportunities, and a "color-blind" civil democracy. By then, enough black people had registered to vote in Tuskegee to affect the results of closely contested local elections. Gomillion's Tuskegee Civic Association became the voice of Tuskegee's black community. Its moderate pursuit of African American interests won some improved public services for black Tuskegeeans. In 1957, however, Alabama's state legislature redrew the city boundaries to exclude most of its four hundred black voters and assure continued white rule in Tuskegee. Gomillion successfully challenged this move in *Gomillion v. Lightfoot* (q.v.), a case in which the Supreme Court rejected the legislature's gerrymander in 1960. By then, however, younger movement activists had turned to direct action in boycotts, Freedom Rides, picket lines, and sit-ins. The new activism cast Gomillion's moderation in a conservative light. He continued to be active until the early 1970s, when he retired and moved to Washington, D.C. Gomillion died on 4 October 1995 in Montgomery, Alabama.

GOMILLION v. LIGHTFOOT, 364 U.S. 339 (1960). A case in which the Supreme Court found that an Alabama statute redrawing the lines of Tuskegee, Alabama, had the effect of excluding African American voters and was, therefore, unconstitutional.

In order to reduce the influence of African American voters in Tuskegee, Alabama, the state legislature redrew the city's boundaries in May 1957. The 4-sided figure of the old city map was replaced by a 28-sided figure that excluded almost all of Tuskegee's 400 black voters. Led by Charles G. Gomillion (q.v.) and the Tuskegee Civic Association (q.v.), the disfranchised black voters sued Mayor Philip Lightfoot and the city of Tuskegee for the denial of rights guaranteed by the Fourteenth and Fifteenth Amendments. A federal district court held that the legislature was authorized to draw municipal boundaries, regardless of the motive. A three-judge Fifth Circuit Court of Appeals panel divided two to one, with Judge John Robert Brown in dissent, to sustain that verdict. The Supreme Court noted that the exclusion violated constitutional rights that black Tuskegeeans had previously enjoyed and unanimously ordered the district court to review its decision in that light. In February 1961, the trial court set aside the city's discriminating boundaries. *Gomillion v. Lightfoot* set a precedent for federal judicial intervention in state redistricting and for later one-person, one-vote decisions that would affect legislative apportionments across the country.

GOODMAN, ANDREW (1943–64). Civil rights activist.

Andrew Goodman was born on 23 November 1943 in New York City. He was the son of wealthy, liberal Jewish parents. From the age of 3 until he was 18, Andrew Goodman was enrolled in the private Walden School in New York. At 15, he tasted life outside the city and his social class on a visit with a friend to poor sections of West Virginia. When he left the Walden School at 18, Goodman enrolled at the University of Wisconsin, but he dropped out after a short time there. Returning to New York, he enrolled in Queens College and was a junior, majoring in anthropology, when early in 1964 he volunteered to join the Council of Federated Organizations' (COFO; q.v.) Freedom Summer (q.v.) project in Mississippi. He was assigned to work with two more experienced civil rights workers, James Chaney (q.v.), a 21-year-old black Mississippian, and Michael Schwerner (q.v.), a Jewish 24-year-old from New York, in Meridian, Mississippi.

Goodman joined Chaney and Schwerner in Meridian on 20 June 1964. On the following day, they went to nearby Neshoba County to investigate the burning of an African American church. They were arrested in Philadelphia, Mississippi, and released from custody to return to Meridian. Then, they vanished. On 23 June, their automobile was found in a canal. A massive search for the missing young men ended on 4 August, when their bodies were found in a pit, next to an earthen dam. They had apparently been abducted and shot to death before their burial on 21 June 1964. The deaths of Chaney, Goodman, and Schwerner drew national attention to the real threat of racial violence for black people and their allies in Mississippi. Andrew Goodman was reburied in Brooklyn's Mount Judah Cemetery on 9 August 1964.

GOSS v. BOARD OF EDUCATION OF KNOXVILLE, 373 U.S. 683 (1963). A case in which the Supreme Court rejected Knoxville, Tennessee, school desegregation plans that allowed a student to transfer from a desegregated school to one in which his or her racial group was the dominant group.

Responding to the federal desegregation requirements of *Brown v. Board of Education* (q.v.), the Knoxville and Davidson County, Tennessee, school boards developed plans for school desegregation. They included an option that allowed a student to transfer from a desegregated school to one in which his or her racial group was the dominant group. Believing that this option was intended to allow white students to avoid attending a desegregated school, the parents of African American students sued to prevent the implementation of the transfer option. The transfer plan was found acceptable by both a federal district court and the Sixth Circuit Court of Appeals. The Supreme Court rejected the transfer plan as unconstitutional because its effect would be to perpetuate segregation in the public school system.

GRANGER, LESTER BLACKWELL (1896–1976). The third executive director of the National Urban League (q.v.).

Lester B. Granger was born on 16 September 1896 at Newport News, Virginia. His father, William Randolph Granger, was a native of Barbados, who as a cabin boy had jumped ship, come to the United States, and studied at Bucknell University and the University of Vermont to become a medical doctor. His mother, Mary Turpin Granger, was a school teacher. When the Grangers' oldest son finished the seventh grade, the highest grade open to African Americans in Newport News, the family moved to Newark, New Jersey, to complete the children's public education. Following their father's vocation, all five of Lester Granger's brothers earned medical degrees and practiced medicine. He entered Dartmouth College and graduated in 1918. Granger served as an artillery officer with the American Expeditionary Force's 92nd Division in France in World War I. Returning from the war, he became an industrial relations officer of the Newark, New Jersey, chapter of the National Urban League.

From 1920 to 1922, Granger taught at two North Carolina schools, the Slater Normal School in Winston and St. Augustine's College in Raleigh. In 1922, Granger became an extension worker at the New Jersey Manual Training School in Bordentown, New Jersey. There, he met and, in 1923, married the school's bookkeeper, Harriett Lane. Until 1934, Granger was a counselor, teacher, and athletic coach at the Bordentown school. He developed an interest in social work and took courses at New York University and the New York School of Social Work. In 1930, during a year's leave of absence, he organized the Los Angeles chapter of the National Urban League. Four years later, he joined the Urban League's national staff as business manager for its periodical, *Opportunity,* and secretary of its workers' education bureau. He was secretary of the New York Welfare Council from 1938 to 1940, when he returned to the Urban League as assistant executive secretary.

In 1941, Granger succeeded Eugene K. Jones as the Urban League's executive secretary and continued in that position until he retired in 1961. He supported the demand by A. Philip Randolph (q.v.) for fair industrial employment. Granger called for desegregation of the armed forces and, in 1945, as a special assistant to Secretary of the Navy James Forrestal, he was responsible for racial equity in the navy. Granger worked to end racial discrimination in the armed forces, employment, housing, and organized labor, but by the 1950s there was growing criticism of him as being too conservative. Granger retired from the leadership of the Urban League in October 1961. Thereafter, he became the first

American to serve as president of the International Conference of Social Work. Granger taught at several universities, becoming finally the first Edgar B. Stern professor at Dillard University in New Orleans. At 79, he died on 9 January 1976 at Alexandria, Louisiana, of a heart attack.

GREEN v. SCHOOL BOARD OF NEW KENT COUNTY, VIRGINIA, 391 U.S. 430 (1968). A case in which the Supreme Court found a school district's "freedom of choice" plan in public schools was unconstitutional.

New Kent County in eastern Virginia was a rural county of 4500 people, about half of them black and half white. There was no pattern of racial segregation in housing in the rural county, but the two public schools included a traditionally white school in the eastern part of the county and a black school in the western part of the county. After three years of the school board's "freedom of choice" policy which allowed students to enroll at the school of their own choice, the traditionally white school had 550 white students and 115 black students. The black public school had 625 black students and no white students. The plaintiff in this case held that the freedom of choice policy largely maintained public school segregation in the district. In one of the last school segregation cases heard by the Warren Court, the Supreme Court unanimously held the freedom of choice plan violated black students' equal protection rights under the Fourteenth Amendment. The local school board had a long history of defying its mandate to desegregate the schools, the results of its policy minimized the effects of desegregation and its policy placed the burden of desegregation on African American parents, argued Justice William J. Brennan. The effect of the Court's decision was to emphasize the responsibility of school boards to take positive action to abolish dual school systems.

GREENSBORO, NORTH CAROLINA, SIT-IN MOVEMENT. The sit-in by African American college students in Greensboro, which launched the sit-in movement (q.v.).

On 1 February 1960, four African American students at North Carolina Agricultural and Technical College sat down at Woolworth's lunch counter in Greensboro, North Carolina, and asked for service. This action by Ezell Blair, Jr., Franklin McCain, Joseph McNeil, and David Richmond was largely spontaneous. On the evening of 1 February, 50 Greensboro students organized the Student Executive Committee for Justice. The next day 50 students from North Carolina A & T, Bennett College, and the Women's College of the University of North Carolina participated in the sit-in. Within days, there were hundreds of students sitting in at lunch counters in downtown Greensboro. On 5 February, the students agreed to halt the protests for negotiations, but when they produced no tangible results the demonstrations were resumed on 1 April. On 21 April, 45 students were among the first arrested for sit-ins. The combined pressure of continued sit-ins and an economic boycott of white merchants in Greensboro forced desegregation of the city's lunch counters in July 1960.

Scattered sit-ins had occurred in cities from North Carolina to Florida and Oklahoma between 1957 and 1960, but within days after the Greensboro sit-in began it prompted others in cities across North Carolina to Virginia, Maryland, South Carolina, Tennessee, Georgia, Florida, Louisiana, and Texas. By the end of February 1960, there were sit-in demonstrations in thirty-one cities in eight Southern states. Student leaders of the sit-in movement in cities across the South met at Shaw University in Raleigh, North Carolina, in April 1960 to organize the Student Nonviolent Coordinating Committee (SNCC; q.v.).

GREGORY, RICHARD CLAXTON (Dick; 1932–   ). Civil rights activist and entertainer.

One of six children, Dick Gregory was born on 12 October 1932 in St. Louis, Missouri, to Lucille Gregory, a domestic worker. He learned survival skills on the streets of St. Louis and graduated from its segregated Sumner High School. On a cross country and track scholarship, Gregory attended Southern Illinois University and was named its outstanding athlete in 1953. He broke into the entertainment field after college and, by the early 1960s, Gregory was earning as much as $5,000 a week in nightclub appearances as a comedian. He was drawn into the civil rights movement, initially as a headliner for NAACP, SCLC, and SNCC fund raising events, at the peak of his popularity as an entertainer. By 1963, Gregory joined Martin Luther King (q.v.), Fred Shuttlesworth (q.v.) and others in Birmingham, Alabama, Movement (q.v.) demonstrations and spent some time in jail for it. In 1964, he drew national attention to voter registration efforts in Mississippi's Freedom Summer (q.v.), promoted food, clothing, and book drives to help its student volunteers, and offered a substantial reward for information leading to the arrest of the murderers of James Chaney (q.v.), Andrew Goodman (q.v.), and Michael Schwerner (q.v.). In 1965 and 1966, Gregory led civil rights demonstrations in Chicago, volunteered to continue the march of James Meredith (q.v.) from Memphis, Tennessee, to Jackson, Mississippi, and was shot while trying to calm the rioting in the Watts section of Los Angeles.

Subsequently, Dick Gregory explored other means of protest. In electoral politics, he ran against Richard J. Daley for mayor of Chicago in 1967 and against Richard M. Nixon for president of the United States in 1968. In 1967, Gregory fasted from Thanksgiving to Christmas to protest the Vietnam War. The experience transformed his life. Personally, he became a vegetarian; and, politically, he was increasingly preoccupied by the problem of hunger. By 1974, Gregory moved his wife and ten children from Chicago's South Side to a 400-acre farm near Plymouth, Massachusetts, and made a 900-mile run from Chicago through Gary, Detroit, and Cleveland to Washington, D.C., to draw attention to the national and world problem of hunger. In the next decade, Gregory turned his interest in diet and hunger into a business empire. Despite business reversals, however, he continued his record of social protest with a forty-four-day fast against drug use in Atlanta in 1987 and a vigil against the Gulf War in 1990.

GRIFFIN v. BRECKINRIDGE, 403 U.S. 88 (1971). A case in which the Supreme Court ruled that individuals can be prosecuted for violations of civil rights even if they are not acting in cooperation with the state.

In 1951, the United States Supreme Court held in *Collins v. Hardyman* that in order to sustain a charge of conspiracy to deprive another person of the equal protection of the laws an action had to have been ordered by a state official or had the support of the state. It reversed that finding 20 years later in *Griffin v. Breckinridge.* Two African Americans, Eugene Griffin and R. G. Grady, were driving through Mississippi, where they were taken for civil rights workers by James C. Breckinridge and other white men. Breckinridge and the others forced Griffin and Grady off the road, threatened them with guns, and beat them. Griffin and Grady brought charges against their assailants under 42 United States Code section 1985(3): "If two or more persons conspire or go in disguise on the highway or on the premises of another, for the purposes of depriving any person or class of persons the equal protection of the laws, or of equal privileges and immunities under the laws the party so injured or deprived may have a cause of action against the conspirators."

Relying on the *Collins* precedent, a Mississippi federal district court dismissed the case against Breckinridge on the grounds that the plaintiffs had failed "to state a cause of action." The district court's judgment was upheld by the Fifth Circuit Court of Appeals. When Griffin appealed to the Supreme Court, however, it reversed its precedent in *Collins* and acknowledged private conspiracies to deprive other persons the equal protection of the laws. Justice Potter Stewart spoke for the Court in finding that Congress had authority to pass 42 U.S.C. 1985(3) under its power to protect interstate travel and section 2 of the Thirteenth Amendment.

GRIFFIN v. PRINCE EDWARD SCHOOL BOARD, 377 U.S. 218 (1964). A case in which the Supreme Court ordered the Prince Edward County, Virginia, school board to reopen its public schools.

The case had its origin in 1951 as one of several cases that were resolved in the Supreme Court's decision in *Brown v. Board of Education* (q.v.). Until 1959, Prince Edward County maintained its public schools on a segregated basis. Under the pressure of federal court desegregation orders, however, the Prince Edward County school board ordered the closing of all of its public schools in that year. Thereafter, state education funds to Prince Edward County were used in the form of tuition grants to send white students only to the private Prince Edward Academy. The litigation continued for years, until the Supreme Court ruled in 1964 that the school board's action violated the equal protection rights of Prince Edward County's African American school children. In the language of the Court's 1955 *Brown* decision, Justice Hugo Black drolly observed that Prince Edward County had moved with "entirely too much deliberation and not enough speed" to desegregate its schools. Under direct court orders, Prince Edward County began levying public school taxes again and reopened its public schools in 1964. The years of delay and the entrenched feelings in the white community, however, meant that few white parents chose to send their children to the county's public schools.

GRIGGS v. DUKE POWER COMPANY, 401 U.S. 424 (1971). A case in which the Supreme Court ruled that the use of an education qualification or standardized tests must have a job-related justification and not be used merely to screen applicants on racial grounds.

Willie S. Griggs and other African American employees of North Carolina's Duke Power Company believed that the company was using an education requirement and a standardized test requirement to discriminate against hiring or promoting African Americans in the company. Griggs and others filed a class action lawsuit against the company under Title VII of the Civil Rights Act of 1964 (q.v.) to bar those requirements as discriminatory against African Americans. The federal district and appellate counts held that Title VII did not preclude the use of an education requirement or standardized testing. The Supreme Court, however, unanimously reversed the lower courts' findings. It held that, when there was a record or prior discrimination, when the education requirement or standardized testing did not relate specifically to job performance and when the requirements eliminated African American candidates at a significantly higher rate than white candidates, the company was in violation of Title VII of the Civil Rights Act of 1964.

H

HALEY, ALEXANDER PALMER (Alex; 1921–92). Writer.

Alexander Palmer (Alex) Haley was born on 11 August 1921 in Ithaca, New York. For two years in the late 1930s, he studied to become a teacher at Elizabeth City State Teacher's College in North Carolina. As the war clouds gathered over Europe at the beginning of World War II, however, Haley chose a career in the armed forces. He spent the next 20 years in the military, retiring in 1959. Sustained by his military pension, Alex Haley began a second career as a free-lance writer. In 1962, *Playboy* published his interview with Malcolm X (q.v.), which became the genesis for Haley's first important book, *The Autobiography of Malcolm X* (1965). Based on extensive interviews with Malcolm X, the book was Haley's artistic creation and has won an important place in American biography.

Alex Haley's second important book, *Roots: The Saga of an American Family* (1976), was even more his own story. An historical novel which invited acceptance as a work of history, *Roots* was inspired by stories told to Haley by his grandmother about the family's origins in West Africa, its experience in slavery, and its subsequent history. To recollections of his grandmother's stories, Haley added 12 years of historical research and claimed to have discovered the name of a Gambian ancestor, Kunta Kinte. A best-selling book that had even greater impact when it was made into a gripping television miniseries, *Roots* did much to stimulate interest and pride in the African American experience and had a much greater immediate effect than *The Autobiography*. Subsequent renewed interest in Malcolm X and criticism of the originality and reliability of *Roots* may reverse early judgments about the relative importance of the two books. Alex Haley died on 10 February 1992 in Seattle, Washington.

HAMER, FANNIE LOU TOWNSEND (1917–77). Civil rights activist.

Born on 6 October 1917, Fannie Lou Townsend Hamer was the last of twenty children born to Jim and Ella Townsend in Montgomery

County, Mississippi. Her father, who had been born a slave, and her mother were impoverished sharecroppers, who moved to Sunflower County in 1919. She began working in its plantation fields when she was six and received only six years of formal education in black public schools. Jim Townsend died in 1939 and, until her death in 1961, Ella Townsend lived with her youngest daughter. In 1944, when she was twenty-seven, Fannie Lou Townsend married Perry "Pap" Hamer, a young black farm worker who had moved to the Delta from the hill country near Kilmichael, Mississippi. In 1961, Fannie Lou Hamer was hospitalized for the removal of a uterine tumor. After the surgery, she was told that she had been accidentally given a hysterectomy. The Hamers adopted two daughters and when one of them died in 1967, they raised her two daughters as well.

Fannie Lou Hamer had a reputation as a leader among the workers on the W. D. Marlowe plantation near Ruleville, Sunflower County, Mississippi, where she was a timekeeper. The county was the home of Senator James Eastland, the birthplace of the Citizens Council (q.v.), and the site of the state's notorious Parchman Prison. Two-thirds of Sunflower County's population was black, but white people owned 90 percent of the land. Of 13,000 black people of voting age, less than 200 were registered to vote in August 1962, when Fannie Lou Hamer went to a meeting sponsored by the Student Nonviolent Coordinating Committee (SNCC; q.v.). There, she was motivated by James Bevel (q.v.) and James Forman (q.v.) to try to register to vote. She was rejected by the registrar for failing to be able to interpret a section of the Mississippi constitution as required by law.

For trying to register, Marlowe fired Fannie Lou Hamer and drove her off the plantation. Ten days later, night riders pumped sixteen bullets into the bedroom of the house in Ruleville where she took refuge. Unhurt and more determined than ever, Hamer began attending and addressing SNCC-sponsored mass meetings and SCLC workshops. By 1963, at age 46, she registered to vote and became SNCC's newest and oldest field secretary. As they returned from an SCLC workshop at Charleston, South Carolina, in August 1963, Hamer and others were arrested, jailed, and severely beaten by white law officers and black inmates in Winona, Mississippi. The Justice Department brought charges against five men. Despite photographs of the injuries and FBI testimony against the accused, a federal court jury of white men in Oxford, Mississippi, found all of the accused innocent.

In 1964, Fannie Lou Hamer welcomed the Northern white college students who came to Mississippi as volunteers in Freedom Summer (q.v.). She helped to found the Mississippi Freedom Democratic Party (q.v.) and, as vice-chairman of its delegation which challenged the seating of the all-white regular delegation to the Democratic National Convention in 1964, she offered dramatic testimony to the experience of racial repression in Mississippi. In 1965, Hamer, Annie Devine and Victoria Gray unsuccessfully challenged the seating of white congressmen from Mississippi in the United States House of Representatives. In 1966, she resigned from SNCC to protest its decision to exclude white people from its work. Fannie Lou Hamer remained active in the movement from her modest apartment in Ruleville. She made several races for public office and helped to organize the Delta Ministry (q.v.) and the Freedom Farms Foundation, a nonprofit effort to offer support to impoverished plantation families. She supported the Child Development Group of Mississippi (CDGM), spoke out against the war in Vietnam and attended the Democratic National Conventions of 1968 and 1972 as a delegate from Mississippi. In July 1971, she was a founding member of the National Women's Political Caucus (NWPC). In the end, however, after raising thousands of dollars to help others, Fannie Lou Hamer died penniless from the ravages of breast cancer, diabetes, and heart disease in a Mound Bayou, Mississippi, hospital on 14 March 1977.

HAMILTON v. ALABAMA, 376 U.S. 650 (1964). A case in which the Supreme Court reversed the conviction of an African American woman on contempt of court charges.

Mary Hamilton, a black Alabama woman, refused to answer questions on cross-examination in a hearing about a writ of habeas corpus when the white examining attorney addressed her by her first name. Commonly, prior to the mid-1960s, black witnesses were addressed in demeaning or familiar terms by examining attorneys. Insisting that she be addressed as "Miss Hamilton" rather than as "Mary," Hamilton refused to answer the offending attorney's questions and was fined and jailed on a charge of contempt of court for her refusal. When the Alabama supreme court refused to hear her case, Hamilton appealed to the United States Supreme Court. It reversed her conviction and set a mark for the equally courteous treatment of African Americans in American courts.

HARMAN v. FORSSENIUS, 380 U.S. 528 (1965). A case in which the Supreme Court held that a state's attempt to levy a poll tax was unconstitutional.

Virginia had imposed a poll tax in 1902 as a part of its effort to disfranchise African American voters in the state. Prior to the Twenty-fourth Amendment's banning such fees in federal elections, three challenges to the legality of Virginia's poll tax were grouped together in the Supreme Court's hearing of this case. Harman, the black plaintiff, sued Forssenius, a white state elections officer, for relief from paying Virginia's poll tax, which would become illegal under the Twenty-fourth Amendment. A federal district court found Virginia's poll tax illegal on several grounds. On 27 April 1965, the Supreme Court confirmed that finding. "The poll tax is abolished absolutely as a prerequisite for voting in federal elections," wrote Chief Justice Earl Warren, "and no equivalent or milder substitute may be imposed."

HARPER v. VIRGINIA BOARD OF ELECTIONS, 383 U.S. 663 (1966). A case in which the Supreme Court found that Virginia's poll tax was an unconstitutional bar to citizen participation in state and local elections.

Annie E. Harper, a black domestic worker, and others sought a federal court decision that poll taxes, already unconstitutional in federal elections, according to the Twenty-fourth Amendment, were unconstitutional in state and local elections, as well. In *Breedlove v. Suttles* (1937), the Supreme Court had found that Virginia's requirement that potential voters must have paid their poll tax for the previous three years or lose their right to vote was constitutional. A lower federal court had followed the *Breedlove* precedent in denying Harper the relief that she sought. The Fifth Circuit Court of Appeals had already barred poll taxes in state and local elections in Alabama and Texas. Mississippi and Virginia continued to apply them, however, and an effort to rescind them had recently failed in Virginia's state legislature. On 24 March 1966, the Supreme Court reversed both its own precedent and the lower federal court decision. By a six-to-three decision, with Justices Hugo Black, John Marshall Harlan, and Potter Stewart in dissent, the Court held that the poll tax in state and local elections violated the equal protection requirements of the Fourteenth Amendment.

HASTIE, WILLIAM HENRY (1904–76). Civil rights attorney and judge.

William Henry Hastie was born on 17 November 1904 in Knoxville, Tennessee. He earned his B.A. from Amherst College in 1925. Entering law school at Harvard University, Hastie earned an LL.B. in 1930 and an S.J.D. in 1933. He joined the faculty of Howard University's law school in 1930. In 1933, Hastie was admitted to the bar of the District of Columbia and joined his colleague, Charles H. Houston (q.v.), in the firm of Houston and Houston. With Houston, Hastie handled many legal cases for the National Association for the Advancement of Colored People (NAACP; q.v.) in the 1930s and 1940s, including the unsuccessful application of Thomas R. Hocutt to the University of North Carolina school of pharmacy and several salary equalization and employment discrimination cases. Despite Southern opposition to his "leftist leanings" and his involvement with the NAACP and the New Negro Alliance, Secretary of Interior Harold Ickes recruited Hastie to serve as an assistant solicitor in his department from 1933 to 1937.

In 1937, Hastie resigned from the Howard University faculty and the Interior Department to accept an appointment as federal district judge for the Virgin Islands. He was the first African American appointed to the federal bench. In 1939, Hastie resigned from that appointment to return to Howard as professor of law and dean of the law school. From 1940 to 1943, he took a leave of absence from that position to serve as a civilian aide to Secretary of War Henry L. Stimson. In 1943, Hastie resigned in protest of racial segregation and discrimination in the armed forces. He returned to his position at Howard University's law school until 1946, when President Truman appointed him territorial governor of the Virgin Islands. In 1949, President Truman appointed Hastie to the Third Circuit Court of Appeals in Philadelphia. He served in that position until he retired in 1971 and as its chief judge from 1969 to 1971. William H. Hastie died on 14 April 1976.

HEART OF ATLANTA MOTEL, INC. v. UNITED STATES, 379 U.S. 241 (1964). A case in which the Supreme Court upheld the constitutionality of Title II, the public accommodations clause, of the Civil Rights Act of 1964 (q.v.).

When President Lyndon Johnson signed the Civil Rights Act of 1964, the owners of the Heart of Atlanta Motel sued the United States in federal court for relief from the requirement of its Title II that the motel must not discriminate on racial grounds in renting its facilities. Attorneys for the motel noted that in 1883 the Supreme Court had found a similar requirement in the Civil Rights Act of 1875 violated the commerce clause in Article 1, Section 8 of the Constitution. They argued that such a requirement was beyond the powers of the Congress to regulate interstate commerce, that it violated management's right to choose its own customers, and that it subjected management to "involuntary servitude." Attorneys for the Justice Department countered that the commerce clause authorized Congress to remove barriers, such as racial discrimination, to interstate commerce, that the Fifteenth Amendment authorized reasonable regulation of private property, and the plaintiff's reference to slavery was "frivolous." On 14 December 1964, the Supreme Court ruled unanimously that Title II of the Civil Rights Act of 1964 was constitutional. Speaking for the Court, Justice Tom Clark doubted that management would sustain long-term economic losses from the act's requirement and found that it violated neither the commerce clause nor the due process rights of the plaintiff. Rather, said Justice Clark, it was justified by the equal protection rights of African American citizens. The Court reached similar conclusions in *Katzenbach v. McClung* (q.v.).

HEIGHT, DOROTHY IRENE (1912–   ). President of the National Council of Negro Women and civil rights activist.

Dorothy Height was born on 24 March 1912 in Richmond, Virginia, the first of two daughters of Fannie Burroughs and James Edward Height. In 1916, the Heights moved to Rankin, Pennsylvania, a small community near Pittsburgh, where Dorothy attended integrated public schools. With a $1000 scholarship from a national oratorical contest sponsored by the black Elks, Height enrolled in New York University, where she earned both bachelor's and master's degrees in four years. She did additional postgraduate work at the New York School of Social Work. During the 1930s, Height was a caseworker for the New York Welfare Department and an assistant director of the Emma Ransom branch of the Young Women's Christian Association (YWCA) in Harlem. From there, she moved to the Phyllis Wheatley branch of the YWCA in Washington, D.C. When she met Mary McLeod Bethune on 7 November 1937, the pattern for Height's career was established. She was a YWCA staff member and a volunteer worker with the National Council of Negro Women (NCNW q.v.). From 1944 to 1977, Height was a national staff member of the YWCA. In 1965, she founded its Center for Racial Justice and was its director until she retired from the YWCA in 1977. Elected national president of Delta Sigma Theta sorority in 1947, Height held that office until 1956. She left that position to become president of the NCNW, a position she has held for forty years.

Coming to power as the civil rights movement crested, she was often included with James Farmer (q.v.), Martin Luther King (q.v.), John Lewis (q.v.), A. Philip Randolph (q.v.), Roy Wilkins (q.v.), and Whitney Young (q.v.) among its leading national advocates. She supported King's leadership of demonstrations in Birmingham, addressed the March on Washington (q.v.), and led an intensive drive to desegregate the YWCA in 1963. A year later, Height and the NCNW brought black and white women from other parts of the country to open lines of communication among women in Alabama and Mississippi. Throughout the 1960s and 1970s, Height often testified before congressional committees on major social legislation. In 1966, she participated in the White House Conference "To Fulfill These Rights" (q.v.). Five years later, she was a founding member of the National Women's Political Caucus (NWPC). In the 1980s, she chaired the Black Leadership Forum, which drew leaders of 14 African American organizations together for joint strategic planning. The NCNW was forced to scale its operations back during the Reagan and Bush administrations, but Height and the NCNW launched the annual Black Family Reunion celebrations in 1986 to emphasize the resilience and strength of the African American family.

HENDERSON v. U.S. INTERSTATE COMMERCE COMMISSION AND SOUTHERN RAILWAY, 339 U.S. 816 (1950). A case in which the Supreme Court held that racially segregated dining facilities on railroad cars violated Section 3 of the Interstate Commerce Act of 1887.

In 1942, Elmer W. Henderson boarded a Southern Railway train in Washington, D.C., for a trip to Atlanta, Georgia. When the train passed into Virginia, he found that curtains were drawn across the dining car, dividing it into sections for white and for black diners. Tables were set at a ratio of five tables for white people for every one table for black people. If additional white diners appeared, the curtain was drawn back, white diners served at tables reserved for black people, and black people were asked to eat later. When Henderson entered the dining car, he took a seat at the only available table and was asked to leave. He did so, with the promise that he would be called when white diners had finished eating. Henderson was never called and the dining car closed without serving him. Later, he complained to the Interstate Commerce Commission, which would not hear his case.

When Henderson sued in federal district court to win a hearing of his grievance, the court ruled that the railroad's policy violated Section 3 of the Interstate Commerce Act of 1887. In response to the ruling, the railroad changed its ratio of white to black tables from five to one to five to two. Henderson sued again, but the district court ruled that the railroad's revised policy complied with its previous decision and the separate but equal requirements of *Plessy v. Ferguson*. Henderson appealed his case to the Supreme Court. For the first time, the Justice Department intervened in this case, as well as *McLaurin v. Oklahoma State Regents* (q.v.) and *Sweatt v. Painter* (q.v.), which were decided on the same day, to challenge the constitutionality of *Plessy*. On 5 June 1950, the Supreme Court ruled that the railroad's revised policy still denied equal access to public accommodations in violation of Section 3 of the Interstate Commerce Act. Justice Harold Burton spoke for a unanimous Court in arguing that "the right to be free from unreasonable discriminations belongs . . . to each particular person." Yet, the Court addressed only the issue of equality of service and avoided the issue of the *Plessy* precedent's endorsement of the constitutionality of racial segregation.

HENRY, AARON (1922–   ). Civil rights activist, pharmacist, and politician.

Aaron Henry was born on 2 July 1922 in Dublin, Mississippi. He studied in Coahoma County's public schools for African American children. Henry served in the military for three years during World War II in the Pacific. Thereafter, he studied pharmacy at Xavier University in New Orleans, where he graduated in 1950. Henry settled in Clarksdale, Mississippi, married Noelle Michael, and managed a drugstore, which he soon bought. He helped to establish Coahoma County's branch of the NAACP (q.v.) and became known in the 1950s as a young radical who challenged both Mississippi's white segregationists and its cautious older NAACP leaders. In 1960, Aaron Henry was elected president of Mississippi's NAACP branches and foresaw that the movement would lead many of its members to jail for freedom's sake. When the Freedom Riders (q.v.) arrived in Jackson, Mississippi, a year later, he was there to receive them and was arrested with them. At the center of the movement in Clarksdale, he led an economic boycott of white merchants and civil rights demonstrations to force improvements in the treatment of black people and a voter registration drive to increase their influence in local and state politics.

Aaron Henry's white opponents retaliated by arresting and convicting him of conducting an illegal boycott and on a dubious morals charge and by vandalizing and firebombing his home and business. His wife, Noelle, was fired from her teaching position. Henry persisted, and in

February 1962 he organized the Council of Federated Organizations (COFO; q.v.), which drew the major civil rights organizations working in the state into a united front. He was its candidate for governor of Mississippi in the "Freedom Ballot Campaign" of 1963. As its president, he directed Freedom Summer (q.v.) in 1964, when Northern college students came to Mississippi to help staff freedom schools and voter registration campaigns. He was also the founding chairman of the Mississippi Freedom Democratic Party (MFDP; q.v.), which unsuccessfully challenged the seating of the all-white regular Mississippi delegation to the Democratic National Convention in 1964. In 1968, he chaired the biracial loyalist delegation, which successfully unseated the all-white regular delegation to the Democratic National Convention. Later, Aaron Henry served as a member of the Mississippi state legislature from Clarksdale.

HIGH POINT, NORTH CAROLINA, SIT-IN MOVEMENT. One of the first sit-in movements (q.v.) after their beginning in Greensboro, North Carolina.

Ten days after the sit-in movement began in Greensboro, 26 black students at High Point's William Penn High School assembled at a local black church, where Birmingham, Alabama's Fred Shuttlesworth (q.v.) was a guest preacher, and marched downtown to sit-in at the W. F. Woolworth's lunch counter. Surprised by the move, Woolworth's management first closed its lunch counter and later announced the closing of the store in order to forestall continuing demonstrations. Several other stores in downtown High Point followed Woolworth's lead in closing their doors to the public. Despite some violent white reactions, the sit-in movement in High Point was ultimately successful. High Point's downtown lunch counters were peacefully desegregated in mid-1960, about the same time lunch counters in Charlotte and Greensboro were desegregated.

HIGHLANDER FOLK SCHOOL. A center for labor and civil rights education in southeastern Tennessee.

Inspired by both the folk school movement among Danish-American immigrants to the United States and the settlement house movement in American cities, Myles Horton and Donald West founded the Highlander Folk School at Monteagle, Tennessee, in 1932. Folk schools often emphasized the preservation of traditional folk ways, but at Highlander that could mean preservation by resistance to the disruptions of industrial capitalism. Thus, in its first two decades, Highlander Folk School was a center for labor education in the South. Its program focused on economic and social problems by studying cultural geography, psychology, and radical literature. During World War II, Highlander developed a commitment to racial justice.

By the 1950s, Highlander had become a training center for the civil rights movement. Rosa Parks (q.v.), for example, attended a retreat there shortly before she refused to yield her seat on a Montgomery public bus, which led to the Montgomery Bus Boycott (q.v.) in December 1955. In 1957, Septima Clark (q.v.) became Highlander's director of education. By then, it had become a target of state and federal police harassment, FBI surveillance, Internal Revenue Service audits, and state investigations. State police raided Highlander in July 1959. By December 1961, its charter was revoked, its property seized, and it was closed. In 1964, it was reorganized as Highlander Research and Education Center and moved to Knoxville. Seven years later, Highlander moved to New Market, Tennessee, where it has focused on Appalachia and its problems.

HOBSON v. HANSEN, 265 F. Supp. 902 (D.D.C. 1967). A case in which a federal district court held that ability grouping or tracking in Washington, D.C.'s public schools discriminated against children in lower tracks by failing to provide them with the necessary compensatory and remedial education.

In the mid-1960s, Washington, D.C., civil rights activist Julius Hobson launched a broadscale attack on racial discrimination in the district's public schools. He lost the first phase of his legal attack when a federal district court ruled that congressional legislation authorizing the district court judges to appoint the district's school board was constitutional. Later, Congress itself would change that arrangement by providing for a popularly elected school board. In the second, more controversial phase of his legal assault, Hobson argued that the school board unconstitutionally discriminated against African American children by segregating them in lower tracks of its ability grouping system. In *Hobson v. Hansen,* Judge J. Skelly Wright (q.v.) held that the district's school board was discriminating against African American children. Wright did not conclude that ability grouping itself was unconstitutional, but he held that many African American children did not have access to kindergarten in their neighborhood schools, that they were thus disadvantaged in testing for placement in the tracking system, and that they were further denied the necessary compensatory and remedial education when placed in the lower tracks of the system.

HOLMES v. ATLANTA, 350 U.S. 879 (1955). A case in which the Supreme Court applied the logic of its decision in *Brown v. Board of Education* (q.v.) to require the desegregation of public recreation facilities.

In July 1951, the manager of a municipal golf course in Atlanta, Georgia, refused to allow African Americans access to its facilities. Black citizens petitioned the city officials for the desegregation of the city's golf courses, but the city authorities refused to change the status quo. When black citizens filed a case for desegregation of Atlanta's public golf courses in federal district court, the court found that the city could maintain segregated park and recreation facilities because such a policy was not in conflict with the Fourteenth Amendment. Yet, because the city maintained no golf courses for African Americans, the court ordered the city to comply with the "equal" requirement of the "separate but equal" logic of the *Plessy v. Ferguson* precedent. When the plaintiffs appealed to the Fifth Circuit Court of Appeals (q.v.), the court sustained the federal district court ruling. Six months after its *Brown* decision, which held public school segregation was unconstitutional, however, the Supreme Court overturned the decisions of both lower federal courts to rule that Atlanta must not bar African American citizens from its municipally owned golf courses because of race or color. This was the Court's first extension of its logic in *Brown* to other public facilities.

HOLMES v. DANNER, 191 F. Supp. 394 (M.D. Ga., 1961). A case in which a federal district court ordered the desegregation of the University of Georgia.

In September 1960, two African American students, Hamilton Holmes and Charlayne Hunter, sued the University of Georgia for admission. A federal district court found that they were qualified students and that they had been denied admission to the university because of their race. The district court judge issued a temporary injunction ordering their admission and, in January 1961, Hamilton Holmes and Charlayne Hunter became the first African American students to enter the University of Georgia. Faced with violent demonstrations on the campus, university officials suspended the admission of Holmes and Hunter. The district court revoked the suspension orders and enjoined the state from invoking a statute that would suspend funding to a previously all-white institution that admitted African American students. Governor Ernest Vandiver reluctantly called for compliance with federal court orders and convened a session of the state legislature to amend the statute that the district court held to be unconstitutional. Both Hamilton Holmes and Charlayne Hunter, later Charlayne Hunter Gault, graduated from the University of Georgia and have had distinguished public careers. After Holmes graduated from medical school, he became a prominent physician and medical administrator in Atlanta. Charlayne Hunter Gault became a reporter for the *New York Times* and public television.

HOOKS, BENJAMIN LAWSON (1925–   ). Civil rights activist, attorney, and pastor.

Benjamin L. Hooks was born on 31 January 1925 in Memphis, Tennessee. His paternal grandmother, Julia Hooks, had become a charter member of the Memphis branch of the NAACP (q.v.) in 1912. His father's business, Hooks Brothers Photography on Beale Street, was prosperous and young Ben Hooks grew up in the economic and social security of Memphis's black social elite. He attended local schools for African American youth and completed two years at LeMoyne College in Memphis before joining the army. He served with the 92nd Infantry during World War II, including eight months of duty in Italy. In Georgia, he guarded Italian prisoners of war who could eat in a white restaurant while he could only stand outside the door. With a strong sense of unfinished business at home, Hooks returned to the United States and entered De Paul University's law school, where he earned a J.D. degree in 1948. He began a law practice in Memphis and was also ordained in the Baptist ministry. As a pastor, Hooks served Middle Baptist Church in Memphis and, bimonthly, he held services for Greater New Mount Moriah Baptist Church in Detroit, Michigan. In Memphis, Hooks was active in both the civil rights movement and local politics.

Hooks made unsuccessful bids for election to the state legislature in 1954 and for juvenile court judge in 1959. In 1961, he was appointed assistant public defender for Shelby County, Tennessee. Four years later, Governor Frank Clement appointed Hooks to the Shelby County criminal court bench. He was the first African American to hold such a position in Tennessee since the end of Reconstruction. In 1966, Hooks won reelection as a criminal court judge. He left the bench in 1969, however, to enter a private business partnership which failed in 1972. During his 1968 presidential campaign, Richard M. Nixon had promised to appoint an African American to the Federal Communications Commission and, in 1972, he kept that promise by naming Hooks as the first African

American to serve on the commission that regulates the American radio, telephone, and television industries. As an FCC commissioner, he defended freedom of speech rights, even of speakers whose views he abhorred.

In November 1976, the NAACP chose Hooks to succeed Roy Wilkins (q.v.), who retired as its executive director in August 1977. He came to the leadership of the nation's oldest, largest, and most prestigious civil rights organization at a time of diminishing national commitment to its goals. During his 16 years as the NAACP's executive director, Hooks sought to redefine an agenda for the movement and, with diminished resources, fought rearguard actions to protect and extend its accomplishments. He fought for home rule for the District of Columbia and against antibusing legislation in Congress and the nomination of Clarence Thomas to the Supreme Court. Following his retirement from the leadership of the NAACP in 1993, the organization continued a painful struggle to redefine its direction.

HOUSTON, CHARLES HAMILTON (1895–1950). Civil rights attorney and professor of law.

Charles H. Houston was born on 3 September 1895 in Washington, D.C., to William and Mary Houston. His father, a graduate of Howard University Law School, practiced law and taught at the university's law school. His mother was a public school teacher, hairdresser and seamstress. Young Houston attended the city's public schools for African American youth, graduating at 15 from Dunbar High School. He studied at Amherst College, where he won membership in Phi Beta Kappa and was class valedictorian in 1915. After two years as an instructor at Howard University, Houston served two years with the American Expeditionary Force in France and Germany before returning to the United States to study law at Harvard University Law School. There, he studied with the future Supreme Court Justice Felix Frankfurter and became the first African American member of the *Harvard Law Review*'s editorial board. He earned the LL.B., cum laude, in 1922. Harvard University Law School awarded him the J.D. degree in 1923 and Houston studied civil law for a year at the University of Madrid before returning to Washington to join his father's legal practice.

Houston was associated with his father and with William Henry Hastie (q.v.) in private legal practice until his death in 1950. Houston also joined the faculty of Howard University Law School. In 1929, he became the first African American dean of the law school and from 1933 to

1935 he was a member of the District of Columbia's Board of Education. From 1935, when in *Hollins v. Oklahoma* Houston won a Supreme Court reversal of an Oklahoma death sentence of a black man convicted of rape because black people were excluded from his trial jury, until 1939, Houston was the full-time special legal counsel for the NAACP (q.v.). In 1938, his case in *Missouri ex rel. Gaines v. Canada* (q.v.) persuaded the Supreme Court to insist upon equal access to legal education for African American students. From 1939 to 1950, he was counsel for the Association of Colored Railway Trainmen and Locomotive Firemen and for the International Association of Railway Employees. In *Steele v. Louisville & Nashville R.R.* (1944) and *Tunstall v. Brotherhood of Locomotive Firemen & Engineermen* (1944), Houston's arguments persuaded the Court to require railroad unions to give fair representation to black railroad workers.

In his last fifteen years, Houston worked closely with Thurgood Marshall, James M. Nabrit, Jr., and others to lay the legal groundwork for a full-scale assault on de jure racial segregation. In 1944, President Franklin D. Roosevelt appointed Houston to the Fair Employment Practice Committee (FEPC; q.v.). He resigned from the FEPC a year later, however, because he believed that President Truman was undermining its work. In 1948, his last major cases before the Supreme Court, *Hurd v. Hodge* (q.v.) and *Urciolo v. Hodge* (q.v.), ended legal enforcement of racially restrictive covenants in real estate. At 54, Charles H. Houston died suddenly of a coronary occlusion on 20 April 1950 in Washington, D.C. He was posthumously awarded the NAACP's Spingarn Medal in 1950. Eight years later, Thurgood Marshall referred to his teacher and legal colleague as "The First Mr. Civil Rights."

HURD v. HODGE, 334 U.S. 24 (1948). A case in which the Supreme Court found that judicial action to enforce racially restrictive covenants in real estate violated the Civil Rights Act of 1866.

In 1906, a hundred Washington, D.C., real estate owners signed a covenant excluding black people from future rental or sale of their properties. Forty years later, an African American by the name of Hurd purchased one of the affected properties on Bryant Street in Washington. Hodge, a white neighbor, sued Hurd to prevent him from taking possession of the property. Both a federal district court and the federal appeals court upheld the legality of the racially restrictive covenant. The case was appealed to the Supreme Court by the NAACP Legal Defense and Educational Fund (LDEF; q.v.), which coordinated it with the appeal of four restrictive covenant cases addressed by the Court in 1948: *Shelley v. Kraemer* (q.v.), tried by George Vaughn; *McGhee v. Sipes,* tried by Thurgood Marshall (q.v.); and *Hurd v. Hodge* and *Urciolo v. Hodge,* tried by Charles H. Houston (q.v.). The Supreme Court found that restrictive covenants violated the Civil Rights Act of 1866, which guaranteed to all citizens equally the right to convey, hold, inherit, purchase, rent, and sell real or personal property. *Hurd* and its companion cases were significant legal milestones in undermining de jure racial segregation.

HURLEY, RUBY (1909–80). Civil rights activist.

Ruby Hurley was born in 1909 in Washington, D.C. She graduated from Washington's public schools for African American students. Later, she attended Miners Teachers College and the Robert H. Terrell Law School, both in Washington. During the 1930s, Hurley worked for the Industrial Bank of Washington and for the federal government. In 1939, Hurley began organizing an NAACP (q.v.) youth council in the District of Columbia. Four years later, she became national youth secretary for the NAACP, a position she held from 1943 to 1951. During that time, the number of youth and college branches of the NAACP increased from 86 to 280. In 1951, Hurley went to Birmingham, Alabama, on a temporary assignment to coordinate membership drives in NAACP branches from Tennessee to Florida. Subsequently, the southeast region of the NAACP was organized to include state conferences and local branches from North Carolina to Mississippi and Hurley was named its southeast regional director.

In 1955, Hurley investigated the murders of the Reverend George W. Lee and Emmett Till (q.v.) for the NAACP. Shortly thereafter, she stood by Autherine Lucy when rioting mobs of white students and adults greeted her admission to the University of Alabama. With little police protection from a department run by Eugene "Bull" Connor (q.v.), Hurley developed a stress disorder, losing weight and suffering from persistent illness. In June 1956, when Alabama sought to bar the NAACP from operating within the state in *NAACP v. Alabama* (q.v.), she moved her offices from Birmingham to Atlanta. There, Hurley saw new civil rights organizations such as Southern Christian Leadership Conference (SCLC; q.v.) and SNCC (q.v.) seize the initiative of nonviolent direct action. In 1961–62, she monitored the participation of the Albany, Georgia, NAACP branch in the Albany Movement (q.v.) for the NAACP's national office. In the subsequent turbulent decade, Hurley embodied a word of cautious encouragement from an older generation.

I

"I HAVE A DREAM." The most famous address by Martin Luther King, Jr. (q.v.), given at the March on Washington (q.v.).

On 28 August 1963, two to three hundred thousand people—black and white, poor and rich, laborers and bosses, athletes and celebrities, professional women and housewives, Protestants, Catholics, Jews, and others—gathered at the Lincoln Memorial in Washington, D.C., and stretched away from it as far as the eye could see. A brilliant array of musicians on stage—Marian Anderson, Joan Baez, Bob Dylan, Mahalia Jackson, Odetta, Josh White, Peter, Paul, and Mary, and SNCC's Freedom Singers from Albany, Georgia—celebrated the joy of common purpose. Norman Thomas, the elder statesman of American socialism, thanked God that he had lived long enough to see the day; Roy Wilkins (q.v.) soberly announced that W. E. B. Du Bois, the elder statesman of black radicalism, had not. He had died that very morning in Accra, Ghana. At the end of a long program, when ABC and NBC joined CBS for live television coverage of the movement's largest mass meeting, A. Philip Randolph (q.v.) introduced Martin Luther King, Jr., "the moral leader of our nation."

For the first five minutes of his speech, King followed a prepared text. When he came to its paraphrase of the prophet Amos, "we will not be satisfied until justice runs down like waters and righteousness like a mighty stream," however, the crowd's approving roar moved him to lay aside the prepared text and begin to preach. Words came to him from many earlier sermons and speeches, but with unprecedented authority and power. "Go back to Mississippi; go back to Alabama . . . ," he urged them. "Let us not wallow in the valley of despair." From behind him on the platform, Mahalia Jackson called out: "Tell 'em about the dream, Martin." Despite all the difficulties, he responded, "I still have a dream."

> It is a dream deeply rooted in the American dream. I have a dream
> that one day this nation will rise up and live out the true meaning
> of its creed—we hold these truths to be self-evident, that all men
> are created equal.

In Georgia, the dream would seat "the sons of former slaves and the sons of former slave-owners" at the "table of brotherhood"; it would transform Mississippi's "sweltering heat of oppression" into "an oasis of freedom and justice"; it would let his own children be judged, not "by the color of their skin but by the content of their character"; in Alabama, it would allow little black boys and girls to join hands with little white girls and boys "as brothers and sisters. I have a dream today!" The dream lifted King from words of Amos to those of Isaiah:

> I have a dream that one day every valley shall be exalted, every hill and mountain shall be made low, the rough places will be made plain, and the crooked places will be made straight and the glory of the Lord shall be revealed and all flesh shall see it together.

This hope, this faith, said King, could "transform the jangling discords of our nation into a beautiful symphony of brotherhood."

With each cadence, the massive crowd lifted its approving roar. Then, King took up the first stanza of "My Country 'Tis of Thee" to ring the bells of freedom. He rang them from the hills of New Hampshire to those of New York, from the mountains of Pennsylvania to those of Colorado and the "curvaceous slopes of California." He rang them from Georgia's Stone Mountain to Tennessee's Lookout Mountain, "from every hill and molehill of Mississippi, from every mountainside, let freedom ring."

> When we let freedom ring from every village and every hamlet, from every state and every city, we will be able to speed up that day when all of God's children—black men and white men, Jews and Gentiles, Protestants and Catholics—will be able to join hands and sing in the words of the old Negro spiritual, 'Free at last, free at last; thank God Almighty, we are free at last.'

With that conclusion to his most powerful public address, King stepped aside.

King's address was a patchwork of ideas and themes, some of which he had been using for eight years. In this form, he had given it twice in the previous six months, in Birmingham and Detroit. Yet, fed by the enthusiastic response of his vast audience, it took on fresh power and vitality. The *New York Times*'s headline over James Reston's story about the March on Washington read: " 'I Have a Dream . . .' Peroration by Dr. King Sums Up a Day the Capital Will Remember." Like Lincoln's "Gettysburg Address," King's "I Have a Dream" has outlasted all the other speeches given on that day. It ranks among the classic orations of American history and, together with his "Letter from Birmingham Jail," it summarized the powerful moral appeal of the Civil Rights Movement.

J

JACKSON, JESSE LOUIS (Jesse Burns; 1941–   ). Civil rights activist, preacher, and politician.

The child of Noah Louis Robinson and Helen Burns, Jesse L. Jackson was born on 8 October 1941 in Greenville, South Carolina. Two years later, Helen Burns married Charles Henry Jackson, who adopted her young son. He attended local public schools for African American students, graduating from Greenville's Sterling High School. Young Jackson won admission to the University of Illinois on an athletic scholarship. After his first year there, Jackson transferred to North Carolina Agricultural and Technical College at Greensboro, the institution whose students had launched the sit-in movement (q.v.). There, he won attention as an athlete and officer in his social fraternity, Omega Psi Phi. In 1962, Jackson married Jacqueline Lavina Davis and was elected president of the North Carolina A & T student body. As leader of the campus chapter of the Congress of Racial Equality (CORE; q.v.), Jackson promised that "I'll go to jail and I'll go to the chain gang if necessary." In June 1963, 278 civil rights demonstrators led by Jesse Jackson were arrested in Greensboro. He graduated from North Carolina A & T with a major in sociology.

Jackson was torn between his desire to prepare for the ministry and his determination to be on the movement's front lines. He was ordained in the Baptist ministry and enrolled for study at Chicago Theological Seminary, but in 1965 he enlisted in the voting rights campaign of the Southern Christian Leadership Conference (SCLC; q.v.) in Selma, Alabama, where he met Martin Luther King, Jr. (q.v.). Thereafter, with other SCLC staff members, including James Bevel (q.v.), Diane Nash (q.v.), and Bernard Lafayette, Jackson returned to Chicago and played an important role in SCLC's civil rights campaign there. From 1966 to 1971, he directed SCLC's Operation Breadbasket, which encouraged private industries to end employment discrimination and sought contracts for black businesses with the threat of an economic boycott.

Among SCLC staff members, Jackson was very young and very ambitious. He was with King at the assassination in Memphis, but his claim that he stood next to the fallen leader when he was shot and his wearing a shirt with King's blood on it for days after the assassination irritated many SCLC insiders as crass exploitation of the tragedy. Restive with the lackluster leadership of Ralph D. Abernathy (q.v.), Jackson left SCLC in 1971 to organize People United to Save Humanity (PUSH). Intended to be a multiracial coalition to mobilize the economic and political power of poor people, it was an exclusively black vehicle for his campaigns against drugs, teenage pregnancy, and violence. Charges of financial irregularities attended Jackson's departure from both Operation Breadbasket and PUSH.

In 1971, Jackson lost his first political campaign, a race against Chicago's Mayor Richard J. Daley. A year later, his delegation to the Democratic National Convention unseated one led by Mayor Daley. For another decade, Jackson promoted Democratic Party reform, black voter registration, and the election of African Americans to office. In 1983, he was active in the election of Harold Washington as the first African American mayor of Chicago. A year later, Jackson made his first bid for the Democratic Party's presidential nomination. His campaign was marred by growing tension between African Americans and Jewish Americans when his private reference to New York City as "Hymietown" became public; he refused to repudiate the political support of the Nation of Islam's Louis Farrakhan; and he conferred with the Palestine Liberation Organization's Yasser Arafat about a Palestinian homeland in Israel. Yet, Jackson's "rainbow coalition" won about 3,250,000 votes in Democratic primaries, the third largest group of delegates to the convention, and considerable leverage in the design of the party's platform. In 1988, Jackson ran again for the Democratic presidential nomination, winning over 7,000,000 votes and nine state primaries. During the 1980s, he gained increasing international stature, negotiating the release of an American pilot shot down in Syria in 1983; of 48 prisoners, including 22 American citizens, from Cuba in 1984; and 47 American hostages in Iraq in 1990.

JACKSON, JIMMIE LEE (1938–65). Civil rights activist.

Jimmie Lee Jackson was born in December 1938 in Marion, Alabama. He was a church deacon, who farmed and cut pulpwood for a living. Jackson tried unsuccessfully many times to register to vote in Wilcox County. In 1964, SCLC (q.v.) began organizing voter registration activities there. On 18 February 1965, the Reverend C. T. Vivian led a protest march for voter registration at Marion. Colonel Al Lingo of the Alabama State Patrol ordered the street lights shut off and his troops began to beat demonstrators and drive them from the street. Jackson, his mother, Viola Jackson, and his eighty-two-year-old grandfather, Cager Lee Jackson, took refuge in Mack's Cafe near Zion's Chapel Methodist Church, the movement's local headquarters. Troopers followed them and hit Jackson's mother and grandfather several times before he leaped to their defense.

The troopers beat Jimmie Lee Jackson with billy clubs and shot him in the stomach. Admitted to a Perry County hospital, Jackson was transferred to Selma's Good Samaritan Hospital. While he still lived, Colonel Lingo had Jackson formally arrested for assault and battery with intent to kill. Charges were never brought against the Alabama state troopers. Jimmie Lee Jackson died on 26 February 1965. At his funeral on 3 March, SCLC's Martin Luther King (q.v.) and James Bevel (q.v.) revealed plans for its voting rights march from Selma to Montgomery (q.v.) in Jackson's memory. It began on 7 March with another confrontation with Colonel Lingo that marked the day as "Bloody Sunday."

JACKSON, JOSEPH HARRISON (J. H.; 1900–1990). Pastor and president of the National Baptist Convention (q.v.).

In 1900, Joseph Harrison Jackson was born in Mississippi. He received his B.A. from Jackson State College in 1926. Called to the Baptist ministry, he earned a B.D. from Colgate Rochester Divinity School in 1932. While serving a congregation in Nebraska, Jackson earned an M.A. from Creighton University in Lincoln. In 1941, after serving congregations in Pennsylvania and Mississippi, he succeeded the Reverend Lacey Kirk (L. K.) Williams, president of the National Baptist Convention, as pastor of Chicago's Olivet Baptist Church, one of the country's largest congregations. He served as pastor and pastor emeritus of Olivet for 49 years. Jackson also served as secretary of the foreign mission board and vice-president of the National Baptist Convention. In 1953, when David V. Jemison stepped down as president of the convention, Jackson was elected his successor.

Although he had been a friend of the King family and his church had sent financial support to the Montgomery Bus Boycott (q.v.), Jackson grew suspicious of the popularity of Martin Luther King, Jr. (q.v.), and his desire to mobilize the National Baptist Convention behind the civil rights movement. He barred the sale of King's book, *Stride toward Freedom* (1958), at the convention's gathering in 1958 and was critical of the sit-in movement (q.v.) two years later. In 1960 and 1961, Jackson fended off Gardner C. Taylor's challenges to his leadership of the convention. Because King had supported Taylor's candidacy, Jackson ousted the civil rights leader as an officer of the convention. Many of the supporters of King and Taylor left the National Baptist Convention after 1961 to organize the Progressive National Baptist Convention. In 1964, Jackson criticized the use of boycotts to promote social change. Two years later, he opposed King's leadership of civil rights demonstrations by the Chicago

Movement (q.v.). In 1967, Jackson convened a group of 100 African American clergymen who issued a manifesto repudiating "Black Power." His books include: *Unholy Shadows and Freedom's Holy Light* (1967) and *A Story of Christian Activism: The History of the National Baptist Convention, U.S.A., Inc.* (1980). In 1982, Jackson left the presidency of the National Baptist Convention to his successor, Theodore J. Jemison (q.v.). Jackson died eight years later in Chicago.

JACKSON, MISSISSIPPI, MOVEMENT. The movement in Mississippi's capital city.

Although Medgar Evers (q.v.) became Mississippi field secretary for the National Association for the Advancement of Colored People (NAACP; q.v.) in 1954 and Aaron Henry (q.v.) replaced a more conservative president of the state's branches of the NAACP in 1960, the movement in Mississippi was largely dormant until March 1961, when Tougaloo College students sat in at Jackson's public library. After their arrest, the city's police attacked black sympathizers who waited outside the courthouse as the Tougaloo students were tried and convicted. In subsequent months, Jackson youth branches of the NAACP protested segregation in the city's public parks, swimming pools and zoo. In May 1961, the Freedom Rides (q.v.) drew national attention and both the Congress of Racial Equality (CORE; q.v.) and the Student Nonviolent Coordinating Committee (SNCC; q.v.) to the Mississippi Movement. Clarie Collins Harvey's Womanpower Unlimited gave the Freedom Riders local support. By summer's end, 328 of them had been arrested in Jackson and packed into Mississippi prisons. As they were released, some of the "outside agitators," such as CORE's David Dennis and Tom Gaither and SNCC's James Bevel (q.v.), Diane Nash (q.v.), and Bernard LaFayette, remained in the state as a cadre of civil rights organizers to work with black Mississippians.

After the Council of Federated Organizations (COFO; q.v.) was reorganized in February 1962, CORE and the NAACP focused on voter registration, and the SNCC-influenced Jackson Nonviolent Movement sponsored a bus boycott, which, with an NAACP lawsuit, removed signs designating segregated seats on city buses. Even without the signs, Jackson's buses remained segregated and Mississippi justice had jailed enough of its activists to derail the Jackson Nonviolent Movement in 1962. Late in 1962, however, advised by Tougaloo College sociology professor John Salter, the north Jackson youth branch of the NAACP launched a boycott of downtown merchants. Six months later, as Martin Luther King (q.v.)

focused national attention on Birmingham, the NAACP's national office rallied to support the Jackson boycott and sit-in demonstrations at downtown lunch counters began on 28 May 1963. The police stood by for two hours, while white civilians beat up the demonstrators.

Television coverage of the violence and Mayor Allen Thompson's reneging on promises made in private transformed the languid boycott into a mass movement. Within days, movement activity charged through Jackson's black community and hundreds of people were arrested. Quickly, however, the NAACP's Roy Wilkins (q.v.) stepped in, took local decision making from the hands of Medgar Evers and John Salter and throttled the movement's momentum. In the early hours of 12 June, Evers was assassinated and the mass movement was momentarily recharged. Yet, conservative black leaders, backed by the NAACP's national office and the Kennedy administration, won a commitment to end the Jackson demonstrations in return for limited concessions that left segregation untouched. Jackson never again sustained a mass movement. Desegregation came to the city, not on the wings of a mass movement, but on the passage of the Civil Rights Act of 1964 (q.v.) and the surprising recommendation of the local Chamber of Commerce that, however offensive it might be, Jackson, Mississippi, should obey it.

JACKSON STATE COLLEGE POLICE RIOT (1967). An armed assault by Jackson policemen and Mississippi national guardsmen on African American students at Jackson State College.

Jackson, Mississippi, policemen entered the Jackson State College campus on 9 May 1967 to arrest a student for speeding. The following day, a thousand Jackson State students gathered to protest the incident and were confronted by hundreds of Jackson policemen and Mississippi national guardsmen. When police opened fire in a similar confrontation on 11 May, several people were wounded. A bystander, Ben Brown, was killed. The killing led to more demonstrations. Student leaders at Tougaloo College feared that fellow students would be caught in downtown Jackson and arrested for violating the police department's 10:00 P.M. curfew, so they took the school's bus to bring them back to campus. When a college official charged them with taking the bus off campus without authorization, Tougaloo students boycotted classes and closed the campus to outside traffic. The incident renewed student protests at Tougaloo with demands for a black studies program and additional black faculty.

Jackson authorities said Ben Brown had been caught in cross fire between the police and students, but local civil rights activists did not believe it. A movement activist since the Freedom Rides, Brown worked in voter registration drives in 1964, demonstrated in Jackson in 1965, and worked with the Delta Ministry until late 1966. Having been arrested seven times in civil rights demonstrations in Jackson, he was well known to local police. He had married another civil rights activist, settled in Jackson, and worked as a truck driver. Out to buy hamburgers for himself and his pregnant wife on the night of the massacre, Brown was hit by a shotgun blast into his back and the back of his head. He died the following morning, his twenty-second birthday. Over a thousand people attended Ben Brown's funeral. Owen Brooks of the Delta Ministry (q.v.), Charles Evers (q.v.) of the NAACP (q.v.), and Lawrence Guyot of the Mississippi Freedom Democratic Party (MFDP; q.v.) charged that Ben Brown had been murdered by Klansmen who wore badges. "We must organize Mississippi," said Guyot, "or we will keep returning to this hall for more funerals."

JEMISON, THEODORE JUDSON (T. J.; 1918–   ). Civil rights activist and pastor.

The youngest child of the Reverend David V. Jemison, president of the National Baptist Convention (q.v.) from 1941 to 1953, Theodore J. Jemison was born in 1918. He grew up and went to public schools for African American youth in Selma, Alabama, where his father was pastor of a Baptist church. Young Jemison received his B.S. from Alabama State College in Montgomery in 1940 and studied for the ministry at Virginia Union University, where he received a B.D. in 1945. As the pastor of Mount Zion Baptist Church in Staunton, Virginia, Jemison organized the community's first branch of the NAACP (q.v.). In 1949, he succeeded Gardner C. Taylor as the pastor of Mount Zion Baptist Church in Baton Rouge, Louisiana. He has been the pastor of that congregation for over 45 years.

Two events in 1953 shaped T. J. Jemison's future career. Early in the year, the Baton Rouge city council passed an ordinance allowing passengers to be seated on a first come, first served basis. Black passengers would occupy seats from the back of the bus forward and white passengers from the front of the bus backward, but no seats would be strictly reserved for either race. When bus drivers ignored the ordinance, black passengers staged a one-day boycott of the buses. Louisiana's attorney general held that the city ordinance was unconstitutional. Jemison helped to organize the United Defense League and, from 18 to 25 June 1953, he led black Baton Rouge in a boycott of city buses. Against the bus company's wishes, the city council reinstated the ordinance, which maintained racial segregation but under conditions less offensive to black passengers. The Baton Rouge bus boycott became a model for the more famous and protracted Montgomery bus boycott (q.v.) two years later and Jemison advised its leaders about a car-pooling system to help sustain it.

In September 1953, Jemison's father, David V. Jemison, stepped down as president of the National Baptist Convention and was replaced by J. H. Jackson (q.v.). At the same time, the younger Jemison was elected general secretary of the convention. In 1957, he was elected secretary of SCLC (q.v.). As tension mounted between Jackson and Martin Luther King, Jr. (q.v.), within the National Baptist Convention, however, Jemison had to make choices. He resigned as secretary of SCLC in 1958 and served as general secretary of the National Baptist Convention throughout Jackson's 29 years as its president. In 1982, Jemison succeeded J. H. Jackson as president of the National Baptist Convention. He served in that position for 12 years. His last years in office were clouded by allegations that he sought to intervene in the trial of boxer Michael Tyson on rape charges in return for a promised contribution to pay off the convention's debt on its national headquarters in Nashville, Tennessee.

JIM CROW. A term which refers to a wide variety of legal and extralegal practices of racial discrimination in the United States in the nineteenth and first half of the twentieth centuries.

The term had its origin in a white minstrel show popular across the North in the 1830s. In it, Thomas Dartmouth "Daddy" Rice, appearing in blackface, danced and sang a number called "Jump Jim Crow." Later, the white South reacted to emancipation and the end of Reconstruction by enacting laws separating the races, restricting the franchise of African Americans and confirming social mores that discriminated against them. These laws and mores were called "Jim Crow." In law, they banned intermarriage, disfranchised African Americans by a variety of provisions and mandated separate housing, public accommodations, schools, and transportation.

Jim Crow's social mores commonly barred black people from eating at the same table with white people, required that they deferentially step aside when white folks passed on the sidewalk, and allowed black people to enter a white family's home only through the back door. They reached ridiculous extremes in some places, such as Fulton County, Georgia, where a court had separate Bibles for swearing in black and white witnesses. Although it varied significantly from one locale to another, the practice of Jim Crow was invariably to subordinate the interests of people of color to white hegemony. It was given legal sanction by the United States Supreme Court in the case of *Plessy v. Ferguson* in 1896, which was reversed in 1954 in the case of *Brown v. Board of Education of Topeka, Kansas* (q.v.). The civil rights struggle of the twentieth century has been to obliterate both the de jure and the de facto manifestations of Jim Crow.

JOHNS, VERNON (1892–1965). Preacher and civil rights pioneer.

Vernon Johns was born near Farmville, Prince Edward County, Virginia, to Willie and Sallie Price Johns in 1892. His grandfathers were a black slave, who cut his white owner in two with a scythe, and a white slave owner, who murdered a white man who tried to rape his black lover. Young Vernon Johns attended public and private elementary and secondary schools near his home in Virginia. He compensated for his weak eyesight, the result of being kicked in the face by a mule, by committing long passages of scripture and poetry to memory. In 1915, he received an A.B. degree from Virginia Theological Seminary and College in Lynchburg. In 1918, he earned a B.D. degree from Oberlin College and was ordained in the Baptist ministry. Johns taught homiletics and New Testament at Virginia Theological Seminary and was a graduate student in theology at the University of Chicago before he became the pastor of Lynchburg's Court Street Baptist Church in 1920. He remained there and farmed until 1926, when an early sermon, "Transfigured Moments," was the first one by an African American to be published in *Best Sermons*. In 1927, Johns married Altona Trent, the daughter of William Johnson Trent, the fourth president of Livingstone College, and succeeded Mordecai Johnson as pastor of First Baptist Church in Charleston, West Virginia.

Vernon Johns was a man of obvious intellectual power, but he scorned the refined ways of the black bourgeois. From 1929 to 1934, he was the president of Virginia Theological Seminary and College. During the depression and World War II, Johns intermittently farmed, operated a grocery store, and traveled the countryside on the black church and college lecture circuits. In 1947, he became the pastor of Dexter Avenue Baptist Church in Montgomery, Alabama. An advocate of both economic self-sufficiency and civil rights militancy, Vernon Johns offended local white authorities with sermons such as "Segregation after Death," "It's Safe to Murder Negroes in Montgomery," and "When the Rapist Is White." Other sermons, however, such as "Mud Is Basic," offended his own congregation's bourgeois sensibilities. After five tempestuous years at Dexter Avenue, Vernon Johns left the church in 1952. He served as the director of the Maryland Baptist Center between 1955 and 1960, but he never was the pastor of a church again. On 11 June 1965, Vernon Johns died from a heart attack at Freedmen's Hospital in Washington, D.C.

JOHNSON, CHARLES SPURGEON (1893–1956). Sociologist and educator.

Charles S. Johnson was born on 24 July 1893 in Bristol, Virginia. He was the oldest of six children born to Charles Henry Johnson, a Baptist minister, and Winifred Branch Johnson. Young Charles Johnson left Bristol's public schools for black students for Wayland Academy in Richmond, Virginia, in 1908. In 1913, he entered Virginia Union University, where he became editor of the college newspaper and a member of the Lyceum, the debate team, and the student council. In 1916, he graduated with a B.A. in sociology. Johnson entered the University of Chicago to study race relations with Robert E. Park. Chicago awarded him the Ph.B. in 1917. Named director of research and records of the Chicago Urban League, Johnson took a leave of absence to enlist in the army and served in the Meuse-Argonnes offensive in France. A week after his return to Chicago to continue studies with Park, Johnson witnessed the Chicago race riot of 1919. As associate executive director of the Chicago Commission on Race Relations, he coauthored its report, *The Negro in Chicago: A Study of Race Relations and the Race Riot*, a pioneering study in American race relations. In 1920, he married Marie Antoinette Burgette. They became the parents of four children.

Charles Johnson moved to New York in 1921 to become director of research and investigation for the National Urban League (q.v.). In 1923, he founded and, from 1923 to 1928, edited its periodical, *Opportunity,* which fostered the "Harlem Renaissance" by publishing the work of its most important writers. Johnson left the Urban League in 1928 to chair the Social Science Department at Fisk University. There, he created its nationally regarded program in race relations and published *The Negro in American Civilization* (1930). As director of Swarthmore College's Institute of Race Relations after 1933, he published *Shadow of the Plantation* (1934), *Growing Up in the Black Belt* (1941) and *Patterns of Negro*

Segregation (1943), the result of his participation in Gunnar Myrdal's massive study resulting in *An American Dilemma* (q.v.). In 1947, Johnson became the first African American president of Fisk University. In his ten years as Fisk's president, the faculty was strengthened and several buildings were added to the campus. After the Supreme Court's decision in *Brown v. Board of Education* (q.v.), Johnson helped to organize the Southern Educational Reporting Service (SERS), which monitored and published its findings on the desegregation of public schools across the South in *Southern School News.* Charles Johnson died in Louisville, Kentucky, from a massive heart attack on 27 October 1956.

JOHNSON, FRANK MINIS, JR. (1918–   ). Attorney and federal judge.

Frank M. Johnson, Jr., was born on 30 October 1918 in Delmar, near Haleyville, Alabama. He was the oldest of seven children of a high school teacher, farmer, and Republican state legislator. Young Frank Johnson attended local public schools, Gulf Coast Military Academy at Gulfport, Mississippi, and several colleges before entering the University of Alabama, where he earned a law degree in 1943. Serving in the armed forces, he was wounded in the Normandy invasion and spent the remainder of the war as a military aide in England. When he returned to the United States in 1945, Johnson opened a law office with two friends in Jasper, Alabama. In 1952, he helped to organize Alabama Veterans for Eisenhower. In August 1953, President Eisenhower appointed Johnson United States attorney for the Northern District of Alabama. In November 1955, a month before the launching of the Montgomery Bus Boycott, Eisenhower appointed him as federal district judge for the Middle District of Alabama. At the time, he was the youngest person ever appointed a federal judge.

In June 1956, Frank M. Johnson and Richard Taylor Rives (q.v.) ruled in *Browder v. Gayle* (q.v.) that racial segregation on Montgomery's public buses was unconstitutional. Their decision was upheld by the Supreme Court six months later. Thereafter, Johnson played a crucial role in Alabama's civil rights revolution, often clashing with his law school classmate and friend, Governor George Wallace (q.v.). In 1961, he issued an injunction against Ku Klux Klan (q.v.) violence against the Freedom Rides (q.v.). In 1965, Johnson ordered Alabama state officials to protect Martin Luther King (q.v.) and his voting rights marchers from Selma to Montgomery. Later, he presided over the conviction of the men who murdered Viola Liuzzo (q.v.) for violating her civil rights. Johnson joined in a decision that abolished the state's poll tax (q.v.) and ordered the state to reapportion its legislative districts. In the first such statewide ruling, he ordered Alabama to desegregate all of its school districts in 1967. Two years later, Johnson was rumored as a likely successor to Justice Abe Fortas on the Supreme Court, but the Nixon administration bowed to Southern white segregationist sentiment by nominating another candidate. In 1977, President Jimmy Carter nominated him to be director of the Federal Bureau of Investigation, but Johnson withdrew his name because of ill health. In 1979, President Carter elevated Johnson to membership on the Fifth Circuit Court of Appeals (q.v.), where he served until his retirement in 1993.

JOHNSON v. VIRGINIA, 373 U.S. 61 (1963). A case in which the Supreme Court reversed the contempt of court conviction of an African American who refused an order to sit in a segregated section of a Virginia courtroom.

Ford T. Johnson, Jr., an African American student at Virginia Union University, was in a Richmond, Virginia, traffic court on 27 April 1962 for a traffic violation. He refused to obey regulations that required him to sit in a section of the courtroom reserved for black people and was convicted of contempt of court. Challenging the constitutionality of racial segregation in courtrooms, Johnson appealed to Virginia's supreme court, which sustained his conviction as "plainly right." Johnson appealed his conviction to the Supreme Court, which reversed the state court's finding. "State-compelled segregation in a court of justice," said the Supreme Court justices, "is a manifest violation" of the Fourteenth Amendment's equal protection requirements.

JONES, LEROI (Imamu Amiri Baraka; 1934–   ). Black cultural nationalist writer.

LeRoi Jones was born into a middle-class family in Newark, New Jersey, on 7 October 1934. He studied in local public schools, demonstrating a particular talent for oratory and graduating from high school two years early. Jones entered Rutgers University in 1951, but transferred to Howard University the following year. At Howard, Jones appreciated Sterling Brown's courses in jazz criticism, but he was alienated by the social distinctions drawn among the students. The contempt of the light-skinned for the dark-skinned, of Northern for Southern, of urban for rural, and of African American for Caribbean and African, he thought, was an internalized acquiescence in a "white aesthetic." Jones left Howard in 1954, apparently without graduating, and joined the Air Force, which assigned him to a base in Puerto Rico. There, he read widely in Western literature. On furlough, he visited New York's Greenwich Village where friends introduced him to Beat culture circles. Discharged from the Air Force in 1957 on suspicion of having Communist sympathies, Jones settled in Greenwich Village. There, he worked as a stock clerk in a record shop, married a white coworker, Hettie Cohen, in 1958, edited several obscure Beat generation literary magazines, and published his first book of poetry, *Preface to a Twenty Volume Suicide Note* (1961).

In 1961, Jones visited Cuba, where he met Robert F. Williams (q.v.), a civil rights militant who had fled from Monroe, North Carolina, after arming African Americans there to defend themselves. Jones won his greatest acclaim from white critics between 1961 and 1964, but his relations with white colleagues grew strained as Williams's militance, the Cuban revolutionary spirit, and the African revolutionary struggle against European colonialism inspired Jones's critique of liberal, nonviolent integrationism in the name of a black cultural nationalism. His new attitude was exemplified in *Dutchman* (1964), a play which won an Obie, and two anthologies of essays, *Home* (1966) and *Black Fire* (1968). The assassination of Malcolm X (q.v.) in February 1965 reenforced Jones's nationalist inclinations. He separated from his white wife and moved to Harlem, where his work centered in the Black Arts Repertory Theatre/School (BART/S), which he had founded in 1964. There, Jones and other black artists explored the possibilities of a "black aesthetic," but his work was increasingly criticized for its anti-Semitic, antiwhite, and homophobic themes and confrontational style.

In 1967, when BART/S lost its funding from the Office of Economic Opportunity, Jones left Harlem for Newark, New Jersey, where he founded Spirit House, and married his second wife. Later in the year, he took a position at San Francisco State University, where he met Maulana Karenga (q.v.). Soon, Jones accepted Karenga's Kawaida religion, an eclectic mix of Moslem and sub-Saharan African religious traditions, and adopted the name Imamu Amiri Baraka. When he returned to Newark in 1968, Baraka organized the Committee for a Unified Newark to promote the election of black officials and help elect Kenneth Gibson as the city's first black mayor in 1970. Two years later, Baraka chaired the National Black Political Convention, which was hopelessly divided between advocates of mainstream and of separatist politics. After 1974, Baraka abandoned racially separatist politics in favor of a Marxist critique of capitalist society. His national visibility had peaked between 1964 and 1970, but since then Baraka has taught at Rutgers, Yale, and the State University of New York at Stony Brook.

JONES v. ALFRED H. MAYER CO., 392 U.S. 409 (1968). A case in which the Supreme Court found racial discrimination in housing rentals and sales was unconstitutional.

In 1917, the Supreme Court had found residential segregation ordinances unconstitutional in *Buchanan v. Warley* and, in 1948, the Court had ruled in *Shelley v. Kraemer* (q.v.) and *Barrows v. Jackson* (q.v.) that racially restrictive covenants were unconstitutional. Yet, these decisions had limited effect on residential segregation because they still tolerated racial discrimination in housing rentals and sales, so long as it was not enforced by state action. Joseph Lee Jones, an African American, sought to purchase a house owned by the Alfred H. Mayer Company in St. Louis County, Missouri, and was refused on racial grounds. Jones sought injunctive relief but was denied it in both federal district and federal appeals courts. His appeal to the Supreme Court, however, had the support of both the NAACP (q.v.) and the Justice Department. By a seven-to-two decision, the Supreme Court reversed the lower courts' decisions. Justice Potter Stewart spoke for the court majority. Finding precedent as early as the Civil Rights Act of 1866, Stewart argued that its ban on "racial discrimination, private as well as public, in the sale or rental of property" was a "valid exercise of the power of Congress to enforce the Thirteenth Amendment." Under section 1982 of the U.S. Code, the Court held, Congress had the authority to bar racial discrimination in real estate transactions and it had done so, again, in the Civil Rights Act of 1968 (q.v.). The Civil Rights Act of 1968 (q.v.) and the Supreme Court's decision in *Jones* finally committed the federal government to an antidiscrimination policy in housing.

JORDAN, BARBARA CHARLINE (1936–96). Attorney, politician, and professor of law.

Barbara Jordan was born on 21 February 1936 in Houston, Texas, to the Reverend Benjamin Jordan, a Baptist minister, and his wife, Arlyne. She studied in Houston's public schools for African American students and at Texas Southern University. There, in 1956, she graduated magna cum laude in history and political science. From 1956 to 1959, Jordan was in law school at Boston University. Upon graduation, she was admitted to the bar in Massachusetts and Texas. Returning to Houston, Jordan opened a law office in her parents' home and continued practicing from there until 1962. From 1959 to 1966, she also served as an administrative assistant to the county judge of Harris County, Texas. Jordan lost races for election to the Texas state legislature in 1962 and 1964. In 1966, however, she was elected to the Texas state senate, the first African American to be seated there since 1883 and the first African American woman ever to serve there. Two years later, she was elected to a full four-year term in the office. In the state legislature, Jordan focused on legislation on fair employment, workmen's compensation, and nondiscrimination in state contracts with private businesses.

A careful political insider, Jordan was elected president pro tempore of the Texas state senate by 1972, when she was elected to the United States House of Representatives. Named to the powerful House Judiciary Committee, she received national attention as a powerful voice in that body for the impeachment of Richard M. Nixon in 1973. In 1975, as a member of the Congressional Black Caucus, she led the effort to extend the Voting Rights Act of 1965 (q.v.). A year later, she became the first African American woman to give the keynote address to the Democratic National Convention. She is the recipient of many honors, including an honorary degree from Harvard University in 1977. She left the Congress voluntarily in that year to teach law and public policy at the University of Texas. Jordan served on the president's Advisory Board on Ambassadorial Appointments during the Carter administration, but multiple sclerosis and confinement to a wheelchair limited her public activity. In 1990, Jordan nearly drowned in a swimming accident at her home. She returned to public life as a keynote speaker at the Democratic National Convention in 1992 and to serve in an advisory capacity on immigration policy during the Clinton administration. In 1994, President Clinton awarded her the Presidential Medal of Freedom. Barbara Jordan died from leukemia-complicated pneumonia on 17 January 1996.

JORDAN, VERNON EULION, JR. (1935–   ). Attorney and civil rights activist.

Vernon Jordan was born on 15 August 1935 in Atlanta, Georgia, and educated in its public schools for African American students. He earned a B.A. in political science from DePauw University in 1957 and a J.D. from the Howard University Law School in 1960. As a law clerk for Atlanta civil rights attorney Donald Hollowell, who tried the case of *Holmes v. Danner* (q.v.), Jordan escorted Charlayne Hunter through a mob of angry white segregationists when she enrolled at the University of Georgia. From 1962 to 1964, he was field secretary of Georgia branches of the NAACP (q.v.). In that capacity, he worked with the NAACP's regional secretary, Ruby Hurley (q.v.), and the local branch to advise the Albany Movement (q.v.) and led a boycott of Augusta's white merchants who refused to hire black employees. In 1964, Jordan became the director of the Southern Regional Council's Voter Education Project (q.v.). Four years later, he joined the federal government's Office of Economic Opportunity to fight the War on Poverty. In March 1970, Jordan became executive director of the United Negro College Fund. When Whitney Young (q.v.), executive director of the National Urban League (q.v.) drowned in Lagos, Nigeria, a year later, the Urban League chose Jordan as his successor.

Under Vernon Jordan's leadership from 1972 to 1981, the Urban League grew dramatically: from 99 to 118 affiliates, from 2100 to 4200 employees and from a $40,000,000 to a $150,000,000 budget. The league's voter registration drives added 30,000 black voters in 10 cities across the country. Jordan expanded the Urban League's traditional interest in black employment, health, and welfare to campaign for a national full-employment policy and a national health system. Finally, he began the publication of *The State of Black America,* annual reports on the conditions of life for African Americans. On 29 May 1980, after an address to the Fort Wayne, Indiana, Urban League affiliate, Vernon Jordan was near-fatally wounded by a gunshot fired by a white supremacist. He survived and continued to lead the Urban League until the end of December 1981. Jordan then entered private legal practice in Washington, D.C. He returned to public life briefly in 1992 and 1993 as a member of the transition team that paved the way from the Bush to the Clinton administrations.

JOURNEY OF RECONCILIATION (1947). A test of the Supreme Court's ruling in *Morgan v. Virginia* (q.v.) that called for the desegregation of interstate public transportation.

In June 1946, the United States Supreme Court ruled against segregation of interstate public transportation in *Morgan v. Virginia.* In 1947, 16 black and white male members of the Congress of Racial Equality (CORE; q.v.), the Fellowship of Reconciliation (FOR; q.v.) and the Workers Defense League traveled by bus through the Upper South to test compliance with the Court's decision. Outside the bus station at Chapel Hill, North Carolina, four of them—Joe Felmet, Andrew Johnson, Igal Rodenko, and Bayard Rustin (q.v.)—were arrested. They were convicted and sentenced to serve 30 days on a North Carolina road gang.

Except for Johnson, they served 22 days of their sentences. This "Journey of Reconciliation" was a model for CORE's Freedom Rides (q.v.) in 1961.

K

KARENGA, MAULANA (Ronald McKinley Everett; 1941–   ). Black cultural nationalist.

Ronald McKinley Everett was born on 14 July 1941 in Parsonsburg, Maryland. His father was a preacher, but little else is known of his family background and childhood. At eighteen, young Everett joined an older brother in Los Angeles, where he attended Los Angeles City College. Active in student politics there, he became the first black president of its student body. Everett received his B.A. in 1963 and an M.A. in political science with a major in African studies in 1964 from the University of California, Los Angeles. At UCLA, he was active in a black student union and, from 1963 to 1965, in the Los Angeles branch of the Afro-American Association, which sponsored civil rights activity in alliance with the Congress of Racial Equality (CORE; q.v.) and the Student Nonviolent Coordinating Committee (SNCC; q.v.), as well as tutorials, studies in history and languages, and street speaking. The death of Malcolm X and the Watts riot in 1965 were turning points in Everett's life. He adopted the name Maulana Karenga ("keeper of the tradition" or "master teacher") and organized US. Provoked in part by J. Edgar Hoover's Federal Bureau of Investigation, the heat of West Coast black power politics in the late 1960s put Karenga's US organization in collision with Huey Newton's Black Panther Party. There were several shoot-outs between members of the two groups by 1969. The conflict had its ideological origin in Karenga's rejection of class analysis and his insistence that the recovery of an authentic African American tradition must come before a successful political revolution.

In the early 1970s, Karenga served time in prison for a felonious assault on a female member of US. During that time, he rethought the highly patriarchal attitudes of his earlier teachings and became more sympathetic with African socialist traditions. At the same time, he articulated more fully the religious tradition of *Kawaida* based upon seven principles: *Umoja* (unity), *Kujichagulia* (self-determination), *Ujima* (collective work and responsibility), *Ujamaa* (cooperative economics), *Nia* (purpose in community-building), *Kuumba* (creativity), and *Imani* (faith). This tradition, which is both authentic and frankly artificial, included its own holidays and ritual services, including *Kwanzaa* (26 December–1 January), a celebration of the community's historic achievements; *Kuanzisha* Founder's Day (February), anniversary of the founding of US in 1966; *Kuzaliwa* (19 May), the birthday of Malcolm X; *Uhuru* Day (11 August), the anniversary of the Watts Riot in 1965; *Arusi,* a wedding ceremony; *Akiki,* a nationalization ceremony for children; and *Maziko,* a funeral ceremony. Having chaired the Department of Black Studies at the California State University at Long Beach, Karenga has also actively promoted the institutionalization of African and African American Studies programs throughout the United States.

KATZENBACH v. MCCLUNG, 379 U.S. 294 (1964). A case in which the Supreme Court upheld the constitutionality of Title II, the public accommodations clause, of the Civil Rights Act of 1964 (q.v.).

The McClung family of Birmingham, Alabama, had owned and operated a restaurant in the city, Ollie's Barbecue, for nearly 30 years. The restaurant served African American customers in its take-out service, but its owners refused to serve them in its dining room. After the passage of the Civil Rights Act of 1964, Attorney General Nicholas Katzenbach sued the restaurant's owner to force compliance with the act's provisions. Legal justification for congressional action requiring hotels and restaurants to serve customers regardless of race lay in the authority of Congress to regulate interstate commerce. Ollie's Barbecue was a neighborhood restaurant, located far from interstate traffic and serving local people almost exclusively. Attorneys for the defense argued that the restaurant's only significant link to interstate commerce was the remote one of its buying and selling meat from a distributor who brought it in from out of state and that being coerced to serve certain customers in its dining room was a denial of due process in trade under Article I of the Constitution. Justice Tom Clark spoke for the Supreme Court, which held that Congress had acted within its authority to regulate commerce. The Court reached similar conclusions in *Heart of Atlanta Motel v. United States* (q.v.).

KATZENBACH v. MORGAN, 384 U.S. 641 (1966). A case in which the Supreme Court found that Congress had the authority to prohibit literacy tests for voting.

In 1965, the state of New York had an English literacy requirement for voting. Section 4(e) of the Voting Rights Act of 1965 (q.v.) provided that persons who completed the sixth grade in a non-English speaking school in Puerto Rico could not be disfranchised merely because they did not read or write English. In *Morgan v. Katzenbach,* a New York state resident sued the attorney general of the United States to prevent Puerto

Ricans who could not read or write English from voting. A lower court sustained his claim that Congress had no authority to bar New York's English literacy requirement for voting. In *Katzenbach v. Morgan,* the Supreme Court reversed the lower court's ruling by a vote of seven to two, with Justices John Marshall Harlan and Potter Stewart in dissent. Writing for the Court majority, Justice William Brennan held that Congress had acted within its authority to enforce the equal protection requirements of the Fourteenth Amendment.

KENNEDY v. BRUCE, 298 F.2d 860 (5th Cir., 1962). A case in which the Fifth Circuit Court of Appeals (q.v.) authorized the Justice Department to examine local voter registration lists when there were reasonable grounds to think that some citizens were being denied the right to vote.

In Wilcox County, Alabama, African Americans outnumbered their white neighbors by more than two to one. In 1960, its voter registration lists carried the names of more white people than the white voting-age population of the county. By contrast, none of its 6,085 black people of voting age were registered to vote. Attorney General Robert Kennedy brought suit against the registrar of Wilcox County to secure the voting rights of black people in Wilcox County. In an Alabama federal district court, the registrar testified that no African Americans had been denied the right to register or vote in his county and the district court found for the defendant. The Fifth Circuit Court of Appeals reversed the lower court's finding, however, arguing that the registrar's testimony was incredible in light of the disparity between the percentages of white and black potential voters on the registration books. This decision, which the Appeals Court reenforced three years later in *United States v. Lynd,* found that the Justice Department had the authority to examine local voter registration lists if there were reasonable grounds to believe that some citizens were being denied the right to vote.

KERNER COMMISSION (National Advisory Commission on Civil Disorders). A presidential commission which studied conditions which fed racial unrest in American cities in the mid-1960s.

Between 1965 and 1968, some 500,000 African Americans in 300 American cities took part in riots. They resulted in 50,000 arrests, 8,000 injuries, and over $100 million in property damage. The riots drew attention to conditions in urban ghettoes, largely outside the South, where inadequate housing, job opportunities, political representation and public education combined with strained relations with law enforcement authorities to create tinderbox conditions. On 27 July 1967, after major race riots in Detroit, Michigan, and Newark, New Jersey, President Lyndon Johnson appointed a National Advisory Commission on Civil Disorders, unofficially known as the Kerner Commission.

Chaired by Illinois governor Otto Kerner, Jr. (q.v.), the commission's members included Roy Wilkins (q.v.), executive director of the National Association for the Advancement of Colored People (NAACP; q.v.), Senators Edward W. Brooke (q.v.) of Massachusetts and Fred Harris of Oklahoma, I. W. Abel, president of the United Steelworkers, New York mayor John V. Lindsay, and five other prominent Americans. On 1 March 1968, the commission reported to President Johnson that the "nation is moving toward two separate societies, one black, one white—separate and unequal." Its report examined the origins and course of the race riots, placing them in a tradition of black political protest. Examining the texture of life in the urban ghettoes, it called for massive remedial programs to alleviate hunger, ignorance, poverty, and social disorganization. By then, however, the nation was dramatically divided by the Vietnam War and was in no mood for new domestic social programs.

KERNER, OTTO, JR. (1908–76). Politician.

Otto Kerner, Jr., was born on 15 August 1908 in Chicago, Illinois. His father, Otto Kerner, Sr., was prominent in Chicago's Czech community, a noted attorney and judge on the Seventh Circuit Court of Appeals. Young Kerner attended elementary and secondary schools in Chicago's wealthy River Forest suburb before studying at Brown University, where he won his undergraduate degree in 1930. Kerner went to England in 1930–31 for study at Trinity College of Cambridge University and entered law school at Northwestern University, where he took a degree in 1934. From 1936 to 1946, Kerner served in the Black Horse Troop of the Illinois National Guard, rising to the rank of major general in the field artillery. In 1947, his close ties to Chicago's Democratic political machine brought an appointment as United States attorney for the Northern District of Illinois. In 1954, Kerner was elected Cook County judge and was reelected to that position in 1958.

In 1960, Kerner defeated incumbent Republican governor William G. Stratton in a closely contested race for governor of Illinois and was reelected to that position in 1964. Kerner had a reputation as an able and honest administrator and had won adoption of a fair employment practices law in Illinois, but he was not known as an aggressive advocate of civil rights when, on 27 July 1967, President Lyndon Johnson named him as chairman of the National Advisory Commission on Civil Disorders. On 1 March 1968, the Kerner Commission (q.v.) submitted its report to the president. On 22 May 1968, President Johnson appointed Kerner to the Seventh Circuit Court of Appeals. He was forced to resign four years later, when he was indicted and found guilty of having secured advantageous racing dates for the state's race tracks in exchange for stock in the tracks during his first term as governor. Losing an appeal in July 1974, Kerner began serving a three-year prison sentence. Within months, however, his wife died, he suffered a mild heart attack, and was diagnosed as dying of an incurable lung cancer. Kerner was paroled and died on 9 May 1976.

KESTER, HOWARD ANDERSON (Buck; 1904–77). Civil rights activist.

Howard Anderson "Buck" Kester was born on 21 July 1904 in Martinsville, Virginia. He studied at Lynchburg College, Princeton Theological Seminary, and Vanderbilt University. As a student, he was active in the interracial work of the Student Volunteer Movement, the collegiate Young Men's Christian Association (YMCA), and the Fellowship of Reconciliation (FOR; q.v.). During the 1920s, he organized interracial discussions among college students in Lynchburg, Virginia. One of the first white students to attend black intercollegiate conferences of the YMCA, he also sought to desegregate the white YMCA conference center near Asheville, North Carolina. Employed by the Committee on Economic and Racial Justice and FOR in the 1920s and 1930s, he promoted student interracial conferences, worked with the Southern Tenant Farmers' Union and reported on lynchings, race riots, and peonage cases for the NAACP (q.v.). In the late 1930s, Kester became secretary of the Fellowship of Southern Churchmen, a nondenominational, interracial organization of Southern Christians working for social justice. He left that position in the mid-1950s to become the principal of Penn Normal, Agricultural and Industrial School, a school and conference center in the South Carolina Sea Islands. Throughout his life, Buck Kester worked for Christian solidarity across lines of race and social class. He died on 12 July 1977.

KEYES v. SCHOOL DISTRICT NO. 1, DENVER, COLORADO, 413 U.S. 189 (1973). A case in which the Supreme Court held that a Denver, Colorado, school board had acted to reenforce de facto racial segregation in its schools and was obliged to counteract it.

Denver, Colorado's public schools were not racially segregated by legal mandate; indeed, they operated under a law barring racial segregation. Yet, local African Americans, including Keyes, backed by the NAACP Legal Defense and Educational Fund (LDEF; q.v.), complained that the school board of Denver's School District No. 1 made decisions reenforcing tendencies to segregation in housing patterns that created racially segregated public schools. In a landmark decision about racially segregated public schools outside the South, the Court majority found for the plaintiff in a seven-to-one decision. Writing for the Court, Justice William Brennan distinguished between de jure segregation (segregation mandated by law) and de facto segregation (segregation deriving from residential patterns and other factors not sustained by law or state action).

The Court majority found that the school board for Denver's District No. 1 had reenforced de facto segregation with decisions that drew school attendance zones along racial lines, placed mobile classrooms at overcrowded schools for black children, and assigned African American teachers to schools whose students were predominantly African American. Given de facto segregation in its schools, said the Court, the school board's responsibility was to act against it. Justice William Rehnquist dissented from the decision. Justice Lewis Powell, Jr., partially concurring with and dissenting from the majority decision, objected primarily to the usefulness of distinguishing between de facto and de jure segregation. *Keyes* set precedents for further litigation against de facto segregation outside the South.

KEYS v. CAROLINA COACH COMPANY, 64 M.C.C. 769 (1955). A case in which the Interstate Commerce Commission (ICC) found separate but equal seating on interstate public transportation violated the Interstate Commerce Act.

Sarah Keys was an African American from New York City who was stationed by the Women's Army Corps at Fort Dix, New Jersey. On 1 August 1952, she boarded a bus at Trenton, New Jersey, for Washington, North Carolina. She sat toward the front of the bus until it arrived at Roanoke Rapids, North Carolina. There, according to Keys, employees of the Carolina Coach Company refused to allow her further passage and had her arrested and jailed. A month later, Keys brought charges against the Carolina Coach Company. Basing its defense on the Supreme Court's finding in *Plessy v. Ferguson,* the company claimed that its rules gave the company complete authority over the seating of passengers and that only white passengers were allowed to sit at the front of the bus. Section

216 of the Interstate Commerce Act held that public vehicles offering interstate transportation could not subject any passengers to "unjust discrimination or any undue or unreasonable prejudice or disadvantage in any respect whatsoever."

Based on Supreme Court decisions from *Morgan v. Virginia* (q.v.) in 1946 to *Brown v. Board of Education* (q.v.) in 1954, the ICC found that separate but equal was unacceptable. In a companion case, *NAACP v. St. Louis-San Francisco Railroad* (q.v.), the ICC banned racial segregation of interstate passengers on railroads and in railway terminals. Yet, interstate public transportation in the South continued to be segregated, in violation of the *Morgan, Keys,* and *NAACP* decisions, until the widespread challenge offered by the Freedom Rides (q.v.) in 1961.

KING, CHEVENNE BOWERS (C. B.; 1923–88). Civil rights attorney.
C. B. King was born on 12 October 1923 in Albany, Georgia. He was one of seven sons of C. W. King, a prosperous Albany builder and real estate broker. The young Kings were well educated, several of them studied abroad, and at least two of them became college professors. Young C. B. King attended Albany schools for African American youth and served in the United States Navy during World War II. Returning to civilian life, he earned an undergraduate degree at Fisk University in Nashville and a law degree at Case Western Reserve University in Cleveland. When C. B. King opened a law office in Albany, he was one of only three black attorneys in Georgia outside Atlanta. In Albany, he and his brother Slater King, an insurance agent and real estate broker, were the only sons of C. W. King who returned to be pillars of the city's small black middle class. In 1958, C. B. King won the release of his oldest brother, Clennon, from a Mississippi insane asylum, where a local judge committed him when he tried to desegregate the University of Mississippi.

In 1961, C. B. and Slater King helped to organize the Albany Movement (q.v.), a coalition of the black community's major civic organizations working to desegregate the city. Working with Atlanta attorney Donald Hollowell, C. B. King was the lead attorney for the Albany Movement. During the summer of 1962, Slater King's pregnant wife, Marion, was beaten at the Mitchell County jail and, as he tried to represent the interests of a Student Nonviolent Coordinating Committee (SNCC; q.v.) organizer, C. B. King was beaten by Daugherty County sheriff D. C. "Cull" Campbell. Two years later, King was defeated in a race for Congress. In 1970, he became the first African American ever to run for election as governor of Georgia. Winning 8 percent of the vote, he placed third in a Democratic primary won by Jimmy Carter. C. B. King died of cancer on 15 March 1988 in San Diego, California.

KING, MARTIN LUTHER, JR. (Mike, M. L.; 1929–68). Civil rights activist and pastor.

Martin Luther King, Jr., was born on 15 January 1929 in Atlanta, Georgia. He was the second child and older son of Martin Luther King, Sr., the pastor of Atlanta's Ebenezer Baptist Church, and Alberta Christine Williams King, whose father had been the pastor of the church from 1894 until his death in 1931. Encouraged by his parents, who were among the city's black elite, young King skipped three grades through public schools, graduating from high school and entering Atlanta's Morehouse College at 15. He was ordained in the Baptist ministry in 1947 and graduated from Morehouse in 1948, with a major in sociology. From 1948 to 1951, King studied at Crozer Theological Seminary in Chester, Pennsylvania. President of the student body in his senior year, King was class valedictorian and won two awards at commencement. From 1951 to 1954, King was a graduate student in philosophical theology at Boston University. There, he met Coretta Scott, a student at the New England Conservatory of Music. They married in the summer of 1953. A year later, the Kings moved to Montgomery, Alabama, where he became pastor of Dexter Avenue Baptist Church. In his first year there, King finished his dissertation and was awarded his Ph.D. by Boston University in June 1955.

On 1 December 1955, an African American seamstress, Rosa Parks (q.v.), was arrested for refusing to give up her seat on a city bus to a white passenger. In protest, the Montgomery Improvement Association (MIA; q.v.) was organized, young Martin Luther King was drafted as its president, and the MIA spearheaded the Montgomery Bus Boycott (q.v.), which was resolved by the desegregation of the city's buses in December 1956. Long before that, however, King had won national and, even, international attention as an eloquent spokesman for militant nonviolent social protest. In 1957, with other Southern black clergymen, King sought to build on the success in Montgomery by organizing the Southern Christian Leadership Conference (SCLC; q.v.). He retold the story of the Montgomery Bus Boycott in *Stride toward Freedom* (1958), which explained his understanding of nonviolent resistance to injustice. On trips to Africa in 1957 and India in 1959, King identified the Afro-American civil rights movement with third world struggles against colonialism and deepened his own commitment to Gandhian nonviolent resistance.

In January 1960, King left Montgomery's Dexter Avenue Baptist Church to become copastor with his father of Ebenezer Baptist Church and be closer to SCLC headquarters in Atlanta. When the sit-in movement (q.v.) spread from Greensboro, North Carolina, across the Upper South, King supported it by convening a meeting of student activists at Shaw University in Raleigh, North Carolina, which organized SNCC (q.v.). Later that year, King's arrest and imprisonment led to intervention by Democratic candidate John Kennedy to win his release. Kennedy's intervention may have substantially increased black support for his candidacy in a close presidential contest with Richard Nixon. Yet, King resisted Kennedy administration pressure to halt the Freedom Rides (q.v.) when they met violence at Anniston, Birmingham, and Montgomery, Alabama. In December 1961, he went to Albany, Georgia, to support the attack of the Albany Movement (q.v.) on racial discrimination in the city. After a year of economic boycotts and massive demonstrations, however, King and the Albany Movement had won no significant concessions from the city's white leadership.

With better planning, King and SCLC went to the aid of the Birmingham, Alabama, Movement (q.v.) in 1963. After his arrest there on Good Friday, 12 April, King's famous "Letter from Birmingham Jail" (q.v.) summarized the grievances of the black community and the justification for his nonviolent protest for social change. On 28 August, he gave his equally famous address, "I Have a Dream" (q.v.), at the March on Washington (q.v.). For his efforts, King was awarded the Nobel Peace Prize on 10 December 1963 and in its 1964 New Year's issue, *Time* magazine chose him as its Man of the Year. After the adoption of the Civil Rights Act of 1964 (q.v.), King led major campaigns in St. Augustine, Florida, and Selma, Alabama. The latter led to the Selma to Montgomery March (q.v.) and the enactment of the Voting Rights Act of 1965 (q.v.).

Thereafter, the Watts race riot in 1965, the invocation of "black power" by Stokely Carmichael (q.v.) on the Meredith March in 1966, the war in Vietnam, and the Detroit race riot in 1967 redirected King's attention to a broader range of issues. His campaign against discrimination in education, employment, and housing in Chicago ended in disappointing results. In his last five years, threats on King's life became commonplace. J. Edgar Hoover's Federal Bureau of Investigation monitored his contacts with suspected Communists and attempted to use reports of his personal life to destroy his marriage or drive him to suicide. Yet, he continued to cry out for economic and social justice at home and an end to the war in Vietnam abroad. On 4 April 1968, Martin Luther King was killed by an assassin's bullet as he prepared to lead demonstrations in support of city sanitation workers in Memphis, Tennessee.

KING, R. EDWIN, JR. (Ed; 1936–   ). Civil rights activist and pastor. R. Edwin King, Jr., was born on 20 September 1936 into a prominent white family in Vicksburg, Mississippi. He was active in interracial meetings in Jackson, Mississippi, while he studied at Millsaps College, where he took a B.A. in sociology in 1958. King prepared for the Methodist ministry by entering the Boston University School of Theology that year and earned his B.D. in 1961. The white Mississippian became committed to the civil rights movement during his seminary years and was arrested in Montgomery, Alabama, in 1960. He was awarded an M.A. in social theology from Boston University in 1963. By then Ed King had plunged into Mississippi's civil rights struggle by becoming the chaplain at Jackson's Tougaloo College, a historically black institution.

Early in 1963, King and his wife, Jeanette, began working with Tougaloo sociology professor John R. Salter, Jr., and Medgar W. Evers (q.v.) in the Jackson, Mississippi, Movement (q.v.). Later that year, the Council of Federated Organizations (COFO; q.v.) nominated Aaron Henry (q.v.) and King to run for governor and lieutenant governor in its unofficial "Freedom Vote Campaign," which garnered the support of 83,000 disfranchised Mississippians. In 1964, Ed King was among the delegates of the Freedom Democratic Party (q.v.) to challenge the all-white regular Mississippi delegation to the Democratic National Convention and one of its two nominees for membership on the Democratic National Committee. In 1966, as the Freedom Democratic Party's candidate for Congress from the Jackson area, he won 22 percent of the vote against the incumbent white Democrat, John Bell Williams. Although as a native white Mississippian King courageously pioneered in biracial politics and continued to be active in civil rights efforts in the state, he was later shunned by Mississippi's white moderates in rebuilding the state's Democratic Party as a biracial political coalition. In the 1990s, King was employed as a sociologist at the University of Mississippi Medical Center in Jackson.

L

LASSITER v. NORTHAMPTON ELECTION BOARD, 360 U.S. 45

(1959). A case in which the Supreme Court found that an equitably administered literacy requirement for voting was constitutional.

Literacy tests for voting were common in the United States until the 1960s. In the South, between 1890 and 1915, such tests were often used in conjunction with a grandfather clause, which commonly exempted persons who had been eligible to vote on 1 January 1867 and their descendants. The effect was to allow otherwise qualified white illiterates to vote, while excluding by definition black illiterates. In *Guinn v. United States* and *Lane v. Wilson,* the Supreme Court had found grandfather clauses unconstitutional, but it had found literacy tests that did not discriminate on the basis of race were acceptable. In the 1950s, North Carolina's constitution still contained a grandfather clause, but its voter registration statute of 1957 did not. Louise Lassiter tried to register to vote in Northampton County, North Carolina. The registrar rejected her application when Lassiter refused to take a required literacy test. In court, she challenged the use of the test for voter registration, claiming that it violated the Fourteenth and the Seventeenth Amendments to the Constitution. In *Lassiter,* the Supreme Court ruled unanimously that a literacy test that did not discriminate on racial lines was constitutional. Literacy tests for voting continued in use until Congress barred them in the Voting Rights Act of 1965 (q.v.) and its subsequent extensions.

LAWSON, JAMES M., JR. (1928–   ). Civil rights activist and pastor.

James M. Lawson, Jr., was born on 22 September 1928 in Uniontown, Pennsylvania. His father was a Methodist minister and a Republican, who commonly carried a gun for self-defense. Educated in local public schools, Lawson was a champion debater by 1946, when he argued for a preemptive atomic strike on the Soviet Union to prevent the spread of Communism. He wrestled with issues of conscience and social ethics at Ohio's Baldwin-Wallace College. There, Lawson became committed to nonviolence, believing that both military service and racial segregation violated Christian principles. In 1951, while he was president of the national Methodist Youth Fellowship, Lawson refused induction into the army and served over a year in federal prison. During the ordeal, Bayard Rustin (q.v.) and Glenn Smiley of the Fellowship of Reconciliation (FOR; q.v.) counseled him in his pacifism. Sponsored by the American Friends Service Committee, Lawson spent three years teaching and studying Gandhian nonviolence in India. There, he read about the Montgomery

Bus Boycott (q.v.) in the *Nagpur Times*. His trip back to the United States included a month in Africa, conferring with leaders of independence movements there. At Oberlin College in February 1957, Lawson met Martin Luther King, Jr. (q.v.), who urged him to come South to help lead the nonviolent movement.

Lawson traveled the country as an FOR field secretary and, in March 1958, was sent to Nashville, Tennessee, where he began theological studies at Vanderbilt University. There, his workshops in nonviolence led black students from American Baptist Theological Seminary, Fisk University, Meharry Medical College, and Tennessee State University to participate in demonstrations in November 1959 and to respond quickly when news reached Nashville of the sit-ins at Greensboro, North Carolina. With Kelly Miller Smith's First Baptist Church as their headquarters and James Lawson as their tutor, students of the Nashville, Tennessee, Movement (q.v.) launched their own sit-in movement (q.v.). Pressured by his trustees, Vanderbilt's chancellor expelled Lawson on 3 March 1960 for his activity, but when 400 members of the university faculty threatened to resign in protest, he was readmitted to Vanderbilt. In April, Lawson drafted the declaration of purpose for the Shaw University conference in Raleigh, North Carolina, which organized the Student Nonviolent Coordinating Committee (SNCC; q.v.) and was its keynote speaker. He attacked the bourgeois bureaucracy of the National Association for the Advancement of Colored People (NAACP; q.v.) for failing to mobilize black people to assert their rights and urged the student activists to pack Southern jails.

In May 1961, Lawson led a group of Nashville student activists who continued the Freedom Rides (q.v.) from Montgomery, Alabama, to Jackson, Mississippi, and served time in Parchman Prison. Yet, Mississippi justice was so harsh that even Lawson had doubts about the possibility of a nonviolent social protest movement in the state. After his appointment as pastor of Centenary Methodist Church in Memphis, Lawson helped Martin Luther King plan and execute the attack on segregation in Birmingham. It was modeled in part on the Nashville, Tennessee, Movement (q.v.) and Lawson conducted the nonviolence workshops in preparation for it. The origins of the Selma to Montgomery March (q.v.) lay in conversations among Lawson, James Bevel (q.v.) and Diane Nash (q.v.) about the creation of a "nonviolent army" to lay siege to Alabama until civil rights were secure for black people throughout the state. In June 1966, when James Meredith (q.v.) was shot on his march from Memphis to Jackson, Mississippi, Lawson joined Stokely

Carmichael (q.v.), Floyd McKissick (q.v.), King, and others in the last great march of the civil rights movement. Twenty-one months later, he asked King to come to Memphis to support the city's sanitation workers' strike. As the local leader of the strike's supporters, however, Lawson alienated a black youth gang, the Invaders, and their violent behavior embarrassed King's nonviolent leadership. After King's death in Memphis, James Lawson accepted appointment to Holman United Methodist Church in Los Angeles, where he has served for many years. In 1995, he was elected chairman of the national council of the Fellowship of Reconciliation.

LEE, HERBERT (1912–61). Civil rights activist and farmer.

Herbert Lee was born on 1 January 1912. He was an Amite County, Mississippi, farmer and the father of nine children. In 1954, Lee and E. W. Steptoe, another local farmer, became charter members of Amite County's branch of the NAACP (q.v.). In August 1961, when Robert Moses (q.v.) of SNCC (q.v.) launched a voter registration drive in the county, Lee volunteered to drive him around the county. On the morning of 25 September 1961, state representative E. H. Hurst shot and killed Herbert Lee. A coroner's jury acquitted Hurst on a plea of self-defense the following day. A black eyewitness, Louis Allen, told FBI agents that Lee had made no threatening gestures toward Hurst, but he was denied federal protection and, thus, corroborated Hurst's story before a grand jury, which confirmed the coroner's jury's finding. The murder of Herbert Lee temporarily suspended all black voter registration activity in Amite County. Word circulated among local white people that Allen had confided in federal officials, however. In the next two years, the independent logger and father of four children was harassed economically, jailed on false charges, and had his jaw broken by a deputy sheriff. In January 1964, hearing that his life was in jeopardy, Louis Allen planned to leave Amite County on 1 February to live with a brother in Milwaukee, Wisconsin. On the evening of 31 January 1964, Louis Allen was killed when two loads of buckshot were fired into his face. The sheriff and the FBI investigated Louis Allen's murder, but no one was ever charged in the case.

LEE v. MACON COUNTY BOARD OF EDUCATION, 267 F. Supp. 458 (M.D. Ala., 1967). A case in which an Alabama federal district court ordered the state of Alabama to desegregate its public schools.

In January 1963, Detroit Lee and other African American parents in Tuskegee, Macon County, Alabama, sued the county's board of education for an end to racial segregation in its public schools. In September 1963, Federal District Judge Frank M. Johnson (q.v.) ordered the board to admit thirteen African American students to the all-white Tuskegee High School. The board attempted to comply with the federal court order, but Governor George C. Wallace (q.v.) and his state board of education intervened to postpone the school's opening and allowing it to open only under federal court injunction. In January 1964, Wallace and the state board of education closed Tuskegee High School, moved the black students to an all-black high school in Tuskegee, and transferred Tuskegee High School's white students to white schools in the county. The plaintiffs in *Lee v. Macon County Board of Education* then asked Judge Johnson for a federal court injunction to compel Governor Wallace and the state board of education to end racial segregation in all of Alabama's public schools. Declining to issue the more sweeping order, Johnson ordered the desegregation of Macon County's public schools. In 1967, when Wallace and the state board of education tried to impede the court's orders to desegregate public schools in other counties, Johnson issued a sweeping order to desegregate Alabama's public schools. In 1970, the Supreme Court upheld the federal district court's action.

LEE v. MISSISSIPPI, 332 U.S. 742 (1948). A case in which the Supreme Court reversed the conviction of a black Mississippi adolescent on a charge of assault with intent to rape.

Albert Lee, a black, seventeen-year-old Mississippian, was convicted in a Hinds County, Mississippi, circuit court on a charge of assault with intent to rape. The court's finding was based on a confession by Lee of his guilt. In an appeal to Mississippi's supreme court, Lee maintained both that he had not confessed to being guilty of the crime and that his confession was coerced by threats and physical violence. Citing the contradictions in Lee's appeal, Mississippi's supreme court confirmed the lower court's finding. When the case was appealed to the United States Supreme Court, Lee's conviction was overturned. Speaking for the Court, Justice Frank Murphy found that Lee had confessed to the crime and that the confession was extorted. The Court's ruling set an important legal precedent for the treatment of confessions.

LEGAL DEFENSE AND EDUCATIONAL FUND. *See* **NAACP Legal Defense and Educational Fund.**

LESTER, JULIUS BERNARD (1939–   ). Jewish African American writer and educator.

Julius Lester was born on 27 January 1939 in St. Louis, Missouri, the son of a middle-class, African American Methodist minister and his wife. The family moved to Kansas City, where young Julius Lester attended segregated public schools for African American youth. Even in his youth, Lester was aware of a complex family history that included a Jewish maternal great-grandfather and, in his youthful struggles for self-identity, he rebelled against his father's formal religion by declaring himself an atheist. In 1956, Lester entered Nashville's Fisk University. Among the faculty members there, he was particularly influenced by the poet Robert E. Hayden. Lester received a B.A. from Fisk in 1960 and worked for a time thereafter as a social caseworker. As a volunteer in 1964, he sang at mass meetings and held music workshops for the Student Nonviolent Coordinating Committee (SNCC; q.v.) in Mississippi's Freedom Summer (q.v.). Thereafter, Lester made several blues records for Vanguard Records, directed the Newport Folk Festival from 1966 to 1968, published *Look Out Whitey! Black Power's Gon' Get Your Mama* (1968), produced a radio show, "The Great Proletarian Cultural Revolution," for New York's WBAI, and worked in television for New York's WNET from 1968 to 1975. In 1971, he joined the Afro-American Studies Department at the University of Massachusetts.

Behind these public activities lay an intense private spiritual quest during which Lester married, fathered two children, divorced, married again interracially, and became the father of a third child. He reassessed his experience in *All Is Well* (1976), an autobiography. Lester's grappling with the problem of suffering led to publication of "The Uses of Suffering" in 1979. He was severely attacked by his colleagues in Afro-American Studies for having greater empathy with Jewish than with African American suffering. Their hostility may have confirmed the direction in which Lester was already moving. In 1983, he became a Jew. His conversion threatened Lester's relations, not only with his professional colleagues, but with his wife and children. His wife eventually became a Jew, but his children refused to join them. Lester revisited those experiences in *Lovesong: On Becoming a Jew* (1988). By then, he had left the Afro-American Studies program at the University of Massachusetts and served as a professor of Judaic and Near Eastern Studies.

"LETTER FROM BIRMINGHAM JAIL." Martin Luther King's apologia for nonviolent demonstrations for racial justice in Birmingham, Alabama.

Martin Luther King (q.v.) was arrested and jailed for leading a civil rights demonstration in Birmingham, Alabama, on Good Friday, 14 April 1963. As he was being arrested, eight of the city's leading moderate white Christian and Jewish clergymen published a plea for an end to the "unwise and untimely" demonstrations. They were led by "outsiders" who agitated issues that were more appropriately handled by the courts, said the clergymen. Two days later, the criticism prompted King to write, scribbling his prose on scraps of paper and around the edges of newspaper. In the next few days, he passed pieces of it out of jail through the hands of visiting attorneys. On the outside, his secretary transcribed them under the editorial supervision of Wyatt Tee Walker (q.v.).

King's letter from the Birmingham jail began with a critique of what he called the clergymen's "myth of time." Time was neutral, he told them, never productive of inevitable progress. It must be used creatively and the time to do the right thing was always at hand. Like St. John the revelator in exile on the isle of Patmos, King spewed out the righteous wrath of God on the sin of moderation. "Over the last few years I have been gravely disappointed with the white moderate," he wrote. "I have almost reached the regrettable conclusion that the Negro's great stumbling block in the stride toward freedom is not the White Citizen's Counciler [sic] or the Ku Klux Klanner, but the white moderate who is more devoted to "order" than to justice; . . . who paternalistically believes that he can set the timetable for another man's freedom; who lives by the myth of time and who constantly advised the Negro to wait until a 'more convenient season'." Like St. Paul, said King, he had been summoned by his fellow Christians to make known their grievances. His letter continued with his justification for disobedience to unjust law and a discussion of the grievances of Birmingham's black citizens.

King closed his long letter on a note of gracious humility. "If I have said anything in this letter which is an overstatement of the truth and is indicative of an unreasonable impatience, I beg you to forgive me," he concluded. "If I have said anything in this letter that is an understatement of the truth and is indicative of my having a patience with anything less than brotherhood, I beg God to forgive me." King's "Letter from Birmingham Jail" was a compelling apologia for the movement. Popular reconstructions of events in Birmingham often mistakenly suggest that its eloquence turned national opinion in favor of the movement. More immediately persuasive were the media's accounts and pictures of the violent reaction of police against Birmingham's civil rights demonstrators, for King's letter from the Birmingham jail did not receive widespread circulation for months after the crisis in Birmingham.

LEVITT AND SONS, INCORPORATED v. DIVISION AGAINST DISCRIMINATION, STATE OF NEW JERSEY, WILLIE JAMES AND FRANKLIN TODD, 363 U.S. 418 (1959). A case in which the Supreme Court rejected the use of Federal Housing Administration (FHA) mortgage insurance to maintain residential segregation.

Abraham Levitt built huge tracts of prefabricated housing to satisfy a large post-World War II demand for low cost private homes. He built 12,000 houses at Levittown, New York, and 17,300 houses at Levittown, Pennsylvania. His policy, however, was to refuse to sell houses to African Americans. In May 1954, Levitt began buying land in Willingboro Township, New Jersey, for a third Levittown. In 1957, the New Jersey branches of the NAACP (q.v.) persuaded the state legislature to extend state laws against racial discrimination in employment, public accommodations, and public schools to ban discrimination in publicly assisted housing. Announcing that New Jersey's Levittown would also be an all-white community in June 1958, Levitt refused to sell houses to Willie James, a black military officer at Fort Dix, and to Franklin Todd, an engineer for the Radio Corporation of America. As the state antidiscrimination office investigated the complaints of James and Todd, Levitt filed a suit challenging the new state legislation. It both lacked effective enforcement provisions and, if it applied to Levittown, Levitt's attorneys argued, was an unconstitutional restriction by a state law of a federal program, FHA mortgage insurance. Confirming prior decisions by New Jersey's appellate and supreme courts, the Supreme Court rejected the claims of Levitt's attorneys in 1959.

LEWIS, JOHN ROBERT (1940–   ). Civil rights activist and politician.
Born on 21 February 1940, John Lewis was the third of 10 children of sharecrop-farming parents near Troy, Alabama. He grew up on the farm and attended local public schools for African American children. In 1958, Lewis moved to Nashville, Tennessee, where he studied at Fisk University and American Baptist Theological Seminary. There, he joined Marion Barry (q.v.), James Bevel (q.v.), James M. Lawson, Jr. (q.v.), and Diane Nash (q.v.) to form the core leadership of the Nashville, Tennessee, Movement (q.v.). In that capacity, he was a leader in its sit-in movement (q.v.) and took part in the Freedom Rides (q.v.).

Lewis was among the founding members of SNCC (q.v.) and served as its chairman from 1963 to 1966. As SNCC's newly chosen chairman, he gave the most controversial and militant speech at the March on Washington (q.v.) in 1963. He coordinated SNCC's voter registration drives and community action programs during Mississippi Freedom Summer (q.v.) in 1964. On 7 March 1965, Lewis and Hosea Williams (q.v.) of SCLC (q.v.) led over 500 to 600 marchers across Selma, Alabama's Edmund Pettus Bridge to face Alabama state troopers. On that "bloody Sunday," he suffered a brain concussion as they attacked the marchers. The Selma to Montgomery March (q.v.) and the passage of the Voting Rights Act of 1965 (q.v.) followed quickly thereafter. Defeated in a bid for reelection as its chairman by Stokely Carmichael (q.v.) in 1966, John Lewis withdrew from SNCC as it abandoned nonviolence and increasingly espoused a racial nationalism. One of the civil rights movement's most courageous young leaders, Lewis was arrested 40 times and assaulted or injured many times.

From 1966 to 1977, John Lewis continued to work in civil rights as a director of the voter registration projects for the Field Foundation, the Southern Regional Council, and the Voter Education Project (q.v.). After losing a race for Congress in 1977, Lewis was appointed by President Carter to direct ACTION, a federal agency of 250,000 volunteer workers. He left ACTION in 1980 to become community affairs director of Atlanta's National Consumer Co-op Bank. The following year, Lewis was elected to Atlanta's city council. He served on the council for five years, resigning in 1986 to make a race for Congress from Atlanta. Lewis defeated Julian Bond (q.v.) in a bitterly contested Democratic primary, was easily elected to Congress in November 1986, and has subsequently been returned to Congress with overwhelming majorities. He rose quickly in the House of Representatives, becoming chief deputy majority whip and a member of the Steering and Policy Committee and the Ways and Means Committee in 1989. After the Democratic Party's electoral reversals in 1994, Lewis continued as the chief deputy minority whip and became cochair of the Congressional Urban Caucus.

LITTLE, MALCOLM. *See* **Malcolm X.**

LIUZZO, VIOLA FAUVER GREGG (1925–65). Civil rights activist.
Viola Fauver Gregg was born on 11 April 1925. She grew up and went to public schools in Tennessee and Georgia. In a first marriage, she gave birth to two daughters. Following a divorce, she married a

Teamsters Union local official, Anthony J. Liuzzo, and gave birth to three children. She was employed as a medical laboratory assistant in hospitals in Detroit, Michigan. While watching television in March 1965, she saw Alabama state troopers attack civil rights marchers at Selma's Edmund Pettus Bridge on "bloody Sunday." Viola Liuzzo drove to Selma to volunteer her support. At the end of the Selma to Montgomery March (q.v.) on 25 March 1965, she and a young black man, LeRoy Moton, were driving marchers back to Selma. They returned through Lowndes County to Montgomery to pick up more passengers. Near the White Chapel community, a car carrying four Klansmen pulled alongside their car. They shot Viola Liuzzo twice in the face, killing her instantly. Moton was uninjured, but he pretended to be dead when the murderers checked the automobile.

One of the Klansmen, Gary Thomas Rowe, Jr., was an FBI undercover agent, who notified his superiors of the incident. The men were arrested the next day. Despite Rowe's testimony, a Lowndes County jury acquitted Collie LeRoy Wilkins, Jr., of the murder of Viola Liuzzo. In December 1965, Rowe's testimony in a federal court helped to convict Wilkins, William Orville Eaton, and Eugene Thomas of violating Liuzzo's civil rights and they received ten-year prison sentences. Twelve years later, when they accused Rowe of firing the shot that killed Liuzzo, he was indicted for her murder. Justice Department officers found that there was no "credible evidence" that he had done so and federal courts ruled that Rowe could not be tried for the crime. In 1983, the Liuzzo family's two million dollar suit against the FBI for negligence in Viola Liuzzo's death was rejected in federal court.

LOMBARD v. LOUISIANA, 373 U.S. 267 (1963). A case in which the Supreme Court held that the intention of government officials to maintain racial segregation, even in the absence of segregation laws, violated the Fourteenth Amendment.

On 17 September 1960, four students, three black and one white, were arrested in a sit-in at a McCrory Five and Ten Cent Store in New Orleans. There was no state law or city ordinance requiring that restaurants and lunch counters be segregated, but the mayor and police superintendent had condemned sit-in demonstrations and said that they would not be tolerated in New Orleans. The four students were refused service and asked to leave by the store manager. When they failed to do so, the students were arrested and convicted of "criminal mischief." They were fined $350 each and sentenced to serve 60 days in jail; in lieu of the fine, they would have to serve an additional 60 days in jail. Louisiana's supreme court upheld the convictions and sentences. On 20 May 1963, speaking for a Supreme Court majority, Chief Justice Earl Warren denied that the refusal of service to the students was private action. The statements of public officials articulated state policy as clearly as any law. The Court reversed the students' convictions, holding that they violated the Fourteenth Amendment's equal protection requirement.

LOS ANGELES RACE RIOT. *See* **Watts Race Riot** (1965).

LOUISIANA, Ex Rel. GREMILLION, ATTORNEY GENERAL v. NAACP, 366 U.S. 293 (1961). A case in which the Supreme Court struck down a Louisiana law which required organizations to file lists of their officers and members with the state.

In the mid-1950s, some Southern states, including Alabama and Louisiana, and some localities, such as Little Rock, Arkansas, adopted laws requiring organizations to register their membership lists and other information with local or state authorities. Their legal precedent was a 1928 United States Supreme Court decision in *Bryant v. Zimmerman,* in which the Court upheld a New York state law which required that the Ku Klux Klan make its membership list available to the public. Similar laws in the South 30 years later led to a series of cases, including *Bates v. Little Rock* (q.v.), *Louisiana, Ex Rel. Gremillion, Attorney General v. NAACP,* and *NAACP v. Alabama* (q.v.), in which the Court reversed itself. In 1956, Louisiana's attorney general sued to force the NAACP (q.v.) to comply with a state law requiring it to file a list of its officers and members.

Seeking relief from alleged harassment, the NAACP countersued. When a federal district court enjoined the state from enforcing the law, Gremillion appealed to the Supreme Court on behalf of the state. The Supreme Court unanimously upheld the lower court's decision. "If it be shown that disclosure of the Association's membership lists results in reprisals and hostility to members," said Justice William O. Douglas for the Court, "such disclosure may not be required consistently with the First Amendment, made applicable to the states by the Due Process Clause of the Fourteenth Amendment."

LOVING v. VIRGINIA, 388 U.S. 1 (1967). A case in which the Supreme Court found state laws against interracial marriage were unconstitutional.

In June 1958, two Virginia residents, Mildred D. Jeter, an African American woman, and Richard P. Loving, a white man, were married in the District of Columbia and returned to Virginia to live together in Caroline County, Virginia. Indicted by a grand jury for violating the state's antimiscegenation law, they pled guilty and were each given the law's minimum sentence of a year in prison. The judge agreed to suspend their sentences if they agreed to leave the state for 25 years, at the end of which they could return if they were divorced. The Lovings moved to Washington, D.C., and in 1963 asked a trial court to set aside the ruling and allow them to return to Virginia as a married couple. When the court refused, they appealed unsuccessfully to a federal district court and a federal appeals court.

The federal courts held that Virginia's antimiscegenation law was constitutional and the Lovings' convictions were acceptable applications of it. The Lovings appealed to the United States Supreme Court for relief. On 12 June 1967, the Court unanimously agreed that Virginia's ban on interracial marriage was an unconstitutional violation of the couple's due process and equal protection rights under the Fourteenth Amendment. "It is simply not possible," wrote Justice Potter Stewart, "for state law to be valid under our Constitution which makes the criminality of an act depend upon the race of the actor." The Supreme Court's ruling signalled the end of antimiscegenation statutes that were still on the books in 16 states.

LOWERY, JOSEPH ECHOLS (Joe; 1921–   ). Civil rights activist and pastor.

Joseph E. Lowery was born on 6 October 1921 in Huntsville, Alabama. His grandfather was the founding pastor of Huntsville's Lakeside Methodist Church; his father managed a pool hall and store. Young Joseph Lowery studied at Knoxville College, Alabama A & M College, Paine College and Wayne State University. He received his theological education at Ohio's Payne Theological Seminary, Garrett Theological Seminary, and Chicago's Ecumenical Institute. In 1948, he was appointed pastor of St. James Methodist Church in Birmingham, Alabama. A year later, Lowery moved to the Methodist church at Alexander City, Alabama, where he served as president of the local interdenominational ministerial alliance. He married Evelyn Gibson. In 1952, Lowery was appointed pastor of Warren Street Methodist Church in Mobile, Alabama, one of the largest Methodist congregations in the state. As president of Mobile's interdenominational ministerial alliance and its Alabama Civic Affairs

Association, Lowery gave financial support to the Montgomery Bus Boycott (q.v.) and led black Mobile's demands for desegregation of its public transportation.

In January 1957, Lowery joined Martin Luther King (q.v.), Ralph D. Abernathy (q.v.), T. J. Jemison (q.v.), Fred Shuttlesworth (q.v.), C. K. Steele (q.v.), and other African American clergymen to organize SCLC to coordinate their struggle for racial justice throughout the South. In its early years, Lowery served as a vice president of the organization. In March 1960, apparently without their knowledge or consent, the names of Lowery, Abernathy, Shuttlesworth, and S. S. Seay, Sr., of Montgomery were signed to a controversial full-page advertisement, written by Bayard Rustin (q.v.) and headlined HEED THEIR RISING VOICES, in the *New York Times* to raise money to defend King. In response to charges in the ad, Montgomery, Alabama, police commissioner L. B. Sullivan sued them and the *Times* for libel in the case of *Sullivan v. New York Times* (q.v.). In a Montgomery trial court, a jury awarded Sullivan $500,000 in damages. Montgomery mayor Earl James won another suit for $500,000 in damages and Governor John Patterson won a third for a larger amount. Birmingham Police Commissioner Eugene "Bull" Connor followed with a fourth suit. Total damage awards approached $3,000,000. By 1962, Alabama had seized the automobiles of the four clergymen and begun proceedings against other personal property. The case dragged on for four years, ending in the United States Supreme Court, which reversed the Alabama courts' findings.

In 1961, Lowery moved to Nashville, Tennessee, to be administrative assistant to Bishop Charles F. Golden and to lead Nashville's Inter-Civic Coordinating Council. He helped King plan SCLC's actions in support of the Birmingham, Alabama, Movement (q.v.) in 1963 and, from 1965 to 1968, he was pastor of St. Paul United Methodist Church in Birmingham. There, Lowery urged the city and state to end police brutality, to expand voter registration opportunity and to hire and promote black police officers and other employees. In 1966, he led the demand of black delegates to the general conference of the Methodist Church to eliminate racial segregation in the denomination's official structures. In 1968, Lowery became the pastor of Atlanta's Central United Methodist Church and, at King's request, chairman of SCLC's board of directors.

When Ralph Abernathy resigned as president of SCLC in 1977, Joseph Lowery was unanimously chosen as his successor. From 1986 to 1992, when he retired from the ministry, Lowery was the pastor of Atlanta's Cascade United Methodist Church. President of SCLC for nearly as long as both his predecessors combined, Lowery has grappled with the problem of leading a major civil rights organization in reduced financial straits in the "post civil rights era." His leadership has focused on the struggle against apartheid in South Africa, extensions of the Voting Rights Act (q.v.), economic justice through Operation Breadbasket, and the struggle against drugs and violence in the African American community.

LOWNDES COUNTY FREEDOM ORGANIZATION (LCFO). An African American political organization founded in Lowndes County, Alabama, by SNCC (q.v.) and local activists to challenge the local white Democratic organization.

After the Democratic National Convention refused to seat delegates from the Mississippi Freedom Democratic Party (q.v.) in 1964, SCLC (q.v.) encouraged black voters to continue organizing within the Democratic Party for representation. Increasingly scornful of biracial politics, Stokely Carmichael (q.v.) and other SNCC organizers in Lowndes County, Alabama, promoted the idea of an independent black political party. Four-fifths of Lowndes County's 15,000 voting-age population were black, but early in 1965 no black people were registered to vote in the county. After the Selma to Montgomery March (q.v.), Carmichael helped to found the Lowndes County Freedom Organization. Its ballot symbol, the black panther, represented the power of organized black people and contrasted with the Democratic Party's ballot symbol, a white rooster. After federal registrars appeared in Lowndes County in August 1965, the LCFO helped to register black voters. In November 1966, it nominated candidates for sheriff, tax assessor, tax collector, coroner, and three seats on the board of education. All of its candidates were defeated, but the LCFO had made its mark in local politics. At the same time, the West Coast's Black Panther Party was co-opting LCFO's symbol and giving it broader national currency as a symbol of black nationalist autonomy. In Alabama's Democratic Party, however, biracial politics had begun to prevail by the 1970s.

LUCY v. ADAMS, 134 F. Supp. 235 (W.D. Ala., 1955). A case in which a federal district court ordered the admission of Autherine Juanita Lucy to the University of Alabama.

In 1952, two well-qualified candidates for professional studies, Autherine Lucy and Polly Myers were admitted to the University of Alabama. They registered for classes and received dormitory assignments by mail. When they arrived for classes, however, university officials turned them away because they were black. After further negotiations, the two women sued for admission to the university. Finding that they could not be excluded on racial grounds, a federal district judge ruled in their favor. That ruling was reversed in a federal appellate court, but attorneys for Autherine Lucy appealed to the United States Supreme Court. Under order from the Supreme Court, the university reluctantly admitted the Birmingham English teacher for professional studies in January 1956. White students, residents of Tuscaloosa, and people from outside the community rioted and burned crosses on the campus, however, to protest the admission of a black student. Suspended for her own safety initially, Lucy was later expelled by university trustees when she allegedly criticized the university's racial policies in public. The Alabama legislature supported the trustees' action and threatened to suspend appropriations to black colleges in the state and its payment of tuition for Alabama's black students in graduate and professional programs outside the state.

M

MALCOLM X (Malcolm Little, El Hajj Malik El-Shabazz; 1925–65). Militant black nationalist.

Malcolm X was born Malcolm Little on 19 May 1925 in Omaha, Nebraska. He was the son of Louise and the Reverend Earl Little, a Baptist preacher and follower of Marcus Garvey. In Malcolm's childhood, the family moved to Lansing, Michigan. There, the family's home burned and Earl Little died in 1931 under the wheels of a streetcar. The Little family believed that Klansmen had burned the house and that white people had also murdered Earl Little. When Louise Little was committed to a mental institution in the late 1930s, the children were placed in a foster homes. Malcolm was raised thereafter by a white couple. In 1940, when he finished the eighth grade, Malcolm quit school and moved to Boston to live with a sister. During World War II, he took to the streets of Boston and Harlem, running numbers, dealing drugs, and pimping for black and white prostitutes. To support a $20-a-day cocaine addiction, Malcolm committed a series of burglaries, which, in 1946, led to his arrest in a Boston suburb and a prison sentence of eight to ten years.

During the six-and-a-half years that Malcolm actually served in prison, he became a follower of Elijah Muhammad, the leader of the Lost-Found Nation of Islam or Black Muslims. When he was paroled in 1952, he shed his "slave name," Little, and replaced it with "X," according to the practice of Elijah Muhammad's followers. He met with Muhammad in Chicago, became a Black Muslim minister and was appointed in June

1954 to lead Temple #7 in Harlem. When New York policemen beat Johnson Hinton, a member of the Nation, in April 1957, Malcolm led 2,000 people in surrounding the local precinct to demand that he receive medical attention. In 1958, Malcolm married Betty X Shabazz, with whom he had six children. By then, Malcolm had become the Black Muslims' spokesman, who organized temples across the country and was popular on the college lecture circuit as well. In 1959, he was Elijah Muhammad's emissary to African and Middle Eastern countries.

When President Kennedy was assassinated in November 1963, Malcolm X referred to it as "a case of chickens coming home to roost." By then, Elijah Muhammad and Malcolm X had grown suspicious of each other. Muhammad distrusted Malcolm's popularity within and outside the Nation of Islam and Malcolm was disturbed by rumors that Muhammad was an adulterous father of many illegitimate children. Muhammad placed Malcolm on suspension for his remark about Kennedy's death. On 12 March 1964, Malcolm X resigned from the Nation of Islam. After organizing his own religious community, the Muslim Mosque, Inc., he made the *hajj* or pilgrimage to Mecca in April 1964 and toured the Middle East. During the trip, Malcolm met white people who he knew were not racists, began to modify his antiwhite rhetoric, and adopted the name, El Hajj Malik El-Shabazz, and a more traditional form of Moslem thought. In June 1964, after his return to the United States, Malcolm founded the Organization of Afro-American Unity to promote black unity and cooperate with sympathetic white people to defeat racism, which he believed was deeply rooted in Western culture.

Later in 1964, Malcolm traveled to Africa and conferred with leaders of newly emerging African nations. When Malcolm dismissed Elijah Muhammad as a "racist" and a "religious faker," tensions with the Nation of Islam intensified. Louis X Farrakhan ominously declared that Malcolm X was "worthy of death." The Nation of Islam secured a court order to evict Malcolm and his family from their house in Queens, New York. When Malcolm refused to comply with it, the house was firebombed on 14 February 1965. No one was injured then. On 21 February 1965, as he began to speak to a crowd at the Audubon Ballroom in upper Manhattan, however, Malcolm was fatally wounded. Three Black Muslims, Talmadge X Hayer, Norman 3X Butler and Thomas 15X Johnson, were eventually convicted of and served time in prison for the murder of Malcolm X. Debate about responsibility for Malcolm's death continues. Butler and Johnson were innocent, Hayer later testified, but he was responsible for the vengeful act by followers of Elijah Muhammad. Although Malcolm's specific accomplishments were limited, he has become in death an even more powerful symbol of African American dignity than he was in life.

MARCH ON WASHINGTON (March on Washington for Jobs and Freedom; 1963). The largest of the civil rights movement's five marches on Washington between 1957 and 1968.

In 1941, at the outset of World War II, discrimination against hiring African Americans in government and industry was common. A. Philip Randolph (q.v.), president of the Brotherhood of Sleeping Car Porters and Maids, summoned 100,000 African Americans to march on Washington in protest of employment discrimination. On 25 June, a week before it was to occur, President Franklin Roosevelt issued Executive Order 8802 (q.v.), banning discrimination based on race, color, creed, or national origin in the federal government, the armed forces, and defense industries and establishing a Fair Employment Practice Committee (q.v.) to oversee the policy. Only then did Randolph cancel the March on Washington. Between 1957 and 1968, the civil rights movement marched on Washington five times. Randolph, Martin Luther King (q.v.) of the Southern Christian Leadership Conference (SCLC; q.v.), and Roy Wilkins (q.v.) of the National Association for the Advancement of Colored People (NAACP; q.v.) led the Prayer Pilgrimage to Washington (q.v.) in 1957 and the Youth Marches for Integrated Schools (q.v.) in 1958 and 1959. These marches emphasized desegregation and voting rights, but they drew disappointing crowds of only 10,000 to 26,000 people.

Early in 1963, Randolph, King, and Bayard Rustin (q.v.) agreed that the time was ripe for a massive March on Washington. In the following months, SCLC's efforts with the Birmingham, Alabama, Movement (q.v.) mounted, Governor George Wallace (q.v.) of Alabama barred black students from entering the University of Alabama, Medgar Evers (q.v.) was assassinated in Mississippi, and the Kennedy administration proposed new civil rights legislation. By June, Roy Wilkins of the NAACP, Whitney Young (q.v.) of the National Urban League (q.v.), James Farmer (q.v.) of the Congress of Racial Equality (CORE; q.v.), John Lewis (q.v.) of the Student Nonviolent Coordinating Committee (SNCC; q.v.), and King agreed to cochair the March on Washington, with Randolph as its national director and Rustin as deputy director. They set 28 August as its date and support of Kennedy administration civil rights legislation as its purpose. Subsequently, four prominent white leaders were added to the list of cochairs: Mathew Ahmann, executive director of the National Catholic Conference for Interracial Justice, the Reverend Eugene Carson Blake of the National Council of Churches, Rabbi Joachim Prinz, and Walter Reuther, president of the United Automobile Workers.

Two to three hundred thousand people—black and white, poor and rich, laborers and bosses, athletes and celebrities, professional women and housewives, Protestants, Catholics, Jews, and others—gathered on 28 August 1963 at the Lincoln Memorial in Washington, D.C., and stretched away from it as far as the eye could see. A last-minute conflict was avoided when SNCC's John Lewis agreed to modify the tone of his speech in deference to the objections of Washington's Patrick Cardinal O'Boyle, who offered the invocation. Brilliant musicians, from Marian Anderson, Mahalia Jackson, Odetta, and Josh White to Joan Baez, Bob Dylan, Peter, Paul, and Mary, and SNCC's Freedom Singers from Albany, Georgia, sang freedom's song that day. Norman Thomas, the grand old man of American socialism, thanked God that he had lived long enough to see it; Roy Wilkins soberly announced that W. E. B. Du Bois, the grand old man of black radicalism, had not. He had died that very morning in Accra, Ghana. At the end of a long program, as ABC and NBC joined CBS for live television coverage of the movement's largest mass meeting, A. Philip Randolph introduced Martin Luther King as "the moral leader of our nation."

King launched into a prepared text and, then, abandoned it for an extemporaneous rendering of his "I Have a Dream" (q.v.) speech. It was a patchwork of ideas and themes, some of which he had been using now for eight years. In this form, he had given it twice in the last six months, in Birmingham and Detroit. Yet, fed by the enthusiastic response of this vast audience, the speech took on fresh power and vitality. Like Lincoln's "Gettysburg Address," King's "I Have a Dream" has outlasted all the other speeches given on that day in the public mind. As he finished, King stepped aside and Bayard Rustin asked for the audience's endorsement of the March's goals: passage of the Kennedy administration's civil rights bill, a $2 minimum wage, school desegregation, a federal public works job program, and federal action to bar racial discrimination in employment. With that approval, the March on Washington was concluded with a benediction by Morehouse College president Benjamin Mays.

MARSHALL, THURGOOD (1908–93). Civil rights attorney and Supreme Court justice.

Thurgood Marshall was born on 2 July 1908 in Baltimore, Maryland. His father was a Pullman car porter, waiter, and chief steward for several white social clubs. His mother was a teacher in Baltimore's public elementary schools for African American children. Young Marshall attended local public schools and graduated with honors from Douglass High School in 1926. He entered Pennsylvania's Lincoln University and worked his way through college by doing odd jobs. Graduating with honors from Lincoln in 1930, Marshall entered Howard University Law School, where he met Charles Hamilton Houston (q.v.), the school's assistant dean. He graduated from Howard magna cum laude in 1933, began practicing law in Baltimore, and became legal counsel for the city's branch of the NAACP (q.v.). From 1936 to 1938, Marshall served as assistant to Houston as the NAACP's legal counsel. Succeeding Houston as its legal counsel in 1938, Marshall became director of the NAACP Legal Defense and Educational Fund (LDEF; q.v.) in 1939.

For the next 22 years, Thurgood Marshall was the NAACP's point man in its long legal battle against racial segregation. From *Missouri Ex Rel. Gaines v. Canada* (q.v.) in 1938 through *Sipuel v. Board of Regents of the University of Oklahoma* (q.v.) in 1948 and *Sweatt v. Painter* (q.v.) in 1950 to *Brown v. Board of Education* (q.v.) in 1954, Marshall took a long series of cases to the United States Supreme Court to undermine the legal foundations of racial segregation in public education. On 23 September 1961, President Kennedy nominated Marshall to serve on the Second Circuit Court of Appeals. Southern white opponents delayed his confirmation to serve on the court of appeals for another year. Marshall wrote over a hundred opinions on a wide variety of subjects as an appellate court judge. In June 1965, President Johnson nominated him to serve as solicitor general of the United States, the officer who argues the federal government's cases before the Supreme Court.

In July 1967, President Johnson nominated Thurgood Marshall to the Supreme Court, the first African American to serve on the nation's highest court. By then, he had won 29 of 32 cases that he argued before the Court. Justice Marshall served on the Supreme Court for 23 years. During those years, he was the most reliable member of the liberal, activist wing of the Court. An ardent defender of individual and civil rights, Marshall opposed the death penalty and supported abortion rights for women, busing (q.v.), and affirmative action (q.v.) for women and ethnic minorities. As conservative justices appointed in the Nixon, Ford, Reagan, and Bush administrations replaced his older liberal colleagues from the Warren Court, Marshall was increasingly in a liberal minority.

In declining health and doubtful that he could outlive the Bush administration, Justice Marshall resigned from the Court on 27 June 1991. His successor, Clarence Thomas, would prove to be as ardent a judicial conservative as Marshall had been a judicial liberal. On 24 January 1993, four days after the inauguration of a liberal president, William Clinton, Justice Thurgood Marshall died at Bethesda Naval Medical Center.

MAYOR AND CITY COUNCIL OF BALTIMORE CITY v. DAWSON, 350 U.S. 877 (1955). A case in which the Supreme Court held that racially segregated public beaches violated the equal protection clause of the Fourteenth Amendment.

In 1954, Robert M. Dawson filed suit in a federal district court challenging racially segregated public beaches in Maryland. His attorney argued that legally mandated segregation violated the Fourteenth Amendment's equal protection clause. Relying on earlier federal court precedents that tolerated segregation, the federal district judge dismissed Dawson's case. Dawson appealed to the Fourth Circuit Court of Appeals. Based on the Supreme Court's recent decisions in *Brown v. Board of Education* (q.v.), its companion, *Bolling v. Sharpe* (q.v.), and earlier Supreme Court decisions barring racial discrimination in interstate commerce, real estate sales, and schools, the appeals court reversed the district court's finding. When the city of Baltimore appealed to the Supreme Court, its opinion read: "The motion to affirm is granted and the judgment is affirmed." Having made its case against legally mandated racial segregation in *Brown,* thereafter the Court commonly struck down state segregation laws without further comment.

MCDONALD v. KEY, 224 F.2d 608 (10th Cir., 1955). A case in which a federal appeals court held that racial designations on ballots violated the Fourteenth Amendment's equal protection requirement.

Oklahoma law required that a person of African descent who was a candidate for public office be identified as "Negro" on the ballot; all other persons were presumed to be "white" and were not racially identified. A. B. McDonald, an African American, was a candidate for the United States Senate from Oklahoma in 1954. He sued members of the state election board for identifying him as a "Negro" after his name on the ballot. His attorneys argued that the requirement was in violation of the equal protection requirement of the Fourteenth Amendment. A federal district court in Oklahoma dismissed his complaint, arguing that the racial designation was descriptive rather than discriminatory. When

McDonald appealed to the Tenth Circuit Court of Appeals, however, the district court's ruling was reversed. Oklahoma's requirement that people of African descent be given a racial designation on the ballot, while all others were not racially identified, the court held, was a violation of the equal protection requirement. Although Oklahoma's board of elections appealed to the United States Supreme Court, it refused to hear the case, allowing the appellate court's decision to stand.

MCKISSICK, FLOYD BIXLER (1922–91). Civil rights activist and attorney.

Floyd B. McKissick was born on 9 March 1922 in Asheville, North Carolina. He studied in local public schools for African American students. After he was attacked at a local athletic event in his youth because of his race, McKissick was determined to fight racial oppression. He graduated from high school, enlisted in the United States Army, and served as a sergeant in World War II, earning a Purple Heart for bravery. McKissick entered Morehouse College after his return from Europe. In 1947, he participated in CORE's Journey of Reconciliation (q.v.) to contest racial segregation in interstate public transportation. At Morehouse, he chaired Henry Wallace's presidential campaign on the Progressive Party ticket in campus mock elections in 1948. McKissick transferred to North Carolina College, where he received his bachelor's degree in 1951. Denied admission to law school at the University of North Carolina, he continued to study law at North Carolina College until Thurgood Marshall (q.v.) and the NAACP LDEF (q.v.) won his case in a federal appeals court. In 1952, McKissick was the first African American to receive a degree in law from the University of North Carolina at Chapel Hill.

McKissick opened a law office in Durham, North Carolina, and served as youth advisor for the North Carolina conference of the NAACP (q.v.). His children were among the first African American students to desegregate Durham's public schools. He was a consultant and legal counsel to students who conducted early sit-in demonstrations in Greensboro and Durham, North Carolina. He continued to play an active advisory role as demonstrations shifted from lunch counters to other public accommodations. In 1962, as director of a new Durham chapter of CORE (q.v.), McKissick shifted from the NAACP to CORE as the primary vehicle for his civil rights efforts and became a rising star in CORE's orbit. He helped to plan and organize its massive "Freedom Highways" demonstrations in North Carolina in 1962 and 1963. First named CORE's lead legal counsel, on 29 June 1963 he became the first African American to serve as its national chairman. In that capacity, he was one of the featured speakers at the March on Washington (q.v.) in August 1963. As CORE's national chairman, McKissick was both part of a shift toward exclusively black leadership of the organization and identified with its increasingly influential militant wing.

On 3 January 1966, McKissick replaced James Farmer (q.v.) as CORE's national director, placing him in the leadership of the civil rights movement's five key organizations. It was a coalition already, however, badly fraying. When James Meredith (q.v.) was shot in June 1966, other civil rights leaders rushed to continue his march from Memphis, Tennessee, to Jackson, Mississippi. Yet, this last great march of the civil rights movement drew attention to its internal divisions over "black power" and separatist politics, as Stokely Carmichael and McKissick emphasized the latter and Roy Wilkins (q.v.) of the NAACP (q.v.) and Whitney Young (q.v.) of the National Urban League (q.v.) refused to be identified with them. In September 1967, McKissick left CORE to direct a Ford Foundation program in training young African American leaders.

Later in the decade, McKissick began to lay the groundwork for his vision of a model town and industrial community in rural North Carolina. Soul City, 60 miles northeast of Raleigh, was his dream. In 1972, he surprised the civil rights community by becoming a Republican and urging the reelection of Richard Nixon as president. The Nixon and Ford administrations rewarded him with $18 million in federal grants to Soul City. Yet, his vision seemed unfruitful. Hoping for a city of 45,000 African Americans by 2000, McKissick had a community of 105 black people and 30 white people by 1978, when federal funding ended. McKissick continued to practice law in the region through the 1980s and served as pastor of Soul City's First Baptist Church. In June 1990, North Carolina governor James Martin appointed him to fill a vacancy on the bench of North Carolina's Ninth Judicial District Court. Floyd McKissick died of lung cancer on 28 April 1991.

MCLAUGHLIN v. STATE OF FLORIDA, 379 U.S. 184 (1964). A case in which the Supreme Court reversed a lower court's conviction of an unmarried interracial couple for occupying the same room at night.

Florida law had a different standard of punishment for unmarried interracial couples than it did for unmarried couples of the same race. An unmarried interracial couple, Dewey McLaughlin and Connie Hoffman (or Connie Gonzalez), was convicted by Florida courts of occupying the same room at night. On appeal, the United States Supreme Court overturned their conviction on many points of constitutional law. Florida law and its courts had violated the couple's civil rights on five major counts: the law denied an unmarried interracial couple equal protection of the law; the law ignored the purpose of the equal protection clause to bar discrimination by the state; the law's racial categories were irrelevant to any legislative purpose under the United States Constitution; Florida courts had disregarded equal protection requirements in the state's use of racial categories in criminal law; and Florida's legal system tolerated a malicious racial discrimination in the adjudication of the same crime by different people.

MCLAURIN v. OKLAHOMA STATE REGENTS, 339 U.S. 637 (1950). A case in which the Supreme Court ruled that racial segregation within a public institution violated the equal protection clause of the Fourteenth Amendment.

In 1948, the Supreme Court's decision in *Sipuel v. Board of Regents of the University of Oklahoma* (q.v.) led to the admission of a woman of color, Ada Louise Sipuel Fisher, to the University of Oklahoma Law School. At nearly 70, another African American, George McLaurin, sought admission to the university's doctoral program in education. While he pursued the issue, Oklahoma's state legislature passed a law requiring "segregated facilities" within the state's institutions of higher education. Conforming to the new law, the university admitted McLaurin to attend classes with its white students, but it seated him at a desk marked "reserved for colored" and set apart from the other students' desks. Both his study space in the library and his dining space in the cafeteria were similarly segregated. When McLaurin challenged the constitutionality of Oklahoma's new law, both federal district and appellate courts refused to hear his case. On 5 June 1950, however, the Supreme Court's unanimous verdict found in McLaurin's favor. Oklahoma's new segregation law violated the Fourteenth Amendment's equal protection clause, said Chief Justice Fred M. Vinson. Students in public institutions may not be racially segregated by administrative practice or law. Yet, the Vinson Court would continue to limit its modification of *Plessy v. Ferguson* to narrow interpretations of specific cases before it. *McLaurin* was, nonetheless, an important building block toward the Supreme Court's sweeping *Brown v. Board of Education* (q.v.) decision under the leadership of a new chief justice.

MEREDITH, JAMES HOWARD (1933–   ). Civil rights activist.

James Meredith was born on 25 June 1933 near Kosciusko, Mississippi. He studied in public schools for African American children in Mississippi and Jacksonville, Florida. After his graduation from high school, Meredith enlisted and served in the air force until 1960. From 1960 to 1962, he was a student at Mississippi's Jackson State College, an African American institution. Wishing to enroll in the segregated University of Mississippi, Meredith enlisted the support of Medgar Evers (q.v.) to persuade the NAACP LDEF (q.v.) to take up his case. In *Meredith v. Fair* (q.v.) on 3 September 1962, the Fifth Circuit Court of Appeals (q.v.) ordered Mississippi governor Ross Barnett to allow Meredith to enroll in the University. Barnett continued to defy the federal court, forcing President Kennedy to call on the National Guard to secure his admission to the university. The resulting confrontation led to the most severe campus riot of the 1960s, but Meredith persevered, earning a bachelor's degree in political science in 1964.

After studying at Nigeria's University of Ibadan in 1964–65, Meredith entered law school at Columbia University. He published an autobiography, *Three Years in Mississippi,* in 1966. Shortly thereafter, Meredith began a "March Against Fear" from Memphis, Tennessee, to Jackson, Mississippi, and was wounded by an unknown sniper on 5 June. Martin Luther King (q.v.), Stokely Carmichael (q.v.), Floyd McKissick (q.v.), and others continued the "Meredith March," which ended in Jackson on 26 June. Yet, this last great march of the civil rights movement publicized its internal divisions over "black power" and separatist politics, when Charles Evers (q.v.) and Roy Wilkins (q.v.) of the NAACP (q.v.) and Whitney Young (q.v.) of the National Urban League (q.v.) refused to sign the March's Manifesto. Meredith returned to Columbia, where he earned a J.D. degree in 1968.

The national crisis of the late 1960s largely dissolved the tense alliances that composed the civil rights movement and sent some of its activists in unusual directions. After graduating from law school, James Meredith became an investor and stock broker, an exemplar of "black capitalism." In 1972, he lost a primary race for the Republican nomination for the United States Senate from Mississippi. Thereafter, Meredith became a more strident critic of the civil rights establishment's belief in racial reform through action by the federal government. By the 1980s, he supported the conservative Republican Reagan and Bush administrations. The surviving black and white leadership of the established civil rights organizations was, he argued, the "greatest enemy" of the African American people. In 1989, Meredith became the first African American to join the professional staff of North Carolina senator Jesse Helms, an archenemy of the civil rights movement. Two years later, Meredith supported the campaign of former Ku Klux Klan grand dragon David Duke for governor of Louisiana.

MEREDITH v. FAIR, 305 F.2d 343 (5th Cir., 1962). A case in which the Fifth Circuit Court of Appeals (q.v.) ordered the desegregation of the University of Mississippi.

In June 1958, when Clennon King attempted to desegregate the University of Mississippi's summer school, state police arrested him and a local judge committed him to a mental institution. Two-and-a-half years later, James Meredith (q.v.) was twice denied admission by the university before he filed suit in federal district court on 31 May 1961, charging racial discrimination. The district court sided with university officials, who claimed that Meredith failed to meet admission requirements. On appeal, however, the Fifth Circuit Court of Appeals (q.v.) ruled in a two-to-one decision that Meredith had been denied admission on racial grounds and that Mississippi maintained an unconstitutional policy of racial segregation in higher education. It ordered the federal district court to enjoin university officials from interfering with Meredith's admission to the university. The court's decision led to a bitter struggle between state and federal authorities over Meredith's admission to the university. Only a federalized Mississippi National Guard ensured his admission in 1963 and that led to the most severe campus riot of the decade.

MILLIKEN v. BRADLEY, 418 U.S. 717 (1974). A case in which the Supreme Court narrowly overturned a massive busing plan for Detroit, Michigan's public schools.

Detroit, Michigan, had never segregated its public schools by law. Like many Northern and Western cities, however, its schools were largely segregated because of the concentration of black people in its inner city and of white people in outlying suburbs. Believing that African American students would receive an inferior education in racially segregated urban schools, the NAACP (q.v.) challenged this de facto segregation. In *Swann v. Charlotte-Mecklenburg Board of Education* (q.v.), the Supreme Court seemed to agree that cities should bus students away from neighborhood schools if necessary to achieve desegregation. In 1970, Detroit was ordered to desegregate its schools. An overwhelming majority of students in its public schools were black, however, so desegregation within the city's school system alone seemed impossible. Federal district and appeals courts ordered Detroit and suburban school districts to desegregate their schools by busing students across school district lines.

When the Supreme Court agreed to hear the case in 1974, *Milliken v. Bradley* subsumed two other cases, *Allen Park Public Schools v. Bradley* and *Grosse Point Public School System v. Bradley,* which had resulted from this order. By a narrow five-to-four vote, the Supreme Court reversed the lower federal court orders. The suburban school districts had never practiced de jure racial segregation, argued Chief Justice Warren Burger for the Court majority, and the Court could not impose a busing plan on them merely to remedy de facto segregation in one school district. The decision coincided with angry white protests against busing in Boston, Denver, and Pontiac, Michigan, and, together, the Court's decision and the public opposition to busing slowed the pace of school desegregation in Northern and Western public schools.

MILLIKEN v. BRADLEY, 433 U.S. 267 (1977). A case in which the Supreme Court upheld lower court orders for compensatory programs in Detroit's public schools.

The Supreme Court's 1974 decision in *Milliken v. Bradley* (q.v.) remanded the case to a lower federal court for trial. As an alternative to busing students across school district lines, the trial court ordered Detroit public schools to institute remedial or compensatory education programs, new training programs for teachers in urban schools, and enhanced guidance programs and testing procedures. The plaintiffs in *Milliken* appealed the court order for compensatory programs to the federal appeals court and the United States Supreme Court. In 1977, the Supreme Court upheld the trial court's order that Detroit's public schools should adopt compensatory programs to benefit African American students.

MIRANDA v. ARIZONA, 384 U.S. 436 (1966). One of four cases which the Supreme Court heard in 1966 in which it held that statements obtained by police interrogation from suspects uninformed of their rights to counsel or to be silent or of the possible use of their statements as evidence are inadmissible as evidence.

Early in 1963, a woman was robbed and an 18-year-old woman was kidnapped and raped after being threatened with a knife in Phoenix, Arizona. On 13 March, an impoverished 23-year-old with a ninth grade education, Ernesto Miranda, was arrested by Phoenix police and taken to a police station where both women identified him in a lineup as their assailant. He was taken to an interrogation room, where he wrote and signed a confession on paper with a typed paragraph on it stating that the confession was made voluntarily, with full knowledge of his legal rights, and with the understanding that any statement he made might be used against him. Over the objection of his attorney, Miranda's confession was admitted in evidence by an Arizona trial court. He was convicted of robbery and of kidnapping and rape and sentenced to 40 to 55 years in prison on the two charges.

The Arizona supreme court upheld the trial court's decisions, but the United States Supreme Court reversed it. It had held in earlier cases that the right not to incriminate one's self is protected against state action by the Fourteenth Amendment. Now, by a vote of five to four, with Justices Tom Clark, John Marshall Harlan, Potter Stewart, and Byron White in dissent, the Court found that Miranda had not been advised of his right to counsel nor was his privilege against self-incrimination protected in any way. Speaking for the Court majority, Chief Justice Earl Warren said that suspects must be warned prior to questioning of their right to remain silent and to the presence of an attorney and that any statement they make may be used as evidence against them.

MISSISSIPPI FREEDOM DEMOCRATIC PARTY (MFDP). The creation of Mississippi's Council of Federated Organizations (COFO; q.v.) in the mid-1960s as an alternative to Mississippi's all-white regular Democratic Party.

Excluded from participating in formal Mississippi politics through the mid-1960s, black Mississippians challenged it with alternative structures. Faced with white harassment and violence when they tried to register to vote, few black Mississippians were registered to vote in August 1963, when over 700 of them presented petitions at the Democratic primary that they had been illegally denied the right to register. Pursuing a different tactic for the run-off primary for governor three weeks later, COFO members nominated Aaron Henry (q.v.) and the Reverend Edwin King (q.v.), the white chaplain at Tougaloo College, for governor and lieutenant governor. With the help of about a hundred Northern white college students, COFO offered black Mississippians alternate polling places in black churches, as well as alternate candidates, and 83,000 black Mississippians took part in this unofficial "freedom election."

In subsequent months, COFO leaders planned "Freedom Summer" (q.v.) in which students from Stanford and Berkeley to Harvard and Yale converged on Mississippi in the summer of 1964. Despite 3 murders, 67 arson and bombing incidents, 80 beatings, and a thousand arrests, Northern student volunteers helped to organize the Mississippi Freedom Democratic Party. In June, the state's regular Democratic Party included in its platform a plank opposing the national party's commitment to civil rights. Charging the state's white Democratic organization with disloyalty to the national party, the MFDP held precinct, county, and state conventions open to all loyal Democrats and elected a slate of delegates to the Democratic National Convention, which met in August at Atlantic City, New Jersey. There, Fannie Lou Hamer (q.v.) gave eloquent testimony before the convention's credentials committee and a national television audience about political oppression in Mississippi.

Determined to control disturbances to the renomination of President Lyndon Johnson, nationally prominent liberal Democrats, including Hubert Humphrey, Walter Mondale, Joseph Rauh (q.v.), Walter Reuther, and Bayard Rustin (q.v.), offered both the state's regular and the MFDP delegations a compromise. It would have seated all delegates from the regular organization who would sign an oath of loyalty to the national party as Mississippi's delegation to the convention. In addition, it would have seated two members of the MFDP delegation as at-large delegates to the convention. The "compromise" failed to satisfy the expectations of either Mississippi's white or its black Democrats. All but three of the state's regular delegates walked out of the convention, refusing to sign any loyalty oath. Fannie Lou Hamer spoke for grass roots black Mississippians in saying that she had not come all this way for "no two votes." Most MFDP loyalists left Atlantic City disillusioned about alliances with white liberals. In Mississippi, the MFDP supported candidates for election to local and state offices. In 1968, it joined a broader biracial coalition in a successful challenge to the seating of the state's white regulars at the Democratic National Convention.

MISSOURI ex rel. GAINES v. CANADA, 305 U.S. 337 (1938). A case in which the Supreme Court found Missouri's lack of an equal law school for African American students violated the equal protection requirement of the Fourteenth Amendment.

Lloyd Gaines, an honors graduate of Lincoln University in Jefferson City, Missouri, was denied admission to the University of Missouri Law School because he was an African American. There was little demand for legal education by African Americans, said the state. Rather than maintain a separate law school for Missouri's few African American law students, Missouri offered to pay the tuition of the state's black students at law schools in the contiguous states of Illinois, Iowa, Kansas, or Nebraska. Gaines sued Canada, the registrar at the University of Missouri, for admission to its law school. Federal district and appellate courts found the university's admissions policy and the state's tuition payment program as meeting the equal protection requirement of the Fourteenth Amendment and the Supreme Court's "separate but equal" interpretation of the law in *Plessy v. Ferguson.*

In one of his first cases for the NAACP (q.v.), Thurgood Marshall took Lloyd Gaines's case to the Supreme Court. Speaking for the Court, Chief Justice Charles Evans Hughes reversed the lower federal courts' decision. Demand was an acceptable basis for state policy, he acknowledged, but where a service was offered, it must represent substantial equality of treatment. The state must offer "other and proper provision for his legal training within the state," said Hughes, or admit him to the university's law school. Faced with that choice, Missouri established a law school at Gaines's alma mater, Lincoln University. By then, however, he had entered a law school in Michigan. *Gaines* was an early case in the NAACP's long litigation against racial segregation in public schools. At this stage in the struggle, however, it was argued and settled within the limits of the Supreme Court's earlier "separate but equal" precedent in *Plessy v. Ferguson.*

MITCHELL v. UNITED STATES, 313 U.S. 80 (1941). A case in which the Supreme Court held that African Americans could sue for discrimination in interstate transportation.

In 1937, United States representative Arthur Weigs Mitchell, an African American Democrat from Chicago, booked first class Pullman car accommodations on the Illinois Central Railroad from Chicago to Memphis and on the Chicago, Rock Island & Pacific Railway from Memphis to Hot Springs, Arkansas. His trip on the Illinois Central was uneventful. On transferring to the Chicago, Rock Island & Pacific at Memphis, however, Mitchell was asked and, then, ordered to move to a lesser-quality railroad car reserved for black people. This was in compliance with Arkansas law, which required "separate but equal" accommodations for black and white passengers in public transportation. Despite his objections, Mitchell complied with the state law.

Later, Mitchell filed charges against the railway company with the Interstate Commerce Commission (ICC), claiming racial discrimination in interstate commerce. After a hearing on his charges, the ICC dismissed his case. He then sued for damages, naming the United States as defendant because the ICC was a federal agency. A federal district court found in favor of the ICC, but Mitchell appealed the case to the Supreme Court. On 28 April 1941, Chief Justice Charles Evans Hughes spoke for a unanimous Court which found in Mitchell's favor. The ICC was wrong to dismiss his complaint, said Justice Hughes, and the "separate coach laws of the several states do not apply to interstate commerce." Public interstate transportation in the South would continue to be segregated for another twenty years, but the *Mitchell* decision was an important precedent for the Court's decision in *Morgan v. Virginia* (q.v.) and subsequent actions by the ICC.

MOBILE v. BOLDEN. *See* **City of Mobile v. Bolden.**

MONROE v. PAPE, 365 U.S. 167 (1961). A case in which the Supreme Court determined that police brutality was state action under the United States Code and a violation of civil rights.

Chicago police suspected Monroe, the African American plaintiff in this case, of murder. They entered his house in the middle of the night without a warrant, searched it, and arrested and detained him for ten hours without a lawyer being present. When Monroe sued the city of Chicago under Revised Statutes section 1979, his attorneys claimed that the police had violated his "rights, privileges and immunities secured by the Constitution." The city asked the federal district court to dismiss the suit because it could not be held liable for actions which were part of "normal" responsibilities of government. The district court acted in the city's favor and an appeals court upheld the district court's dismissal of Monroe's claim. When he appealed to the United States Supreme Court, however, it reversed the lower courts' decisions in an eight-to-one decision, with Justice Felix Frankfurter dissenting. While the city was not liable under section 1979, acknowledged Justice William O. Douglas for the Court majority, the police were liable. The Fourth Amendment's guarantee against "unreasonable searches and seizures," said Douglas, was "made applicable to the States by the Due Process Clause of the Fourteenth Amendment." The decision in *Monroe v. Pape,* which allowed for lawsuits against police officers for brutality under the color of state action, was the legal basis for later decisions, such as in *United States v. Price* (q.v.).

MONTGOMERY BUS BOYCOTT. The first major nonviolent social action of the modern civil rights movement.

On 1 December 1955, Rosa Parks (q.v.) refused to give up her seat on a public bus in Montgomery, Alabama, to a boarding white passenger and was arrested for violating a local ordinance. In response, black Montgomery organized the Montgomery Improvement Association (MIA; q.v.), which conducted a successful 381-day boycott of the city's buses from 5 December 1955 to 21 December 1956. Initially, the MIA demanded only a less offensive form of racial segregation on the city's buses, the hiring of African American drivers on some buses, and more courteous treatment of African Americans on the buses. The intransigence of the bus company's white officers and the city's white political leadership transformed what might have been a short-term protest leading to minimal reform into a year-long confrontation that won international attention and ended in the desegregation of Montgomery's city buses.

MONTGOMERY IMPROVEMENT ASSOCIATION (MIA). An organization formed originally to conduct the Montgomery Bus Boycott (q.v.).

After the arrest of Rosa Parks (q.v.) on 1 December 1955 for refusing to give up her seat on a Montgomery, Alabama, bus to a boarding white passenger, the city's black leadership organized a successful one-day boycott of the buses on 5 December. That afternoon, they organized the Montgomery Improvement Association to conduct a continuing boycott of the city's buses. Martin Luther King, Jr. (q.v.), the young pastor of Dexter Avenue Baptist Church, and E. D. Nixon (q.v.), a former president of the local branch of the NAACP (q.v.), were chosen its president and treasurer. Pastors of local churches and leaders of local civic organizations made up its 35-member executive committee. These plans were confirmed at a mass meeting that evening at Holt Street Baptist Church. The city's white leaders rejected the MIA's initial demands for a less offensive form of racial segregation on the city's buses, the hiring of African American drivers on some buses, and more courteous treatment of African Americans on the buses. The city's buses were desegregated by federal court order a year later.

After the organization of SCLC (q.v.) in January 1957, the MIA became its local affiliate and pursued other interests of the local African American community, such as desegregation of schools and public accommodations, employment opportunities, improved public services, and voter registration. When Martin Luther King moved to Atlanta in January 1960 to become copastor with his father of Ebenezer Baptist Church, Ralph D. Abernathy (q.v.), the pastor of Montgomery's First Baptist Church, was his successor as president of the MIA. In 1962, when Abernathy moved to Atlanta to become the pastor of West Hunter Street Baptist Church, his successor as president of the MIA was Solomon Snowden Seay, Sr., the pastor of Montgomery's Mt. Zion A.M.E. Zion Church. Seay moved to Selma, Alabama, in 1965. Under the presidency of Mrs. Johnnie R. Carr since 1973, the MIA has been less active in its later years than earlier.

MOORE, AMZIE (1911–82). Civil rights activist.

Amzie Moore was born on 23 September 1911 between Le Flore and Elliott on the border between Carroll and Grenada counties, Mississippi. He studied in local public schools for African American children. After Moore served in the armed forces during World War II, he returned to live and work in Cleveland, Mississippi. There, Moore became a post office employee and owner of a gas station. He was also an active member of the NAACP and, in 1951, he worked with Dr. T. R. M. Howard as a founding member of the Delta's Regional Council of Negro Leadership. In 1954, the Supreme Court's decision in *Brown v. Board of Education* (q.v.) was followed by the organization of the Citizens Council (q.v.). Moore was not intimidated. In 1955, he became president of Cleveland's branch of the NAACP.

After the murder of Emmett Till (q.v.), Amzie Moore cooperated with Medgar Evers (q.v.) and Ruby Hurley (q.v.) in investigating Emmett Till's murder for the NAACP. In retaliation for his civil rights activity, Moore's bank in Cleveland called in the $6,000 mortgage it held on his house and service station. Less concerned with destroying segregation and less interested in direct social action than with enabling black people to defend their own interests, Amzie Moore was an ardent advocate of voter registration. He persuaded Robert Moses (q.v.) to place much of SNCC's emphasis there when Moses came to Mississippi in 1961. In 1962, Moore helped to organize the Council of Federated Organizations (COFO; q.v.), a coalition of all the major civil rights organizations working in Mississippi. Throughout the 1960s, Moore was a tower of strong indigenous leadership of the civil rights movement in the Mississippi Delta. He died on 1 February 1982 in Mound Bayou, Mississippi.

MOORE, HARRY TYSON (1905–51). Civil rights activist.

Harry T. Moore was born on 18 November 1905 in Mims, Florida. His parents had little education, but they encouraged him to aspire to more than they had. He graduated from high school at Florida Baptist Institute in Cocoa Beach, Florida, in 1924 and began teaching at the institute that year. In 1931, he received a bachelor's degree from Bethune-Cookman College. He married Harriette Simms and they helped to organize the Brevard County, Florida, branch of the NAACP (q.v.) in 1935. Three years later, Moore filed a lawsuit to win equal pay for black and white teachers in Florida's public schools. He was increasingly active in the NAACP throughout the state and, in 1941, was elected president of Florida's conference of branches of the NAACP. After the Supreme Court held that the white primary was unconstitutional in 1944, Moore and Edward D. Davis organized the Progressive Voters' League of Florida. It tripled black voter registration in the state and encouraged black people to vote in primaries from which they had been excluded.

In July 1949, when three black men were convicted of the rape of a white woman in Groveland, Florida, Moore and others contested the convictions. Two years later, the Supreme Court ordered a new trial in the case. Before they could be retried, however, Lake County, Florida, sheriff Willis McCall shot and killed one of the men and wounded another while they were in his custody. Harry Moore called for the sheriff's suspension. At 10:20 P.M. on Christmas, 25 December 1951, a month after the shooting, a bomb exploded in the Moores' bedroom. Their bed was blown through the roof of the house. They were found, severely injured, under some debris. Harry Moore was dead on arrival at the hospital. His wife, Harriette, lingered for nine days before dying from her wounds. Members of the Ku Klux Klan were suspected in the bombing, but no one was brought to trial. In 1955, Governor LeRoy Collins (q.v.) reopened the rape case and commuted the sentence of the only surviving prisoner. Florida writer Stetson Kennedy believed that local law enforcement officers were Klan sympathizers, either complicit in the killing of Harry and Harriette Moore or guilty of suppressing evidence against the guilty parties. Kennedy persuaded Governor Lawton Chiles to reopen the investigation of the Moores' murder 40 years later.

MOOSE LODGE #107 OF HARRISBURG v. IRVIS, 407 U.S. 163 (1972). A case in which the Supreme Court held that private clubs unrelated to the state may not be sued for racial discrimination.

K. Leroy Irvis, an African American who was the Democratic Party's minority leader in Pennsylvania's House of Representatives, sought membership in Moose Lodge #107 in Harrisburg, Pennsylvania. When he was rejected on racial grounds, Irvis sued the Moose Lodge. Attorneys for Irvis argued that the lodge's liquor license was a sufficient bond with the state to make its racial discrimination a matter of "state action" and that the license should be suspended until the lodge ceased its discrimination. A federal district court upheld the claims of Irvis's attorneys. When the lodge appealed the decision to the Supreme Court, the Court overturned the district court's ruling. By a six-to-three vote, the Court held that the Moose Lodge was a private club and that its racial discrimination was not an appropriate reason to suspend its license. "Where the impetus for the discrimination is private," wrote Chief Justice William Rehnquist for the majority, "the State must have 'significantly involved itself with invidious discriminations,' in order for the discriminatory action to fall within the ambit of the constitutional prohibition."

MORGAN v. VIRGINIA, 328 U.S. 373 (1946). A case in which the Supreme Court found state laws requiring racial segregation in public transportation did not apply to interstate passengers.

On 14 July 1944, Irene Morgan boarded a Greyhound bus in Gloucester County, Virginia, with a ticket for Baltimore, Maryland. Shortly, thereafter, the bus driver told her and another African American woman to move to seats further back in the bus so that white passengers who were standing could be seated. The driver was acting in compliance with Virginia law, which required that buses be segregated by rows of seats. When Morgan refused to move, she was removed by force, arrested, and convicted of resisting arrest and violating Virginia's segregation statute. Virginia's supreme court upheld both the state segregation law and Irene Morgan's conviction. Morgan appealed to the United States Supreme Court. In June 1946, her conviction was overturned by a seven-to-one vote. The state might require racial segregation of intrastate passengers, said the Court, but its law could not extend to interstate passengers. In the Journey of Reconciliation (q.v.) in 1947, black and white members of CORE (q.v.), the Fellowship of Reconciliation (q.v.), and the Workers Defense League tested compliance with the Court's *Morgan* decision. Not only did they find it unenforced in the Upper South, but they were convicted of violating North Carolina law and served time in its state prison. The Supreme Court's ruling in *Morgan* would be ignored throughout the South until after the Freedom Rides (q.v.) in 1961.

MOSES, ROBERT PARRIS (Robert Parris; 1935–   ). Civil rights activist.

Robert Moses was born on 23 January 1935 in New York City. His grandfather was a Baptist preacher, active in the National Baptist Convention (q.v.). His father's professional career was truncated by the depression and he supported his family by work as a janitor. Young Robert Moses was a bright student, who graduated from Stuyvesant High School and Hamilton College. In 1958, Moses earned an M.A. in philosophy from Harvard University. He began teaching at New York's Horace Mann High School. In 1960, Moses visited an uncle who taught at Hampton Institute and participated in a civil rights demonstration there. In nearby Newport News, he met Wyatt Tee Walker (q.v.), who was about to become the executive director of SCLC (q.v.), and decided to work with Bayard Rustin (q.v.) on the Committee to Defend Martin Luther King when he returned to New York. During the summer of 1960, Rustin persuaded Moses to go to Atlanta to work on voter registration for SCLC. At SCLC headquarters, he met young SNCC (q.v.) volunteers. At the suggestion of Ella Baker (q.v.), SCLC's interim executive director and inspirational mother of SNCC, Moses volunteered to work for SNCC in Mississippi.

In Mississippi, Amzie Moore (q.v.) persuaded Moses that political power through voter registration would do more for black Mississippians than nonviolent direct action, such as picket lines or sit-in demonstrations. In 1961, Robert Moses began his voter registration work in McComb, a town in southwestern Mississippi. When local white people realized what he was doing, they reacted severely. He was beaten and arrested; an assistant was killed. Yet, Moses persevered. In 1962, he was named program director for the Council of Federated Organizations (COFO; q.v.) and administered funds from the Voter Education Project (VEP; q.v.). In vain, Moses called for federal intervention to force Mississippi election officials to allow black people to register to vote without fear of retribution. In 1963, Moses and COFO organized parallel elections in which black Mississippians could cast votes for unofficial candidates for public office. A year later, he directed Freedom Summer (q.v.) in which large numbers of white college students came from the North to work with black Mississippians in freedom schools and voter registration efforts.

Moses was also a key figure in the challenge of the Mississippi Freedom Democratic Party (q.v.) to the all-white regular delegation from Mississippi at the Democratic National Convention. Disillusioned and shocked by the MFDP's treatment by powerful white Democrats, Robert Moses left Mississippi, used the name "Robert Parris," and cut off contact with white people. In 1966, he left the country to avoid the draft. For several years, he and his wife, Janet, taught in a small village in Tanzania. After President Carter established an amnesty program in 1977, Moses and his family returned to the United States. Subsequently, he was awarded a five-year grant from the McArthur Foundation to found the Algebra Project to teach mathematics to children in Boston's public schools. By involving local people in issues related to their own lives, he hoped to communicate a math and computer literacy that would prevent their reduction to the status of serfs. By 1992, the Algebra Project was being replicated in ten states across the country, including Mississippi.

MOTLEY, CONSTANCE BAKER (1921–   ). Civil rights attorney and judge.

Constance Baker Motley was born on 14 September 1921 in New Haven, Connecticut. Her parents were recent immigrants from the West Indies. While Motley was a law student at Columbia University, she began working for the NAACP LDEF (q.v.). Upon graduation from Columbia's law school, Motley began to work full time with the LDEF in its long litigation against racial segregation in public schools. At 27, soon after her graduation from law school, Motley made her first trip to Mississippi to argue a wage equalization case for African American teachers. Although she lost that case on a legal technicality, Motley would argue nine NAACP LDEF cases before the United States Supreme Court, including *Lucy v. Adams* (q.v.), which won the admission of Autherine Lucy to the University of Alabama in 1955, and *Meredith v. Fair* (q.v.), which won the admission of James Meredith to the University of Mississippi in 1962.

Despite the professional obstacles to a black female attorney, Motley won wide recognition for her work in the field. In 1964, she became the first African American woman elected to the New York State Senate. A year later, Motley won election as the president of the borough of Manhattan in New York City. She was the first woman to hold the position, the highest elective office held by an African American woman at the time. In 1966, Motley was appointed a judge in a New York federal district court by President Lyndon Johnson. She was the first African American woman ever appointed as judge in a federal district court. Motley continued to serve on the court until she became its chief judge in 1982. In 1986, Motley became a senior judge on the court, a semiretired position in which she continued to sit on some, but not a full schedule of, cases.

MUIR v. LOUISVILLE PARK THEATRICAL ASSOCIATION, 347 U.S. 971 (1954). A case in which the Supreme Court held that racial segregation in public facilities leased to a nonpublic agency is unconstitutional.

A black resident of Louisville, Kentucky, James W. Muir, filed suit against the Louisville Park Theatrical Association, which refused to sell him a ticket to one of its productions in a city-owned amphitheater. His attorney claimed that the equal protection requirement of the Fourteenth Amendment barred racial segregation in publicly owned facilities. Muir lost his case in lower courts, which held that the Fourteenth Amendment protection did not extend to a private agency, even if it were operating in a publicly owned facility. The long shadow of the Supreme Court's logic in *Brown v. Board of Education* (q.v.) extended to its judgment in *Muir.* The Court unanimously reversed the lower courts' findings and held that its ruling in *Brown* applied to publicly owned facilities, whether they were operated by a public or by a private agency.

MURPHY, CARL (1889–1967). Journalist and civil rights activist.
Carl Murphy was born on 17 January 1889 in Baltimore, Maryland. He was the son of John Henry Murphy and Martha Howard Murphy. Born a slave, John Henry Murphy served in the Civil War and founded and edited the *Baltimore Afro-American* from 1892 until his death in 1922. Young Carl Murphy graduated from Howard University in 1911, earned an M.S. at Harvard University in 1913, and studied at the University of Jena in Germany during the summer after his work at Harvard. From 1913 to 1918, Murphy chaired Howard University's German Department. In 1918, he married Vashti Turley of Washington, D.C., and joined his father's staff at the *Afro-American.* The swelling tide of African American migration from the South during those years vastly increased the audience and operations of Northern black newspapers, such as Robert Abbott's *Chicago Defender,* the Murphys' *Baltimore Afro-American,* and Robert Vann's *Pittsburgh Courier.*

From his father's death in 1922 until his own retirement in 1961, Carl Murphy was the editor of the *Afro-American.* During his tenure, it was published biweekly in Baltimore and Washington and weekly in Newark, Philadelphia, and Richmond. Murphy was for many years a member of the Board of Directors and, in 1954–55, was president of the National Newspaper Publishers Association. Murphy became a major force in the legal struggle of the NAACP (q.v.) for civil rights from the 1920s to the 1960s. He helped to make the NAACP's Baltimore branch one of the largest in the nation. In 1931, Murphy joined the NAACP's Board of Directors. For years, as chairman of its legal redress and administration committee, he supported the battle directed by Charles H. Houston (q.v.) and Thurgood Marshall (q.v.) against racial segregation. In 1955, the NAACP honored Carl Murphy by awarding him its Spingarn Medal.

MYRDAL, KARL GUNNAR. *See An American Dilemma.*

N

NAACP v. ALABAMA, 377 U.S. 288 (1964). A case in which the Supreme Court overturned an Alabama court's decision to bar the National Association for the Advancement of Colored People (NAACP; q.v.) from operating within the state.

In 1928, the United States Supreme Court upheld a New York state law which required the Ku Klux Klan to make its membership list available to the public in *Bryant v. Zimmerman.* Thirty years later, similar laws in the South led to a series of cases, including *Bates v. Little Rock* (q.v.), *Louisiana, Ex Rel. Gremillion, Attorney General v. NAACP* (q.v.), and *NAACP v. Alabama,* in which the Court reversed itself. *NAACP v. Alabama* was itself a series of four cases before the Supreme Court in 1958, 1959, 1961 and 1964, in which the state of Alabama sought to bar the NAACP from operating in the state. In June 1956, during the Montgomery Bus Boycott (q.v.), Alabama attorney general John Patterson sued the NAACP. He sought to enjoin its operations in the state because it did not comply with a state law requiring a corporation or organization chartered outside the state to register its charter with the state of Alabama, indicate where it did business in the state, and identify its agent or agents in the state. An Alabama trial court judge ordered the NAACP to cease operations in the state until it complied with the law and set a date by which it must submit all pertinent records to the state. NAACP attorneys submitted all the requested records except its membership list, arguing that release of the latter would violate the civil rights of its members to free association and speech. The judge's fine of $100,000 against the NAACP was appealed to the Alabama supreme court, which affirmed the lower court's decision.

When the NAACP appealed to the United States Supreme Court, it unanimously found the Alabama law unconstitutional, voided the fine, and ordered the Alabama court to try the case on its merits. Refusing to do so, the Alabama court maintained its injunction on NAACP operations in the state through two more NAACP appeals to the Supreme Court, in 1959 and 1961, before it ruled on the original charges. In 1962, the Alabama court made permanent its ban on NAACP operations in the state. Two years later, the United States Supreme Court unanimously found the Alabama court's ruling was unconstitutional. The "freedom of individuals to associate for the collective advocacy of ideas" was a fundamental constitutional right, said the Court, as it ordered Alabama to register the NAACP as a legal organization. By then, however, the costly litigation had effectively barred the NAACP from operating in Alabama through much of the civil rights era. During that time, civil rights activists from Birmingham to Montgomery and Mobile rallied to affiliates of the Southern Christian Leadership Conference (SCLC; q.v.), including the Alabama Christian Movement for Human Rights (ACMHR; q.v.) and the Montgomery Improvement Association (MIA; q.v.), to carry on their battle for civil rights. Alabama officials could not bind SCLC with the same litigation because it was not a membership organization, but the state attacked SCLC with a costly court battle in *Sullivan v. New York Times* (q.v.).

NAACP v. ST. LOUIS–SAN FRANCISCO RAILROAD, 297 I.C.C. 335 (1955). A case in which the Interstate Commerce Commission (ICC) found that racial segregation on trains and in waiting rooms serving interstate passengers violated the Interstate Commerce Act of 1887.

In 1951, the NAACP (q.v.) began gathering evidence of racial discrimination in railroad transportation. In July 1954, NAACP attorneys presented its evidence against 15 railroad companies in ICC hearings. The Eisenhower administration's Justice Department joined the case as amicus curiae. The NAACP attorneys proved that 14 of the 15 railroads practiced racial segregation on trains and coaches and in their waiting rooms. Section 216 of the Interstate Commerce Act held that public vehicles offering interstate transportation could not subject any passengers to "unjust discrimination or any undue or unreasonable prejudice or disadvantage in any respect whatsoever." In November 1955, the ICC ruled that segregated facilities caused "undue and unreasonable disadvantages" to black passengers in violation of the Interstate Commerce Act. The ICC ruling did not extend either to intrastate railroad passengers or to restaurants or lunch counters operating within railroad stations. In a companion case, *Keys v. Carolina Coach Company* (q.v.), however, the ICC sought to bar racial segregation of interstate passengers on buses and in bus terminals. It ordered the buses and railroads to correct their policies by 10 January 1956. Yet, interstate public transportation in the South continued to be segregated, in violation of the *Keys* and *NAACP* decisions, until it was challenged by the Freedom Rides (q.v.) in 1961.

NAACP LEGAL DEFENSE AND EDUCATIONAL FUND (LDEF). A nonprofit corporation, organized apart from the NAACP (q.v.), to carry the burden of its litigation.

Prior to 1939, the NAACP handled its litigation through independent attorneys' offices or through the office of its counsel. In 1939, the NAACP Legal Defense and Educational Fund, Inc., was established as a nonprofit, tax-exempt corporation to carry on its civil rights litigation and educational work. Organized by Thurgood Marshall (q.v.), the LDEF operated independently of the NAACP. It began with a staff of two persons, including Marshall, who was its first executive director. The LDEF carried on the long series of court battles from 1939 to 1954, which resulted in the Supreme Court's decision in *Brown v. Board of Education* (q.v.), which found that it was unconstitutional to mandate racially segregated public schools in the law.

NASH, DIANE (Diane Nash Bevel; 1938–   ). Civil rights activist.

Diane Nash was born on 15 May 1938 in Chicago, Illinois. She grew up on the city's South Side with her mother and stepfather, Dorothy Nash Baker and John Baker. Raised a Roman Catholic, Nash attended a parochial elementary school and the public Hyde Park High School. After graduating from high school, she entered Howard University in Washington, D.C. After a year at Howard, Nash transferred to Fisk University in Nashville, Tennessee, where she first experienced Southern racial segregation. Nash gravitated to the workshops on nonviolence conducted by James Lawson (q.v.). She soon became a central figure in the group of student activists Lawson was training. Elected chairperson of the Student Central Committee, Nash was among the organizers of student sit-ins at downtown Nashville lunch counters. She attended the founding meeting of the Student Nonviolent Coordinating Committee (SNCC; q.v.) on 15–17 April 1960 in Raleigh, North Carolina.

In February 1961, Nash was one of eleven students who were jailed in Rock Hill, South Carolina, and, refusing to be bailed out, she served a full month's sentence. When it appeared that the Freedom Rides (q.v.) might collapse, Nash coordinated student efforts from Nashville that renewed the Freedom Rides to desegregate interstate transportation. In August 1961, after heated debates over SNCC's future direction, Nash was appointed to lead its direct-action efforts, while Charles Jones was to direct its work in voter registration. Later in 1961, Nash married fellow Nashville student activist James Bevel (q.v.) and moved with him to Jackson, Mississippi, where they continued to organize for the movement. In April 1962, pregnant and faced with a two-and-a-half-year jail sentence, she was prepared to give birth to her child in a Southern jail in order to dramatize the plight of black people in the South. After serving a reduced sentence and joining the SCLC (q.v.) staff, Diane Nash gave birth to her first child, Sherrilynn, on 5 August 1962 in Albany, Georgia.

As field staff organizers for SCLC, Diane Nash and James Bevel played key roles in its campaign with the Birmingham, Alabama, Movement (q.v.) and the March on Washington (q.v.) in 1963. When their second child, Douglass, was born on 15 May 1964, Nash and Bevel were organizing the Selma voter registration drive, which led to the Selma to Montgomery March (q.v.) in 1965. SCLC gave them its highest honor, the Rosa Parks Award, in 1965. Near the end of 1966, Diane Nash traveled with a group of women from the United States to visit North Vietnam. For her, the civil rights movement, the peace movement, and the women's movement were continuous expressions of the struggle for peace and social justice. Through the 1970s, 1980s, and 1990s, Diane Nash continued the struggle in housing advocacy, tenant organizing, and welfare support organizations in Chicago.

NASHVILLE, TENNESSEE, MOVEMENT. The civil rights movement in Tennessee's state capital, which produced many leaders of the Southern movement.

In March 1958, the Fellowship of Reconciliation (FOR; q.v.) sent its field secretary, James Lawson (q.v.), to Nashville, Tennessee, where he began theological studies at Vanderbilt University. Lawson's workshops in nonviolence led black students from American Baptist Theological Seminary, Fisk University, Meharry Medical College, and Tennessee State University to a sit-in demonstration as early as November 1959. When news reached Nashville of the sit-ins at Greensboro, North Carolina, Nashville students launched their own sit-in movement (q.v.) on 13 February 1960. From their headquarters at First Baptist Church, whose pastor, Kelly Miller Smith, led the Nashville affiliate of the SCLC (q.v.), students such as Marion Barry (q.v.), James Bevel (q.v.), Bernard Lafayette, John Lewis (q.v.), and Diane Nash (q.v.) quickly emerged as leaders in their own right. The numbers of Nashville's sit-in demonstrators grew daily and sit-ins at Kress, Woolworth, and McLellan lunch counters spread to those at W. T. Grant and Walgreens. Some demonstrators were beaten and hundreds were arrested, 81 on 27 February alone.

In April 1960, Lawson was the keynote speaker and drafted the declaration of purpose for the Shaw University conference in Raleigh, North Carolina, which organized SNCC (q.v.). By then, tensions in Nashville mounted dramatically. The sit-in demonstrations were supplemented by a black boycott of white merchants. In late April, an explosion demolished the home of the students' 72-year-old attorney, Z. Alexander Looby, and blew out 147 windows at Meharry Medical College across the street. When two to three thousand black and white people marched ten miles to Nashville's City Hall in protest, the city's white leaders agreed to form a biracial committee to negotiate a compromise. On 10 May 1960, four theaters and six lunch counters in downtown Nashville were desegregated. A year later, when it appeared that the Freedom Rides (q.v.) might collapse, Bevel, Lawson, Lewis, and Nash led a group of Nashville student activists who continued them from Montgomery, Alabama, to Jackson, Mississippi.

NATIONAL ADVISORY COMMISSION ON CIVIL DISORDERS. *See* **Kerner Commission.**

NATIONAL ASSOCIATION FOR THE ADVANCEMENT OF COLORED PEOPLE (NAACP). One of five major organizations at the heart of the civil rights movement.

The older and more bureaucratic of the civil rights organizations, the NAACP and the National Urban League (q.v.), formed the conservative or traditional wing of the civil rights coalition of the 1960s. In the first decade of the twentieth century, several organizations were founded to reverse the tide of racism and racial segregation which swept the post-Reconstruction South. None of them achieved longevity until a National Negro Conference on 12 February 1909 called for a biracial "neo-abolitionist" movement. In its early days, the NAACP was an extension of the mutual commitment of W. E. B. Du Bois, the eloquent African American scholar, and Mary White Ovington, a white social worker, to their network of contacts in progressive reform, including Jane Addams,

John Dewey, William Dean Howells, and Ida B. Wells-Barnett. Du Bois was the NAACP's director of research and editor of its periodical, *The Crisis,* and in forty years as an NAACP officer Ovington held many of its other major offices. Rejecting Booker T. Washington's strategy of racial accommodation, they intended to fight for equality and social justice by litigation and lobbying, protest and publicity.

From 1920 to 1930, James Weldon Johnson was the NAACP's first African American executive secretary. He had developed its major campaign against racial violence, organizing a silent protest march against lynching in New York in 1917 and investigating race riots two years later. In 1919, the NAACP published *Thirty Years of Lynching in the United States, 1889–1918,* which documented more than 2500 lynchings in the previous thirty years. It failed to persuade Congress to adopt the Dyer antilynching bill in the early 1920s, but the NAACP's lobbying and publicity campaign helped to create a national climate in which lynching declined. Walter White (q.v.) spearheaded the NAACP's campaign to defeat the nomination of John J. Parker to the Supreme Court. In 1931, when White succeeded Johnson as executive secretary, he began to weave alliances among church, civil liberties, ethnic, labor, and women's organizations that had an early success in the struggle to defeat Parker's nomination. In 1939, the separate organization of the NAACP LDEF (q.v.) under the direction of Thurgood Marshall (q.v.) created the primary vehicle for its long series of court battles against racial segregation. As executive secretary of the NAACP until his death in 1955, however, Walter White made racial justice a fixed plank in progressive American politics.

In 1955, Roy Wilkins (q.v.) succeeded White, his mentor, as executive secretary of the NAACP. Named to the position shortly after the Supreme Court's decision in *Brown v. Board of Education,* Wilkins steered the venerable organization through the crucial years of the civil rights movement and desegregation in the South. He was staunchly committed to desegregation through the NAACP's traditional methods of legislation and litigation, protest and publicity. Many of its local branches spearheaded nonviolent social action on local levels, but the NAACP's national office under Wilkins was cautious in its approach to direct action. He supported the Montgomery Bus Boycott (q.v.), but Wilkins's NAACP initiated neither the sit-in movement (q.v.) nor the Freedom Rides (q.v.). He participated in the March on Washington (q.v.) in 1963 and the Selma to Montgomery March (q.v.), but he did so as a way of mobilizing public support for federal civil rights legislation, in which he placed great confidence. After 1965, Wilkins was an outspoken critic of the politics of racial separatism and the rhetoric of black power. When his health began to fail in 1977, Roy Wilkins resigned his position of leadership.

Unlike White and Wilkins, who became NAACP executive secretary after years of experience on its staff, Benjamin Hooks brought the experience of a minister, attorney, judge, and federal official to the position. He struggled to maintain financial support for the NAACP through difficult years for civil rights organizations and to articulate a new civil rights agenda after the common platform had been largely achieved. For Hooks, that new agenda included civil rights for black South Africa, renewal of voting rights legislation, and home rule for the District of Columbia. Too often, the agenda meant fighting rearguard actions, such as staving off antibusing legislation or fighting President Bush's nomination of Clarence Thomas to succeed Thurgood Marshall (q.v.) on the United States Supreme Court.

In 1993, when Benjamin Chavis succeeded Hooks, who was 23 years his senior, much was made of the passage of leadership in civil rights to a new generation. Chavis had belonged to the NAACP, CORE, and SCLC in the 1960s. Yet, he matured in its later years, when the politics of racial separatism was fashionable, and he came to power as the memory of Malcolm X (q.v.) achieved iconic status among African Americans. When Chavis sought to move the venerable NAACP in a radical new direction by reaching out to the followers of Louis Farrakhan, he seemed to threaten both its historic commitment to racial integration and its sources of financial support. He was forced from office within a year and, in the aftermath, the chairman of the NAACP's national board was also forced from office. For a new chairperson, the NAACP turned to Myrlie Evers, the accomplished widow of Medgar Evers (q.v.); on 9 December 1995, the NAACP chose Maryland congressman Kweisi Mfume as president and chief executive officer. Together, they face the difficult task of rejuvenating a dispirited but venerable civil rights organization.

NATIONAL BAPTIST CONVENTION, U.S.A. The largest African American organization in the United States.

From the earliest date of reliable statistics, about half of African Americans have identified themselves as Baptists. Commonly part of biracial congregations in the antebellum South, the freedmen quickly established separate black Baptist congregations throughout the region during Reconstruction. Offended by attitudes and treatment in white-dominated local associations, state conventions, and the Southern and Northern Baptist Conventions, African American Baptists developed parallel organizations between 1865 and 1895. In 1895, that development was capped by the organization of the National Baptist Convention in Atlanta, Georgia. A division within the convention twenty years later led to the creation of the National Baptist Convention of America. Nonetheless, the larger body was able to establish a national headquarters and a publishing house in Nashville, Tennessee, five independent black colleges, and missions in West Africa and the Caribbean. Since 1924, the National Baptist Convention and the Southern Baptist Convention have jointly operated the American Baptist Theological Seminary in Nashville.

Between 1953 and 1956, National Baptist Convention pastors Theodore J. Jemison (q.v.) in Baton Rouge, Martin Luther King (q.v.) in Montgomery, and C. K. Steele (q.v.) in Tallahassee led bus boycotts which anticipated the ministerial activism of the next decade. The convention's president, Joseph H. Jackson (q.v.) of Chicago, supported the bus boycotts. In 1957, activist National Baptist Convention pastors joined King in organizing SCLC (q.v.) in numbers so large as to dominate its leadership. Soon, American Baptist Seminary was producing such student leaders of the movement as James Bevel (q.v.) and John Lewis (q.v.), and King hoped to make the convention a primary vehicle of the movement. Yet, as Jackson warily eyed King's growing popularity, his National Baptist Convention and King's SCLC seemed to become alternative centers of loyalty. Heir apparent in the convention, Jemison quietly dropped his affiliation with SCLC; challenged for reelection as president by King's associates, Jackson fired King from a lesser office in the convention.

In 1961, the National Baptist Convention split a second time, as Jackson's opponents left to form the Progressive National Baptist Convention. J. H. Jackson served as the convention's president until his retirement in 1982, when Jemison was elected as his successor. Despite the two divisions in the National Baptist Convention, it still claimed eight million members. In 1989, NAACP (q.v.) executive secretary Benjamin Hooks (q.v.) and Jesse L. Jackson (q.v.) joined Jemison in dedicating the convention's new national headquarters in Nashville and, symbolically, rededicating the convention to the cause of civil rights. Five years later, the Reverend Henry J. Lyons succeeded Jemison as president of the National Baptist Convention.

NATIONAL COUNCIL OF NEGRO WOMEN (NCNW). A coalition of African American women's organizations in the twentieth century.

The National Council of Negro Women was founded on 5 December 1935 by Mary McLeod Bethune, the president of Florida's Bethune-Cookman College. From 1896 to 1935, the foremost national organization of black women was the National Association of Colored Women (NACW). Bethune had served as its president from 1924 to 1928. Believing that the NACW was a weak vehicle for new challenges facing African American women, Bethune won the support of leaders of fourteen national organizations of black women to affiliate with the NCNW. Thereafter, the NACW declined in national significance. As director of Negro Affairs for the National Youth Administration, Bethune was the highest ranking African American woman in Franklin D. Roosevelt's administration. She and the NCNW exposed racial discrimination in job training and employment during World War II and lobbied for desegregation of the armed forces. Bethune continued as president of the NCNW until 1949, when she was succeeded by Dorothy Bolden Ferebee, who served from 1949 to 1953, and by Vivian Carter Mason, who served from 1953 to 1957. Their presidencies were largely transitional from the Bethune era and their accomplishments were limited by scarce resources.

In 1957, Dorothy I. Height (q.v.) was elected president of the NCNW. She brought to the position 20 years of experience in appointive positions in the NCNW, 13 years on the national YWCA staff and 8 years as national president of Delta Sigma Theta sorority. Coming to power just as the civil rights movement crested, Height was often included with James Farmer (q.v.), Martin Luther King (q.v.), John Lewis (q.v.), A. Philip Randolph (q.v.), Roy Wilkins (q.v.), and Whitney Young (q.v.) among its leading national spokespersons. She won nonprofit, tax-exempt status for the NCNW. This enabled it to win grants from the Agency for International Development, the Department of Health, Education and Welfare and the Ford Foundation to expand its staff and develop programs for youth and women at home and abroad. Although forced to scale back during the Reagan and Bush administrations, the NCNW seized the initiative in 1986 to launch the annual Black Family Reunion celebrations to emphasize positive images of the strength and resilience of the African American family.

NATIONAL URBAN LEAGUE (Urban League). One of five major organizations at the heart of the civil rights movement.

The older and more bureaucratic of the civil rights organizations, the NAACP (q.v.) and the National Urban League, formed the conservative or traditional wing of the civil rights coalition of the 1960s. Responding to problems arising from the great migration, three separate organizations were founded in New York between 1905 and 1910 to help Southern black migrants adjust to problems of urban life. They were merged in October 1911 as the National Urban League. George Edmund Haynes, the first African American to earn a doctorate from Columbia University, was its executive secretary from 1911 to 1917. Haynes was succeeded by Eugene Kinckle Jones, who was the Urban League's executive secretary from 1917 to 1941. Haynes and Jones largely shaped the Urban League's approach to problems arising from the great migration. On issues of employment, housing, and social welfare, they worked with corporations, foundations, and sympathetic government officers to improve economic conditions for black people in the city. From 1923 to 1949, the Urban League published *Opportunity* as its official publication.

Lester B. Granger (q.v.) was the Urban League's executive secretary from 1941 to 1961. In the tradition of Haynes and Jones, Granger worked with sympathetic corporate, foundation, and government insiders to achieve modest reforms. He moved the Urban League toward closer cooperation with organized labor and lobbied for denying federal funds to housing developments that practiced discrimination and desegregating the armed forces after World War II. By his retirement in 1961, however, Granger and the Urban League were much criticized for their caution and conservatism. His successor, Whitney M. Young (q.v.), moved the Urban League into a firmer alliance with the other major civil rights organizations. Young was careful to retain the confidence of the league's powerful inside contacts, but he insisted that it join the March on Washington in 1963. His most important influence lay in his call for a domestic "Marshall Plan," outlined in his book, *To Be Equal.* His proposals influenced President Lyndon Johnson's War on Poverty. As the civil rights coalition frayed in 1966, Young and the NAACP's Roy Wilkins (q.v.) refused to sign a manifesto drafted by other civil rights leaders when they continued the march of James Meredith (q.v.) from Memphis, Tennessee, to Jackson, Mississippi. Young shunned the black power rhetoric popular with leaders of CORE (q.v.) and SNCC (q.v.), but he responded to the black power movement and urban violence in the late 1960s by concentrating Urban League resources on young people in the urban black underclass. He drowned on a visit to Nigeria in 1971.

After Arthur Fletcher served briefly as interim executive director, Young's successor at the Urban League was Vernon E. Jordan (q.v.). Unlike his predecessors, whose background was in social work, Jordan was an experienced attorney. A former director of the Southern Regional Council's Voter Education Project (q.v.), he focused Urban League resources on black voter registration. Jordan initiated the league's publication of *The State of Black America,* annual reports on conditions in the African American community, and worked for a full employment national economic policy and a consumer-oriented national health system. After Jordan addressed the Urban League's Fort Wayne, Indiana, affiliate on 29 May 1980, a white supremacist wounded him in an assassination attempt. He recovered from the near-fatal wound and continued to lead the Urban League until the end of 1981. When Jordan retired to private legal practice, John Jacob, his chief assistant at the Urban League, became his successor. Jacob renewed Whitney Young's call for a Marshall Plan for American cities, continued Vernon Jordan's emphasis on black voter-registration, and has summoned the African American community to attend to self-help programs on issues such as black-on-black crime, single-parent households and teenage pregnancy.

NEW YORK TIMES v. SULLIVAN, 376 U.S. 254 (1964). A case in which the Supreme Court reversed a lower court's finding and award of damages in a libel case.

In March 1960, apparently without their knowledge or consent, the names of Ralph D. Abernathy (q.v.), Joseph E. Lowery (q.v.), Fred Shuttlesworth (q.v.) and S. S. Seay, Sr., of Montgomery, Alabama, were signed to a controversial full-page advertisement in the *New York Times.* Written by Bayard Rustin (q.v.) and headlined HEED THEIR RISING VOICES, it sought to raise money to defend Martin Luther King (q.v.). In response to its accusations, Montgomery, Alabama, police commissioner L. B. Sullivan sued them and the *Times* for libel in the cases of *Sullivan v. Abernathy* and *Sullivan v. New York Times.* In a Montgomery trial court, the plaintiff was awarded $500,000 in damages. Montgomery mayor Earl James won another suit for $500,000 in damages and Governor John Patterson won a third suit for a larger amount. Birmingham police commissioner Eugene "Bull" Connor (q.v.) followed with a fourth suit. Total damage awards approached $3,000,000. When the Alabama supreme court confirmed the trial court's decision in 1962, Alabama seized the automobiles of the four clergymen and began proceedings against other property. In part to avoid the continued seizure of their property, Abernathy moved to Atlanta to be pastor of West Hunter Street Baptist Church; Lowery moved to Nashville, Tennessee, where he led the Inter-Civic Coordinating Council; and Shuttlesworth took a church in Cincinnati, Ohio. When the two cases reached the United States Supreme Court in 1964, it unanimously reversed the trial court's decision.

NEWARK, NEW JERSEY, RACE RIOT (1967). Of 59 urban race riots in the United States in 1967, this was one of the most severe.

By the late 1960s, Newark, New Jersey, was already a city in economic and social trouble. The concentration of new black residents and the flight of white home-owners and businesses in the city of 400,000 had transformed it from a majority white to a majority black city. Economic and political power remained overwhelmingly white, however, even as the tax base necessary to meet increasing social needs was eroding. Public education and public services were deteriorating. Newark's African American community had a high rate of dependence on welfare, high unemployment statistics, and a high rate of complaints about police brutality. When white policemen beat a black cab driver in Newark on 12 July 1967, Newark's cauldron bubbled over. Angry black protesters gathered at the police station near the Hayes Homes housing project, and a firebomb hit the wall of the station. Policemen poured out of the building and beat everyone they could reach. The incident triggered rioting in Newark for the next six days. Windows were smashed, businesses were looted, and fires were set. The governor sent 475 state troopers and more than 4,000 national guardsmen to augment Newark's 1300-person police force in the effort to quell the riot. The guardsmen fired on suspected arsonists, looters, and snipers. Once they fired on suspected snipers, anyone framed in a window could become a target. The 23 people who were killed in the riot included six black women and two black children, a white policeman and a white fireman. About $10 million in property damage and losses were attributed to the riot.

NEWTON, HUEY PERCY (1942–89). Founder of the Black Panther Party.

Huey P. Newton was born on 17 February 1942 in Monroe, Louisiana, and named for Louisiana's favorite son, Huey Long. He was the son of Armelia and Walter Newton, a sharecropper and Baptist minister. The large Newton family moved to Oakland, California, in Huey's youth. Although he attended Oakland's public schools, Huey Newton was arrested for gun possession at 14 and was still functionally illiterate when he graduated from high school. In 1965, he earned an A.A. degree from Merritt Junior College in Oakland, where he met Bobby Seale (q.v.). In October 1966, Newton and Seale founded the Black Panther Party (q.v.) in Oakland. In April 1967, shortly after meeting Eldridge Cleaver (q.v.), they persuaded him to become the Black Panther's minister of information to launch and edit *The Black Panther.* A month later, 30 armed Black Panthers disrupted the California state assembly in Sacramento as it considered a gun control law. In October, when white policemen stopped a car in which Newton rode, there was an exchange of gunfire. A policeman was killed; Newton was injured and charged with first degree murder of the policeman. He became the Party's symbolic hero in "Free Huey Newton" campaigns by black and white radicals across the country, but he was convicted of voluntary manslaughter in July 1968.

Newton's cause drew attention to the Black Panthers. Membership in the Bay area grew from 60 to several hundred and new chapters sprang up across the country. Newton remained in prison until 1970, when the California supreme court overturned his conviction on manslaughter charges and released him. During his imprisonment, the Black Panther Party's fortunes declined. Its membership dropped from about 2,000 in 1968 to half that in 1970, when Cleaver's defection further divided the Panthers. After his release from prison, Newton shifted the party's emphasis to free health clinics, breakfasts for children, and voter registration drives. In his last two decades, Newton spent three years as a cement worker in Cuban exile from 1974 to 1977 and was in and out of California jails on a variety of criminal charges, including diverting public funds to his personal use, possession of guns and drug paraphernalia, and murdering a 17-year-old prostitute. He won a doctorate in social philosophy from the University of California at Santa Cruz in 1980, but he lurched through highs and lows on alcohol, drugs, and violence in his last ten years. In August 1989, Huey Newton was killed outside an Oakland crack house, allegedly by a 25-year-old crack cocaine dealer for the Black Guerilla Family, whom he had attempted to rob.

NIXON, EDGAR DANIEL (E. D.; 1899–1987). Pullman car porter and civil rights activist.

E. D. Nixon was born on 12 July 1899 in Montgomery, Alabama. He was the fifth of eight children born to Wesley M. Nixon, an untrained Baptist preacher, and Sue Ann Chappell Nixon, a cook and maid. When Sue Ann Nixon died, her children went to live with Wesley Nixon's sister, Pinky, in rural Autauga County, Alabama. Subsequently, Wesley Nixon remarried and became the father of nine more children. Sue Ann Nixon's children were needed for work on the farm where Pinky Nixon lived and the nearest school for black children was ten miles away. When E. D. Nixon returned to Montgomery in 1914, he had never attended school more than a few months a year and had no more than a third grade education. Young Nixon took odd jobs before he was hired in the baggage room of Montgomery's railroad station. In 1923, Nixon became a Pullman car porter. He married Alease Curry Nixon in 1926 and they became the parents of a son, Edgar Daniel Nixon, Jr., in 1928.

In 1928, E. D. Nixon helped to found a Montgomery branch of the NAACP (q.v.) and joined the Brotherhood of Sleeping Car Porters and Maids, recently organized by A. Philip Randolph (q.v.). After a divorce from his first wife, Nixon married Arlet Nixon in 1934. Active members of Montgomery's Holt Street Baptist Church, their union lasted for 53 years. In 1934, Nixon organized the Montgomery Welfare League, which sought to assure black people in the community of equal access to government assistance during the depression. During the 1930s, he worked with Myles Horton of Highlander Folk School (q.v.) to organize Alabama's cucumber pickers. As the founder and president of Montgomery's local of the Brotherhood of Sleeping Car Porters and Maids in 1938, Nixon became Randolph's chief aide in Alabama. He organized the Montgomery Voters League in 1940 and led a march of 750 black citizens to demand the franchise in 1944. From 1939 to 1951, he was president of Montgomery's branch and, from 1951 to 1953, he was president of the Alabama conference of branches of the NAACP. In 1954, Nixon conducted the first political contest by an African American in twentieth-century Alabama, when he ran for election to the Montgomery County Democratic Party Executive Committee.

When Rosa Parks (q.v.) was arrested on 1 December 1955 for refusing to give up her seat on a Montgomery bus to a white passenger, Nixon and Clifford J. Durr (q.v.) bailed Mrs. Parks out of jail. Nixon played a key role in organizing the MIA (q.v.), which protested Mrs. Parks's arrest and racial discrimination on the city buses by carrying on the Montgomery Bus Boycott (q.v.) for a year, until the Supreme Court ordered the desegregation of the city buses. During that time, Nixon served as treasurer of the MIA. Subsequently, in a disagreement with Martin Luther King (q.v.), the president of the MIA, about leadership and decision making in the organization, E. D. Nixon resigned. Through the 1960s and 1970s, he continued to support the civil rights movement and was active in the Alabama Democratic Party. Nixon died of cancer at Montgomery's Baptist Medical Center on 25 February 1987.

NORTH CAROLINA STATE BOARD OF EDUCATION v. SWANN, 402 U.S. 43 (1971). A case in which the Supreme Court found a North Carolina law against busing students to desegregate schools unconstitutional.

In 1965, only two percent of African American students in the Charlotte-Mecklenburg, North Carolina, school district attended school with white students. Black parents filed suit, claiming that the board of education had an obligation not merely to desegregate the schools but to create a unified, integrated school system. Federal courts were initially unsympathetic to the claims of the plaintiffs. In 1968, however, the Supreme Court ruled in *Green v. School Board of New Kent County, Virginia* (q.v.) that school boards had an "affirmative duty to take whatever steps" necessary to create a unified, nonsegregated school system. The plaintiffs in *Swann v. Charlotte-Mecklenburg Board of Education* (q.v.) re-opened their case. In the meantime, the North Carolina legislature had adopted a law which said that:

> No students shall be assigned or compelled to attend school on account of race, creed, color or national origin, or for the purpose of creating a balance or ratio of race, religion or national origins. Involuntary busing of students in contravention of this article is prohibited, and public funds shall not be used for any such busing.

North Carolina State Board of Education v. Swann tested the constitutionality of that law. It reached the United States Supreme Court at the same time as *Swann v. Charlotte-Mecklenburg Board of Education.* In *North Carolina State Board of Education v. Swann,* the Supreme Court found that North Carolina's antibusing legislation violated the Fourteenth Amendment.

NORTON, ELEANOR HOLMES (1937–   ). Civil rights attorney and politician.

Eleanor Holmes Norton was born on 13 June 1937 in Washington, D.C. The oldest of three daughters born to Coleman and Vela Holmes, she studied in Washington's public schools for African American students, graduating from Dunbar High School in 1955. Eleanor Holmes majored in history at Antioch College in Yellow Springs, Ohio, and graduated in 1960. In graduate and professional studies at Yale University, she earned an M.A. in American studies in 1963 and an LL.B. from the

University Law School in 1964. As a Yale student, Holmes was active in SNCC, worked on the staff of the March on Washington (q.v.) in 1963, and founded the New Haven chapter of CORE (q.v.). In the mid-1960s, she married another young attorney, Edward Norton. As assistant legal director of the American Civil Liberties Union (ACLU) from 1965 to 1970, Eleanor Holmes Norton helped to prepare the case of Julian Bond (q.v.), when the Georgia legislature refused to seat him because of his opposition to the Vietnam War. As a civil libertarian, however, her clients also included George Wallace (q.v.) and the National States Rights Party, a white supremacist group. Norton was also supportive of the emerging feminist movement. At the ACLU, she filed a class action suit against *Newsweek*, charging gender bias in both hiring and promotions. In 1973, she was a founder of the National Black Feminist Organization.

Norton left the ACLU staff in 1970 to chair the New York City Commission on Human Rights, where she served for seven years. The position offered her renewed opportunity to fight discrimination in education, employment, and housing. In 1977, President Jimmy Carter appointed Norton to the Equal Employment Opportunity Commission (EEOC; q.v.). She spearheaded the EEOC's reorganization in 1978 and served as its chairperson from 1979 to 1981. Upon leaving the EEOC, Norton became a faculty member of the Georgetown University Law Center in Washington. In 1990, she took a leave of absence from her position there to run for the nonvoting delegate seat from the District of Columbia in the House of Representatives. Despite the embarrassing discovery that Norton and her husband, whom she subsequently divorced, had not filed local income tax forms for eight years, she was elected in 1990. In subsequent elections, she was returned by large majorities. Recipient of honorary doctorates from over 50 colleges and universities, Norton has served on the Board of Trustees of Antioch University and as a board member of the Yale Corporation.

O

O'DELL, JACK (1924–). Civil rights activist.

Jack O'Dell was born in 1924. He was raised in the Detroit, Michigan, home of his grandfather, a janitor in a public library, and his grandmother, who raised young Jack as a devout Roman Catholic. He graduated from parochial schools in Detroit and attended Xavier University in New Orleans, where he joined a fraternity. During World War II, O'Dell ferried war cargoes under destroyer escort for the Coast Guard merchant marine. At the time, he read widely in African and

African American history. After the war, he worked in New Orleans as an organizer for the National Maritime Union, the first international seamen's union to ignore the color line. An anti-Communist faction of the union purged O'Dell from its ranks in 1950 for circulating peace petitions. His home in New Orleans was raided by the police. In 1956, he published an article on Louisiana racial politics in a Communist periodical.

After selling burial insurance in Birmingham, in 1957 O'Dell became the branch manager of the insurance firm's Montgomery office. There, as a lapsed Catholic, he heard Martin Luther King (q.v.) preach several times at Dexter Avenue Baptist Church. O'Dell lost his position with the insurance company after he was called to testify before the House Un-American Activities Committee as a suspected Communist. He moved to New York for graduate study and helped Bayard Rustin (q.v.) and Stanley Levison coordinate the Youth March for Integrated Schools in 1959. Two years later, O'Dell helped promote a Carnegie Hall benefit for the Southern Christian Leadership Conference (SCLC; q.v.) which featured Sammy Davis, Jr., Dean Martin, and Frank Sinatra.

In 1961, Levison recommended O'Dell to King who hired him to supervise a mass mail fund-raising office for SCLC in New York. O'Dell studied advanced marketing at New York University's Business School to prepare himself. By August 1961, his efficient Harlem office had a master list of 9,000 "proven contributors" and was raising over half of SCLC's annual budget. In January 1962, King anticipated grants to SCLC from the Voter Education Project (VEP; q.v.) and asked O'Dell to commute between New York and Atlanta to apply his fund-raising skills to SCLC's voter registration project. Within months, the Federal Bureau of Investigation was monitoring contacts among King, Levison, O'Dell, and others to verify Communist influence on the civil rights movement. The FBI told Attorney General Robert Kennedy that O'Dell was elected to the Communist Party's executive committee under a false name several years earlier. Its agents thought Levison's suggestions that O'Dell might become SCLC's public relations assistant or even replace Wyatt Tee Walker (q.v.) as its executive director were particularly significant.

King reacted to early warnings from the Kennedy administration about his ties to Levison and O'Dell by barring O'Dell from appearing in Birmingham in 1962 and 1963. Even so, the FBI leaked a story on O'Dell's role in SCLC to the press. It appeared in five newspapers and increased pressure on King to fire him. O'Dell readily admitted to King that he had attended some Communist Party meetings, had once supported its program and continued to have friends in the party, but he denied being a member of the party or supporting its program any longer. King stalled, publicly denying the significance of O'Dell's role in SCLC and saying that he had resigned.

O'Dell gave up supervision of SCLC's voter registration work, but he remained central to SCLC's New York fund-raising effort and only his assurances of solid financial support allowed King to proceed with the Birmingham campaign. Dramatic news stories about the Birmingham Movement (q.v.) reaped unprecedented financial support for SCLC through O'Dell's New York office. On 22 June 1963, however, Assistant Attorney General Burke Marshall, Attorney General Robert Kennedy, and President John Kennedy all spoke to King about the necessity of severing O'Dell's relationship with SCLC. King had the temerity to ask even the president for proof of the charges against O'Dell, but the administration's pressure had its effect on him. On 26 June, King told O'Dell to begin looking for work elsewhere. Four days later, a Birmingham newspaper featured a story leaked by the FBI or the Justice Department that O'Dell, a known Communist, had helped to plan SCLC's campaign in Birmingham. On 3 July, King dismissed him from SCLC's staff. O'Dell left SCLC, taking his valuable mailing lists with him to *Freedomways,* a journal founded by followers of W. E. B. Du Bois, including several prominent black Communists. Yet, Georgia's attorney general and the *Atlanta Constitution* took up the accusations of Communist influence in SCLC with renewed vigor, until Stanley Levison also agreed to have no contact with King. In more recent years, O'Dell has worked with Jesse Jackson (q.v.) and the Rainbow Coalition.

OPEN HOUSING ACT OF 1968. *See* **Civil Rights Act of 1968.**

ORANGEBURG STATE COLLEGE POLICE RIOT (1968). An armed assault by South Carolina state patrolmen on African American students at South Carolina State College in Orangeburg.

In 1963, the sit-in movement (q.v.) failed to desegregate local lunch counters in Orangeburg, South Carolina. Five years later, the South Carolina State College chapter of the National Association for the Advancement of Colored People (NAACP; q.v.) led by John Stroman sought to desegregate Harry Floyd's All Star Bowling Lanes near the campus. On 5 February 1968, Stroman led a group of students to Floyd's bowling alley. Some of them got in, but the bowling alley was then closed. Led on the next night by Stroman and Student Nonviolent Coordinating Committee (SNCC; q.v.) organizer Cleveland Sellers, African American students returned to the bowling alley in larger numbers. They were confronted by local police, who beat several male and female students in the resulting brawl. South Carolina State College students organized a grievance committee the next day and planned a march on city hall and a boycott of local businesses unless their demands were met. As tension mounted, Governor Robert McNair sent national guardsmen to supplement the state highway patrolmen who were already in Orangeburg.

On 8 February, President M. Maceo Nance ordered South Carolina State College students to remain on the campus. That evening, as some of the students tried to start a bonfire at the edge of the campus near the highway patrolmen's command post, a fencepost was thrown and struck a patrol officer. Thinking that he had been shot, other patrolmen began firing on the students. Three students were killed and several dozen others were wounded. Although the white press claimed that there had been an exchange of shots, later investigations proved that the students had not fired any weapons. Governor McNair declared a state of emergency in Orangeburg. Nine patrolmen were tried for their role in the killings, but they were found not guilty. Cleveland Sellers was arrested and found guilty of inciting to riot, although his sentence was eventually commuted. Subsequent legal action forced the desegregation of Harry Floyd's bowling alley.

P

PALMER v. THOMPSON, 403 U.S. 217 (1971). A case in which the Supreme Court decided that segregated facilities which were closed to everyone were not a denial of the equal protection rights of African American citizens.

When a federal district court ruled that all public facilities in Jackson, Mississippi, must be open to black and white citizens alike, city officials claimed that they could no longer guarantee security at the city's public swimming pools. They sold four of the pools and leased a fifth pool to the YMCA, which continued to operate it for white people only. Claiming that closing of the pools denied them equal protection of the law, Palmer and other African American plaintiffs sued Jackson's mayor, Allen Thompson. Federal district and appeals courts found in favor of Mayor

Thompson. The plaintiffs appealed to the Supreme Court and, on 14 June 1971, the lower courts' ruling was sustained by a narrow five-to-four majority. There was no discrimination as such against black citizens, said Justice Hugo Black for the Court's majority, when the pools were closed to all the citizens.

PALMORE v. SIDOTI, 466 U.S. 429 (1984). A case in which the Supreme Court reaffirmed its finding in *Loving v. Virginia* (q.v.) that state laws against interracial marriages were unconstitutional.

When Anthony and Linda Sidoti, a Florida couple, were divorced, a Florida court awarded custody of their daughter to Linda Sidoti. Subsequently, Mrs. Sidoti met and moved in with an African American man, Clarence Palmore, Jr. Anthony Sidoti sued his former wife for custody of their daughter, claiming that housing her in a black man's home was traumatic. When lower courts sided with Mr. Sidoti's claim, Palmore and Mrs. Sidoti appealed to the Supreme Court. The social pressures on a child living with an interracial couple may be very difficult, Chief Justice Warren Burger acknowledged in a unanimous Court verdict, but they were unacceptable grounds for denying Mrs. Sidoti custodial rights to her daughter. To rule otherwise, he argued, would reinstitute racial segregation in housing and deny Mrs. Sidoti the equal protection of the law.

PARKS, ROSA MCCAULEY (1913–   ). Civil rights activist.

Rosa Parks was born on 4 February 1913 in Tuskegee, Alabama. Her father was a carpenter. She attended local public schools for African American children until 1924, when she was sent to Montgomery to attend a private school for African American children. Rosa McCauley graduated from a Montgomery high school in 1931 and, eventually, took some courses at Alabama State College in Montgomery. She married a local barber, Raymond Parks, in 1932 and, during her married life, Rosa Parks worked as a clerk and a seamstress. She became active in civic affairs, joining the Montgomery branch of the National Association for the Advancement of Colored People (NAACP; q.v.) in 1943, registering to vote in 1945, and joining the Montgomery Voters League. She was advisor to the NAACP's Montgomery youth council and served as secretary of both the Montgomery branch and the state conference of branches of the NAACP.

On 1 December 1955, Rosa Parks was riding a city bus home from her work as a seamstress. When additional white passengers boarded the bus, the bus driver asked her to give up her seat to a white passenger and move to the back of the bus. Tired from a long day's work, Parks refused. She was arrested and jailed. E. D. Nixon (q.v.) and Clifford J. Durr (q.v.) came to the jail to bail her out. As news of her arrest swept through black Montgomery, members of the Women's Political Council and of the Interdenominational Ministerial Alliance organized a one-day boycott of the city's buses on 5 December. When it succeeded beyond expectations, they organized the Montgomery Improvement Association (MIA; q.v.), which sustained the Montgomery Bus Boycott (q.v.) for a year, until the Supreme Court found segregation on Montgomery's city buses unconstitutional in *Browder v. Gayle* (q.v.). In 1957, Rosa Parks and her family left Montgomery for Detroit, Michigan. There she worked in the office of United States representative John Conyers. The quiet lady from Montgomery continues to be a powerful symbol of African American resistance to oppression.

PARRIS, ROBERT. *See* **Robert Moses.**

PASADENA BOARD OF EDUCATION v. SPANGLER, 427 U.S. 424 (1976). A case in which the Supreme Court held that, once a school district had been desegregated, it was not necessary to modify its school attendance policies.

In 1968, African American students in Pasadena, California, sued their school board for operating racially segregated schools. The "resegregation" of Pasadena's public schools occurred, in part at least, from "white flight" out of the area and minority groups, including African Americans, moving into it. In 1970, a federal district court ordered the Pasadena school board to submit a desegregation plan in which no school had a majority of its students from an ethnic minority group. The board was ordered to review its plan annually in order to guarantee continuing compliance with the court order. In 1974, noting that the court order implied a perpetual supervision of Pasadena's public schools to monitor racial segregation deriving from demographic changes over which the school board had no control, the Pasadena school board asked the district court to modify its orders.

When the district court refused to modify its orders, the school board went to the Ninth Circuit Court of Appeals. While also refusing to modify the district court order, the appeals court held that the district court should not attempt to supervise Pasadena's public schools in perpetuity. When the school board took the case to the Supreme Court, it overruled the lower courts by a six-to-two vote, with Justices Thurgood Marshall and William J. Brennan in dissent. Once Pasadena's public schools were desegregated, said Chief Justice William Rehnquist for the Court majority, the school board was not obliged to adjust its school attendance policies annually in a vain attempt to compensate for normal patterns of human migration which were not a function of any official action. Justices Brennan and Marshall, in dissent, held that, due to the school board's lack of cooperation, Pasadena's public schools had never really been desegregated.

PATTON v. MISSISSIPPI, 332 U.S. 463 (1947). A case in which the Supreme Court held that the systematic exclusion of African Americans from grand or trial court juries was grounds for the dismissal of convictions of African American defendants.

Eddie "Buster" Patton, an African American, was indicted by an all-white grand jury and convicted of the first degree murder of a white man by an all-white trial court jury in Lauderdale County, Mississippi. The Mississippi supreme court refused to consider evidence that no African American had served on a Lauderdale County grand jury or trial court jury as reason for quashing Patton's indictment or reversing his conviction because of violations of his equal protection rights under the Fourteenth Amendment. NAACP (q.v.) attorneys, led by Thurgood Marshall (q.v.), made that case before the United States Supreme Court. Mississippi's attorney general argued that juries were selected from voter registration lists and that, since few or no African American people were registered to vote in Lauderdale County, there was no racial discrimination in the makeup of the county's grand or trial juries. Writing for a unanimous Supreme Court, Justice Hugo Black held that "the fact that no Negro had served on a criminal court grand or petit jury for a period of 30 years created a strong presumption that Negroes were systematically excluded from jury service because of race." Patton might be reindicted and retried, Black said, but only by juries more representative of the community.

PEONAGE. The holding of a person in bondage or in coerced labor for the payment of a debt.

In spite of the Thirteenth Amendment and the federal government's Peonage Abolition Act of 1867, peonage, debt bondage, or forced labor for the discharge of a debt was common in the post-Reconstruction rural South. Early in the twentieth century, peonage drew widespread attention as a new form of bondage in the rural South. In *Clyatt v. United States* (1905), the United States Supreme Court seemed to find peonage an acceptable means of debt collection. In an important subsequent series of cases, *Bailey v. Alabama* (1911), *United States v. Reynolds* (1914), *Taylor v. Georgia* (q.v.; 1942), and *Pollock v. Williams* (q.v.; 1944), however, the Court reversed course. The Justice Department filed some peonage cases in the 1950s. Thereafter, practices in some migrant labor camps appeared to verge on peonage, but the practice of peonage largely disappeared in the post–World War II era.

PETERSON v. CITY OF GREENVILLE, 373 U.S. 244 (1963). A case in which the Supreme Court held that African American patrons who protested segregated dining facilities could not be arrested for trespass if city law required racially segregated dining facilities.

James Richard Peterson and nine other African American youths sat in at the S. H. Kress lunch counter in Greenville, South Carolina, on 9 August 1960. Ordered to leave, they refused, were arrested by Greenville policemen, and were convicted of trespass by a local court. When Peterson and the others appealed their convictions to the United States Supreme Court, the convictions were reversed by an eight-to-one Court majority. Speaking for the majority, Chief Justice Earl Warren noted that the defendants were refused service because of their race and that the city's racial segregation ordinance made their exclusion a violation of their equal protection rights under the Fourteenth Amendment. Greenville's racial segregation ordinance was unconstitutional, said Warren, and its police could not constitutionally be used to enforce segregation in public accommodations or private businesses.

POLL TAX. A tax, commonly levied by the state, on the right or privilege of voting.

When Reconstruction amendments to the United States Constitution guaranteed African American men access to the ballot box equal to that of white men, Southern states commonly imposed a poll tax on voting rights. Men who were otherwise qualified to vote, but who failed to pay their annual poll tax, were barred from voting. The nominal annual fee of $1 to $3 tended to discourage impoverished black and white men from voting. After the enfranchisement of women, Southern states commonly continued to impose the poll tax, thus discouraging impoverished women, black and white, from voting. In 1937, the United States Supreme Court held in *Breedlove v. Suttles* that the imposition of a poll tax, equitably administered, violated no constitutional right. Thus, poll taxes continued in many Southern states in the post–World War II era and were not finally abolished until the ratification of the Twenty-fourth Amendment in 1964, passage of the Civil Rights Act of 1964 (q.v.) and the Voting Rights Act of 1965 (q.v.), and the Supreme Court's decisions in *Harman v. Forssenius* (q.v.) in 1965 and *Harper v. Virginia Board of Elections* (q.v.) in 1966.

POLLOCK v. WILLIAMS, 322 U.S. 4 (1944). A case in which the Supreme Court sustained federal anti-peonage legislation.

James Pollock, an African American who lived in Florida, agreed to do a job for a $5 advance wage. He failed to do the work and was subsequently arrested, convicted, and jailed. His breach of contract, held the trial court, was prima facie evidence of an intent to defraud his employer. Pollock then sued Williams, his jailer, for holding him in violation of federal antipeonage legislation and Supreme Court decisions in *Bailey v. Alabama* (1911), *United States v. Reynolds* (1914) and *Taylor v. Georgia* (q.v.; 1942). After a circuit court reversed the trial court's decision, the Florida supreme court reversed the circuit court's decision. Pollock appealed to the United States Supreme Court. Justice Robert Jackson wrote the Supreme Court's decision which reversed the Florida supreme court's judgment and found the Florida law under which Pollock was convicted unconstitutional. "A statute which makes guilty of a misdemeanor any person who, with intent to defraud, obtains an advance upon an agreement to render services, and which provides further that failure to perform the services for which the advance was obtained shall be prima facie evidence of intent to defraud," said Jackson, violates the Thirteenth Amendment and federal antipeonage legislation.

POOR PEOPLE'S MARCH ON WASHINGTON (Poor People's Campaign; 1968). The last of the civil rights movement's five marches on Washington between 1957 and 1968.

The Poor People's March on Washington had its origin in the growing conviction of Martin Luther King (q.v.) after 1965 that the movement must turn its attention to the problem of poverty in the United States. By November 1967, the idea of organizing poor people to march on Washington to encamp and, if necessary, engage in civil disobedience there until the government adopted policies and programs to offer them a more hopeful future had begun to take shape in his discussions with SCLC (q.v.) associates. In January 1968, King announced that the minimal demands of the Poor People's March on Washington would be: a full-employment economic policy, a guaranteed annual income, and funds for the construction of 500,000 units of low-cost housing per year. Yet, he entered the campaign with a larger sense of its likely failure than ever before. CORE (q.v.), the NAACP (q.v.), SNCC (q.v.), and the National Urban League (q.v.) offered no support of SCLC's Poor People's March on Washington and Bayard Rustin (q.v.), who had organized the previous marches, was publicly critical of plans for this one. In March, at the urgent request of James Lawson (q.v.), King went to Memphis, Tennessee, in support of the city sanitation workers' strike. When a King-led demonstration on 28 March in Memphis broke up in violence, the media began predicting a similar end for the Poor People's March on Washington. A week later, King returned to Memphis and was assassinated there on 4 April.

As King's successor, Ralph D. Abernathy (q.v.) decided to push ahead with plans for the Poor People's March on Washington. King's death prompted much more support for the march than had been apparent before 4 April. Buses full of poor people began arriving in Washington on 11 May. Robert Kennedy and Coretta Scott King addressed the SCLC's poor people on 12 May. The demonstrators' quarters, Resurrection City, a town of canvas, plywood, and tarpaper near the Washington Monument, was intended to dramatize the plight of the poor. Rain turned it into a muddy, squalid center of petty crime. In early June, Bayard Rustin (q.v.) was briefly brought in to organize plans for a massive rally on 19 June, but his earlier criticism of plans for the march and his attempt to redefine its goals alienated the SCLC staff. He was replaced by Sterling Tucker of the Washington bureau of the Urban League. "Solidarity Day" on 19 June attracted 50,000 people. Five days later, when the march's camping permit expired, District of Columbia police moved in to raze Resurrection City. Abernathy and 300 other marchers were arrested when they marched on the Capitol to protest the police action. Shortly thereafter, SCLC evacuated Washington, D.C., with a few minor concessions from several federal agencies.

PORTSMITH, VIRGINIA, SIT-IN MOVEMENT. *See* **Tidewater, Virginia, Sit-In Movement.**

POWELL, ADAM CLAYTON, JR. (1908–72). Pastor and politician.
Adam Clayton Powell, Jr., was born on 29 November 1908 in New Haven, Connecticut. His father, the Reverend Adam Clayton Powell,

moved the family to New York City, where the elder Powell became the pastor of Abyssinian Baptist Church. Young Powell attended public schools in New York City and the City College of New York before completing his B.A. at Colgate University in 1930. Thereafter, he earned an M.A. in religious education at Columbia University in 1932. He received the first of several honorary degrees, a D.D. from Shaw University, in 1935. In 1930, young Powell began working with his father as assistant manager of Abyssinian Baptist Church. During the depression, he organized private relief efforts in black Manhattan and fought to protect the jobs and extend the employment of black professional people and workers in the city.

When his father retired from the pulpit of Abyssinian Baptist Church in 1936, the congregation chose Adam Clayton Powell, Jr., to succeed him. Powell, Jr., was elected to New York's city council in 1941. In 1944, he was elected to the United States House of Representatives from New York City. Powell would serve eleven successive terms in that position, leaving office, finally, in 1971. During his years in office, Powell succeeded in desegregating congressional dining facilities and winning admission of black journalists to the press galleries. He fought for federal antilynching and anti-poll tax legislation and an end to racial discrimination in the armed forces. Powell won the passage of legislation to deny federal money to any project that practiced racial discrimination. As chairman of the House Committee on Education and Labor from 1960 to 1967, he spearheaded the adoption of antipoverty and minimum wage legislation.

A flamboyant preacher and politician, who made many enemies over the years, Powell was criticized for mismanaging public money and taking excessively expensive trips at public expense. By 1966, he was avoiding trips to his congressional district, where he was wanted for his refusal to pay a judgment for slander. In March 1967, the House of Representatives ousted him from his congressional seat. When he won a special election to choose his successor the next month, the House of Representatives refused to let him take his seat. Powell was reelected in 1968, but he refused to take his seat when congressional colleagues stripped him of his seniority. In 1970, Powell was defeated for renomination in the Democratic primary and as an independent candidate in the general election by Charles Rangel. His career in politics over, Powell retired as pastor of Abyssinian Baptist Church at the end of 1971. After suffering a heart attack, he died on 4 April 1972.

PRAYER PILGRIMAGE TO WASHINGTON (1957). The first of the civil rights movement's five marches on Washington between 1957 and 1968.

Early in 1957, civil rights leaders were irritated by the Eisenhower administration's failure to address civil rights issues or to meet with them. The idea for a march on Washington originated within the fledgling SCLC (q.v.) and won support from A. Philip Randolph (q.v.) and Roy Wilkins (q.v.) of the NAACP (q.v.). Bayard Rustin (q.v.) did much of the work coordinating preparations for the Prayer Pilgrimage. Held on the third anniversary of the Supreme Court's decision in *Brown v. Board of Education* (q.v.), 17 May 1957, the Prayer Pilgrimage was intended to demonstrate black unity, Northern support for civil rights, protest of attacks on the NAACP by several Southern states, protest racial violence in the South, and support for the passage of the Civil Rights Act of 1957 (q.v.). Randolph presided over the event. It featured appearances by Harry Belafonte, Sammy Davis, Ruby Dee, Mahalia Jackson, Sidney Poitier, and Jackie Robinson and speeches by Mordecai Johnson, Adam Clayton Powell (q.v.), Fred Shuttlesworth (q.v.), and Roy Wilkins. Martin Luther King (q.v.) spoke at the end of the program and his cry "Give us the ballot" was the message from the Prayer Pilgrimage that caught the attention of the press. Although its organizers hoped for a crowd of 50,000 people, estimates of the actual attendance ranged from 15,000 to 27,000.

R

RANDOLPH, ASA PHILIP (1889–1979). Civil rights activist and labor leader.

A. Philip Randolph was born on 15 April 1889 in Crescent City, Florida. The sons of a Methodist minister, young Randolph and an older brother attended Cookman Institute in Jacksonville, Florida. A. Philip Randolph graduated from the Methodist elementary and secondary mission school in 1907. After holding a series of odd jobs in Florida, Randolph moved to New York City. Working as an elevator operator, a porter, and a waiter during the day, he attended classes at the City College of New York at night. After he met Chandler Owen, a black law student at Columbia University, they founded a Harlem employment agency called the Brotherhood of Labor and sought to organize black workers. In November 1917, Owen and Randolph launched *The Messenger,* a radical black newspaper. Backing black labor unions, the Russian Revolution, socialism, and women's suffrage, it attacked capitalism, Garveyism, the racism of President Woodrow Wilson's administration, World War I and, occasionally, the National Association for the Advancement of Colored People (NAACP; q.v.) and older black leaders as puppets of white authority. By the 1920s, when it was a vehicle for Harlem's cultural renaissance, Randolph's newspaper was critical of the Russian Revolution's brutality. *The Messenger* survived until 1928, when financial difficulties forced its closure.

Angered by the treatment of black Pullman car porters and maids, A. Philip Randolph organized the Brotherhood of Pullman Car Porters and Maids in 1925. Randolph struggled with the Pullman Car Company and white labor unions to win recognition for his union. After the adoption of federal legislation protecting the right of laboring men and women to organize, Randolph's union won recognition when the Pullman company signed a union contract in 1937. Four years later, Randolph summoned 100,000 African Americans to march on Washington in protest of employment discrimination. On 25 June, a week before the March was to occur, President Franklin Roosevelt signed Executive Order 8802 (q.v.), banning discrimination based on race, color, creed, or national origin in the federal government, the armed forces, and defense industries and establishing a Fair Employment Practice Committee (q.v.) to oversee the policy. Only then did Randolph cancel the March on Washington. Through World War II and the early postwar years, he lobbied the Roosevelt and Truman administrations to end racial segregation in the armed forces.

Randolph led the Brotherhood of Pullman Car Porters and Maids into the merger of the American Federation of Labor (AF of L) and the Congress of Industrial Organizations (CIO) in 1955 and was an original member of the AFL-CIO executive council. In 1957, he became an AFL-CIO vice president. Randolph believed that African American interests were best served by solidarity with the labor movement, that those interests were often ill-served by the bourgeois leadership of the American labor movement, and that black Americans must become a more powerful force within organized labor. Thus, in 1960, Randolph organized the Negro American Labor Council. The AFL-CIO leadership censured Randolph for dividing black and white workers by giving black workers a voice separate from the AFL-CIO leadership, but Randolph was undaunted. He organized the Prayer Pilgrimage to Washington (q.v.) in 1957 and the Youth Marches for Integrated Schools (q.v.) in 1958 and 1959. By 1963, when he was the national director for the March on Washington (q.v.), A. Philip Randolph was widely regarded as the elder statesman of African American civil rights leaders. Two years later, he secured AFL-CIO funding for the A. Philip Randolph Institute in New York. Directed by Bayard Rustin (q.v.), the institute was a black think tank, which studied living and working conditions for African Americans. Randolph died on 16 May 1979.

RAUH, JOSEPH LOUIS, JR. (1911–92). Civil liberties attorney and civil rights activist.

Joseph Rauh, Jr., was born on 3 January 1911 in Cincinnati, Ohio. He attended Harvard University and graduated magna cum laude with a major in economics. Rauh then entered Harvard's law school and graduated in 1935. In his first position, he was law clerk to Supreme Court justices Benjamin Cardozo and Felix Frankfurter. He served as counsel to several New Deal agencies and to the Lend Lease Administration. In 1941, he helped to draft Executive Order 8802 (q.v.), which banned employment discrimination and established the Fair Employment Practice Committee (q.v.). During World War II, Rauh served as an aide to General Douglas MacArthur in the Pacific. After the war, he returned to Washington, going into private practice and specializing in civil liberties law. In the postwar "red scare," his clients included Lillian Hellman, Arthur Miller, and Joseph A. "Jock" Yablonski of the United Mine Workers. He was a founding member of Americans for Democratic Action (ADA).

At the 1948 Democratic National Convention, Rauh and others led the fight to adopt a civil rights plank in the platform that drove Southern white Democrats to walk out of the convention to form the States Rights Party. During the 1960s, he served as counsel to the Leadership Conference on Civil Rights, the Freedom Riders (q.v.), and the Mississippi Freedom Democratic Party (q.v.). In the latter capacity, Rauh alienated many MFDP activists by urging them to accept the compromise offer of two votes at the Democratic National Convention in 1964. He continued to be active for another 25 years and testified before the Senate Judiciary Committee against all of the Reagan and Bush administrations' nominees to the Supreme Court during the 1980s. He died in Washington on 3 September 1992.

REEB, JAMES J. (1927–65). Unitarian minister and civil rights activist.

James Reeb was born on 1 January 1927 in Wichita, Kansas, the son of Harry D. Reeb, a prosperous oil-well equipment dealer. In young Reeb's youth, the Reebs moved to Casper, Wyoming, where he attended public schools. After graduating from high school, he entered the United States Army in June 1945. Discharged in 1946, he entered St. Olaf College in Northfield, Minnesota. After earning his undergraduate degree in 1950, Reeb entered Princeton Theological Seminary, graduating in 1953. Ordained in the Presbyterian ministry in Casper, he began graduate study in theology at Temple University's Conwell School of Theology and served as assistant chaplain at the Philadelphia General Hospital. After a period of doubt, Reeb left the Presbyterian ministry to become a Unitarian. He directed the youth division of the West Branch YMCA in Philadelphia and then became assistant pastor of All Souls Unitarian-Universalist Church in Washington, D.C.

In Washington, Reeb urged white churches to remain in the city to serve black residents and organized the [Howard] University Neighborhood Council, which later became the United Planning Organization, an affiliate of federal antipoverty programs. In September 1964, Reeb moved to Boston as director of the American Friends Service Committee's Metropolitan Boston Low-Income Housing Program, a neighborhood action program with offices in Dorchester, Roxbury and the South End. Moved by the violence of Alabama state police on "Bloody Sunday," 7 March 1965, Reeb left for Selma the next day. On Tuesday, 9 March, he marched with Martin Luther King (q.v.) across Selma's Edmund Pettus Bridge and, with King, turned back to Selma. That evening he had dinner with other ministers at the Silver Moon Cafe, a black diner. As they left the cafe, four white men attacked them. Reeb suffered multiple skull fractures, resulting in a blood clot on the left side of his brain. There were delays in transporting him to a Birmingham hospital and he died on 11 March 1965.

REITMAN v. MULKEY, 387 U.S. 369 (1967). A case in which the Supreme Court found a California constitutional amendment on the rental or sale of housing unconstitutional.

In 1964, California voters passed Proposition 14, which amended the state constitution to prevent the state from interfering with the right of property owners to rent, lease, or sell their property to persons of their own choosing. Subsequently, an African American couple, the Mulkeys, claimed that they had been denied the rental of an apartment by the Reitmans solely because of their race. The Mulkeys sued, claiming that the constitutional amendment violated the equal protection clause of the Fourteenth Amendment and sections 51 and 52 of the California Civil Code. The Reitmans claimed that the constitutional amendment superseded sections 51 and 52 of the California code. A California trial court threw the Mulkeys' claim out of court, but they appealed. The California supreme court ruled that the state constitutional amendment violated the Fourteenth Amendment. On 29 May 1967, Justice Byron White wrote the opinion for a Supreme Court majority of five which sustained the decision of California's supreme court. Justices Hugo Black, Tom Clark, John Marshall Harlan, and Potter Stewart, in dissent, held that the equal protection clause allows individuals acting on their own to discriminate on racial grounds.

RESURRECTION CITY. *See* **Poor People's March on Washington.**

REYNOLDS, A JUDGE v. SIMS, 377 U.S. 533 (1964). A case in which the Supreme Court held that a reapportionment of state legislatures which disenfranchises any citizen is unconstitutional and that federal courts had the authority to prevent it.

In 1962, the Supreme Court held in *Baker v. Carr* (q.v.) that federal courts had the authority to examine the constitutionality of state legislative reapportionments. Urban voters in Georgia quickly challenged that state's county unit system in *Gray v. Sanders.* In Alabama, African American voters who believed that legislative districts left them underrepresented filed suit to test the constitutionality of the state's legislative apportionments. In 1962, when a three-judge federal panel required the state to reapportion legislative districts, it was not satisfied that the state's new map of legislative districts met the equal representation requirement. State officials appealed to the Supreme Court by suing one of the federal judges. Grouped with several others deriving from Alabama's reapportionment problems, this case was heard by the Supreme Court in 1963. On 15 June 1964, the Court issued a ruling that the federal district court was correct in finding both Alabama reapportionment plans in violation of the equal protection clause of the Fourteenth Amendment.

RICE v. ARNOLD, 340 U.S. 848 (1950). A case in which the Supreme Court ordered Florida's supreme court to review segregation in Miami's public accommodations.

African American golfers in Miami, Florida, had access to the city's public golf course only on Monday. White golfers had the course to themselves for the other six days of the week. Joseph Rice, a black Miamian, believed that this restriction violated his Fourteenth Amendment equal protection right of access to public accommodations. When he sued H. H. Arnold, the superintendent of the Miami Springs Country Club, Rice's claim was denied in a lower court. He appealed to the Supreme Court, which ordered Florida's supreme court to examine the case in the light of the Supreme Court's recent decisions in *Sweatt v. Painter* (q.v.) and *McLaurin v. Oklahoma State Regents* (q.v.). Florida's supreme court decided that the stark inequalities in segregated public higher education in those two cases were not found in this case. The Florida court reasoned, in the first place, that Rice and other black golfers in Miami had access to the same golf course as white golfers and, in the second place, that the Supreme Court had not yet turned its back on the "separate but equal" doctrine of the *Plessy v. Ferguson* precedent. It rejected Rice's petition, therefore, because it did not properly raise issues of access to equal facilities and because it challenged local laws which were not held to be unconstitutional. The Supreme Court then refused to hear Rice's appeal of the Florida court's decision.

RICE v. ELMORE, 165 F.2d 387 (4th Cir., 1947). A case in which the Fourth Circuit Court of Appeals extended the Supreme Court's ruling in *Smith v. Allwright* (q.v.) that party primaries were public events from which African Americans could not be excluded.

In 1944, the Supreme Court ruled in *Smith v. Allwright* that the Democratic Party in Texas could not exclude African Americans from voting in its primary elections. South Carolina lawmakers then reasoned that if the state had no rules regulating primary elections they would be private affairs operating outside the scope of the Fifteenth Amendment's bar against racial discrimination in the free exercise of the suffrage. Thus, the South Carolina legislature dispensed with all state laws relating to primary elections. George Elmore, a black South Carolinian, who was represented by Thurgood Marshall (q.v.) of the NAACP Legal Defense and Educational Fund (LDEF; q.v.) challenged the legislature's action in *Rice v. Elmore.* Federal District Judge Julius Waties Waring (q.v.) ruled in Elmore's favor, asserting that black people were entitled to participate in the Democratic primary as long as it was effectively the state's only election. Fourth Circuit Court of Appeals Judge John J. Parker upheld Waring's ruling and the Supreme Court refused to hear an appeal. In August 1948, 35,000 African American voters participated in South Carolina's Democratic primary.

RICHARDSON, GLORIA HAYES (Gloria St. Clair Hayes Richardson Dandridge; 1922–   ). Civil rights activist.

Gloria Hayes Richardson was born on 6 May 1922 in Baltimore, Maryland. She was the only child of John Edwards Hayes, a successful pharmacist, and Mabel St. Clair Hayes. In 1928, the Hayes family moved to Cambridge, Maryland, where Gloria Hayes's maternal grandfather, H. Maynadier St. Clair, served on the Cambridge city council from 1912 to 1946. She graduated from Frederick Douglass High School in Cambridge and Howard University. She married and gave birth to a daughter, Donna. Cambridge was still rigidly segregated; poverty and unemployment were widespread among the one-third of its citizens who were African Americans. Inspired by the example of young Freedom Riders and sit-in demonstrators from New York and Baltimore, Gloria Richardson and members of the St. Clair family formed the core of the Cambridge Nonviolent Action Committee (CNAC) in 1962. It was cochaired by Richardson and Inez Grubb. They won outside support from the Student Nonviolent Coordinating Committee (SNCC; q.v.).

On 25 March 1963, Richardson asked that the city council desegregate the city. Days later, students from Baltimore, Philadelphia, and New York joined black residents of Cambridge in an economic boycott, marches, picket lines, and sit-ins. Richardson was among the 80 demonstrators arrested within seven weeks. Early in May 1963, they were tried, convicted, given suspended sentences, and fined a penny each. Richardson then renewed the demonstrations. On 14 May, 62 demonstrators, including Richardson, her mother, and her daughter were arrested. White authorities agreed to release them and establish a human relations committee to prepare to implement the demonstrators' demands. Richardson vowed to continue the demonstrations until the demands were met. Believing that white authorities in Cambridge had violated constitutional rights of local activists, she asked Attorney General Robert Kennedy to intercede.

On 11 June, windows of white-owned stores were broken and shots were exchanged. The governor declared martial law in Cambridge three days later and national guardsmen surrounded black neighborhoods. The guardsmen were withdrawn a month later, demonstrations were renewed, and violence broke out again. The guardsmen returned to Cambridge, negotiations with state officials broke down, and Richardson was arrested again. On 22 July, Attorney General Robert Kennedy interceded to negotiate commitments to desegregate public accommodations and schools, a public housing project, and a biracial commission to deal with issues of jobs and poverty. Desegregation of public accommodations in Cambridge was delayed until June 1964, when President Lyndon Johnson signed the Civil Rights Act of 1964 (q.v.) into law. Two months later, Gloria Richardson left Cambridge to marry Frank Dandridge and live in New York. There, she has worked with the city's Department of Aging.

RICHMOND v. UNITED STATES. *See* **City of Richmond v. United States.**

RIVES, RICHARD TAYLOR (1895–1982). A member of the Fifth Circuit Court of Appeals (q.v.).

Richard Taylor Rives was born on 15 January 1895 in Montgomery, Alabama. He was educated in Montgomery's public schools. In 1911, Rives entered Tulane University in New Orleans on scholarship, but he left it after a year for financial reasons. After studying law with Montgomery attorney Wiley Hill, Rives was admitted to the Alabama bar in 1914. He served as president of both the Montgomery and the Alabama bar associations. During the 1940s, Rives's son, who was studying in the North for a career in the law, encouraged his father to read Gunnar Myrdal's *An American Dilemma* (q.v.). President Harry Truman appointed Rives to the Fifth Circuit Court of Appeals in 1951. From 1960 until his retirement in 1966, Rives served as its chief judge. A close friend of Supreme Court Justice Hugo Black, Rives became allied with Fifth Circuit Court of Appeals judges John Robert Brown (q.v.), Elbert Tuttle (q.v.), and John Minor Wisdom (q.v.) to ensure that the Supreme Court's mandate in *Brown v. Board of Education* would be implemented in the Deep South and in expanding it to secure equal justice for African Americans in employment, jury selection, and voting rights. Richard Taylor Rives died on 27 October 1982.

ROBESON, PAUL BUSTILL (1898–1976). Actor, singer, and civil rights activist.

Paul Robeson was born on 9 April 1898 in Princeton, New Jersey. His father, William Drew Robeson, was a runaway North Carolina slave who served in the Union Army and worked his way through Lincoln University to become the pastor of Witherspoon Street Presbyterian Church in Princeton. His mother, Maria Louisa Bustill Robeson, gave birth to five children before she died in 1904 from burns suffered in a house fire. In 1909, William Drew Robeson moved his family to Somerville, New Jersey, where he was pastor of St. Thomas A.M.E. Zion Church. Paul Robeson graduated from Somerville High School and entered Rutgers College in 1915 on a scholarship. He was a scholar-athlete, earning 13 letters in baseball, basketball, football, and track, entering Phi Beta Kappa as a junior and graduating as class valedictorian in 1919. His senior thesis was on "The Fourteenth Amendment, the Sleeping Giant of the American Constitution." Robeson moved to Harlem, entered law school at Columbia University, and played professional football to pay his way through school. After graduating in 1923, he practiced law briefly with a white law firm, but resigned in protest when a white secretary refused to take dictation from him.

Robeson's career as an actor and vocalist began with appearances in *Taboo* (1922), two plays by Eugene O'Neill, *All God's Chillun* and *The Emperor Jones* (1925), and concerts of black spirituals and folk songs. From 1927 to 1939, he lived and worked primarily in Europe, appearing in concerts across the continent, including the Soviet Union, and identifying the black freedom struggle with that of working class people everywhere. On the American stage and screen, he starred in wide-ranging productions of *Othello, Porgy and Bess,* and *Show Boat* and won a Donaldson Award for best acting performance of the year and the American Academy of Arts and Sciences' Gold Medal Award. Widely acclaimed during the "united front" period in the 1930s and during World War II, Robeson's political loyalties became suspect in the post–World War II era. In 1947, for example, Adolphe Menjou testified before the House Un-American Activities Committee that government agents could assume that anyone who attended a Robeson concert or bought his records was a Communist. From 1950 to 1958, he was denied a passport to travel abroad because he refused to deny that he was a member of the Communist Party. Robeson spent his last years traveling, writing, and giving occasional public lectures. He died on 23 January 1976.

ROBINSON, AMELIA BOYNTON *See* **Amelia Boynton.**

ROBINSON, JO ANN OOIMAN GIBSON (1912–   ).

Jo Ann Gibson Robinson was born on 17 April 1912 near Culloden, Georgia. She was the youngest of six boys and six girls born to Owen Boston Gibson and Dollie Webb Gibson. The Gibsons farmed their own land, but after Owen Gibson's death in 1918, Dollie Gibson sold the farm. With her younger children, she moved to Macon to live with an older son. Jo Ann Gibson attended Macon's public schools for African American youth and graduated as valedictorian from high school. The first in her family to finish college, she earned a B.S. from nearby Fort Valley State College and began teaching public school in Macon. There, she married Wilbur Robinson, but after the death of their only child in infancy the marriage ended. After teaching for five years in Macon, Jo Ann Robinson moved to Atlanta and earned an M.A. in English at Atlanta University. Later, she had additional graduate study at Teachers College of Columbia University and at the University of Southern California. In 1949, after a year chairing the English department at Mary Allen College in Crockett, Texas, Robinson accepted a position in the English department at Alabama State College in Montgomery. There, she joined Dexter Avenue Baptist Church and the Women's Political Council (WPC). During the Christmas season in 1949, Robinson was humiliated on a bus in Montgomery and resolved to work to improve conditions on the city's buses for African Americans.

Five years later, as president of the WPC, Robinson lobbied the city government for those improvements. When Rosa Parks was arrested on 1 December 1955 for refusing to yield her seat to a white passenger, Robinson mass-produced and distributed the leaflets that launched the Montgomery Bus Boycott (q.v.). She was one of the most active members of the executive committee of the Montgomery Improvement Association (MIA; q.v.), which was created to direct the boycott; she edited the MIA's newsletter and was among those arrested and charged with conducting an illegal boycott. Although she attempted to remain in the background in order to protect her colleagues at Alabama State College, Robinson was one of the civil rights activists who was forced to leave its faculty in 1960. She taught for a year at Grambling College in Grambling, Louisiana, and then moved to Los Angeles, where she taught English in public schools until she retired in 1976. In 1987, her memoir, *The Montgomery Bus Boycott and the Women Who Started It,* was published. For the first time, it recognized the crucial role women played in launching and sustaining the bus boycott. Her health was deteriorating seriously when the book was published. In 1989, when the Southern Association of Women Historians honored her with a publication prize, Jo Ann Robinson was unable to accept it in person.

ROBINSON, RUBY DORIS (Ruby Doris Smith-Robinson; 1942–67). Civil rights activist.

Ruby Doris Smith was born on 25 April 1942 in Atlanta, Georgia. She was the second of seven children born to Alice and J. T. Smith in Atlanta's Summerhill neighborhood. Despite the security of family and a separate black community, Smith was aware of another, a hostile white community. "My only involvement was in throwing rocks at them," she remembered. A strong student, she graduated from Atlanta's public schools for African American youth and entered Spelman College in 1960. As early as February 1961, Smith was active in local desegregation efforts with SNCC (q.v.). She participated in the early Freedom Rides (q.v.) and helped to shape SNCC's "jail, no bail" policy. Smith's bold attitudes and actions made her a leader in the Atlanta student movement and SNCC. By 1963, she was a member of its central office staff.

After graduating from Spelman with a major in physical education in 1964, she married Clifford Robinson and, a year later, they had a son, Kenneth Toure Robinson. Marriage and motherhood did not tame her spirit. In the fall of 1964, when a delegation of SNCC staff members was to board a plane for Africa, an airline representative said that the flight was overbooked and asked them to wait for another flight. Without consulting the others, Robinson sat in on the runway and refused to move until the SNCC delegation was assured of passage on the flight. "You could feel her power in SNCC on a daily basis," recalled one of SNCC's freedom singers. She had a "100 percent effective shit detector," said a member of its research staff. In 1966, when James Forman resigned as SNCC's executive secretary, Ruby Doris Robinson was elected his successor. Her health deteriorated soon thereafter. Admitted to the hospital in January 1967, she was diagnosed with terminal cancer in April. Ruby Doris Robinson died on 9 October 1967.

ROBINSON v. FLORIDA, 378 U.S. 153 (1964). A case in which the Supreme Court held that state action in support of private racial discrimination was unconstitutional.

In Miami, Florida, Robinson and 17 other students staged a sit-in at a Shell's City Restaurant, which was segregated. When the manager asked the students to leave, they refused. They were arrested and charged with violation of section 509.141 of the Florida Statutes. It allowed a manager to ask undesired customers to leave the premises of his or her store. At their trial, the manager said that the black customers were welcome in all other sections of Shell's Department Store, but that the cafeteria was only for white customers. Attorneys for the defendants argued that their removal constituted state action in support of racial discrimination. Found guilty and sentenced to probation by the trial court, the students appealed to Florida's supreme court, which upheld the decision of the trial court. The students appealed to the Supreme Court. On 22 June 1964, it found that section 509.141 of the Florida Statutes was state action in support of private discrimination and overturned the convictions of Robinson and the other participants in the sit-in at Shell's Department Store.

ROOTS. *See* **Haley, Alexander Palmer.**

RUNYON, DOING BUSINESS AS BOBBE'S SCHOOL v. McCRARY, 427 U.S. 160 (1976). A case in which the Supreme Court upheld the right of African Americans to attend private schools.

Katheryne and Russell Runyon operated the private Bobbe's School in Arlington, Virginia. After receiving a brochure about the school, the parents of Michael McCrary, a black student, sought to enroll their son in the Bobbe's School. When the Runyons declined to admit him because the school was not integrated, the McCrarys sued under 43 U.S.C. 1981, which assured all citizens of equal rights and responsibilities under the law. A federal district court found against the Runyons and awarded the McCrarys compensation for the racial discrimination. The Fourth Circuit Court of Appeals affirmed the district court's decision. In an opinion delivered by Justice Potter Stewart, the Supreme Court unanimously held that the law prohibits racial discrimination in private schools and that that does not violate rights of privacy or free association.

RUSTIN, BAYARD (1910–87). Civil rights activist.

Bayard Rustin was born on 17 March 1910 in West Chester, Pennsylvania. One of 12 children born to a West Indian father and a Quaker mother, he was an honor student at integrated public schools in West Chester. As an athlete at West Chester High School, he was active in football, tennis, and track-and-field events. Young Rustin met discrimination when he was refused service in a local restaurant with his white football teammates. "I sat there quite a long time," he later recalled, "and was eventually thrown out bodily." The experience shaped his determination never to accept racial discrimination. After high school, Rustin traveled, worked at odd jobs, and studied at Cheney State College in Pennsylvania and Wilberforce University in Ohio. In the mid-1930s, he moved to Harlem to study at the City College of New York and work as a singer in local nightclubs. In 1936, he joined the Young Communist League (YCL) as an organizer.

By 1941, however, Rustin's idealism and pacifism revolted against the turns of Communist Party dogma. He resigned from the YCL and became an organizer for the pacifist Fellowship of Reconciliation (FOR; q.v.) and A. Philip Randolph's proposed march on Washington. Summoned by the draft board, Rustin refused service in the armed forces and spent 28 months in the federal penitentiary at Lewisburg, Pennsylvania, between 1942 and 1945. After his release, he returned to FOR and worked with its young affiliate, the Congress of Racial Equality (CORE; q.v.). In the spring of 1947, Rustin and other members of FOR and CORE tested compliance with the Supreme Court's 1946 decision in *Morgan v. Virginia* (q.v.) in the Journey of Reconciliation (q.v.). They rode on a bus without incident through Virginia. At Chapel Hill, North Carolina, Rustin and three others were arrested and he served 22 days on a North Carolina chain gang for violating segregation laws. When he was released, Rustin continued working with CORE and FOR. After an incident in the back seat of an automobile with other men in 1951, he was convicted on a morals charge in Pasadena, California.

The climate of Senator Joseph McCarthy's "red scare" forced Rustin's resignation from CORE and FOR because of both his former affiliation with a Communist organization and his homosexuality. In 1953, he became executive director of the radical pacifist War Resisters League. In February 1956, he visited Montgomery, Alabama, and became a behind-the-scenes advisor to Martin Luther King (q.v.) and the Montgomery Bus Boycott (q.v.). With Ella Baker (q.v.) and Stanley D. Levison, he helped to organize "In Friendship," a New York effort to raise money for civil rights work in the South, and proposed the idea of organizing the Southern Christian Leadership Conference (SCLC; q.v.). From New York, Rustin continued as an aide to Martin Luther King and A. Philip Randolph (q.v.) of the Brotherhood of Sleeping Car Porters and Maids. In 1963, he promoted the idea of a March on Washington (q.v.). When Randolph agreed to be the chief public organizer of the march, other major church, civil rights, and labor organizations signed on as its sponsors, but Rustin was its chief manager behind the scenes.

In 1965, A. Philip Randolph and Rustin founded New York's A. Philip Randolph Institute and, for the rest of his life, Rustin was its director. Moderate civil rights leaders like Roy Wilkins (q.v.) and Whitney Young (q.v.) had long regarded him as an embarrassment to the movement because of his Communist background and his sexual orientation. After the March on Washington, more radical leaders of the movement criticized him for other reasons. When the Mississippi Freedom Democratic Party (MFDP; q.v.) challenged the seating of the regular white delegation from Mississippi to the Democratic National Convention in 1964, Joseph Rauh (q.v.), Walter Reuther, and Rustin urged the MFDP to accept a compromise that would give it two votes on the convention floor. He believed that coalition politics was crucial to the success of the civil rights movement and was scornful of those who were alienated from it by black power rhetoric and separatist politics. He opposed the establishment of separate black studies programs in colleges and universities for that reason. Similarly, the onetime Communist and longtime radical pacifist was alienated from Martin Luther King as King grew critical of the war in Vietnam because Rustin believed that the criticism threatened the movement's crucial alliance with the Johnson administration. In his last 20 years, Rustin engaged in many controversies. He supported gay liberation and resisted anti-Semitism and scapegoating immigrant workers in the black community. Bayard Rustin died on 24 August 1987.

S

SCHNELL v. DAVIS, 336 U.S. 933 (1949). *See* **Davis v. Schnell.**

SCHWERNER, MICHAEL HENRY (1939–64). Civil rights activist.

Michael Schwerner was born on 6 November 1939 in New York City. The son of a Jewish wig manufacturer, he studied at the Walden School and the public schools of Pelham, Westchester County, New York. After a year at Michigan State University, young Schwerner transferred to Cornell University where he earned a degree in rural sociology in 1961. As a student at Cornell, he insisted that his fraternity admit an African American student. Schwerner entered graduate school in social work at Columbia University, but he dropped out to take a position as a social worker in a public housing project on New York's Lower East Side. In June 1962, Schwerner married Rita Levant. Early in 1963, they became volunteer workers for the Congress of Racial Equality (CORE; q.v.). In July 1963, Schwerner was arrested in a CORE demonstration in Maryland. After the March on Washington and the bombing of the Sixteenth Street Baptist Church in Birmingham, Schwerner asked CORE to send him to work in the South. In January 1964, Michael and Rita Schwerner were sent to Meridian, Mississippi, as staff workers.

In Meridian, the Schwerners established the Meridian Community Center, hired James Earl Chaney (q.v.) to work with them on its staff and began preparations for Freedom Summer (q.v.). In early June, Chaney and the Schwerners helped to train Northern students for the project in Oxford, Ohio. On 20 June 1964, Chaney and Schwerner were joined in Meridian by a Freedom Summer volunteer, Andrew Goodman (q.v.). On the next day, they went to the Longdale community outside Philadelphia in nearby Neshoba County to investigate the burning of Mount Zion Methodist Church, which was to have been used as a Freedom School. They were arrested in Philadelphia and apparently released from custody to return to Meridian. Then, they vanished. They had been taken captive, beaten, and shot. National authorities were notified and FBI agents began a search. On 23 June, their automobile was found in a canal. The massive search for the missing young men ended on 4 August, when their bodies were found in a pit, next to an earthen dam. In October 1967, seven white men including Neshoba County law officers were convicted in federal court of conspiring to deprive Chaney, Goodman, and Schwerner of their civil rights.

SCREWS v. UNITED STATES, 325 U.S. 91 (1945). A case in which the Supreme Court upheld the constitutionality of a Reconstruction-era statute that made it a crime to violate the due process rights of an American citizen.

Under the influence of alcohol, Baker County, Georgia, sheriff Claude Screws and two deputies went to the home of Robert Hall, an African American, arrested him and took him in handcuffs to the courthouse yard. There, in full public view, Screws beat Hall with his fists and a blackjack for at least fifteen minutes. Then, he dragged Hall's dead body feet first into a jail cell. No state murder charges were brought against Screws, but federal prosecutors offered evidence of such brutality against him that an all-white jury convicted Screws of violating Hall's due process rights under the Fourteenth Amendment and Title 18, Section 242 of the Civil Rights Act of 1866, which made it a crime for "whoever, under color of law, . . . willfully" deprives an American citizen of his or her civil rights. Screws's appeal acknowledged that he had intended to murder Hall. ("The defense is not pretty," observed Supreme Court Justice Wiley Rutledge.) The sheriff's counsel held that Section 242 was unconstitutional insofar as it made violations of civil rights a crime. Sheriff Screws could not have known that he was violating Section 242 because the meaning of "due process" itself was vague. Due process condemns vagueness in criminal law and Section 242 thus violated Screws's own due process rights. Screws's own constitutional rights protected him from prosecution under any charge, said his attorney, except the appropriate one of murder under Georgia law.

The Supreme Court held that Section 242 was constitutional and it applied to deprivations of due process rights. Thus, federal authorities could hold state authorities responsible for civil rights violations. The Court's verdict held that "due process" was understandable because "willfully" meant the intent to deprive a person of a specific constitutional right. The "color of law" meant "pretense" of law, rather than authorized by law. This part of the Court's verdict was useful in the later civil rights movement when, local justice failing to indict or convict the murderers of James Chaney (q.v.), Andrew Goodman (q.v.), Viola Liuzzo (q.v.), and Michael Schwerner (q.v.), for example, federal charges could be brought for the deprivation of civil rights. Yet, the Supreme Court reversed Sheriff Claude Screws's conviction, claiming that the trial judge had misinterpreted "willfully." Federal prosecutors had no difficulty proving that Screws had murdered Hall; they had more difficulty proving that he intended to violate Hall's constitutional rights. Sheriff Screws was acquitted when he was retried.

SEALE, ROBERT GEORGE (Bobby; 1936–   ). Founder of the Black Panther Party.

Bobby Seale was born on 22 October 1936 in Dallas, Texas. Despite war-time prosperity during his childhood in World War II, his family had to rent out part of their house to survive. After the war, the family moved to the West Coast. There, Seale grew up amidst the crowded, dirty poverty of Cordonices Village, a public housing project in Berkeley, California. Yet, he finished public school there and joined the air force in the mid-1950s. Seale and white military authority did not take well to each other. He was court-martialed and given a dishonorable discharge. In 1960, he began attending Merritt Junior College in Oakland, California. In 1962, after a term away from classes, Seale returned to school, where he met Huey Newton. He was impressed with Newton's capacity to capture and hold an audience. Over the next four years, Seale and Newton were influenced by a number of sources: Malcolm X (q.v.), Frantz Fanon, and Robert F. Williams (q.v.), as well as the writings of Mao Tse-Tung, Karl Marx, and V. I. Lenin.

At Merritt College, Newton and Seale organized "The Soul Students Advisory Council." By early October 1966, it had evolved into the "Black Panther Party for Self-Defense." The name was inspired by the black panther symbol of the Lowndes County Freedom Organization (LCFO; q.v.) in Lowndes County, Alabama. The Black Panthers issued a Ten Point Program, which assumed that African Americans were a black colony in an imperialist white nation. Committed to liberating the African American colony by any means, the Black Panthers combined militant rhetoric with ameliorating social programs and a readiness to use force if necessary to free black America. They demanded freedom from white power structures, autonomy of black communities to determine their own destiny, exemption from the draft, better education and housing, and social justice. Their social service programs in African American communities included free health clinics and free breakfasts for black children. Seale and Newton met Eldridge Cleaver (q.v.) early in 1967 and persuaded him to become the Black Panther's minister of information and editor of *The Black Panther* in April 1967.

From late 1966 to late 1967, the Black Panthers commonly trailed the Oakland police with cameras, guns, and legal books to monitor police abuse of black people. In October 1967, Newton was charged with the death of a policeman. In February 1968, Bobby Seale and his wife were arrested. Charges of conspiracy to murder were dropped, but Seale was convicted of "disturbing the peace" and sentenced to six months in maximum security in Alameda County. In the meantime, Seale joined demonstrators at the 1968 Democratic National Convention in Chicago. There, he and seven white leaders of the demonstrations were arrested on charges of conspiracy to incite to riot. After serving his time in Alameda County, Seale was tried in Chicago with the "Chicago Seven." During the trial, his protests led to his being gagged and shackled in the courtroom. When the judge declared a mistrial in Seale's case, it was announced that he would be charged with 16 counts of contempt of court. In 1969, Seale and Ericka Huggins were charged with kidnapping and murdering Black Panther Alex Rackley for disloyalty in New Haven, Connecticut. After a trial between late 1970 to May 1971, they were acquitted by a hung jury.

Bobby Seale returned to Oakland and, in 1973, won 43,000 votes in a run-off election against the incumbent Republican mayor. Thereafter, he left the Black Panther Party and moved his family to a comfortable Denver suburb. His life in the subsequent 20 years has been less dramatic than it was during the Black Panther period. His books, *Seize the Time: The Story of the Black Panther Party and Huey P. Newton* (1968), *A Lonely Rage: The Autobiography of Bobby Seale* (1978) and *Barbeque'n with Bobby,* a cookbook (1988), mark an accommodation with realities of life in a capitalist society. Yet, his business ventures have not been marked with success and Seale claims that he continues to be a revolutionary at heart. In the 1990s, he has maintained a part-time relationship with the African American Studies program at Temple University.

SELMA TO MONTGOMERY MARCH (1965). A march which was the climax of the civil rights movement's voting rights campaign in Alabama.

The origins of the Selma to Montgomery March lie in a frustrated voter registration drive in Selma and Dallas County, Alabama. The local movement was led by Amelia Platts Boynton (q.v.) of the local branch of the NAACP (q.v.) and the Dallas County Voters League (DCVL) and Marie Foster, a dental hygienist. Boynton and her husband, Samuel W. Boynton, had testified before the U. S. Civil Rights Commission (q.v.) in 1958 and their son, Bruce, a law student at Howard University, had filed suit to force the desegregation of interstate public transportation in *Boynton v. Virginia* (q.v.). After Samuel Boynton was hospitalized with a heart condition in 1961, his wife became the most influential local leader of the movement in Alabama's western black belt. In July 1964, while she was making an unsuccessful race for Congress, Alabama Circuit Judge James Hare issued a court order banning all public meetings of three or more people in Dallas County. White registrars stymied the efforts of the NAACP branch, the DCVL, and organizers for the Student Nonviolent Coordinating Committee (SNCC; q.v.) to mount a voter registration drive in the African American community.

On 2 January 1965, Martin Luther King (q.v.) and Southern Christian Leadership Conference (SCLC; q.v.) organizers came to Selma to support the voter registration drive by defying Judge Hare's order and holding a mass meeting at Brown's Chapel African Methodist Episcopal Church. Leaders of the DCVL and organizers for SCLC and SNCC mounted daily demonstrations against the denial of African American voting rights in Selma and Dallas County. On 1 February, King and Ralph Abernathy (q.v.) dramatized the need for federal voting rights laws by leading a mass march which ended in the arrest of 770 people. On 16 February, a Dallas County deputy sheriff punched SCLC staff member C. T. Vivian in the face on the steps of the county courthouse as cameras recorded the scene for a national television audience. Two nights later, as Vivian led marchers from a mass meeting at Zion Chapel Methodist Church in nearby Marion, state troopers shut off the street lights and drove marchers from the streets. They tracked Viola Jackson, her son, Jimmie Lee Jackson (q.v.), and his 82-year-old grandfather, Cager Lee Jackson, into Mack's Cafe. They hit Viola and Cager Lee Jackson several times before Jimmie Lee Jackson leaped to their defense. The troopers beat him with billy clubs and shot him in the stomach. While he still lived, state troopers arrested Jackson for assault and battery with intent to kill. Charges were never brought against the state troopers. Jimmie Lee Jackson died on

26 February 1965. At his funeral on 3 March, Martin Luther King and James Bevel (q.v.) revealed plans for a voting rights march from Selma to Montgomery in Jackson's memory.

On 7 March, SNCC's John Lewis (q.v.) and SCLC's Hosea Williams (q.v.) led a column of 500 to 600 marchers out of Selma across the Edmund Pettus Bridge. State troopers and a posse of mounted patrolmen ordered the marchers to turn back and then suddenly charged. Mounted patrolmen beat the marchers and fired tear gas among them, driving the disciplined column into disorderly retreat. Television cameras took graphic footage of Selma's "Bloody Sunday" for the evening news. Two days later, King led another column of marchers across the Edmund Pettus Bridge toward a police line, only to kneel for prayer and turn back in deference to an order from Federal Judge Frank M. Johnson (q.v.). That night, the Reverend James J. Reeb (q.v.), a Unitarian minister who had come to Selma to join the civil rights march, was beaten to death by white segregationists outside Selma's Silver Moon Cafe. The murders of Jimmie Lee Jackson and James Reeb and the dramatic violence of Bloody Sunday finally, on 15 March, prompted President Lyndon Johnson to announce that he was sending new voting rights legislation to the Congress for approval. Two days later, Judge Johnson lifted his ban on a march from Selma to Montgomery. President Johnson nationalized 4,000 Alabama National Guardsmen and mobilized regular troops, FBI agents, and federal marshals to secure the route for the march.

On Sunday, 21 March, Martin Luther King led over 3,000 people out of Selma and over the Edmund Pettus Bridge for the 54-mile walk to Montgomery. Under the eye of law enforcement officers, they covered 7 miles and camped for the night at a farm near Casey, Alabama. A group of 300 people were picked for the remainder of the march to Montgomery and the remainder returned to Selma. The 300 marched 16 miles into rural Lowndes County on Monday and camped at Petronia. A march of 11 miles through heavy rain on Tuesday ended at a muddy site near the Montgomery County line. The group marched 16 miles on Wednesday to the City of St. Jude, a Catholic hospital and school on the outskirts of Montgomery. Their numbers swelled in anticipation of a triumphant entry into the state capital. On Thursday, 22 March, King led 25,000 people through Montgomery's west side and up Dexter Avenue, past the church he had pastored there to the steps of the white state capitol building. There, he gave one of his most memorable addresses. "How long?" would it take to reach the promised land, he asked. "Not long. Because the arc of the moral universe is long but it bends toward justice."

"How long?" "Not long, 'cause mine eyes have seen the glory of the coming of the Lord. . . ." Klansmen sobered that optimism with the murder of Viola Liuzzo (q.v.) that evening, but on 6 August President Johnson signed the Voting Rights Act of 1965.

SHAW v. RENO, ATTORNEY GENERAL, 509 U.S. _____ (1993). A case in which the Supreme Court held that race may not be the exclusive criteria for drawing legislative district lines.

When the North Carolina legislature redrew the lines of its congressional districts based on the 1990 census, the state was entitled to a twelfth congressional seat. The legislature produced a map of congressional districts including one in which the African American population was large enough to make it likely to elect an African American congressman. Under Title V of the Voting Rights Act of 1965 (q.v.), North Carolina had to submit the reapportionment plan to the federal district court for the District of Columbia or the attorney general's office for review. The attorney general's office rejected the legislature's plan with the implication that a different map could produce congressional district lines that were likely to elect two African Americans to Congress from North Carolina. The state legislature redrew the map, producing one congressional district that linked concentrations of black voters along a highway.

Ruth O. Shaw and other white voters brought suit in federal court to challenge the new plan. The federal court rejected an initial suit against North Carolina's governor. The plaintiffs then sued the attorney general, Janet Reno. The Supreme Court issued its opinion on 28 June 1993. By a five-to-four vote, with Justices Harry Blackmun, David Souter, John Paul Stevens, and Byron White dissenting, the Court held that congressional districts created on the basis of race were unconstitutional. "Racial gerrymandering, even for remedial purposes, may balkanize us into competing racial factions," wrote Justice Sandra Day O'Connor for the Court majority; "it threatens to carry us further from the goal of a political system in which race no longer matters—a goal that the Fourteenth and Fifteenth Amendments embody, and to which the Nation continues to aspire."

SHELLEY v. KRAEMER, 334 U.S. 1 (1948). A case in which the Supreme Court found racially restrictive covenants in real estate were illegal.

Shelley, an African American, purchased a house from Fitzgerald, a white man, in St. Louis. Five square miles in St. Louis, including three-fourths of the property in this neighborhood, were covered by contractual agreements that made ethnic, racial or religious minorities ineligible to lease or own it. Kraemer, a neighboring white property owner, sued Shelley, asking the court to enjoin Shelley from taking possession of the property. A state trial court ruled that the restrictive covenant was illegal, but on appeal Missouri's supreme court reversed this decision. The NAACP Legal Defense and Educational Fund (LDEF; q.v.) coordinated the appeal of four restrictive covenant cases to the Supreme Court in 1948: *Shelley v. Kraemer*, tried by George Vaughn; *McGhee v. Sipes*, tried by Thurgood Marshall (q.v.); and *Hurd v. Hodge* (q.v.) and *Urciolo v. Hodge*, tried by Charles H. Houston (q.v.). The NAACP attorneys' briefs depended heavily on sociological data and theory. Chief Justice Fred Vinson spoke for a unanimous Supreme Court in finding that restrictive covenants voluntarily maintained were permissible, but state action to enforce them violated Fourteenth Amendment rights to convey, hold, inherit, purchase, rent, and sell real or personal property. Racial discrimination in private housing did not end with the Supreme Court's 1948 decisions. The federal government's own Federal Housing Administration and Public Housing Administration did not fully comply with them. Even so, the Court's decisions were a major blow to de jure segregation in housing.

SHEPHERD v. FLORIDA, 341 U.S. 50 (1951). A case in which the Supreme Court reversed the rape convictions of two black men who were indicted and sentenced by all-white juries.

In Florida, two black men, Walter Irvin and Samuel Shepherd, were accused of raping a 17-year-old white woman at gunpoint. They were indicted by an all-white grand jury and tried, convicted, and sentenced to death by an all-white trial jury. Attorneys for the NAACP LDEF (q.v.) represented them before the Supreme Court. They argued that, despite the sensational character of the case and the fact that African Americans had fled from the county because of racial animosity there, Irvin and Shepherd had been denied a change of venue for their trial. Moreover, the systematic exclusion of black people from grand and trial jury service was a denial of the defendants' constitutional rights to due process. Justice Robert Jackson wrote the Supreme Court's decision, which reversed the defendants' convictions. The combination of an outraged white public and exclusion of black people from jury selection had violated the defendants' rights to both due process and equal protection of the law.

SHUTTLESWORTH, FRED LEE (1922–   ). Civil rights activist and pastor.

Fred Shuttlesworth was born on 18 March 1922 in Mt. Meigs, Montgomery County, Alabama. He attended rural Alabama schools for African American students. After World War II, Shuttlesworth attended Selma University, where he earned an A.B. degree in 1951, and Alabama State College, where he earned a B.S. degree in 1952. In 1953, Shuttlesworth moved to Birmingham, Alabama, to become the pastor of Bethel Baptist Church. When Alabama attorney general John Patterson filed suit against the NAACP in June 1956 (*NAACP v. Alabama;* q.v.), effectively inhibiting the work of the national civil rights organization in the state, Birmingham pastors R. L. Alford, Edward Gardner, Nelson H. Smith, and Shuttlesworth organized the Alabama Christian Movement for Human Rights (ACMHR; q.v.) as an alternative, parallel to the Montgomery Improvement Association (MIA; q.v.). Chosen as its first president at the founding mass meeting on 5 June 1956 at Birmingham's Sardis Baptist Church, Shuttlesworth became the city's most aggressive advocate of nonviolent direct action as a vehicle for social change. Others, offended by Shuttlesworth's style, looked to the Reverend J. L. Ware's Baptist Ministers' Conference and his Jefferson County Improvement Association (JCIA) for more prudent leadership in civil rights.

In December 1956, when the Supreme Court settled the case in *Browder v. Gayle* (q.v.), Shuttlesworth warned Birmingham authorities that segregation on city buses was unconstitutional. He survived the dynamiting which destroyed his parsonage on Christmas evening to lead an attempt to desegregate Birmingham's buses on the following day. Shuttlesworth and 20 other demonstrators were arrested and convicted of trespass. He was beaten with whips and chains by a white mob when he sought to desegregate Birmingham's public schools by enrolling his daughter at Phillips High School in 1957. The ACMHR became the Birmingham affiliate of SCLC (q.v.) in January 1957 and Shuttlesworth replaced T. J. Jemison (q.v.) as SCLC's secretary in 1958. On 31 October 1958, the ACMHR and Ware's JCIA began a boycott of the city's still-segregated buses. Yet, after two months it failed because of divisions in the African American community, police intimidation, and the failure to win press coverage. The city's buses were officially desegregated by a federal court order on 14 December 1959. In 1960, Shuttlesworth witnessed the sit-in movement (q.v.) in Greensboro, North Carolina, and urged Martin Luther King (q.v.) to get SCLC behind the student demonstrations. ACMHR and Shuttlesworth gave local support for the Freedom Rides (q.v.) in 1961.

In 1960, Shuttlesworth and others became defendants in a libel suit, *New York Times v. Sullivan* (q.v.), when apparently without his knowledge or consent his name was signed to a controversial full-page advertisement in the *New York Times*. In response to charges in the ad, Montgomery, Alabama, police commissioner L. B. Sullivan sued Shuttlesworth, the *Times,* and others for libel. The case dragged on for four years, ending in the United States Supreme Court. By 1962, Alabama had seized Shuttlesworth's automobile and begun proceedings against other property. In order to protect himself from additional seizures and his family from the violence in Birmingham, he became the pastor of Revelation Baptist Church in Cincinnati, Ohio. Yet, Shuttlesworth continued to lead Birmingham's ACMHR and the city remained largely segregated in 1962, when he asked Martin Luther King (q.v.) and SCLC to join the Birmingham, Alabama, Movement (q.v.) in confronting its brutal racism.

The confrontation began on 3 April 1963, when two dozen black college students began sit-ins at four Birmingham stores. Shuttlesworth was arrested in demonstrations on 6 April. The next day, Public Safety Commissioner T. Eugene "Bull" Connor (q.v.) loosed police dogs on civil rights marchers, unintentionally drawing dramatic media attention to the Birmingham story. On Good Friday, 12 April, King, Shuttlesworth, and Ralph Abernathy (q.v.) were arrested and jailed with other marchers for violating a state court injunction against additional demonstrations. Two weeks later, they were convicted of criminal contempt and released on appeal, leading to the case of *Walker v. City of Birmingham* (q.v.). The demonstrations recaptured the nation's attention when SCLC's James Bevel (q.v.) organized school children to march against segregation on 2 May. When "Bull" Connor's police and fire departments used powerful water hoses against the young people the next day, black spectators retaliated by throwing bricks and bottles. Shuttlesworth was hospitalized on 7 May when water from the fire hoses slammed him against a wall. On 10 May 1963, after the Kennedy administration intervened, Shuttlesworth announced a negotiated settlement.

The confrontation in Birmingham led to the passage of the Civil Rights Act of 1964 (q.v.). Shuttlesworth was active in SCLC's campaigns, in St. Augustine, Florida, and the Alabama voting rights campaign that culminated in the Selma to Montgomery March (q.v.), which led to passage of the Voting Rights Act of 1965 (q.v.). In 1966, after an internal struggle in his Cincinnati church, he founded and remains the pastor of the city's Greater New Light Baptist Church. In 1969, Shuttlesworth stepped down as president of the ACMHR and, in 1970, he resigned as secretary of SCLC. He continued to serve on the boards of CORE (q.v.), SCLC, and the Southern Conference Educational Fund (SCEF). He is the director of the Shuttlesworth Housing Foundation in Cincinnati, which helps poor people buy houses. He was, said Martin Luther King, "the most courageous civil rights fighter in the South."

SIMKINS v. CITY OF GREENSBORO, 149 F. Supp. 562 (M.D. N.C., 1957). A case in which a federal district court ordered Greensboro, North Carolina, to provide equal golfing facilities to black and white residents.

Greensboro, North Carolina's Gillespie Park Golf Course was an 18-hole course for white golfers on land leased to the city by the board of education. The city also had a nine-hole course, Nacho Park Golf Course, for black golfers. When a group of African American residents asked to play on the Gillespie Park course in 1949, the city and the board of education leased it to the Gillespie Park Golf Club, a private nonprofit corporation with annual membership and green fees. Informally, white nonmembers were always allowed to play on the course by paying a green fee. If black people asked to play on the course, they were refused because they were not members of the club. In December 1955, Dr. George Simkins, Jr., a Greensboro dentist and leader of the local branch of the NAACP (q.v.), and several black associates were arrested, tried, convicted, and fined for trying to play on the Gillespie Park Golf Course. Their sentences were later commuted, but Simkins brought suit in federal district court against the city of Greensboro for racial discrimination. On 20 March 1957, the court held that the city and the board of education could not lease the course to a private corporation in order to avoid offering equal facilities to black golfers. Rather than desegregating its golf courses, the city closed both Gillespie Park and Nacho Park Golf Courses.

SIMKINS v. MOSES H. CONE MEMORIAL HOSPITAL, 323 F.2d 959 (4th Cir., 1963). A case in which the Fourth Circuit Court of Appeals held that racial discrimination by a hospital subsidized by federal money was unconstitutional.

In 1962, Dr. George Simkins, Jr., a dentist and leader of the local branch of the NAACP (q.v.), and several physicians and patients in Greensboro, North Carolina, brought suit against two local hospitals which excluded black physicians and patients. The two hospitals received federal money under the Hill-Burton Hospital Survey and Construction Act, which included a provision which permitted separate but equal facilities in hospitals benefitted by its funding. The Justice Department and attorneys for the plaintiffs argued that the subsidy by federal money obligated the hospitals to abide by constitutional limits on racial discrimination and that the Hill-Burton Act's toleration of "separate but equal" facilities was unconstitutional. A federal district court ruled in favor of the segregated hospitals, but in a divided vote the Fourth Circuit Court of Appeals ruled in favor of the plaintiffs. The decision set an important precedent against racial discrimination in private medical facilities that received public funds and for the premise of Title VI of the Civil Rights Act of 1964 (q.v.), which banned racial discrimination in agencies that received public funds.

SIPUEL v. BOARD OF REGENTS OF THE UNIVERSITY OF OKLAHOMA, 332 U.S. 631 (1948). A Supreme Court case in which the Court ruled that states must offer equal educational opportunities for qualified African American students.

In 1946, Ada Lois Sipuel was denied admission to the racially segregated University of Oklahoma Law School. The state had no law school for African American students, but it claimed that its provision for tuition grants to African American law students at institutions outside the state satisfied the "separate but equal" requirements of *Plessy v. Ferguson.* Sipuel challenged the state's claim in an Oklahoma district court, which refused to hear her case. On appeal, the Oklahoma supreme court reaffirmed the lower court's decision. Backed by the NAACP LDEF (q.v.) and Thurgood Marshall (q.v.), Sipuel appealed to the United States Supreme Court. In January 1948, the Supreme Court reversed the state courts unanimously. Citing precedent in its decision in *Missouri Ex Rel. Gaines v. Canada* (q.v.), the Court held that Fourteenth Amendment due process requirements meant that the state must provide educational opportunities for African American students within its boundaries that are equal to those offered white students. Oklahoma authorities responded by opening a law school for African American students. It operated in three rooms in the state capitol, had only three white attorneys on its faculty, and offered access to the state law library.

Even so, the new law school could not begin the academic year when the University of Oklahoma Law School did. In the meantime, Sipuel had married, changing her name to Ada Louise Sipuel Fisher, and refused to apply to the new law school. Only one student attended classes during its short existence. In *Fisher v. Hurst* (q.v.), Fisher's attorney returned to Oklahoma courts, arguing that even when it did open, the new law school would not meet the Fourteenth Amendment's due process requirements of equal educational opportunity and asking the court to order Fisher's admission to the University of Oklahoma Law School. Oklahoma courts held that the university's law school could either admit Fisher or suspend the enrollment of white students until the new African American law school was opened and prepared to meet the test of equality. With Justices Frank Murphy and Wiley Rutledge in dissent, the United States Supreme Court held that the state court's ruling met requirements of its ruling in *Sipuel*. In the meantime, faced with the recognition that the state was unlikely to be able to give a racially separate new law school the appearance of equality, Oklahoma authorities reversed course. In 1949, Fisher was admitted to and, in 1951, she graduated from the University of Oklahoma Law School.

SIT-IN MOVEMENT. A tactic adapted from the American labor movement by African American college students in Greensboro, North Carolina, which was replicated by other black students across the South in the early 1960s.

Scattered sit-in demonstrations against racial discrimination occurred in cities from North Carolina to Florida and Oklahoma between 1957 and 1960. On 1 February 1960, four African American students at North Carolina Agricultural and Technical College sat down at Woolworth's lunch counter in Greensboro, North Carolina, and asked for service. This action by Ezell Blair, Jr., and David Richmond of Greensboro, Franklin McCain of Washington, D.C., and Joseph McNeil of Wilmington, North Carolina, was largely spontaneous. That evening, 50 Greensboro students organized the Student Executive Committee for Justice. The next day 50 students from North Carolina A & T College, Bennett College and the Women's College of the University of North Carolina participated in the sit-in. Soon, hundreds of students were sitting in at downtown Greensboro lunch counters. On 5 February, they agreed to halt the protests for negotiations.

Within days after the Greensboro sit-in demonstration began, it prompted others in Charlotte (q.v.), Durham (q.v.), High Point (q.v.), Raleigh and Winston-Salem (q.v.), North Carolina; Tidewater, Virginia (q.v.); Tallahassee, Florida (q.v.); Nashville, Tennessee (q.v.); and Baton Rouge, Louisiana (q.v.). Soon, there were others in Maryland, South Carolina, Georgia, and Texas. By March 1960, there were sit-in demonstrations in 31 cities in nine Southern states. On 19 March, San Antonio, Texas, became the first major Southern city to desegregate its lunch counters. Student leaders of the sit-in movement in cities across the South met at Shaw University in Raleigh, North Carolina, in April 1960 to organize SNCC (q.v.). The results of sit-in demonstrations varied from city to city. Commonly in the Upper South, a tense period of demonstrations and negotiations led to limited desegregation of lunch counters within six months. In Greensboro, for example, when negotiations produced no tangible results, the demonstrations were resumed on 1 April. Among the first arrested for sit-ins there on 21 April were 45 students. The combined pressure of continued sit-ins and an economic boycott of white merchants in Greensboro forced desegregation of the city's lunch counters in July 1960. In Deep South states, sit-in demonstrations commonly did not lead to desegregation of lunch counters for several more years.

SMITH v. ALLWRIGHT, 321 U.S. 649 (1944). A case in which the Supreme Court reversed an earlier finding to hold that the "white primary" is unconstitutional.

In 1932, the Texas Democratic Party adopted a rule that allowed "all white citizens" to vote in its state and national primary elections. That rule passed judicial review three years later in the Supreme Court's decision in *Grovey v. Townsend.* In *Grovey,* the Court held that membership in a political party and participation in its primary elections was a private matter, not subject to state regulation. In 1941, however, the Court ruled in *United States v. Classic* that primary elections were state action because the state delegated to political parties the authority to choose candidates to compete for elective office. Lonnie E. Smith, a dentist in Houston, Texas, was denied a ballot in the 1940 Harris County Democratic primary by election judge S. E. Allwright on the grounds that, as an African American, Smith did not qualify for membership in the Democratic Party. Dallas attorney William J. Durham and Thurgood Marshall (q.v.) of the NAACP LDEF (q.v.) took Smith's case against Allwright to the Supreme Court. In an eight-to-one decision, Justice Stanley Reed wrote for the Court majority in finding that its decision in *Classic* superseded its decision in *Grovey.* The *Allwright* decision removed a major obstacle to African American participation in Southern elections.

SOUTH CAROLINA ELECTRIC AND GAS COMPANY v. FLEMING, 351 U.S. 901 (1956). A case in which the Supreme Court confirmed a Fourth Circuit Court of Appeals decision extending the Supreme Court's decision in *Brown v. Board of Education* (q.v.) to public transportation.

In 1955, Sara Mae Fleming sued the South Carolina Electric and Gas Company, alleging that one of its bus drivers forced her to move to another seat under South Carolina segregation statutes. Attorneys for South Carolina Electric and Gas Company and the driver contended that he was obliged to abide by state transportation laws. Finding against Fleming, the trial court found that South Carolina's law requiring segregation in public transportation was constitutional under *Plessy v. Ferguson*'s "separate but equal" precedent. When Fleming took the case to the Fourth Circuit Court of Appeals, attorneys for South Carolina Electric and Gas Company argued that the Supreme Court's recent decision in *Brown v. Board of Education* applied only to public education. The Fourth Circuit Court of Appeals rejected this narrowing of the implications of *Brown*. "The separate but equal doctrine approved in *Plessy v. Ferguson* has been repudiated," held the appellate court in applying the logic of *Brown* to public transportation. The Supreme Court implied its approval of the appellate court's decision by refusing to hear an appeal.

SOUTH CAROLINA v. KATZENBACH, 383 U.S. 301 (1966). A case in which the Supreme Court upheld the constitutionality of the Voting Rights Act of 1965 (q.v.).

After the passage of the Voting Rights Act of 1965, South Carolina filed suit against Attorney General Nicholas Katzenbach, seeking a court injunction to prevent him from enforcing some of its provisions. South Carolina claimed, for example, that the provision of the act that banned literacy tests for voter registration was an unconstitutional violation of the right of states to establish qualifications for voting. Katzenbach argued that the Voting Rights Act was appropriate legislation based on Section Two of the Fifteenth Amendment, which authorized Congress to enforce the amendment with appropriate legislation. Chief Justice Earl Warren wrote the decision for an eight-to-one court majority, with Justice Hugo Black concurring in part and dissenting in part.

The Court approved the act's formula, which brought those states or subdivisions of states under its coverage which used "tests or devices" as prerequisites for registering and which had less than 50 percent of their otherwise eligible voters registered and voting in the presidential election of 1964. It approved provisions that suspended literacy tests or other devises in the jurisdictions it covered and the authorization of federal agents to register voters. Justice Black dissented from the Court's approval, which required covered jurisdictions to preclear any changes in laws governing elections and voting with the attorney general's office or the federal district court for the District of Columbia before they could become effective. The preclearance requirement violated the principle of federalism, according to Black. The Voting Rights Act of 1965 and the Supreme Court's decision in *South Carolina v. Katzenbach* changed Southern politics dramatically by significantly increasing the numbers of black voters and office holders.

SOUTH v. PETERS, 339 U.S. 276 (1950). A case in which the Supreme Court upheld the constitutionality of Georgia's county unit system of voting.

In 1917, Georgia adopted a county unit system of voting. It gave voters in the state's many small, rural counties a disproportionately large voice in statewide elections and disadvantaged voters in its relatively few but highly populated urban counties. Especially after World War II, African Americans were much more likely to be registered to vote in Georgia's urban counties than in its rural ones. Bernard South and other Atlanta residents argued that the county unit system of counting votes gave a vote cast in a rural county ten times the influence in a statewide election than it would have if it were cast in an urban county. Attorneys for James Peters, chairman of the state's Democratic Party, argued that federal courts had historically refrained from interfering with distributions of power among geographical divisions of a state. Justices Hugo Black and William O. Douglas dissented from the Supreme Court's decision in *South v. Peters*, but the Court majority ruled in favor of Georgia's county unit system. In 1962 and 1964, the Supreme Court decided that it was obliged to ensure equality of voter influence and reversed this decision in *Baker v. Carr* (q.v.) and *Reynolds, a Judge v. Sims* (q.v.).

SOUTHERN BURLINGTON COUNTY NAACP, ETHEL LAW-RENCE v. MT. LAUREL TOWNSHIP, NEW JERSEY, 67 N.J. 151, 336 A.2d 713 (1975). A case in which the New Jersey supreme court ordered a review of zoning laws throughout the state to allow for housing for low- and moderate-income families.

Supported by the local branch of the NAACP (q.v.), Ethel Lawrence sued Mt. Laurel, New Jersey, for adopting zoning ordinances which tended to exclude low-income people. In 1950, the 22-square-mile township 15 miles northeast of Philadelphia was a farming community of about 2800 people. About 400 of them were African Americans, mostly descended from pre-Civil War fugitive slaves, who earned a modest living as farm workers. In the next two decades' suburban expansion, the population quadrupled. Mt. Laurel's township council and zoning board sought to control development in 1964 with the passage of ordinances excluding attached townhouses, mobile home parks, and multiunit apartments. Single-family houses had to include 1100 square feet of living space and be built on lots of 9,375 to 20,000 square feet. Families of more than two children were discouraged from buying or leasing homes in Mt. Laurel. The effect was to preclude low-income people from living in the township. Lawrence, a fourth-generation resident of the community, and the local branch of the NAACP contended that the zoning drove young black people from a community where they could no longer afford to live. New Jersey's superior and supreme courts agreed and found exclusionary zoning so pervasive in the state that it ordered every jurisdiction in the state to revise its policies to provide housing for low-income families.

SOUTHERN CHRISTIAN LEADERSHIP CONFERENCE (SCLC). One of five major organizations at the heart of the civil rights movement.

In January 1957, 60 black leaders from major cities across the South met at Ebenezer Baptist Church in Atlanta, Georgia, to found the Southern Leadership Conference on Transportation and Nonviolent Integration. Like Martin Luther King (q.v.), their first president, most of them were Baptist ministers active in civil rights in their local communities. Most of them were members of the NAACP (q.v.), but they hoped to supplement its commitment to legislation and litigation with nonviolent social action to achieve social justice. Like King, some of them—Ralph D. Abernathy (q.v.) of Montgomery, T. J. Jemison (q.v.) of Baton Rouge, Fred Shuttlesworth (q.v.) of Birmingham, and C. K. Steele (q.v.) of Tallahassee—had recently led bus boycotts in their communities to win better treatment for black people in public transportation. After considering other names, they settled on the less awkward Southern Christian Leadership Conference as the name of their organization. It sponsored the Prayer Pilgrimage to Washington (q.v.) in 1957 and the two Youth Marches for Integrated Schools (q.v.) in 1958 and 1959, but SCLC seemed to lack a coherent or dramatic program for social action until King moved to Atlanta to be near its headquarters and Wyatt Tee Walker (q.v.) became its executive director in 1960.

SCLC did not initiate the two major nonviolent social actions that launched the decade in civil rights, the sit-in movement (q.v.) and the Freedom Rides (q.v.), but it was supportive of them. Once black college students began the sit-in movement in 1960, SCLC's leadership, including Ella Baker (q.v.), James Lawson (q.v.), and King, played major roles in encouraging them to organize their efforts, resulting in the formation of SNCC (q.v.). When CORE (q.v.) launched the Freedom Rides in 1961, SCLC leaders, like King, Abernathy, Lawson, and Shuttlesworth, played important support roles. By then, SCLC had begun its Citizenship Education Project at the Dorchester Center in McIntosh, Georgia, under the leadership of Septima Clark (q.v.), Andrew Young (q.v.) and, later, Dorothy Cotton (q.v.). In December 1961, the Albany, Georgia, Movement (q.v.) asked King and SCLC to assist its attack on segregation there. Despite thousands of arrests and promises of concessions by the city's white leaders, in August 1962 King left Albany in defeat.

Yet, Albany was a testing ground for SCLC's more successful campaign in support of the Birmingham, Alabama, Movement (q.v.) in April and May 1963. After the March on Washington (q.v.) in August, SCLC mounted campaigns in Danville, Virginia, and St. Augustine, Florida. Then at its peak, SCLC had a staff of 50 employees and 85 local affiliates, such as the Alabama Christian Movement for Human Rights (ACMHR; q.v.) in Birmingham, the Baton Rouge Christian Movement, the Montgomery Improvement Association (MIA; q.v.), the Nashville Christian Leadership Council, the Petersburg Improvement Association in Virginia, Tallahassee's Inter-Civic Council, the United Christian Movement in Shreveport, Louisiana, and the Western Christian Leadership Conference in Los Angeles.

After the adoption of the Civil Rights Act of 1964 (q.v.), SCLC joined a voter registration drive in Selma, Alabama. The frustration of that effort led to the Selma to Montgomery March (q.v.) and the enactment of the Voting Rights Act of 1965 (q.v.). Thereafter, the Watts race riot in 1965, the call for "black power" by Stokely Carmichael (q.v.) on the Meredith March in 1966, the war in Vietnam, and the Detroit race riot in 1967 redirected SCLC's attention to a broader range of issues. Its campaign against discrimination in education, employment, and housing with the Chicago, Illinois, Movement (q.v.) ended in disappointing results. Yet, Martin Luther King and SCLC continued to cry out for economic and social justice at home and an end to the war in Vietnam abroad. SCLC was laying plans for the Poor People's March on Washington (q.v.) when Martin Luther King was assassinated on 4 April 1968 as he prepared to lead demonstrations in support of city sanitation workers in Memphis, Tennessee.

In 1965, Ralph Abernathy, the pastor of Atlanta's West Hunter Street Baptist Church, was named King's heir apparent and, after King's death in 1968, at a time when the movement was in disarray, Abernathy succeeded his friend as president of SCLC. Abernathy tried to maintain an agenda for racial justice by leading the Poor People's March on Washington, a demonstration at the Republican National Convention, and an Atlanta sanitation workers' strike in 1968. In succeeding years, he was jailed in a successful Charleston, South Carolina, hospital workers' strike and planned a march from Perry, Georgia, to Atlanta. In 1977, when Abernathy resigned as president of SCLC, Joseph E. Lowery (q.v.) was unanimously chosen as his successor. In 1967, Lowery had become chairman of SCLC's board of directors and, to be closer to its headquarters, he became the pastor of Atlanta's Central United Methodist Church in 1968. From 1986 to 1992, when he retired from the ministry, Lowery was the pastor of Atlanta's Cascade United Methodist Church. President of SCLC for nearly as long as both of his predecessors combined, Lowery has grappled with the problem of leading a major civil rights organization in reduced financial straits in the "post civil rights era." His leadership has focussed on the struggle against apartheid in South Africa, extensions of the Voting Rights Act of 1965 (q.v.), and the domestic fight against drugs and violence in the African American community.

SOUTHERN MANIFESTO. A statement by Southern congressmen and senators which defied the United States Supreme Court's decision in *Brown v. Board of Education* (q.v.).

In 1956, 77 members of the House of Representatives and 19 members of the Senate from Southern states signed the "Southern Manifesto." It was read into the *Congressional Record* by Senator Walter F. George of Georgia on 12 March 1956. The manifesto charged that the Supreme Court's decision in *Brown v. Board of Education* was an "abuse of judicial power," a violation of a century of court decisions and a threat to destroy public education in much of the South. It pledged support for resisting desegregation of schools by "all lawful means" and urged Southerners, however provoked by "the agitators and troublemakers invading our States," to "refrain from disorder and lawless acts." Senators Lyndon Johnson of Texas, Albert Gore and Estes Kefauver of Tennessee, and 24 congressmen from Southern states did not sign the Southern Manifesto.

STATE ATHLETIC COMMISSION v. DORSEY, 359 U.S. 533 (1959). A case in which the Supreme Court extended the logic of its decision in *Brown v. Board of Education* (q.v.) to public athletic contests.

Louisiana law prohibited interracial athletic contests. Joseph Dorsey, Jr., a black professional boxer, challenged the enforcement of the law by the Louisiana State Athletic Commission on the grounds that it was inherently discriminatory and violated the Fourteenth Amendment's equal protection clause. The Supreme Court had ruled in *Brown v. Board of Education* that public school segregation is inherently discriminatory and in violation of the equal protection clause of the Fourteenth Amendment. In *Dorsey,* the Supreme Court confirmed a lower court's decision which extended the logic of its decision in *Brown* to publicly regulated events.

STEELE, CHARLES KENZIE (C. K.; 1914–80). Civil rights activist and pastor.

C. K. Steele was born on 7 February 1914 in Gary, West Virginia. In 1938, he graduated from Morehouse College in Atlanta, Georgia. Steele was the pastor of Baptist churches in Montgomery, Alabama, and Augusta, Georgia, before moving to Tallahassee, Florida, to become the pastor of Bethel Baptist Church, in 1951. There, he served as president of the local branch of the NAACP (q.v.). On 26 May 1956, two students at Florida Agricultural and Mechanical University (FAMU; sat in the only remaining seats that were in the white section of a bus in Tallahassee. When they were arrested for "inciting to riot," FAMU students voted to boycott the bus company. On 29 May, the Interdenominational Ministerial Association created a committee including Steele to meet with city officials about the issue and to hold a mass meeting at Steele's Bethel Baptist Church that evening. When the meeting with city officials proved fruitless, the ministers organized the Inter-Civic Council (ICC) with Steele as its president to lead the bus boycott. Like the Montgomery Improvement Association (MIA; q.v.), it demanded a less oppressive form of segregated seating on a first come, first served basis, more courteous treatment on the buses, and the hiring of black bus drivers.

On 4 June, the bus company appeared to concede the ICC's demands, with the proviso that "members of different races may not occupy the same seat" on the buses. When Steele insisted on desegregation of seating on the city's buses and the bus company retaliated by suspending all service to black sections of the city, a faction in the black community led by the Reverend David H. Brooks argued for acceptance of the bus company's offer. On 1 July, the bus company discontinued all service in the city. The ICC and 21 individual defendants were found guilty of operating an illegal car pool in support of the bus boycott on 20 October. On 13 November, the Supreme Court confirmed an appeals court's decision that segregation on public transportation is unconstitutional, but bus service in Tallahassee did not resume on a desegregated basis until May 1958. In January 1957, Steele joined Ralph D. Abernathy (q.v.), Martin Luther King (q.v.), Joseph Lowery (q.v.), Fred Shuttlesworth (q.v.), and other black ministers active in civil rights to organize SCLC (q.v.). He was chosen its first vice president. In 1960, FAMU students staged sit-in demonstrations in Tallahassee and Steele was among their counselors. When Martin Luther King was jailed in Albany, Georgia, in July 1962, Steele led demonstrations in support of the Albany Movement (q.v.). C. K. Steele continued to serve as pastor of Bethel Baptist Church until his death on 19 August 1980.

STUDENT NONVIOLENT COORDINATING COMMITTEE (SNCC). One of five major organizations at the heart of the civil rights movement.

Students at North Carolina A & T College launched the Greensboro sit-in movement on 1 February 1960. Within days, it prompted others in Charlotte (q.v.), Durham (q.v.), High Point (q.v.), Raleigh, and Winston-Salem (q.v.), North Carolina; Tidewater, Virginia (q.v.); Tallahassee, Florida (q.v.); and Nashville, Tennessee (q.v.). Soon, there were others in Maryland, South Carolina, Georgia, Louisiana, and Texas. By the end of February 1960, there were sit-in demonstrations in 31 cities in nine Southern states. On 15 April 1960, the acting executive director of SCLC (q.v.), Ella Baker (q.v.), convened a meeting of two to three hundred student activists from 58 colleges and universities at Shaw University, her alma mater, to plan for coordinating their efforts. They heard inspiring talks by Martin Luther King (q.v.) and James Lawson (q.v.), but they acted on her advice to remain independent of any existing civil rights organization and formed a Temporary Student Nonviolent Coordinating Committee, chaired by Marion S. Barry (q.v.), a leader of the Nashville, Tennessee, Movement (q.v.). By October 1960, SNCC dropped the word "temporary" from its name, Charles McDew of Orangeburg State College in South Carolina replaced Barry as its chairman, and Ella Baker persuaded Robert Moses (q.v.) to become a SNCC organizer in Mississippi. Baker and Moses nurtured a vision within SNCC of a grassroots movement in which decisions flowed from the bottom up rather than from the top down.

In 1961, James Forman (q.v.), a Chicago journalist, brought experience and maturity to SNCC as its first executive secretary, SNCC activists helped to sustain the Freedom Rides (q.v.) at a moment when they appeared to falter, and SNCC avoided a choice between direct action and voter registration by choosing to do both. With financial support from the Voter Education Project (VEP; q.v.) in subsequent years, SNCC activists gave staff support to voter registration drives from Albany, Georgia, to McComb, Mississippi, where they assisted in the organization of Mississippi's Council of Federated Organizations (COFO; q.v.). In 1963, John Lewis (q.v.) replaced McDew as SNCC's chairman in time to be its spokesman at the March on Washington (q.v.), where the forcefulness of his rhetoric threatened to disrupt events at the last moment.

SNCC activists helped to organize the Mississippi Freedom Democratic Party (MFDP; q.v.) and Freedom Summer (q.v.) in 1964. The Democratic National Convention's refusal to seat the MFDP's biracial delegation in place of the all-white regular delegation to the convention was a profound turning point for many SNCC activists, representing the untrustworthiness of mainstream white liberalism. SNCC did not endorse SCLC's Selma to Montgomery March (q.v.) in 1965, but its leaders were active around it in various ways. John Lewis participated in the march. James Forman was in Montgomery denouncing police repression there. Stokely Carmichael (q.v.) was in Lowndes County, using the aroused interest to organize the Lowndes County Freedom Organization (LCFO; q.v.) as an alternative to biracial politics.

In May 1966, Carmichael took the measure of SNCC's direction by defeating Lewis as its chairman. Carmichael's ally Ruby Doris Robinson (q.v.) replaced James Forman as SNCC's executive secretary and his friend Cleveland Sellers became SNCC's program secretary. The change in SNCC's leadership was just in time to make the Meredith March from Memphis, Tennessee, to Jackson, Mississippi, a vehicle for Carmichael's cry for "black power." By then, there was an exodus of SNCC's early leadership. The early departures of James Bevel (q.v.) and Diane Nash (q.v.) were followed by those of Julian Bond (q.v.), Fannie Lou Hamer (q.v.), John Lewis (q.v.), Robert Moses (q.v.), and white organizers as SNCC shed its commitment to integration and nonviolence. In May 1967, Hubert Gerold (H. Rap) Brown (q.v.) replaced Carmichael as SNCC's national chairman. As SNCC and the Black Panther Party (q.v.)

moved to closer cooperation, Carmichael and Brown joined the Panther organization. In February 1968, the two organizations announced a merger and Carmichael became the Panthers' prime minister. Already under severe pressure from the Federal Bureau of Investigation's counter-intelligence program and police surveillance, however, both organizations were disintegrating even as they announced their merger. Brown still claimed to control SNCC in the summer of 1968, when he sought to change its name to Student National Coordinating Committee. By then, Brown was excommunicating one-time allies—Carmichael, Cleveland Sellers and Willie Ricks—on ideological grounds. By then, too, SNCC itself was dead.

SULLIVAN v. LITTLE HUNTING PARK, 396 U.S. 229 (1969). A case in which the Supreme Court expanded the application of the Civil Rights Act of 1866 to prohibit discrimination in access to facilities conveyed in the sale or lease of property.

In 1968, the Supreme Court ruled in *Jones v. Alfred H. Mayer Co.* (q.v.) that the Civil Rights Act of 1866 prohibited racial discrimination by private individuals in the sale or rental of housing. Paul E. Sullivan was a white home owner in an unincorporated community, Little Hunting Park, in Virginia. He rented his house to an African American, T. R. Freeman, Jr., and assigned his membership in a community recreation organization to Freeman for the duration of the lease. When the organization refused to honor Freeman's membership, he and Sullivan sued Little Hunting Park. When the case reached the Supreme Court, it reasoned that the right to sell or rent property would be impaired if the owner's membership rights in a neighborhood recreation facility could not also be assigned to a new owner or tenant. The Court held that such discrimination violated the Civil Rights Act of 1866. The *Jones* and *Sullivan* decisions significantly strengthened the protections against racial discrimination in property transactions.

SULLIVAN v. NEW YORK TIMES. *See* **New York Times v. Sullivan,** 376 U.S. 254 (1964).

SUMMER COMMUNITY ORGANIZATION AND POLITICAL EDUCATION PROGRAM (SCOPE). An SCLC (q.v.) program to extend Mississippi's Freedom Summer (q.v.) to communities across the Deep South.

In February 1965, Hosea Williams (q.v.) persuaded SCLC to create a Summer Community Organization and Political Education program (SCOPE). It would bring 500 to 1000 Northern college students to work with SCLC field staff members on community organization, political education, and voter registration in as many as 120 communities and 10 cities in the Deep South. The plan transferred responsibility for supervising SCLC's Deep South field staff from James Bevel (q.v.) to Williams. Despite the misgivings of SCLC program director Randolph Blackwell about Williams's capacity to manage so large a program, the staff grew dramatically in anticipation of launching SCOPE in the third week of June 1965. By mid-June, when the students arrived in Atlanta for orientation, SCOPE had been scaled back to teams of four to seven students in 50 counties to work under the supervision of local leaders on community organizing, political education, and voter registration. The scaled-down program cost SCLC $100,000 a month, but Martin Luther King (q.v.) believed it was justified if it produced hundreds of thousands of new black voters in the Deep South.

SCOPE students met white hostility in many small Southern communities and, in places where federal agents were not present to register voters, the results were disappointing. By August, leaders in SCLC's inner circle and in the field had serious doubts about SCOPE. SCLC insiders Blackwell, Stanley Levison, Bayard Rustin, and Andrew Young believed it was poorly administered, financially misfeasant, overstaffed, and unproductive. In the field, local leaders complained that support from the central office was not forthcoming and that the students were unsupervised, more interested in direct action than voter registration, and inclined to experiments with liquor and sex that irritated local community relations. Although SCOPE leaders claimed to have registered 85,000 black voters in the Deep South in the summer of 1965, SCLC did not renew SCOPE in 1966.

SWANN v. CHARLOTTE-MECKLENBURG BOARD OF EDUCATION, 402 U.S. 1 (1971). A case in which the Supreme Court approved an extensive court-ordered busing plan to desegregate Charlotte-Mecklenburg County, North Carolina's schools.

In 1965, only two percent of African American students in the Charlotte-Mecklenburg, North Carolina, school district attended school with white students. James Swann and other black parents filed suit, claiming that the board of education had an obligation not merely to desegregate the schools but to create a unified, integrated school system. Federal courts initially rejected the claims of Swann and the other plaintiffs. In 1968, however, the Supreme Court ruled in *Green v. School Board of New Kent County, Virginia* (q.v.) that school boards had an "affirmative duty to take whatever steps" necessary to create a unified, nonsegregated school system. The plaintiffs in *Swann v. Charlotte-Mecklenburg Board of Education* reopened their case. Now, Federal District Judge James B. McMillan found the Charlotte-Mecklenburg Board of Education not in compliance with the Supreme Court's ruling in *Green*.

The school board submitted several plans that he also found unacceptable, so McMillan ordered the board to implement a consultant's plan that redrew school attendance lines and proposed to bus about a thousand students to desegregate the school district. The Charlotte-Mecklenburg Board of Education took the case to the Fourth Circuit Court of Appeals, which by a vote of four to two upheld McMillan's order to bus junior and senior high school students but rejected massive busing of elementary school students. The board's appeal of that decision reached the Supreme Court at the same time as *North Carolina State Board of Education v. Swann* (q.v.), that tested the constitutionality of a North Carolina law which prohibited the use of tax money to bus public school students for the purpose of achieving racial balance. The Court found that the North Carolina antibusing legislation violated the Fourteenth Amendment and it unanimously upheld McMillan's order to use busing to desegregate Charlotte-Mecklenburg's schools.

SWEATT v. PAINTER, 339 U.S. 629 (1950). A case in which the Supreme Court held that the equal protection clause of the Fourteenth Amendment required the Law School of the University of Texas to admit an African American applicant.

In 1946, Heman Marion Sweatt, an African American postal worker in Houston, applied for admission to law school at the University of Texas. The Texas State Board of Regents denied admission to Sweatt on the grounds that state law required that Texas schools be segregated. Alerted by the Supreme Court's decisions in *Missouri ex rel. Gaines v. Canada* (q.v.) and *Sipuel v. Board of Regents of the University of Oklahoma* (q.v.), the Texas Board of Regents had established a law school for African Americans at the Texas College for Negroes in Houston. They referred Sweatt to the admissions office of that institution. Refusing to attend the segregated law school in Houston, Sweatt filed suit against the admissions officer of the University of Texas Law School, Theophilis Painter, and other school officials, seeking to compel them to admit him to the all-white institution. A Texas trial court, the state's court of appeals and the Texas supreme court all ruled against Sweatt.

Dallas attorney William J. Durham and Thurgood Marshall (q.v.) of the NAACP LDEF (q.v.) took Sweatt's case to the Supreme Court. Chief Justice Fred M. Vinson wrote the decision for a unanimous Supreme Court. The two law schools were clearly separate, reasoned the Court, but they were in no way equal. The newly created law school for African American students could not compare with the outstanding faculty, large library, and national reputation of the law school at the University of Texas. The Houston law school was clearly inferior to the University of Texas school and Sweatt could not get an equal education there. The equal protection requirement of the Fourteenth Amendment required that Sweatt be admitted to the University of Texas law school. While the *Sweatt* decision did not overturn the "separate but equal" precedent of *Plessy v. Ferguson,* it was a major step in that direction.

SWEET BRIAR INSTITUTE v. BUTTON, 280 F. Supp. 312 (1967). A case in which a federal district court refused to enforce a provision of a college's trust that restricted its enrollment to white women.

Sweet Briar College was a private female institution in Virginia. Its trust fund restricted its enrollment to "white girls and young women." By November 1963, its board of directors was considering the possibility of breaking that restriction by desegregating the institution. The passage of the Civil Rights Act of 1964 finally forced the issue with its ban on federal funds to institutions of higher education that could not certify that they admitted students regardless of their race. Sweet Briar sought a resolution to its problem by initiating legal action in state and federal courts for guidance. In July 1967, the federal district court in the Western District of Virginia held that judicial enforcement of the restriction on Sweet Briar's trust fund would be "state action" in violation of the Fourteenth Amendment. In anticipation of this kind of resolution of the case, Sweet Briar had enrolled its first African American student in 1966.

T

TALLAHASSEE, FLORIDA, MOVEMENT. The civil rights movement in Florida's state capital.

On 26 May 1956, two students at Florida Agricultural and Mechanical University (FAMU), Wilhemina Jakes and Carrie Patterson, sat in the only remaining seats that were in the white section of a bus in Tallahassee. They were arrested for "inciting to riot" and FAMU students voted to boycott the bus company. On 29 May, the Interdenominational Ministerial Association created a committee including C. K. Steele (q.v.), the pastor of Bethel Baptist Church and president of the local branch of the National Association for the Advancement of Colored People (NAACP; q.v.), to meet with city officials about the problem and hold a mass meeting at Steele's church that evening. When the meeting with city officials proved fruitless, the ministers organized the Inter-Civic Council (ICC) with Steele as its president to lead the bus boycott. Like the Montgomery Improvement Association (MIA; q.v.), it demanded a less oppressive form of segregated seating on a first come, first served basis, more courteous treatment on the buses, and the hiring of black bus drivers.

On 4 June, the bus company seemed to concede the ICC's demands, with the proviso that "members of different races may not occupy the same seat" on the buses. When Steele insisted on desegregation of seating on the buses and the bus company retaliated by suspending all service to black sections of the city, a faction in the black community led by the Reverend David H. Brooks argued for acceptance of the bus company's offer. On 1 July, the bus company discontinued all service in the city. The ICC and 21 individual defendants were found guilty of operating an illegal car pool in support of the bus boycott on 20 October. On 13 November, the Supreme Court confirmed an appeals court's decision that segregation on public transportation is unconstitutional. In January 1957, Tallahassee's ICC became an affiliate of the Southern Christian Leadership Conference (SCLC; q.v.) and Steele was chosen its first vice president. Bus service in Tallahassee did not resume on a desegregated basis until May 1958.

In February 1960, Patricia and Priscilla Stephens, who were FAMU students and members of the Congress of Racial Equality (CORE; q.v.), staged sit-ins at Tallahassee's Greyhound Bus terminal and the Woolworth lunch counter. On 20 February, they were among 11 students who were arrested when they held a second sit-in at Woolworth's lunch counter. On 17 March, they were tried and found guilty of disturbing the peace and unlawful assembly. Sentenced to pay $300 in fines or serve 60 days in the Leon County jail, 8 of the 11 students chose to serve the jail sentence. It was the first instance of a "jail, no bail" strategy that would become popular among organizers of the sit-in movement (q.v.) and the Freedom Rides (q.v.) a year later. On 5 March and 12 March 1960, students from FAMU and white students from Florida State University held additional sit-in demonstrations. After the police used tear gas on the demonstrators and the governor intervened, 240 students were arrested, the first mass arrests in the Tallahassee movement. Yet, the sit-in movement lost momentum thereafter. Internal divisions among black leaders over the direction of the movement contributed to the loss. Some of them believed that more demonstrations would put them at a disadvantage in negotiating with Tallahassee's white officials and encourage white voters to support the segregationist gubernatorial candidate, Farris Bryant, in the upcoming Democratic primary.

In September 1963, 107 FAMU students were arrested for demonstrating outside Tallahassee's Leon County Jail. Convicted of "trespass with a malicious and mischievous intent," Harriet Adderly and 31 others appealed the decision in *Adderly v. Florida* (q.v.). After losing in a Florida district court and a court of appeals, attorneys Richard Felder and Tobias Simon argued before the Supreme Court that the students had been denied their "rights of free speech, assembly, petition, due process of law and equal protection of the laws under the 14th Amendment." Justice Hugo Black spoke for the Court majority in finding that "the state, no less than a private owner of property, has power to preserve the property under its control for the use to which it is lawfully dedicated." In dissent, Justice William O. Douglas said that the Court's decision did "violence to the First Amendment" by allowing "this 'petition for redress of grievances' to be turned into a trespass action."

TAYLOR v. ALABAMA, 335 U.S. 252 (1948). A case in which the Supreme Court concurred with a decision of the Alabama supreme court in denying an appeal of a man's death sentence on the ground that his confession had been coerced.

Samuel Taylor, a 19-year-old black youth, was arrested for raping a 14-year-old white female in Prichard, Alabama, on 12 April 1946. When arrested, he confessed his guilt to the police. At trial, he pled not guilty, but he did not testify in his own defense. Alabama's supreme court upheld his conviction and Taylor's execution was set for 19 September 1947. On the day before he was to be executed, Taylor petitioned Alabama's supreme court for a stay of execution and claimed that his confession had been coerced. Three of his cell mates supported Taylor's claim by saying that they had heard him being beaten, but since no evidence of coercion had been presented during his trial or appeal the Alabama court refused to give Taylor any relief from his sentence. By a vote of six to three, with Justices William O. Douglas, Frank Murphy, and Wiley Rutledge in dissent, the United States Supreme Court upheld the

Alabama supreme court's decision. Writing for the Court majority, Justice Harold Burton said that neither Alabama's legal processes nor its supreme court's decision had violated Taylor's Fourteenth Amendment due process rights.

TAYLOR v. GEORGIA, 315 U.S. 25 (1942). A case in which the Supreme Court reversed the conviction of a Georgia man of intent to defraud.

In 1911, the Supreme Court struck a major blow against peonage (q.v.) in the case of *Bailey v. Alabama.* It ruled that state laws making it a crime to fail to fulfill a labor contract after receiving advance payment violated both the Thirteenth Amendment and the Peonage Abolition Act of 1867. The practice survived, however, in some places into the World War II era. James Taylor, a black Georgian, was indicted in 1940 of accepting money in advance for work that he did not then do. He was convicted of violating a Georgia law which made breach of a labor contract prima facie evidence of an intent to defraud the employer. The Supreme Court unanimously reversed Taylor's conviction and held the Georgia law violated both the Thirteenth Amendment and the Peonage Abolition Act of 1867. In 1944, the Supreme Court would revisit the peonage issue in *Pollock v. Williams* (q.v.) and strike a more forceful blow against peonage.

TERRY v. ADAMS, 345 U.S. 461 (1953). A case in which the Supreme Court held that a political association's refusal to admit African American participants violated the Fifteenth Amendment.

The Jaybird Democratic Association (JDA) of Fort Bend County, Texas, was organized in 1889 and restricted its membership to white citizens. The candidates it endorsed for nomination in the local Democratic Party primary were usually nominated and, because there was no active Republican Party, usually elected to office. John Terry, an African American, filed suit, asking a federal district court to issue an injunction to force the JDA to allow black voters and candidates to participate in its endorsement process. Attorneys for the JDA argued that it was a private organization, free either to accept or exclude members as it chose. The federal district court found for Terry, holding that the JDA's endorsement processes were state action and ordering it to allow black participation in its activities. The Fifth Circuit Court of Appeals reversed the district court ruling, holding the JDA to be a "private club," free to exclude anyone. When Terry appealed to the Supreme Court, it reversed the appellate court's decision by seven to one, with Justice Sherman Minton in dissent. The

Court majority wrote three concurring opinions that cited precedents in *United States v. Classic* (q.v.) and *Smith v. Allwright* (q.v.). They held, in effect, that the JDA was an "auxiliary" of the Democratic Party and that its exclusion of black voters was state action in violation of the Fifteenth Amendment.

TIDEWATER, VIRGINIA, SIT-IN MOVEMENT. The sit-in movement (q.v.) in Tidewater, Virginia.

When African American students in Greensboro, North Carolina, sat in at downtown lunch counters in February 1960, the movement spread, first to other North Carolina cities and then to cities in Virginia, Tennessee, and elsewhere. In Tidewater, Virginia, the movement was led by youth branches of the NAACP (q.v.) at Hampton Institute, Norcom High School, and Virginia State College in Petersburg. Students from Hampton Institute sat in at lunch counters of the F. W. Woolworth store and a Hampton drugstore. At Rose's lunch counter in Portsmith, 18 African American students sought service and 38 others asked to be served at the F. W. Woolworth lunch counter in Norfolk, while P. L. Artis sought breakfast and lunch at Bradshaw-Diehl's Department Store. These first sit-ins in Tidewater were orderly and no one was arrested. When 150 black students demonstrated at Rose's in Portsmith a week later, there were fights between black and white youth. A crowd of 3,000 people gathered at the shopping center and 27 people, black and white, were arrested on various charges. For the next few days, several stores closed their lunch counters. Months later, the lunch counters were desegregated as a result of court orders and voluntary action.

TILL, EMMETT LOUIS (Bobo; 1941–55). Teenage murder victim.

Emmett Till was the son of Louis and Mamie Bradley Till, who had migrated from Missouri and Tallahatchie County, Mississippi, respectively to Chicago. Emmett Till was born there on the South Side on 25 July 1941. He attended Chicago's McCosh Elementary School. Despite an early bout with polio, which left him with a slight speech impediment, Till completed the seventh grade. In August 1955, Mamie Bradley Till sent her son to visit relatives near Money, Leflore County, Mississippi. There, Till and his cousin, Curtis Jones, stayed with Jones's grandfather, Mose Wright, who was a sharecropper. In the afternoon of 24 August 1955, the cousins went to Bryant's Grocery and Meat Market in Money. In conversation with other black youth outside the market, Till was dared to go in the market and speak to the 21-year-old white woman behind the counter.

Allegedly, Emmett Till went inside, bought some candy, and on his way out said "Bye, baby" and whistled. Mrs. Carolyn Bryant later claimed that he had squeezed her hand and asked her for a date. Determined to avenge the insult to his wife, Roy Bryant and his half-brother, J. W. Milam, awakened Mose Wright after midnight on Sunday, 28 August, and took his grandnephew, Emmett Till, from his house. Three days later, his battered body was discovered, partly submerged in the Tallahatchie River. A 75-pound cotton gin fan was tied to his neck. Roy Bryant and J. W. Milam were charged with murdering Emmett Till, but they were acquitted by a local all-white jury. Five months after they murdered Emmett Till, in return for money, Bryant and Milam acknowledged their guilt to journalist William Bradford Huie.

"TO FULFILL THESE RIGHTS" (1966). The theme of a White House Conference on Civil Rights convened by President Lyndon Johnson in 1966.

In June 1965, President Lyndon Johnson proposed a White House Conference on Civil Rights to find ways to combat the remaining obstacles to African American participation in American life. Initially scheduled for the fall, the conference was postponed when controversy erupted over a report by Assistant Secretary of Labor Daniel Patrick Moynihan on the "pathology" of the black family. A planning session regrouped in November and Johnson appointed a Chicago industrialist, Ben Heinemann, to direct further preparations. A detailed report, "To Fulfill These Rights," was prepared and invitations were sent to 2500 people across the nation. The newly elected chairperson of SNCC (q.v.), Stokely Carmichael (q.v.), announced in advance that it would boycott the conference. Out of favor with the White House because of his criticism of the United States' conduct of the Vietnam War, Martin Luther King (q.v.) was initially not invited to the conference. He received an invitation only after black leaders assured the White House that there would be no White House Conference without him.

On 1 and 2 June 1966, the White House convened the conference on civil rights, but it was handicapped from the beginning by racial tension and divisions over the nation's pursuit of the war in Vietnam. As participants in the conference gathered in Washington, James Meredith (q.v.) announced the beginning of his march from Memphis, Tennessee, to Jackson, Mississippi. Conference participants debated the issues of education, housing, racial justice, and welfare, but their debate was not allowed to modify the report drawn up in advance. Although the results of the conference were predetermined, Floyd McKissick (q.v.) of CORE (q.v.) participated in it. He was very critical of the conference, however, especially when a resolution challenging America's role in the Vietnam War was brushed aside. King addressed a conference session but was otherwise relegated to a role as observer and his name hardly appeared in press reports of the conference. Two days after it ended, James Meredith was shot on the highway to Jackson. When Carmichael, King, and McKissick took up the Meredith March two days later, their manifesto roundly attacked the federal government and the state of Mississippi for failing "to fulfill these rights." Some of the conference report's recommendations did become a part of the Civil Rights Act of 1968 (q.v.), but the issues that divided the conference kept President Johnson from giving its recommendations a very high priority.

TO SECURE THESE RIGHTS (1947). The report of President Harry S Truman's President's Committee on Civil Rights.

When World War II's end refocused national attention on domestic issues, Walter F. White (q.v.) of the NAACP (q.v.) persuaded President Truman to establish the President's Committee on Civil Rights. He did so in Executive Order 9808 (q.v.), which was signed on 5 December 1946. Its 15 members were asked to report on how federal, state, and local governments could strengthen protections of the people's civil rights. Published on 29 October 1947, the committee's report, *To Secure These Rights* (q.v.), was based on the testimony of about 40 witnesses and information from 25 federal agencies. It called for establishing a permanent federal Civil Rights Commission (q.v.), a Congressional Committee on Civil Rights, and a Civil Rights Division of the Justice Department, for strengthening existing civil rights laws, for making lynching a federal crime, for abolishing the poll tax and strengthening protections of the right to vote, for ending segregation in the armed forces, and for establishing a Fair Employment Practice Commission. The committee's report led to President Truman's Executive Order 9981 (q.v.), which ordered the desegregation of the armed services, and it focused national attention on civil rights issues, but it did not lead to significant federal civil rights legislation.

TONKINS v. CITY OF GREENSBORO, 171 F. Supp. 476 (M.D. N.C., 1959). A case in which the federal district court for the Middle District of North Carolina dismissed a complaint about the sale of a Greensboro swimming pool to avoid desegregation.

In 1957, in *Simkins v. City of Greensboro* (q.v.), the federal district court for the Middle District of North Carolina ordered the city to offer equal access to its public golf courses to both races and the city responded by closing both its public golf courses. A year later, Deloris Tonkins and others sought an injunction to keep the city from barring African American citizens from its Lindley Park Swimming Pool by selling it to a private party. The original complaint was dismissed and the pool was sold to the Greensboro Pool Corporation. Attorneys for Tonkins and others, including Thurgood Marshall (q.v.) of the NAACP Legal Defense and Educational Fund (LDEF; q.v.), filed a supplemental complaint that sought to show collusion between the city and the successful bidder in an attempt to perpetuate segregation at the swimming pool. The court found insufficient evidence for the plaintiffs' allegations that the private corporation would default on its annual payments, be given an extended time to make its annual installments, or the city would repurchase the property in a foreclosure sale. The plaintiffs' supplemental complaint was dismissed.

TOURE, KWAME. *See* **Carmichael, Stokely.**

TUREAUD, ALEXANDER PIERRE (A. P.; 1899–1972). Civil rights attorney.

A. P. Tureaud was born on 26 February 1899 in New Orleans, Louisiana. He attended public schools for African American youth in New Orleans and Washington, D.C. In 1922, Tureaud entered Howard University Law School, from which he graduated in 1925. He returned to New Orleans the following year and began working with the New Orleans branch of the NAACP (q.v.). He led a move to oust its lethargic older leaders and transform it into a more progressive vehicle for black Louisianans. Between 1940 and 1943, Tureaud filed actions that led to salary equalization for black public school teachers in East Baton Rouge, Iberville, Jefferson, and Orleans parishes. His brief in *Hall v. Nagel* (1946) helped to open voter registration books to black Louisianans. In 1953, Tureaud filed a class action suit, *Tureaud v. Board of Supervisors* (q.v.), to desegregate graduate and professional schools at Louisiana State University. His suits against parish school boards forced them to begin implementing the Supreme Court's decision in *Brown v. Board of Education* (q.v.). Tureaud was the lead attorney in *Garner v. Louisiana* (q.v.), the first sit-in case to reach the United States Supreme Court. He died in New Orleans on 22 January 1972.

TUREAUD v. BOARD OF SUPERVISORS, 347 U.S. 971 (1954). A case in which the Supreme Court ordered the desegregation of graduate and professional schools at Louisiana State University.

In 1953, New Orleans NAACP attorney A. P. Tureaud was denied admission to a six-year program in arts, sciences, and law at Louisiana State University because, it was claimed, a similar program was available to him at Southern University, an African American institution. He filed a class action suit, claiming that the program at Southern University was not substantially equal to the program at Louisiana State. When a federal district court ordered Tureaud's admission to Louisiana State, the case was appealed to the United State Supreme Court. On 24 May 1954, the Court sustained the district court's order.

TUSKEGEE CIVIC ASSOCIATION. A moderate civil rights organization at Tuskegee, Alabama.

Although they outnumbered white people in Macon County, Alabama, by three to one, most African Americans were unable to vote. Finding the local government of white men unresponsive to African Americans' need of adequate public services, Charles G. Gomillion (q.v.) and other black professional men at Tuskegee Institute and the local Veterans Hospital organized the Tuskegee Civic Association in 1941 to seek better public services for the black community, equal educational opportunities, and a "color-blind" civil democracy. They believed the answer lay in securing African American voting rights. After years of trying, Gomillion and others registered to vote. By 1941, enough of them had registered in Tuskegee to affect the results of closely contested local elections. The Tuskegee Civic Association's moderate pursuit of African American interests won some improved public services for black Tuskegeeans.

In 1957, Alabama's state legislature redrew the city boundaries to exclude almost all of its four hundred black voters and assure continued white rule in Tuskegee. The Tuskegee Civic Association successfully challenged this move in *Gomillion v. Lightfoot* (q.v.), a case in which the Supreme Court rejected the legislature's gerrymander in 1960. By then, however, younger movement activists had turned to direct action in boycotts, Freedom Rides (q.v.), picket lines, and sit-ins. The new activism cast the Tuskegee Civic Association's moderation in a conservative light and it lost initiative by the mid-1960s.

TUTTLE, ELBERT PARR (1897–1996). A member of the Fifth Circuit Court of Appeals (q.v.).

Elbert P. Tuttle was born on 17 July 1897 in Pasadena, California. He grew up in Hawaii, where his father was a cashier for the Hawaiian Sugar Planters Association. Young Tuttle attended the multiracial Punaho School. He attended Cornell University and served briefly in the Army Air Force at the end of World War I. After marrying Sara Sutherland and serving as a reporter for two years, Tuttle returned to law school at Cornell and was editor of its law review. In 1923, the Tuttles moved to Atlanta, where he practiced law in an established firm for a year before entering a partnership with his brother-in-law, William Sutherland. Tuttle was active in civic affairs and served a term as president of Atlanta's chamber of commerce. During World War II, he commanded the 304th Field Artillery Battalion in the Pacific. On 19 April 1945, a Japanese suicide squad staged a predawn attack on his camp on an island near Okinawa. Tuttle was wounded in his neck, back, left hand, and both legs by a grenade that exploded by his tent. Clubbed on his head while overwhelming the Japanese, Tuttle nevertheless told his commander when it was over: "I've never felt better in my life."

After the war, Tuttle returned to his legal practice in Atlanta. In 1951, John Minor Wisdom (q.v.) of Louisiana recruited him to lead a challenge to Georgia's regular Republican organization on behalf of General Dwight Eisenhower's campaign for the Republican nomination for president. When the Eisenhower delegations from Georgia, Louisiana, and Texas were seated by the Republican National Convention in July 1952, Eisenhower became the party's nominee. Tuttle was general counsel to the Treasury Department in the Eisenhower administration from 1953 to 1955, when he was appointed to the Fifth Circuit Court of Appeals. Wisdom joined him on the Fifth Circuit bench two years later. With Richard Taylor Rives (q.v.) and John Robert Brown (q.v.), they implemented and expanded the United States Supreme Court's mandate in *Brown v. Board of Education* (q.v.) in the Deep South.

The presence of Brown, Rives, Tuttle and Wisdom—all devoted to racial justice—would help to ensure the success of the civil rights movement. Beyond desegregation of public schools, their decisions undermined racial discrimination in employment, jury selection, and voting rights. From 1961 to 1967, when he retired from the bench, Tuttle served as chief judge of the Fifth Circuit Court of Appeals. In 1966, in *Bond v. Floyd*, he was the only member of a three-member appeals court panel who held that the Georgia legislature had unconstitutionally refused to seat Julian Bond (q.v.) because of his views on the war in Vietnam. Elsewhere, however, his leadership, particularly in using the civil rights injunction, transformed the due process clause of the Fourteenth Amendment from what Paul Robeson (q.v.) had called the "Sleeping Giant of the American Constitution" into a powerful tool for racial justice.

U

UNITED STATES CIVIL RIGHTS COMMISSION. An agency of the federal government that monitors civil rights in the United States.

On 9 September 1957, President Dwight Eisenhower signed the Civil Rights Act of 1957. It established the United States Civil Rights Commission to investigate the denial of civil rights due to fraudulent practices or discrimination based on color, race, religion, or national origin and recommend corrective action. It has been concerned primarily with rights to equal protection of the law and voting rights. The commission has no enforcement authority. The commission has been chaired by: Michigan State University president John A. Hannah, 1957–69; Notre Dame University President Reverend Theodore Hesburgh, 1969–72; Stephen Thorn, 1972–74; Arthur Fletcher, 1974–82; Clarence Pendleton, 1982–88; Arthur Fletcher, 1988–93; and Mary Frances Berry (q.v.), 1993–

UNITED STATES COURT OF APPEALS FOR THE FIFTH JUDICIAL CIRCUIT. *See* **Fifth Circuit Court of Appeals, United States.**

UNITED STATES ex rel. GOLDSBY v. HARPOLE, 263 F.2d 71 (5th Cir., 1959). A case in which the Fifth Circuit Court of Appeals (q.v.) reversed the conviction of a black Mississippian for murder on the grounds that black people were systematically excluded from jury duty.

A black resident of Carroll County, Mississippi, Robert Lee Goldsby, was indicted, tried, and convicted of the murder of a white couple. Although 57 percent of Carroll County's population of 15,000 was black, Goldsby's jury was all white. Jury duty in Mississippi was restricted to registered voters and because none of Carroll County's registered voters were black, no black people were eligible to serve on a jury. In a landmark case, the Fifth Circuit Court of Appeals reversed Goldsby's conviction because black people were excluded from jury service, remanded the case to Mississippi, and ordered that he be tried by a jury from which black people were not excluded. Goldsby was retried, convicted, and executed, but the case established a principle that trial by a jury of one's peers, who were selected without racial discrimination, was a constitutional right.

UNITED STATES v. FORDICE, GOVERNOR OF MISSISSIPPI, 505 U.S. _____ (1992). A case in which the Supreme Court found Mississippi's dual system of higher education in violation of its decision in *Brown v. Board of Education* (q.v.).

In 1975, Jake Ayers sued the state of Mississippi because its dual system of predominately white and historically black colleges and universities remained overwhelmingly segregated and denied black students equality of opportunity. Later, other black petitioners renewed Ayers's case. In 1990, after Republican Kirk Fordice was elected governor of Mississippi, the Department of Justice brought suit on behalf of the petitioners against Fordice and the state's higher education officials to end racial segregation in Mississippi's higher education. In 1992, Justice Byron White delivered the opinion of a unanimous Supreme Court, which found the state's dual system of higher education in violation of the Constitution as interpreted in its 1954 decision in *Brown v. Board of Education* and of the Civil Rights Act of 1964 (q.v.).

UNITED STATES v. GUEST, 383 U.S. 745 (1966). A case in which the Supreme Court ruled that interstate travel is a protected right under the Fourteenth Amendment.

While Lemuel Penn, an African American teacher, was driving through Georgia, he was stopped and shot by six white men, Herbert Guest, James Spergeon Lackey, Cecil William Myers, Denver Willis Phillips, Joseph Howard Sims, and George Hampton Turner. They were tried by the state of Georgia for conspiracy to deprive Penn of his civil rights under section 6 of the Enforcement Act of 1870, but they were acquitted. In 1964, the six men were indicted by a federal grand jury under Section 241 of the United States Code. Attorneys for the defendants argued that the indictment was invalid because Section 241 protected only against interference with the exercise of the right to equal use of state facilities, which was not a right secured by the Fourteenth Amendment. The federal district court judge threw the indictment out because it did not involve national citizenship rights to which he held Section 241 solely applied. On appeal to the Supreme Court, six justices joined in separate opinions to find that they had no jurisdiction over the part of the indictment that dealt with interference with the right to use public accommodations. The Court also held that interstate travel is a right protected by the Fourteenth Amendment, reinstated the indictments, and returned the case to federal district court in Georgia for further action.

UNITED STATES v. JEFFERSON COUNTY BOARD OF EDUCA-TION, 372 F.2d (5th Cir., 1966). A case in which the Fifth Circuit Court of Appeals (q.v.) rejected "freedom of choice" plans for school desegregation in favor of compulsory racially unitary school integration.

The Civil Rights Act of 1964 (q.v.) mandated that the Department of Health, Education, and Welfare (HEW) establish guidelines for school integration. Some local school districts in Alabama and Louisiana had by 1965 adopted "freedom of choice" desegregation plans which admitted very few African American students to previously all-white schools. They seemed to satisfy the Supreme Court's 1955 mandate in *Briggs v. Elliot* (q.v.) and *Brown v. Board of Education* (q.v.) that school systems must desegregate "with all deliberate speed," but they largely maintained racially separate school systems and did not conform to HEW guidelines. Judge John Minor Wisdom (q.v.) wrote the Fifth Circuit Court's opinion, which adopted HEW's guidelines for a racially unified school system, strengthened the federal government's ability to withhold funds from recalcitrant school districts, and forced those districts to comply with school integration orders. Two years later, the Supreme Court signaled its agreement with the Fifth Circuit Court opinion in *Green v. School Board of New Kent County, Virginia* (q.v.).

UNITED STATES v. LOUISIANA. *See* **United States v. Ward.**

UNITED STATES v. LYND, 349 F.2d 785 (5th Cir., 1965). A case in which the Fifth Circuit Court of Appeals (q.v.) issued an "injunction pending appeal" that ordered a Mississippi voter registrar to cease to discriminate against African American applicants.

In 1959, voters in Hattiesburg and Forrest County, Mississippi, chose Theron Lynd, a 330-pound former football player and member of the Citizens' Council (q.v.), as circuit clerk. His office managed voter registration in the county. When he refused to allow the Justice Department to examine his files, Attorney General William Rogers filed suit to win access. His examiners found that a majority of the 22,431 white voting-age residents of Forrest County were registered but only 25 of the county's 7,431 eligible black residents were registered. Lynd allowed no black people to attempt to register between 1959 and 1961. After federal intervention, some black people tried to register, but all of them, including high school teachers with graduate work in biology, chemistry, and physics, failed the qualifying test. In 1961, the Justice Department filed a second suit, *United States v. Lynd*, which sought an injunction against Lynd's racial discrimination in registering voters.

On 15 July 1963, a three-judge panel of the Fifth Circuit Court found Lynd in civil contempt of a previous order and ordered him to cease racial discrimination or face a jail sentence. Lynd appealed the decision to the Supreme Court and continued to stall. After the passage of the Voting Rights Act of 1965 (q.v.), the Justice Department again sought relief from Lynd's racial discrimination. Federal district judge Harold E. Cox, a Kennedy administration appointee and college roommate of Senator James Eastland, had repeatedly stalled the Justice Department and postponed final decisions in his court. A frustrated Justice Department appealed to the Fifth Circuit Court for relief. The Fifth Circuit Court sharply departed from standard appellate procedure, in which an appeals court reviewed only final district court decisions, by issuing an "injunction pending appeal" against Lynd. That procedure notified district judges that delay of justice by postponement would not be tolerated and it was widely employed thereafter in school desegregation and voter registration cases.

UNITED STATES v. MONTGOMERY COUNTY SCHOOL BOARD, 395 U.S. 225 (1969). A case in which the Supreme Court upheld a federal district court order to desegregate public school faculties in Montgomery, Alabama.

Despite repeated federal court decisions that segregation was unconstitutional and court orders to facilitate integration, the Montgomery County, Alabama, school board had failed to desegregate its school system ten years after the Supreme Court's decision in *Brown v. Board of Education* (q.v.). In order to speed the process, the federal district court ordered the school board to desegregate on a ratio of three to two of white to black faculty and staff members in each school to reflect the county's population ratio and to set the ratio of night, student, and substitute teachers at the same ratio for the whole school system. Schools with fewer than twelve teachers were required to have at least one teacher whose race was different from the majority of the faculty; schools with twelve or more teachers were required to have at least one teacher of a minority race for every six faculty and staff members. On appeal, the Fifth Circuit Court of Appeals (q.v.) reversed the federal district court order. The United States Supreme Court upheld the federal district court order. Justice Hugo Black wrote for a unanimous Court that the desegregation of faculty and staff was important and that, given the board's history of recalcitrance, the district court's action was appropriate and necessary.

UNITED STATES v. NORTHWEST LOUISIANA RESTAURANT CLUB, 256 F. Supp. 151 (W.D. La. 1966). A case in which the federal district court for the western district of Louisiana held that only real private clubs, whose membership was based on an identifiable nonracial condition or requirement, could claim exemption from the public accommodations section of the Civil Rights Act of 1964 (q.v.).

After the passage of the Civil Rights Act of 1964, about 100 restaurant owners in Shreveport and Lake Charles, Louisiana, organized and became voting members of the Northwest Louisiana Restaurant Club. They routinely issued nonvoting membership cards to white customers who dined at restaurants that belonged to the club. African Americans were denied membership cards and were denied admission to or service at the restaurants because they did not belong to the club. Its officers freely acknowledged that the club was formed to circumvent the Civil Rights Act of 1964 by claiming its exemption of a private club. The federal district court for the western district of Louisiana held that only real private clubs, whose membership was based on an identifiable nonracial condition or requirement, could claim exemption from the Civil Rights Act's public accommodations clause. This and similar decisions prevented businesses in public accommodations from evading the act's intentions by forming "private clubs" in order to continue to operate on a racially discriminatory basis.

UNITED STATES v. PARADISE, 480 U.S. 149 (1987). A case in which the Supreme Court limited the use of race-based hiring and promotions as affirmative action (q.v.) to overcome past discrimination.

In 1972, African American plaintiffs sued the Alabama Department of Public Safety (ADPS), claiming its hiring decisions had been racially discriminatory. A federal district court agreed and ordered several remedies. In 1974, the court held that the ADPS was restricting the size of the state police force in order to limit hiring African Americans. Three years later, the African American plaintiffs sued again for relief, alleging that there were no remedies to end hiring discrimination. In 1979, the court agreed to a plan by which the ADPS would implement a fair hiring policy within a year. The policy was tested in 1981, but only a few black applicants were hired. Three years later, the court found that the new policy was not working and ordered the ADPS to adopt a "one for one" hiring and promotion policy in which one black person would be hired or promoted for each white person hired or promoted. The court suspended its order after eight black and eight white applicants were hired under this plan, ordering only that thirteen new officers be hired in this way. The Justice Department asked the Eleventh Circuit Court of Appeals to order the continuation of the federal district court's earlier plan, but it affirmed the district court's decision. By a vote of five to four, with Chief Justice William Rehnquist and Justices Sandra Day O'Connor, Antonin Scalia, and Byron White in dissent, the Supreme Court sustained the federal district court's decision. The conservative minority held that the district court had exceeded its bounds in the 1984 court order.

UNITED STATES v. PRICE, 383 U.S. 787 (1966). A case in which the Supreme Court reinstated the indictments of men accused of the murders of James Chaney (q.v.), Andrew Goodman (q.v.), and Michael Schwerner (q.v.).

Neshoba County, Mississippi, sheriff Lawrence Rainey and deputy sheriff Cecil Ray Price, Philadelphia, Mississippi, policeman Richard Willis and 15 private individuals were indicted for conspiring to deprive James Chaney, Andrew Goodman, and Michael Schwerner of their civil rights. According to the indictments, Price arrested Chaney, Goodman, and Schwerner in Neshoba County, released them, and followed them in a sheriff's car. He picked the three men up again, read the charges against them, and took them to a secret place where the other men joined Price in murdering the three civil rights activists. A federal district judge dismissed the indictments against the 15 private individuals on the grounds that they were not "acting under the color of the law." The federal judge also dismissed the charges against Rainey, Price, and Willis because they did not violate enumerated rights under the Fourteenth Amendment. The Justice Department appealed to the United States Supreme Court to reinstate the indictments of all 18 men. Solicitor General Thurgood Marshall (q.v.) argued its case before the Court.

The Supreme Court ordered reinstatement of the indictment of the 15 private individuals because, as Justice Abe Fortas wrote, "to act 'under color' of law does not require that the accused be an officer of the state. It is enough that he is the willing participant in joint activity with the state or its agents." The Court also ordered reinstatement of the indictment of Rainey, Price, and Willis. Their indictment "sets forth a conspiracy within the ambit of the Fourteenth Amendment," Fortas wrote, and "alleges that the defendants acted 'under color of law' and that the conspiracy included action by the State through its law enforcement officers to punish the alleged victims without the due process of law in violation of the Fourteenth Amendment's direct admonition to the States." In October 1967, seven white men including Rainey, Price, and Willis were convicted in federal court of conspiring to deprive Chaney, Goodman, and Schwerner of their civil rights.

UNITED STATES v. RAINES, 362 U.S. 17 (1960). A case in which the Supreme Court upheld the constitutionality of the Civil Rights Act of 1957 (q.v.).

The Civil Rights Act of 1957 authorized the attorney general to seek a federal court injunction against persons who deprived others of the right to vote because of their race. The defendants in this case were Georgia public officials who the Justice Department accused of discriminating against African Americans who sought to register to vote. Federal district judge T. Hoyt Davis held that the Civil Rights Act of 1957 was unconstitutional and found for the defendants. Davis reasoned that because the act did not refer to persons acting "under color of law," it unconstitutionally authorized the Justice Department to act in cases in which there was only private discrimination and that were beyond the reach of the Fifteenth Amendment. On appeal, the United States Supreme Court reversed Judge Davis. Speaking for the Court, Justice William Brennan wrote that the defendants were acting "under color of law," that they could not challenge it on the grounds of how it might affect others and that it was within the power of Congress to protect private constitutional rights. Had the Court found otherwise, victims of voter discrimination would have had to bring suit for relief themselves rather than relying on the Justice Department to defend their right to register and vote.

UNITED STATES v. SCHOOL DISTRICT OF COOK COUNTY, 286 F. Supp. 786 (W.D. Ill. 1968). A case in which the federal district court for the western district of Illinois held that school board policies perpetuating racial segregation, originally caused by housing patterns, transform legally permissible de facto segregation into unconstitutional de jure segregation.

The Justice Department brought suit to desegregate School District 151 in the Chicago, Illinois, suburbs. Attorneys for the school district contended that racial segregation in the district derived from residential housing patterns beyond the school board's control and that neighborhood schools were permissible under the Supreme Court's decision in *Brown v. Board of Education* (q.v.). The federal district court found, to the contrary, that school district authorities had built schools, drawn attendance zones, and assigned teachers by race to perpetuate racial segregation in violation of both the Fourteenth Amendment and the Civil Rights Act of 1964. Other federal courts had held that *Brown* condoned neighborhood schools in which racial separation derived from natural ethnic housing patterns. If so, school authorities had no legal obligation to correct racial imbalances. In *United States v. School District of Cook County,* the court looked beyond state law to school district policies and procedures as sources of de jure segregation.

UNITED STATES v. SCOTLAND NECK CITY BOARD OF EDUCATION, 407 U.S. 484 (1972). A case in which the Supreme Court found that the creation of a separate school district with the apparent purpose of avoiding racial integration was unconstitutional.

In 1965, African American students were 77 percent of the school-age population in Halifax County, North Carolina, but they attended public schools that were still racially segregated. Between 1965 and 1968, Halifax County operated on a "freedom of choice" plan that minimized the effect of desegregation on the county's schools. When the Justice Department intervened to force more rapid desegregation 14 years after the Supreme Court's decision in *Brown v. Board of Education* (q.v.), 99 percent of Halifax County's white students still attended all-white schools and 97 percent of its black students attended all-black schools. In January 1969, while Halifax County was under a federal court order to desegregate its schools, the state legislature authorized the community of Scotland Neck, a white enclave in Halifax County, to form a separate school district.

A federal district court ruled against allowing Scotland Neck to separate itself from Halifax County's desegregation order, but the Fourth Circuit Court of Appeals reversed the district court's decision. On 22 June 1972, the United States Supreme Court rendered a unanimous opinion against the creation of a separate Scotland Neck school district. "Any attempt by state or local officials to carve out a new school district from an existing district that is in the process of dismantling a dual school system," wrote Justice Potter Stewart, "must be judged according to whether it hinders or furthers the process of school desegregation." Clearly, he concluded, the separation of Scotland Neck schools from the rest of Halifax County schools was intended to create "a refuge for white students" from the desegregation order.

UNITED STATES v. WALLACE, 218 F. Supp. 290 (N.D. Ala. 1963). A case in which the federal district court for the northern district of Alabama ordered Governor George C. Wallace (q.v.) not to interfere with the admission of African American students to the University of Alabama.

On 16 May 1963, the federal district court for the northern district of Alabama ordered the University of Alabama to admit two African American students, James Hood and Vivian Malone, for the summer session. Governor George C. Wallace promised to stand by his 1962 promise to uphold racial segregation even if he had to stand "in the schoolhouse door." On 5 June, the Justice Department won a federal district court injunction against any interference by Governor Wallace in the desegregation of the University of Alabama. On 11 June, Wallace defied the federal court order and stood in the door of a university building to prevent Assistant Attorney General Nicholas Katzenbach from escorting the two black students inside to register. Wallace's action was largely a symbolic gesture. After President Kennedy nationalized the Alabama National Guard and a commanding general returned with the students later that day, Governor Wallace stood aside.

UNITED STATES v. WARD, 352 F.2d 329 (5th Cir., 1965). A case in which the Fifth Circuit Court of Appeals (q.v.) froze restrictive voter registration requirements in Louisiana for two years.

The Justice Department sued Katherine Ward, the registrar of voters in Madison Parish, and the state of Louisiana to halt the application of racially discriminatory state voter registration requirements, such as a literacy test or a requirement that an applicant be able to interpret a passage of the Constitution to the satisfaction of the registrar. The Fifth Circuit Court of Appeals ordered a two-year freeze on the restrictive voter registration requirements to allow all applicants to be registered under the less restrictive requirements that were applied to white applicants. Its ruling would have allowed the more restrictive requirements to have been reapplied on a nondiscriminatory basis after two years. When the Voting Rights Act of 1965 (q.v.) authorized a five-year freeze on restrictive voter registration requirements, the Fifth Circuit Court revised its order to extend the freeze to five years. Federal courts adopted the freeze to compensate for the effect of past discrimination because merely to apply the restrictive registration requirements uniformly to black and white applicants would protect white voters already registered without the restrictions and prevent many black applicants because of the difficult requirements.

UNITED STEELWORKERS v. WEBER, 443 U.S. 193 (1979). A case in which the Supreme Court held that affirmative-action training programs in the skilled crafts were constitutional.

In 1974, the United Steelworkers of America reached an affirmative-action agreement with the Kaiser Aluminum and Chemical Corporation that reserved 50 percent of the company's craft training programs for African American employees. When seven black and six white employees were chosen for a program at Kaiser's plant in Gramercy, Louisiana, several white employees who sought admission to the program, including Brian Weber, had greater seniority than black employees who were chosen for it. Weber sued in federal district court for relief from the union's agreement with Kaiser Aluminum, claiming that it violated the Civil Rights Act of 1964 (q.v.). Both the federal district court and the Fifth Circuit Court of Appeals (q.v.) ruled for Weber, holding that the agreement violated section 701(a), 42 U.S.C., which said it was illegal for an employer "to fail or refuse to hire any individual, or otherwise to discriminate against any individual, with respect to his compensation, terms, conditions, or privileges of employment" because of the individual's color, gender, national origin, race, or religion. The United Steelworkers appealed to the Supreme Court. In a five-to-two decision, with Chief Justice Warren Burger and Justice William Rehnquist in dissent and Justices Lewis Powell and John Paul Stevens not participating in the decision, the Supreme Court reversed the lower courts' ruling. Justice William Brennan wrote the majority opinion, which held that because workers voluntarily entered into the agreement by a collective bargaining process the agreement was not state action and was not a violation of any law, including the equal protection requirement of the Fourteenth Amendment.

UNIVERSITY OF CALIFORNIA REGENTS v. BAKKE, 438 U.S. 265 (1978). A case in which the Supreme Court found that racial quotas in college or university admissions were unconstitutional.

Alan Bakke was a 37-year-old applicant who was twice denied admission to the medical school at the University of California at Davis. The institution set aside 16 of 100 admission's places in each class for minority students. Bakke sued, claiming that the university had admitted minority students who were less well qualified than he was, that were it not for this affirmative action (q.v.) policy, he would have been admitted to the institution and that the affirmative action policy had caused him to be denied the equal protection of the laws. The California supreme court ruled in Bakke's favor and he was admitted to the medical school. In the meantime, however, the school appealed the state supreme court's decision to the United States Supreme Court. When the Court heard the case, Bakke was actually nearing completion of his degree. Four years earlier, the Supreme Court had dodged the substantial issue in a similar case, *DeFunis v. Odegaard* (q.v.).

In 1978, a severely divided Supreme Court issued an opinion in Bakke's favor. By a vote of five to four, with Justices Harry Blackmun, William Brennan, Thurgood Marshall, and Byron White concurring in part and dissenting in part, the Court ruled that denial of admission to Bakke because of his race was a violation of his equal protection rights. In a second five-to-four ruling, the Court held that an institution could use race as one variable among others in admissions if it was attempting to rectify a history of discrimination, which was not evident in the Bakke case. "The fatal flaw," in the University of California's preferential admissions program, wrote Justice Lewis Powell for the majority, "is its disregard of individual rights as guaranteed by the Fourteenth Amendment. Such rights are not absolute. But when a State's distribution of benefits or imposition of burdens hinges on the color of a person's skin or ancestry, that individual is entitled to a demonstration that the challenged classification is necessary to promote a substantial state interest."

URBAN LEAGUE. *See* National Urban League.

V

VOTER EDUCATION PROJECT (VEP). A privately funded, nonpartisan project to encourage African Americans throughout the South to register to vote.

After the sit-in movement (q.v.) and as the Freedom Rides (q.v.) continued in the summer of 1961, Attorney General Robert Kennedy, Southern Regional Council Executive Director Harold C. Fleming, and a wealthy young philanthropist, Stephen R. Currier of the Taconic Foundation, discussed the creation of a privately funded, nonpartisan project to register African Americans throughout the South to vote. Kennedy thought that a voter registration campaign among unregistered black people would be more productive than either a struggle for additional civil rights legislation in Congress or additional nonviolent direct action in the South and he expected sympathetic Democratic candidates to benefit from a harvest of new black voters. Federal money could not be used for the purpose, but Kennedy's Justice Department could file lawsuits to force recalcitrant registrars to open the doors to black applicants and privately encourage philanthropic support for it.

By September 1961, the Congress of Racial Equality (CORE; q.v.), the National Association for the Advancement of Colored People (NAACP; q.v.), the National Urban League (q.v.), the Southern Christian Leadership Conference (SCLC; q.v.), and the Student Nonviolent Coordinating Committee (SNCC; q.v.) were preparing to receive grants from the Voter Education Project (VEP) in support of their voter registration efforts. Sheltered under the tax-exempt status of the Southern Regional Council and directed by civil rights attorney Wiley Branton, VEP was launched in April 1962 and scheduled to extend for two-and-a-half years with $870,000 in grants from the Taconic, Field, and Stern foundations. About 25 percent of eligible black voters in the South were then registered. In Mississippi, where VEP directed much of its attention, only 5 percent of eligible black adults were registered. Activists working for the five civil rights organizations canvassed rural areas and small communities across the Deep South, conducted citizenship and literacy workshops, and encouraged black people to register. In many areas, they faced threats, jailing, beatings, bombing, or killing from determined white opposition. Federal protection, implied by Kennedy's encouragement of the project, was limited to his expansion of the Civil Rights Division of the Justice Department and its prosecution of voting rights cases and violations of the civil rights of activists who were injured or murdered.

Between 1962 and 1964, the percentage of eligible African Americans who were registered to vote in the South rose from 25 percent to over 40 percent, but VEP complained that SCLC failed to generate any voter registration effort in many of the areas assigned to it. VEP sent $50,000 to Mississippi's Council of Federated Organizations (COFO; q.v.) in 1962 and it could count only 3,228 newly registered black voters. The violence against voter registration workers in rural Georgia, Alabama, and Mississippi and the lack of dramatic results helped to convince the Johnson administration of the necessity of additional federal legislation, i.e., the Civil Rights Act of 1964 (q.v.) and the Voting Rights Act of 1965 (q.v.). In 1964, civil rights attorney Vernon Jordan (q.v.) replaced Branton as director of VEP. Despite serious problems in SCLC's Summer Community Organization and Political Education Program (SCOPE; q.v.) in 1965, VEP produced more significant gains with firm federal enforcement of the new legislation. In Mississippi, registered black voters increased from 28,500 in 1964 to 251,000 in 1968 and, across the South, the percentage of eligible black adults who were registered grew from slightly over 40 percent to 62 percent.

VOTING RIGHTS ACT OF 1957. *See* **Civil Rights Act of 1957.**

VOTING RIGHTS ACT OF 1965. Federal legislation that strengthened African American voting rights in the South.

Early in 1965, as Martin Luther King (q.v.) and SCLC (q.v.) increased the pressure in their voting rights campaign at Selma, Alabama, President Lyndon Johnson's Justice Department considered ways to strengthen African American voting rights in the South. After "Bloody Sunday" in Selma, Alabama, in a nationally televised address to the Congress on 15 March, President Johnson introduced the legislation as necessary so that "we shall overcome" America's "crippling legacy of bigotry and injustice." On 26 May, the voting rights legislation passed the Senate overwhelmingly. On 9 July, the House of Representatives passed a similar bill by a similar overwhelming majority. After a conference committee compromised on the two versions of the legislation, it passed both houses of Congress in early August and was signed by President Johnson on 6 August. As adopted, the Civil Rights Act of 1965 banned literacy requirements for registering or voting in states or counties where less than 50 percent of the voting-age population was registered to vote on 1 November 1964 or voted in the 1964 presidential election; it authorized the attorney general to send federal registrars to register voters in those states or counties; it required that in the next ten years those jurisdictions have the permission of the Justice Department or the federal district court for the District of Columbia for any changes in its registration or voting procedures; and it authorized the Justice Department or the court to terminate these procedures if a state or county could prove that it had not discriminated for ten years.

On 10 August 1965, the attorney general sent federal registrars into nine Southern counties. By the end of the year, federal registrars had registered almost 80,000 new voters. In a variety of ways—at-large elections, gerrymandering, or making more offices appointive—some of the affected Southern states sought to minimize the power of the new

African American voters. These changes were generally rejected by federal courts. The United States Supreme Court held the Voting Rights Act of 1965 to be constitutional in *Katzenbach v. Morgan* (q.v.) and *South Carolina v. Katzenbach* (q.v.). Enforcement of the Voting Rights Act of 1965 increased black voter registration in the South dramatically, from just over 40 percent of eligible adults in 1964 to 62 percent of eligible adults in 1968. In Mississippi, the numbers of black voters grew from 28,500 in 1964 to 251,000 in 1968. The increased numbers of black voters led to more black officials and caused white officials to be more sensitive to the needs of black constituents.

W

WALDEN, AUSTIN THOMAS (A. T.; 1885–1965). Civil rights attorney and judge.

A. T. Walden was born on 12 April 1885 in Fort Valley, Georgia. His parents, Jeff and Jennie Tomlin Walden, had been born in slavery. Young Walden studied in Fort Valley's public schools for young African Americans and earned a B.A. at Atlanta University in 1907. He entered law school at the University of Michigan, where he received an LL.B. in 1911. Walden practiced law in Macon, Georgia, from 1912 until he entered the United States Army for service in World War I. He commanded Company I of the 365th Infantry in France and was a trial judge advocate in the 92nd Division. After marrying Mary Ellen Denny of Baltimore on 18 May 1918, Walden moved his legal practice from Macon to Atlanta, Georgia. His general practice there prospered, but he became noted for his role in civil rights cases.

In the 1930s, for example, Walden represented John Downer, an African American who was indicted, tried, convicted, and sentenced to death for rape in Macon only after being rescued from a lynch mob by Georgia national guardsmen under the command of Major Elbert Tuttle (q.v.). Walden and Tuttle won a new trial for Downer with a writ of habeas corpus appeal to the Fifth Circuit Court of Appeals (q.v.). Downer was retried and executed, despite evidence that he was a scapegoat. Yet, Walden and Tuttle had maintained the principle that a defendant has a right to trial free of mob influence. In the 1940s, Walden led a six-year battle to win pay equity for African American school teachers in Georgia. In the 1950s, Walden was the lead attorney in Horace Ward's unsuccessful effort to win admission to the University of Georgia's law school in *Ward v. Regents of the University System of Georgia* (q.v.). In the 1960s, Walden was the lead negotiator in discussions that led to the peaceful desegregation of lunch counters in Atlanta. He also helped to prosecute cases against Blackshirts and Ku Klux Klansmen who sought to obstruct black voting rights.

Walden held many responsible positions: founder and first president of Atlanta's Gate City Bar Association, founder and first cochairman of the Atlanta Negro Voters League, chairman of the executive board of the Atlanta Urban League and the Butler Street YMCA, chairman of the trustee board of Wheat Street Baptist Church, president of the alumni association of Atlanta University, counsel of the National Baptist Convention (q.v.), a national vice president of the National Association for the Advancement of Colored People (NAACP; q.v.) and a member of its legal committee for forty years. In politics, Walden was a Republican until 1940, when he switched to the Democratic Party. He campaigned actively for the Democratic Party's presidential candidates: Truman in 1948, Stevenson in 1952 and 1956 and Kennedy in 1960. In 1962, he was elected to the State Democratic Committee of Georgia. Two years later, Governor Carl E. Sanders appointed him a delegate to the Democratic National Convention and Mayor Ivan Allen appointed him an alternate judge in Atlanta's Municipal Court. Walden died in Atlanta on 2 July 1965.

WALKER v. CITY OF BIRMINGHAM, 388 U.S. 307 (1967). A case in which the Supreme Court held that court injunctions against civil protest were not to be challenged in the streets but in the courts.

In early April 1963, as Martin Luther King (q.v.) and the Southern Christian Leadership Conference (SCLC; q.v.) were mounting major demonstrations with the Birmingham, Alabama, Movement (q.v.), Alabama circuit court judge William A. Jenkins issued a temporary injunction against "unlawful street parades, unlawful processions, unlawful demonstrations, unlawful boycotts, unlawful trespasses, and unlawful picketing or other like unlawful conduct" to King, Fred Shuttlesworth (q.v.) and 136 other people. On Good Friday, 12 April, King, Ralph Abernathy (q.v.), Wyatt Tee Walker (q.v.), and 50 others were arrested and jailed in Birmingham for marching in violation of Jenkins's injunction. The Kennedy administration interceded to be sure that King was safe and from his jail cell he wrote his famous "Letter from Birmingham Jail" (q.v.), which set forth his argument that a Christian has a positive obligation to disobey unjust law.

Despite the arguments of movement attorneys, King and others were found guilty of criminal contempt and sentenced to five days in jail and a $50 fine, which was suspended pending appeal. The Birmingham Movement nevertheless continued its demonstrations in violation of Jenkins's injunction, eventually forcing a crisis in which the Kennedy administration interceded on behalf of the movement. Even so, the Alabama supreme court sustained Judge Jenkins's decision in *Walker* and a severely divided United States Supreme Court upheld its decision. By a vote of five to four, with Chief Justice Earl Warren and Justices William J. Brennan, William O. Douglas, and Abe Fortas in dissent, the Court held that petitioners must appeal the issuing of an injunction, not a contempt conviction, and that until properly challenged a court injunction had the force of law. The Court minority argued that the delay inherent in an appeal process against an injunction that was clearly unconstitutional was a violation of the petitioners' First Amendment rights.

WALKER, WYATT TEE (1929–   ). Civil rights activist and pastor.
Wyatt Walker was born, the tenth of 11 children of a Baptist minister and his wife, on 16 August 1929 in Brockton, Massachusetts. Young Walker grew up and went to public schools in Merchantville, New Jersey. Inspired by Paul Robeson (q.v.) in his youth, he briefly belonged to the Young Communist League as a teenager. Walker studied at Virginia Union University in Richmond, where he earned a B.S. in 1950 and a B.D. in 1953. Ordained in the Baptist ministry in 1952, Walker became the pastor of historic Gillfield Baptist Church in Petersburg, Virginia. By the end of the decade, he embodied Virginia's civil rights movement: president of the local branch of the NAACP (q.v.), director of the Virginia chapter of the Congress of Racial Equality (CORE; q.v.), a founder and president of the Petersburg Improvement Association and the Virginia Christian Leadership Conference, affiliates of the Southern Christian Leadership Conference (SCLC; q.v.), and a member of SCLC's board of directors. Walker organized 2,000 marchers who descended on the state capitol in Richmond on New Year's Day, 1959, on a "Pilgrimage for Integrated Education." Early in 1960, he went to jail for a sit-in at the Petersburg Public Library. In August 1960, Martin Luther King (q.v.) hired Walker as SCLC's executive director.

Ambitious, choleric, and energetic, Wyatt Walker brought a strong sense of direction to SCLC's office. In 1961, after CORE initiated the Freedom Rides (q.v.), Walker helped to coordinate them through the Freedom Rides Coordinating Committee, went on one of the rides to Jackson, Mississippi, and reported on his experience to the Interstate

Commerce Commission. He received his trial by fire in SCLC's campaign with the Albany, Georgia, Movement (q.v.), in which his imperious style antagonized SNCC activists. In developing a master plan for the subsequent campaign with the Birmingham, Alabama, Movement (q.v.), Walker built on lessons learned in Albany. "Project C," as he called it, required advanced planning, a reliable local base of support, clear control over decision making, escalation from small-scale protests to mass demonstrations, and a police force willing to be graphically oppressive. Those conditions made it as successful as Albany had been a failure. In Birmingham, Walker was a torrent of activity: outmaneuvering Police Commissioner Eugene "Bull" Connor (q.v.) by dispatching eight or ten agents to turn in false alarms to draw policemen and firemen away from demonstrators and hovering over a secretary to piece together and edit scraps of paper King sent from his cell to publish as his "Letter from Birmingham Jail" (q.v.). Birmingham was Walker's finest hour, but the city exacted a toll when both he and his wife, Ann, were beaten by the city's policemen.

Shortly after the March on Washington (q.v.), Wyatt Walker sought confirmation of his value to King in a threefold salary increase. The demand came at the same time that staff resentments with Walker were reaching a head. The result was an agreement that he would find work elsewhere. In June 1964, Walker left SCLC to produce a black history series for the Negro History Library. He became the pastor of Canaan Baptist Church in Harlem. In 1975, Walker earned the D.Min. degree from Colgate-Rochester Divinity School. He published 'Somebody's Calling My Name': Black Sacred Music and Social Change in 1979 and The Soul of Black Worship in 1984.

WALLACE, GEORGE CORLEY (1919–   ). Politician.

George C. Wallace was born on 25 August 1919 in Clio, Alabama. He attended local public schools and earned a law degree from the University of Alabama in 1942. During World War II, Wallace rose to the rank of flight sergeant in the United States Air Force. After his return to Alabama, he served as an assistant attorney general of the state from 1946 to 1947. Elected to the Alabama state legislature, Wallace served there from 1947 to 1953. From 1953 until 1962, he was a judge on the bench of Alabama's Third Judicial District. In 1958, Wallace was defeated in a bid for the Democratic Party's nomination for governor by Attorney General John Patterson. Vowing that he would never again be "out-niggered" in a political contest again, Wallace ran for governor of Alabama in 1962 and was elected.

In his inaugural address, George Wallace pledged "Segregation now; segregation tomorrow; segregation forever." On 16 May 1963, the federal district court for the northern district of Alabama ordered the University of Alabama to admit two African American students, James Hood and Vivian Malone, for the summer session. Wallace promised to stand by a 1962 campaign commitment to uphold racial segregation even if he had to stand "in the schoolhouse door." On 5 June, in *United States v. Wallace* (q.v.), the Justice Department won a federal district court injunction against any interference by Wallace in the desegregation of the University of Alabama. On 11 June, Wallace defied the federal court order and stood in the door of a university building to prevent Assistant Attorney General Nicholas Katzenbach from escorting the two black students inside to register.

Wallace's action was largely a symbolic gesture. When President Kennedy nationalized the Alabama National Guard and a commanding general returned with the students later that day, Wallace stood aside. Yet, his gesture made Wallace the symbol of resistance to the federal government's push for desegregation. Unable to run for reelection as governor in 1966, Wallace supported his wife, Lurleen, who was elected. As a candidate of the American Independent Party for president in 1968, he won 13.5 percent of the popular vote and 46 electoral votes. Returned to office as governor of Alabama in 1970, Wallace was campaigning for president in 1972, when he was wounded by Arthur Bremer in an assassination attempt. Now paralyzed from the waist down, Wallace completed his term in office. He was returned to office for a third term in 1982. In his later years, Wallace has been regarded by many observers as a changed man. Modifying his rhetoric and his actions as African Americans swelled the voter registration lists in the years since 1968, Wallace was supported by many of the state's new black voters in his last two gubernatorial victories.

WARD v. REGENTS OF THE UNIVERSITY SYSTEM OF GEORGIA, 191 F. Supp. 491 (N.D. Ga. 1957). A case in which a law school and a federal district court took refuge in procedural justifications for refusing to admit an African American student.

An African American, Horace T. Ward, was denied admission to the University of Georgia's law school in 1950. He appealed to the law school and the Regents of the University System of Georgia without success. In 1952, Ward sought an injunction to prevent the regents from denying his admission on racial grounds. The case was continued when he was drafted into the armed forces and was not renewed until December 1956. Attorneys for the university argued that Ward had been denied, not because of race, but because he had not reapplied for admission after his initial rejection and that, in any case, he was now studying law at Northwestern University. In February 1957, the court held that it had no jurisdiction in Ward's case because: 1) Ward had not applied for admission to the law school since 1950, denying university authorities an opportunity to review his qualifications; 2) Ward had never submitted the character references required by the law school since 1952; and 3) Ward had abandoned his 1950 application for admission as a first-year student by accepting admission to Northwestern University's law school. Subsequently, Ward asked the court to retain jurisdiction because he intended to seek admission to the University of Georgia's law school as a transfer student. The court denied Ward's request in March 1957, claiming that it had already found that it lacked jurisdiction. Ward's declared intention to reapply to the law school, said the court, vindicated its position on the original motion that his refusal to reapply was appropriate grounds for dismissing his case.

WARD v. TEXAS, 316 U.S. 547 (1942). A case in which the Supreme Court defined conditions under which a confession becomes involuntary and its use as evidence a violation of the due process clause of the Fourteenth Amendment.

William Ward was an uneducated African American house servant in Titus County, Texas. Late one evening in 1940, he was arrested without a warrant for the murder of Levi Brown, an old white man. Warned of alleged threats of mob violence, Ward was driven for three days from one Texas county to another and was under continuous interrogation. Finally, he said that although he was innocent he was willing to make any statement that his interrogators wanted. On the basis of his confession alone, Ward was convicted in a state district court of Brown's murder in January 1941 and sentenced to three years in the state penitentiary. The United States Supreme Court heard Ward's appeal in May 1942. Noting that established precedents, which held that confessions drawn from uneducated persons who are kept incommunicado, subjected to protracted questioning, threatened with mob violence, or taken at night to remote places for questioning were involuntary, the Court held that Ward's conviction was reversible on any of these grounds.

WARDS COVE PACKING COMPANY INC. v. FRANK ATONIO,
490 U.S. 642 (1989). A case in which the Supreme Court held that gender or ethnic imbalances in employment were not in themselves sufficient evidence that an employer was discriminating and that the burden of proof of discrimination lay with the employee, not the employer.

Wards Cove Packing Company was one of two companies which operated seasonal salmon canneries in Alaska. They had two kinds of jobs: unskilled cannery line jobs, mostly held by local Alaska natives and by Filipinos; and higher paying white collar bookkeeping and engineering positions, mostly held by white Americans. Frank Atonio and other cannery line workers sued the two companies, alleging racial discrimination under Title VII of the Civil Rights Act of 1964 (q.v.). A federal district court found for the companies, but the Ninth Circuit Court of Appeals overturned the district court ruling. The canneries appealed to the Supreme Court. By a vote of five to four, the Supreme Court reversed the appeals court's ruling. Racial imbalance was not evidence in itself that a company had engaged in racial discrimination in employment, said the Court majority, and the burden of proving discrimination in employment lay with employees. The Civil Rights Act of 1991 (q.v.) reversed the Court's majority's finding on the latter point, placing the burden of proof of nondiscrimination on the employer.

WARING, JULIUS WATIES (1880–1968). Federal district judge.
J. Waties Waring was born on 27 July 1880 in Charleston, South Carolina. His father and two uncles had owned slaves and served in the Confederate army. An eighth-generation Charlestonian, Waring grew up in a privileged family of the city's aristocracy. He studied in private schools and graduated from the College of Charleston in 1900. Waring studied law in the offices of several local firms, passed the state bar examination in 1901, and established a prosperous legal practice. An assistant United States attorney from 1914 to 1920, Waring became an expert in federal litigation. From 1920 to 1942, he was a member of a prominent Charleston law firm and served as Charleston corporate counsel. In 1938, Waring was a campaign advisor to Senator "Cotton" Ed Smith of South Carolina, one of the South's most racist members of Congress. In 1942, President Franklin D. Roosevelt appointed Waring to the federal district bench for the eastern district of South Carolina. Waring's background offered little sign of the progressive civil rights decisions that lay ahead in his courtroom.

Waring ended the practice of white-only jury lists in his courtroom and ruled in favor of equal pay for black and white schoolteachers in South Carolina. In 1947, he ordered the admission of a black student to the law school at the University of South Carolina and, in *Rice v. Elmore* (q.v.), he held that South Carolina's use of the "white primary" was unconstitutional. The state defied his order in the former case by building a separate law school for African American students. In *Rice,* Waring held that black people were entitled to participate in the Democratic primary as long as it was effectively the state's only election and his decision was sustained by the Fourth Circuit Court of Appeals and the Supreme Court.

When the Democratic Party sought to organize itself as private country clubs, open only to white people and requiring an oath of loyalty to racial segregation, Waring told party leaders that he would tolerate no "further evasions, subterfuges or attempts to get around" the law. In *Brown v. Baskin,* he issued an injunction and threatened to jail anyone who tried to prevent black South Carolinians from voting. In August 1948, 35,000 African Americans voted in South Carolina's Democratic primary. As part of a three-judge Fourth Circuit Court of Appeals panel in *Briggs v. Elliot* (q.v.), he wrote a strong dissenting opinion when the two-judge majority condoned continued racial segregation in Clarendon County, South Carolina's public schools. "Segregation is *per se* inequality," he argued. By then, Southern politicians had been trying for several years to remove Waring from the federal bench. After an attempted bombing on his home in Charleston, he retired from the bench at the end of 1951 and moved his family to New York. J. Waties Waring died on 11 January 1968.

WASHINGTON v. DAVIS, 426 U.S. 229 (1976). A case in which the Supreme Court held that job-related tests could be used in employment, even if their results proved to be discriminatory.

The District of Columbia police department required all applicants for positions to take "Test 21," which measured reading, writing, and comprehension skills. Applicants were required to earn a score of 40 out of 80 points in order to be eligible for employment. Davis and other plaintiffs were among African American applicants who failed the test in greater proportions than white applicants. A federal district court found the test requirement constitutionally acceptable, but its judgment was reversed in a federal appeals court. By a vote of seven to two, the Supreme Court held that the test requirement was acceptable because the test was not inherently discriminatory. "Reading ability is manifestly relevant to the police function," wrote Justice Byron R. White for the Court majority; "there is no evidence that the required passing grade was set at an arbitrarily high level; and there is sufficient disparity among high schools and high school graduates to justify the use of a separate uniform test."

WATSON v. CITY OF MEMPHIS, 373 U.S. 526 (1963). A case in which the Supreme Court ordered the immediate desegregation of parks and recreation facilities in Memphis, Tennessee.

In 1960, I. A. Watson, Jr., and other African Americans in Memphis sued the city to force the desegregation of public parks and recreation facilities. Attorneys for the city questioned whether the Fourteenth Amendment required desegregation of public facilities and maintained that the city's desegregation pace would not threaten to arouse racial violence. A federal district court held that the city must desegregate its facilities and, invoking the mandate in *Brown v. Board of Education* (1955; q.v.), which called for school desegregation "with all deliberate speed," gave city authorities six months to prepare a plan for desegregation. The Sixth Circuit Court of Appeals upheld the district court's decision. The African American plaintiffs appealed to the Supreme Court, which rendered its verdict on 27 May 1963. Justice Arthur Goldberg spoke for a unanimous Court in finding that the Fourteenth Amendment's equal protection clause required the desegregation of public facilities in Memphis and rejecting a plan for a gradual desegregation of them. Fear of racial conflict was not a compelling or convincing reason for delaying the desegregation of public parks and recreation facilities in Memphis, said the Court.

WATTS RACE RIOT (1965). Among the first and largest of many race riots in the latter half of the 1960s.

Watts was a 50-square-mile area of south-central Los Angeles, where 250,000 people, 98 percent of them African American, lived in stuccoed buildings beneath approaches to the city's international airport. In Watts, there were four times as many people per square block as in the rest of Los Angeles. Trash collection was rare and the streets were littered with broken glass, rusty cans, and rotting food. Although 34 percent of adult men in Watts were unemployed and two-thirds of its residents were on welfare, local politicians were struggling over control of $20 million in federal antipoverty funds. Only 5 of 205 policemen who patrolled Watts were black and complaints of police brutality were common.

During a heat wave on 11 August 1965, a routine drunk driving arrest in Watts drew a crowd of bystanders and brewed into a confrontation between white police and black antagonists. Rumors that exaggerated harsh police reactions spread through black neighborhoods. Soon, rocks and bottles began to fly at police targets. In the next two days, 5,000 black people were smashing and looting over a 150-block area. When fires broke out, snipers fixed their gun sights on Los Angeles firemen. By 16 August, the riot was over, but it had taken 14,000 national guardsmen and thousands of local police to bring the Watts riot under control. Most of the 34 people killed in the riot were black, but a sheriff's deputy and a fireman were also killed. There were 900 black people injured and 4,000 were arrested for loitering, looting, vandalism, violence, or simply being in the wrong place at the wrong time. Hundreds of businesses were plundered or burned; hundreds of families were left homeless. The estimates of property losses ranged between $35 and $45 million.

WATTS v. INDIANA, 338 U.S. 49 (1949). A case in which the Supreme Court held that the use of a confession obtained by excessive police measures violated the Fourteenth Amendment's due process guarantees.

Robert A. Watts, an African American, was arrested and held for allegedly committing an assault on 12 November 1947. Later that day, the body of a woman was found in the vicinity of Watts's alleged crime. He was taken to Indiana State Police headquarters and held in solitary confinement for several days. There, after he was interrogated by teams of six to eight officers for eight hours a day for six days, Watts confessed to murder. Denied a prompt preliminary hearing, he was without professional counsel and did not have proper food and rest. Watts was convicted and his appeal was rejected until Thurgood Marshall (q.v.) carried it to the Supreme Court. By a vote of six to three, with Chief Justice Fred M. Vinson and Justices Harold Burton and Stanley Reed in dissent, the Court ruled that the use of a confession obtained by excessive police interrogation in a state court murder trial violated due process guarantees of the Fourteenth Amendment. The Court majority submitted an opinion by Justice Felix Frankfurter, joined by Justices Frank Murphy and Wiley Rutledge. Justices Hugo Black, William O. Douglas, and Robert Jackson submitted a concurring opinion.

WHITE CITIZENS' COUNCIL. *See* Citizens' Council.

WHITE HOUSE CONFERENCE "TO FULFILL THESE RIGHTS." *See* "To Fulfill These Rights."

WHITE v. REGESTER, 412 U.S. 755 (1973). A case in which the Supreme Court offered state legislatures some latitude in redistricting state legislative seats in compliance with its decisions in *Baker v. Carr* (q.v.) and *Reynolds, a Judge v. Sims* (q.v.).

In *Baker v. Carr* and *Reynolds, a Judge,* the Supreme Court had put state legislatures on notice that redistricting plans for the purpose of representation must follow the principle of "one man, one vote" as closely as possible. States would be expected to provide explanation of and justification for any deviation from that principle. In 1970, the Texas legislature reapportioned legislative districts by dividing 150 seats among 90 single and multimember districts. The ideal district would include 74,645 people, but actual districts varied from 71,597 to 78,943 people. A federal district court found that the districting plan violated the Fourteenth Amendment's equal protection requirement and that the state had presented no acceptable justification of the plan's deviations. On appeal, the Supreme Court reversed the district court decision. States would be required to justify deviations of nearly 10 percent in congressional districts, explained the Court majority, but that deviation was insufficient to throw out a state legislative redistricting plan and would not require the same justification as would be required of such a deviation in congressional redistricting. The Court's decision did imply, however, that larger deviations in legislative redistricting would require such accountability.

WHITE, WALTER FRANCIS (1893–1955). Civil rights activist.

Walter White was born on 1 July 1893 in Atlanta, Georgia, to George and Madeline Harrison White. His fair skin, blue eyes, blonde hair, and Caucasian features would have allowed White to pass as such, but he knew the harsh injustice of racism at an early age and cast his lot with his African American kinsmen. Walter White's father was a postman who died when White was young because he could not get proper treatment for an injury. At 13, White saw a mob of white men threaten to invade his house during the Atlanta race riot of 1906. That night, he later recalled, "I discovered what it meant to be a Negro." White attended Atlanta schools for African American students and graduated from Atlanta University in 1916. A year later, when Atlanta's board of education threatened to abolish public education for black students in order to pay for additional white public schools, Walter White helped to organize the Atlanta branch of the NAACP (q.v.) to fight the proposal.

In 1918, James Weldon Johnson invited White to join the NAACP staff in New York as assistant executive secretary. He was in Chicago for the NAACP to organize the defense of African Americans who were accused of attacking white people in the city's race riot of 1919. During the subsequent decades, White investigated lynchings for the NAACP. He skillfully handled administrative details for the executive secretary and the NAACP's legal committee. A talented writer, White contributed two novels to the Harlem Renaissance, *The Fire in the Flint* (1924) and *Flight* (1926), and wrote a major study of lynching, *Rope and Faggot* (1929). When James Weldon Johnson became ill in 1929, Walter White became acting executive secretary of the NAACP and led its successful opposition to the nomination of Appeals Court Judge John J. Parker to the Supreme Court in 1930.

When Johnson resigned as executive secretary of the NAACP in 1931, White was the obvious choice to succeed him. Internally, he survived the depression's financial constraints on the organization and struggles for control of its future direction with a very strong administrative authority. His actions both shifted the weight of decision making from the NAACP's board of directors to the staff and control of the organization from white to black leadership. Externally, White wove a network of alliances among civil liberties, church, ethnic, labor, and women's organizations that became crucial to the civil rights movement's success in subsequent decades. In 1948, he published an autobiography, *A Man Called White.* When he divorced his African American first wife, Gladys Powell, the mother of his two children, to marry a white woman, Poppy Cannon, the NAACP board forced him to take a year's leave of absence in 1949. When he returned to the office in 1950, it delegated authority for all internal affairs to his assistant, Roy Wilkins (q.v.), and made Wilkins directly accountable to the board. White remained responsible for broad policy direction and public relations. He died of a heart attack on 21 March 1955.

WHITUS v. GEORGIA, 385 U.S. 545 (1967). A case in which the Supreme Court ordered the retrial of two African American prisoners in Georgia.

Phil Whitus and Leon Davis were African American prisoners who charged that African Americans were excluded from the selection of grand and trial juries that convicted them of crimes in Mitchell County, Georgia. In *Whitus v. Balcom* (1962), the Supreme Court vacated an earlier judgment and ordered the federal district court to reconsider the case. There, the defendant's attorney testified that he had hoped to win an acquittal on the facts and had not raised the exclusion issue because it "would have filled the air with such hostility that an acquittal would have been an impossibility." Fifth Circuit Court of Appeals (q.v.) Judge John Minor Wisdom (q.v.) noted that by excluding black people from the jury selection process the state forced black defendants to face a Hobson's choice of prejudice by reason of being denied trial by a cross-section of their peers or prejudice arising from their attack upon an all-white jury selection process.

Before 1965, Georgia county commissioners used segregated tax return sheets (white for white tax payers, yellow for black taxpayers) from which they compiled jury lists. Black people were 45 percent of the population of Mitchell County, but none of them had been selected for jury duty within memory. After 1965, tax returns were still segregated, but commissioners chose jurors whom they knew personally. Thus, in 1966, only three of 33 prospective grand jurors were black and only one of 18 selected for service was black; only seven of 90 prospective trial jurors were black and none of them were selected for service. *Whitus v. Georgia* was a reappeal to the Supreme Court. Justice Tom Clark wrote for a unanimous Court in reversing lower court decisions and confirming racial discrimination in the jury selection process. The Court did not order that the petitioners be set free, but that their cases be retried before a jury selected without racial discrimination.

WILDER, LAWRENCE DOUGLAS (1931–   ). Politician.

L. Douglas Wilder was born on 31 January 1931 in Richmond, Virginia. He attended local public schools for African American youth and also experienced racial segregation on the city's buses. Wilder graduated from Virginia Union University in 1951 with a degree in chemistry. Drafted into the army, he served in the Korean War and earned a Bronze Star for valor. After being discharged in 1953, Wilder returned to Richmond and took a position as a chemist with the state medical examiner's office. In 1956, he sought admission to law school at the University of Virginia, but he was excluded on racial grounds. Wilder earned his law degree from Howard University in 1959. He practiced law in Richmond for ten years, specializing in criminal law and personal injury cases, before becoming the first African American elected to the Virginia state senate in 1969. Reelected three times, in 1973, 1977 and 1981, Wilder accumulated the power that accrues with seniority, chairing three senate committees, and sustained a civil rights legislative agenda: opposition to the death penalty and support for fair housing legislation and a state holiday honoring Martin Luther King.

In 1985, the Democratic Party nominated Wilder for lieutenant governor of Virginia. Despite the fact that the state's population was only 20 percent black, he was elected with 51 percent of the vote. Four years later, Wilder was nominated for governor of Virginia. Preelection polls gave him an edge of 4 to 16 percent, but he was eventually declared the winner by less than 7,000 votes or one-third of a percent. Wilder's bid for statewide office also forced a change in his position on the death penalty. Attacked on the issue in both statewide races by Republican opponents, Wilder became a strong supporter of the death penalty. In Virginia's flat economy in the early 1990s, Wilder cut state aid to education and state employment rolls. Briefly a candidate for the Democratic Party's presidential nomination in 1992, Wilder was handicapped by a bitter intraparty rivalry with Virginia's Senator Charles Robb, weak campaign financing, and a poor showing in public opinion polls. Since retiring from public office, Wilder has practiced law and hosted a "talk radio" program in Richmond.

WILKINS, ROY OTTAWAY (1901–81). Civil rights activist.

Roy Wilkins was born on 30 August 1901 in St. Louis, Missouri. He was the son of a Methodist minister. After his mother died when he was four, young Wilkins's aunt and uncle in St. Paul, Minnesota, took him in and instilled middle-class values in him. In 1923, he graduated from the University of Minnesota, where he majored in sociology and minored in journalism. During his college career, Wilkins was the night editor of the university newspaper, the *Minnesota Daily,* and editor of a black weekly newspaper, the *St. Paul Appeal.* Wilkins left Minnesota to become a reporter for the *Kansas City Call.* In both St. Paul and Kansas City, he was active in local branches of the NAACP (q.v.). In 1931, Walter White (q.v.) hired Wilkins to serve as assistant secretary for the NAACP. In that position, he traveled in the Deep South for the first time, investigating working conditions for black people in Mississippi. When W. E. B. Du Bois left the NAACP in 1934, Wilkins became his successor as editor of *The Crisis.*

From 1934 to 1949, Wilkins was both editor of *The Crisis* and assistant secretary of the NAACP. During Walter White's leave of absence in 1949, Wilkins served as interim executive secretary of the NAACP. White returned to his position from 1950 until his death in 1955, but increasingly Wilkins assumed the leadership capacity. When White died in 1955, he was officially elected executive secretary of the NAACP. Coming to that position just after the Supreme Court's decision in *Brown v. Board of Education* (q.v.), Wilkins led the NAACP's fight for desegregation of public schools and public accommodations, for equal opportunity in employment and housing, and for the protection of African American voting rights.

Master of the NAACP's bureaucratic structures, Roy Wilkins was confident that its approach to social change and social justice through legislation, litigation, and lobbying was the more certain path to secure results. Although he was skeptical of the positive benefits of nonviolent direct action, Wilkins joined the Prayer Pilgrimage to Washington (q.v.) in 1957, the second Youth March for Integrated Schools (q.v.) in 1959, and the March on Washington (q.v.) in 1963. On rare occasions, he could be found walking a picket line. Roy Wilkins preferred having direct access to people with power to effect long-term, positive social change. His health began to fail in the mid-1970s and he retired in 1977. His successor was Benjamin Hooks (q.v.), a pastor, attorney, and member of the Federal Communications Commission. Wilkins died on 8 September 1981 from kidney failure and uremia.

WILLIAMS, HOSEA LORENZO (Hosé; 1926–   ). Civil rights activist.

Hosea Williams was born on 5 January 1926 in Attapulgus, Georgia, in the deep southwestern part of the state. Both of his parents were blind. Williams attended public schools for young African Americans in rural south Georgia, but his youth was troubled and violent. He served in the military during World War II and returned to Georgia to study at Atlanta's Morris Brown College and Atlanta University. Williams became a research chemist for the United States Department of Agriculture in Savannah, Georgia. Active in the local branch of the NAACP (q.v.), he was elected its vice president. By 1960, however, Williams was frustrated by rivalry with its dominant figure, Westley W. Law, and restless with the NAACP's commitment to legislation and litigation. In 1960, Williams organized and led the Chatham County Crusade for Voters (CCCV) and the Southeastern Georgia Crusade for Voters. By

1962, when CCCV became an affiliate of SCLC (q.v.) and Williams was elected to SCLC's board of directors, CCCV's ties to the NAACP were severed.

In April 1963, Williams responded to King's call for help by bringing a group of civil rights activists from Savannah to Birmingham, Alabama. When three movie theaters reneged on an agreement to desegregate two months later, Williams replicated the Birmingham campaign in Savannah. Almost daily for six weeks, he spoke to noon crowds of 1,000 and led evening marches of 3,000 people. One demonstration drew 6,000 people. In a week, 500 demonstrators were arrested. As confrontations with the police threatened to become violent, Williams asked King to send James Bevel (q.v.), Dorothy Cotton (q.v.), and Andrew Young (q.v.) to Savannah for nonviolence training. They organized a march of 200 children who were arrested and went to jail. In early July, a local judge jailed Williams under a $100,000 "good behavior" warrant; Bevel and Young assumed direction of the Savannah campaign. On 11 July, Savannah replicated Birmingham as police and national guardsmen used tear gas and water hoses on demonstrators, who responded by throwing rocks, breaking windows, and setting fires. The resources of nonviolence were exhausted, white businessmen were ready to negotiate, and demonstrations were suspended. In return for a 60-day suspension, 100 white businessmen agreed to desegregate Savannah's bowling alleys, hotels, motels, and theaters on 1 October. Williams was released from jail on 9 August.

By 1964, Hosea Williams joined SCLC's staff in Atlanta. He was active in its campaign in St. Augustine, Florida, led SCLC's voter registration drive before the 1964 elections and was working in Selma, Alabama, by February 1965. On Sunday, 7 March, John Lewis (q.v.) and he led marchers out of Brown Chapel, through Selma and over the Edmund Pettus Bridge to confront a phalanx of state troopers. Teargassed, clubbed, and beaten, the marchers scrambled back over the bridge to refuge at Brown Chapel. After the Selma to Montgomery March (q.v.) and passage of the Voting Rights Act of 1965 (q.v.), Williams directed SCLC's Summer Community Organization and Political Education (SCOPE; q.v.) program. Although he claimed to have registered 85,000 voters by the end of the summer, SCOPE was widely criticized as badly administered and was not renewed in 1966. Williams opposed SCLC's attempt to address the problems of the Northern ghetto, but he directed its unsuccessful voter registration effort in Chicago in 1966 and 1967. Active in the Meredith March and the Poor People's March on Washington (q.v.), he was in Memphis when King died. Williams was elected to the Georgia General Assembly in 1974; endorsed Ronald Reagan for president in 1980; and was elected to Atlanta's city council in 1985. Two years later, he led a march to Forsyth County, Georgia, to protest racism and Ku Klux Klan violence there. Subsequently, Hosea Williams served a term as a DeKalb County commissioner.

WILLIAMS, ROBERT F. (1925–   ). Civil rights activist.

Robert F. Williams was born in 1925 in Monroe, North Carolina. He studied in local public schools for African American youth. After service in the United States Marine Corps, Williams returned to Monroe, where he was elected president of the Union County, North Carolina, branch of the NAACP (q.v.) in 1956. Early in 1959, he organized 50 of its men into a gun club for self-defense. Armed and drilled, members of the gun club repelled Ku Klux Klansmen who threatened the home of an NAACP officer. Williams gained notoriety from his call for black people throughout the South to arm themselves for organized self-defense. For this call to arms, Williams was suspended from his office by national NAACP officials. Locally, he was charged with kidnapping a white couple. Williams and his wife fled to Cuba in 1961. There, he published a monthly newsletter, *The Crusader.*

In 1962, Williams published *Negroes with Guns.* his call to revolution. He organized the Revolutionary Action Movement (RAM) in 1963. RAM was much smaller than the Black Panther Party (q.v.), but its 50 or so active young members were armed and vowed to wage urban guerilla warfare in the United States. In 1967, police in New York and Philadelphia raided RAM headquarters and found a machine gun, steel-tipped arrows, 300 grams of potassium cyanide (enough to kill 4500 people), literature on guerilla warfare, and plans to assassinate such moderate civil rights leaders as Roy Wilkins (q.v.) of the NAACP and Whitney Young (q.v.) of the National Urban League (q.v.). Under police pressure, RAM collapsed in 1968. Robert Williams returned to the United States in 1969, but charges against him were not dropped until 1976.

WILLIS AND KENNEDY v. PICKRICK RESTAURANT, 243 F. Supp. 179 (N.D. Ga. 1964). A case in which the federal district court for the northern district of Georgia ordered a Georgia restaurateur not to discriminate against African Americans in his establishment.

Lester Maddox was a colorful, white Atlantan, whose advertisements for his Pickrick Restaurant in the *Atlanta Constitution* and *Journal* in the early 1960s often included editorial attacks on the "Communist conspiracy" to destroy "the Southern way of life." After the passage of the Civil Rights Act of 1964 (q.v.), three African Americans tested his compliance with its public accommodations requirement. Waving an ax handle, Maddox drove them from The Pickrick. "You're dirty Communists and you'll never get a piece of fried chicken here," he said. They sought an injunction to force Maddox to comply with the Civil Rights Act. Maddox claimed that it was unconstitutional, but the Justice Department entered the case on the side of the plaintiffs. When the constitutionality of Title II of the Civil Rights Act, its public accommodations clause, was confirmed by the United States Supreme Court in *Heart of Atlanta Motel, Inc. v. United States* (q.v.), the federal district court in Georgia ordered Maddox to comply with it. Briefly, Maddox closed The Pickrick and, then, reopened it as The Lester Maddox Cafeteria. On 5 February 1965, the federal district court held that he was bound by the original court order to desegregate his restaurant and was found guilty of contempt of court for refusing to serve African Americans. Faced with the threat of a fine of $200 a day dating from the date of the original court order if he did not comply, Maddox closed his restaurant. On 27 September 1966, Lester Maddox won the Democratic Party's nomination for and subsequently was elected governor of Georgia.

WINSTON-SALEM, NORTH CAROLINA, SIT-IN MOVEMENT. One of the first sit-in movements (q.v.) after their beginning in Greensboro, North Carolina.

After four African American students sat in at Woolworth's lunch counter in Greensboro, North Carolina (q.v.), on 1 February 1960, the movement spread rapidly to other North Carolina cities, including Charlotte (q.v.), Durham (q.v.), High Point (q.v.), Raleigh, and Winston-Salem. In Winston-Salem, Carl Matthews, Jr., launched a sit-in at the S. H. Kress Company lunch counter on 8 February. African American students at Winston-Salem State College had already planned to sit in. Within hours, they joined Matthews at the S. H. Kress lunch counter. Sit-ins were held at other lunch counters in Winston-Salem on 9 February. On the evening of 12 February, Winston-Salem's African American community held the first mass meetings in support of the sit-in movement. By April, lunch counters throughout the city were closed. After a period of negotiations, they were reopened on a desegregated basis on 25 May 1960.

WISDOM, JOHN MINOR (1905–   ). A member of the Fifth Circuit Court of Appeals (q.v.).

John Minor Wisdom was born on 17 May 1905 into a privileged family in New Orleans, Louisiana. Although his father died when Wisdom was quite young, his mother had enough resources to see her three children through private schools and college. John Minor Wisdom studied at Washington and Lee University in Virginia (A.B., 1925) and did a year of graduate work in English literature before returning to New Orleans, where he took a degree from Tulane University's law school (LL.B., 1929). After graduation, Wisdom entered a partnership with a classmate, Saul Stone, and specialized in corporate law. During World War II, he served in the United States Army's Office of Legal Procurement and rose from the rank of captain to lieutenant colonel. After the war, Wisdom taught part-time in Tulane's law school and worked to build a Republican Party in Louisiana.

In 1952, John Minor Wisdom helped to spearhead General Eisenhower's campaign in the South for the Republican nomination for president. At the Republican National Convention in July, Wisdom chaired an Eisenhower delegation from Louisiana, Elbert Tuttle (q.v.) chaired an Eisenhower delegation from Georgia, and John Robert Brown (q.v.) was on an Eisenhower delegation from Texas. When those three delegations were seated by the Republican National Convention, Eisenhower became the party's nominee. Frank Minis Johnson (q.v.) joined the Eisenhower campaign in Alabama after the convention. They each became Eisenhower nominees to the federal bench. Appointed to the Fifth Circuit Court of Appeals (q.v.) in 1957, John Minor Wisdom joined Richard T. Rives (q.v.), Brown, and Tuttle to give powerful intellectual underpinnings to the Fifth Circuit's crucial decisions that implemented and expanded the Supreme Court's judgment in *Brown v. Board of Education* (q.v.). Those decisions helped to dismantle the Deep South's dual system of public education and undermine racial discrimination in employment, jury selection, and voting rights.

WRIGHT, JAMES SKELLY (1911–88). Federal district and court of appeals judge.

The second of seven children, J. Skelly Wright was born on 14 January 1911 into a Roman Catholic family in New Orleans, Louisiana. His father was a plumbing inspector. Young Wright grew up in a poor working-class neighborhood and attended public schools in New Orleans. He graduated from Loyola University in New Orleans and taught public school after graduation. Wright studied at Loyola University Law School at night after his day of public school teaching. In 1936, he became an assistant United States attorney. As a Coast Guard officer in World War II, he commanded a submarine chaser in the North Atlantic. Later, he was an embassy attaché in London and married Helen Patton, the daughter of an admiral, who worked at the embassy. After the war, Wright returned to New Orleans as senior assistant United States attorney. He became United States attorney in 1948. A year later, Wright was appointed to the federal district court bench. At 38, he was the youngest federal district judge in the United States. Prior to the Supreme Court's 1954 decision in *Brown v. Board of Education* (q.v.), Wright ordered the law school at Louisiana State University (LSU) to admit African American students because the law school for black students at Southern University was inferior.

Although he was initially reversed by the Fifth Circuit Court of Appeals (q.v.), Wright also ordered LSU to admit African American undergraduates for the same reason. Once the Supreme Court ruled in *Brown,* the Fifth Circuit returned this case to Wright's court and he reinstated his original order. His order to desegregate New Orleans's buses and parks won grudging compliance. Litigation over the desegregation of New Orleans's public schools had begun in 1952, but NAACP attorneys agreed with Wright's decision to delay a final decision in *Bush v. Orleans Parish School Board* (q.v.) pending a Supreme Court decision in *Brown.* After the Court had spoken, Wright became the first federal judge in the Fifth Circuit Court's jurisdiction to instruct a board of education to begin desegregation of the public schools "with all deliberate speed."

After repeated delays, in May 1960 Wright ordered the Orleans Parish school board to desegregate in September. With support from the Fifth Circuit Court and the Justice Department, he overcame the opposition of state and local officials who were determined to maintain segregated public schools. During the city's desegregation crisis, Wright became widely disliked in New Orleans's white community. His decisions supporting African American voting rights won him no friends in white Louisiana. Senator Russell Long's opposition to his nomination later prevented President Carter from naming Wright to the Fifth Circuit Court of Appeals. He was, instead, named to the Court of Appeals for the District of Columbia. J. Skelly Wright died on 6 August 1988 in Westmorland Hills, Maryland.

WYGANT v. JACKSON BOARD OF EDUCATION, 476 U.S. 267 (1986). A case in which the Supreme Court held that it was unconstitutional to lay off white teachers with greater seniority in order to preserve the positions of African American teachers.

The Jackson, Michigan, school board signed an agreement with its teachers' union which stipulated, in part, that if layoffs became necessary, white teachers with greater seniority would be fired before newly hired teachers, many of whom were African Americans. When layoffs occurred, Wendy Wygant and several other affected white teachers sued the board of education, claiming that the contract clause was a violation of their Fourteenth Amendment rights. The federal district court for Michigan's eastern district dismissed their complaint, insisting that such practices were necessary if the school district was to overcome years of discrimination. The Sixth Circuit Court of Appeals confirmed the district court's judgment. A divided United States Supreme Court overturned the lower courts' decision, however. Five justices, including Chief Justice Warren Burger and Justices Sandra Day O'Connor, Lewis Powell, William Rehnquist, and Byron White, submitted concurring opinions which held that the school board's interest in "providing minority faculty role models for its minority students" was insufficient reason to justify racial discrimination in the hiring or dismissal of teachers.

Y

YOUNG, ANDREW JACKSON (Andy; 1932–   ). Civil rights activist, clergyman, and politician.

Andrew J. Young was born on 12 March 1932 in New Orleans, Louisiana, the son of a dentist and his wife. Raised in a middle-class suburb of the city, Young and his younger brother attended both a segregated public and a private school, but they were protected from much of the harsh racism of the Deep South. After a year at Dillard University, Young transferred to Howard University where he graduated (B.S., 1951). Then, studying for the ministry, he completed his work at Hartford Theological Seminary (B.D., 1955). While traveling in the South in 1957, he met Martin Luther King (q.v.) who had recently organized the Southern Christian Leadership Conference (SCLC; q.v.). Young was ordained in the United Church of Christ and joined the staff of the National Council of Churches in 1957. Active in civil rights and interracial projects since his years in seminary, he joined the SCLC staff in 1961. Quickly proving his skill as director of its Citizenship Education Project and liaison to the media, Young succeeded Wyatt Walker (q.v.) as SCLC's executive director in 1964. He was active in its crusades from

Albany, Georgia, in 1961–62 to Memphis, Tennessee in 1968 and became its executive vice president in 1967.

After King's death, his successor, Ralph Abernathy (q.v.), appointed Young as his chief lieutenant. In 1970, Young resigned his positions with SCLC to make an unsuccessful race for Congress. Two years later, he won a second race for the House of Representatives, becoming the first African American to represent Georgia in Congress in a century. In Congress, he took an interest in African affairs and was a spokesman both for civil rights and environmental protection. Reelected in 1974 and 1976, Young played a significant role in Jimmy Carter's presidential campaign in 1976. He was appointed as the United States's ambassador to the United Nations by President Carter in 1977, the first African American to hold that position. Two years later, Young violated the public canons of American diplomacy by meeting with representatives of the Palestine Liberation Organization (PLO). Pressured by American Jewish organizations, President Carter asked for and received Young's resignation. He returned to Atlanta and was elected its mayor in 1981. As successor to Maynard Jackson, the first African American to hold the office, Young won reelection in 1985 and left the mayor's office in 1990 to make an unsuccessful bid for the Democratic nomination for governor of Georgia.

YOUNG, PLUMMER BERNARD (P. B.; 1884–1962). Newspaper editor and publisher.

P. B. Young was born on 27 July 1884 in Littleton, North Carolina, the son of Sally Adams Young and Winfield Young, a former slave. Inspired by the self-help philosophy of Booker T. Washington in the 1890s, Winfield Young launched a small weekly temperance newspaper, *The True Reformer.* on which his sons worked. From 1903 to 1905, P. B. Young attended St. Augustine College in Raleigh, North Carolina. He married Eleanor Louise White of Raleigh in 1906. In 1907, he moved to Norfolk, Virginia, and became the plant foreman for the Knights of Gideon's *Lodge Journal and Guide.* Three years later, Young bought the newspaper from the lodge and began publishing the *Norfolk Journal and Guide.* Despite a disastrous fire in 1913, Young built it into the most widely circulated African American newspaper in the South. Its masthead motto—"Build Up, Don't Tear Down"—reflected the conservative influence of Booker T. Washington on Young's journalism. During the 1930s, he abandoned a long affiliation with the Republican Party to become a Democrat. Appointed by President Franklin D. Roosevelt to the Fair

Employment Practice Committee (q.v.) in 1943, Young served two years in that position. In 1946, he turned primary responsibility for managing the newspaper over to his two sons. Young served on the board of trustees of Hampton Institute, Howard University, and Norfolk State University and was a founding officer of the Southern Regional Council.

YOUNG, WHITNEY MOORE, JR. (1921–71). Social worker and civil rights activist.

Whitney M. Young, Jr., was born on 31 July 1921 at Lincoln Ridge, Kentucky. His father was the president of Lincoln Institute, a private African American school founded when Berea College was forced by state law to exclude its African American students. His mother, Laura Ray Young, was a school teacher. Whitney Young, Jr., and his two sisters completed high school at Lincoln Institute. Planning to become a doctor, Young studied at Kentucky State Industrial College (B.S., 1941). After graduating, he was assistant principal and athletic coach at Julius Rosenwald High School in Madison, Kentucky. Drafted in 1942, Young studied engineering at Massachusetts Institute of Technology until 1944, when he was sent to Europe. He served in the all-black 369th Anti-Aircraft Artillery Group. Young's military experience drew him to racial diplomacy. After his military service, he earned a master's degree in social work from the University of Minnesota. Young served as industrial relations secretary of the St. Paul, Minnesota, branch of the National Urban League (q.v.) from 1948 to 1950 and director of the Urban League's branch in Omaha, Nebraska, from 1950 to 1954. In the latter position, he taught in the University of Nebraska's School of Social Work. In 1954, Young became dean of the School of Social Work at Atlanta University. He was on a leave of absence in the 1960–61 academic year as a visiting Rockefeller Foundation scholar at Harvard University.

In January 1961, the Urban League announced Young's appointment to succeed Lester B. Granger (q.v.) as its executive director. He began his new work in August 1961 and led the Urban League for ten years. Young moved the Urban League into a firmer alliance with the other major civil rights organizations. He was careful to retain the confidence of the League's powerful inside contacts, but he insisted that it join the March on Washington in 1963. Young's most important influence lay in his call for a domestic "Marshall Plan," outlined in his book, *To Be Equal*. His proposals influenced President Lyndon Johnson's War on Poverty. As the civil rights coalition frayed in 1966, Young and Roy Wilkins (q.v.) of the NAACP (q.v.) refused to sign the manifesto drafted by other civil rights leaders when they continued the march of James Meredith (q.v.) from Memphis, Tennessee, to Jackson, Mississippi. Young shunned the black power rhetoric popular with leaders of the Congress of Racial Equality (CORE; q.v.) and the Student Nonviolent Coordinating Committee (SNCC; q.v.), but he responded to the black power movement and urban violence in the late 1960s by concentrating Urban League resources on young people in the urban black underclass. At a conference on relations between Africa and the United States in Lagos, Nigeria, Young apparently had a heart attack while swimming in the Atlantic Ocean and drowned on 11 March 1971.

YOUNGE, SAMUEL, JR. (1944–66). Civil rights activist.
    Sammy Younge was born on 17 November 1944 in Tuskegee, Alabama. The 21-year-old student at Tuskegee Institute was a veteran of the United States Navy and SNCC (q.v.). As a SNCC volunteer in voter registration, Younge led 40 black people to the Macon County, Alabama, courthouse, where they were confronted by a knife-wielding registrar on 3 January 1966. That night, he stopped by a service station in Tuskegee to buy cigarettes and use the restroom. When the service station attendant, Marvin Segrest, directed Younge to a bathroom in the rear of the station, which Younge believed was reserved for African Americans, an argument ensued. Younge picked up a golf club and Segrest reached for his gun. As he backed away from the white man, Younge was fatally shot. It was the fifth fatality in the year-old Alabama voter registration drive. After black people marched through the rain to the site of Sammy Younge's death, Segrest was arrested and Mayor Charles Kever of Tuskegee promised that justice would be done "regardless of race." An all-white jury in Lee County, Alabama, found that Segrest had acted in self-defense and acquitted him of the murder of Sammy Younge.

YOUTH MARCHES FOR INTEGRATED SCHOOLS (1958, 1959). Two of the civil rights movement's five marches on Washington between 1957 and 1968.
    When the Eisenhower White House failed to respond to civil rights leaders' call for a White House Conference on Integration in 1958, A. Philip Randolph (q.v.) announced that a coalition of civil rights organizations would hold a "Youth March for Integrated Schools" with Martin Luther King (q.v.) as honorary chairman. When King was wounded by an assailant in September 1958, the Youth March was postponed from 11 October to 25 October. Roy Wilkins (q.v.) and other

NAACP (q.v.) officials chose not to participate in the Youth March. About 11,000 people, mostly college students, walked down Constitution Avenue in Washington, D.C., to the Lincoln Memorial, where the program featured Randolph, Jackie Robinson, Harry Belafonte, and Coretta Scott King, whose husband was still recovering from his injury.

Six months later, Randolph announced that a second Youth March for Integrated Schools would take place on 18 April. Spring weather and the presence of both Martin Luther King and Roy Wilkins made the second Youth March more successful than the first. About 26,000 people attended the second Youth March for Integrated Schools to hear speeches by Kenyan leader Tom Mboya, Randolph, Wilkins, and King. In his address, King won enthusiastic response from the crowd with his cry: "Give us the vote . . . Give us the vote." Planning for both Youth Marches was coordinated from New York by Bayard Rustin (q.v.). They were among the few events in the late 1950s that anticipated the burst of student protest in the sit-in movement (q.v.) and the Freedom Rides (q.v.) of the early 1960s.

Bibliography

Bibliographical Note

Like its leadership, the literature on the civil rights movement is the work of several overlapping generations. From the 1940s through the early 1970s, civil rights advocates and opponents generated a large body of primary literature about the movement. *We Challenged Jim Crow* (1947) by George Houser and Bayard Rustin, Martin Luther King's *Stride toward Freedom* (1958) and Anne Moody's *Coming of Age in Mississippi* (1968) are good examples of that work. It continued to grow as their memoirs, such as Roy Wilkins's *Standing Fast* (1982), James Farmer's *Lay Bare the Heart* (1985) or *Rosa Parks: My Story* (1992), appeared in subsequent decades. A first generation of scholarship on the issues which the movement addressed can be traced from Gunnar Myrdal and his associates' publication of *An American Dilemma* (1944) and other works.

A dozen efforts at a satisfactory one-volume survey of the movement, from Thomas R. Brooks's *Walls Came Tumbling Down* (1974) to Thomas R. West and James W. Mooney, eds., *To Redeem a Nation* (1993), have commonly failed to satisfy their readers' requirements, though Robert Weisbrot's *Freedom Bound* (1990) is perhaps the best of the lot. Other scholars, with more narrowly defined purposes, have published works of magisterial dimension. Studies of the movement's reshaping of civil rights law are particularly impressive. These include: Richard Kluger's *Simple Justice: The History of Brown v. Board of Education and Black America's Struggle for Equality* (1975), Michael R. Belknap's *Federal Law and Southern Order: Racial Violence and Constitutional Conflict in the Post-Brown South* (1987), and Mark V. Tushnet's two volumes: *The NAACP's Legal Strategy against Segregated Education, 1925–1950* (1987) and *Making Civil Rights Law: Thurgood Marshall and the Supreme Court, 1936–1961* (1994). Hugh Davis Graham's *The Civil Rights Era: Origins and Development of National Policy, 1960–1972* (1990) and Steven F. Lawson's two volumes, *Black Ballots: Voting Rights in the South, 1944–1969*

301

(1976) and *In Pursuit of Power: Southern Blacks and Electoral Politics, 1965–1982* (1985) are works of similar quality on their subjects.

The two Pulitzer Prize–winning biographies of Martin Luther King, Jr., David Garrow's *Bearing the Cross: Martin Luther King, Jr., and the Southern Christian Leadership Conference, A Personal Portrait* (1986) and Taylor Branch's *Parting the Waters: America in the King Years, 1954–1963* (1988), manifest the much criticized King-centric inclination of recent literature in the field. Both works are magisterial in conception, but in remarkably contrasting ways. Garrow's scrupulous accuracy of detail is achieved at the expense of literary grace; specialists easily find errors of detail in Branch's brilliant narrative. Two studies of King's rhetoric, Keith D. Miller's *Voice of Deliverance: The Language of Martin Luther King, Jr. and Its Sources* (1992) and Richard Lischer's *The Preacher King: Martin Luther King, Jr. and the Word that Moved America* (1995), contribute immeasurably to our understanding of its power. *The Papers of Martin Luther King* (1992–   ), edited by Clayborne Carson, Ralph E. Luker, and others, is the point of departure for future King scholarship.

The literature on the major civil rights organizations is uneven. August Meier and Elliott Rudwick's *CORE* (1973) and Clayborne Carson's *In Struggle* (1981) do justice to the Congress of Racial Equality and the Student Nonviolent Coordinating Committee. Beyond the two major King biographies, the Southern Christian Leadership Conference is well served by Adam Fairclough's *To Redeem the Soul of America* (1987) and Thomas R. Peake's *Keeping the Dream Alive* (1987). The standard histories of the National Urban League, Jesse Thomas Moore, Jr.'s *A Search for Equality* (1981), Guichard Parris and Lester Brooks's *Blacks in the City* (1971), and Arvarh E. Strickland's *History of the Chicago Urban League* (1966), do not carry its story into the 1960s. They must be supplemented by Nancy J. Weiss's *Whitney M. Young, Jr., and the Struggle for Civil Rights* (1989). The role of the National Association for the Advancement of Colored People is the large untold story. Among important allied organizations, the National Council of Churches is well represented by James Findlay's *Church People in the Struggle* (1993), but others, such as the American Civil Liberties Union, the American Friends Service Committee, the Fellowship of Reconciliation, the National Baptist Convention, the National Council of Negro Women, the National Lawyers Guild, and the United Automobile Workers, need critical attention.

Two "growth areas" in civil rights movement scholarship deserve special mention. The contributions of women to the movement were documented in Daisy Bates, *The Long Shadow of Little Rock* (1962), Septima Clark's *Echo in My Soul* (1962), Moody's *Coming of Age in Mississippi* (1968), and Coretta Scott King's *My Life With Martin Luther King, Jr.* (1969). They were powerfully represented in Sara Evans's *Personal Politics* (1979). Since then, interest in those contributions has been nurtured by Virginia Foster Durr, *Outside the Magic Circle* (1985), Mary King, *Freedom Song* (1987), Jo Anne Gibson Robinson, *The Montgomery Bus Boycott and the Women Who Started It* (1987), Vickie L. Crawford, et al., eds. *Women in the Civil Rights Movement: Trailblazers and Torchbearers, 1941–1965* (1990), Amelia Boynton Robinson, *Bridge across Jordan* (1991), Gayle J. Hardy, *American Women Civil Rights Activists* (1993), and Kay Mills, *This Little Light of Mine: The Life of Fannie Lou Hamer* (1993).

Much of what is yet to be learned about the civil rights movement will come from state and local studies. Several scholars published model local studies during the 1980s, such as William H. Chafe's *Civilities and Civil Rights: Greensboro, North Carolina and the Black Struggle for Freedom* (1980), David Colborn's *Racial Change and Community Crisis: St. Augustine, Florida, 1877–1980* (1985) and Robert J. Norrell's *Reaping the Whirlwind: The Civil Rights Movement in Tuskegee* (1985). In the subsequent decade, other scholars have produced model state studies: John Dittmer, *Local People: The Struggle for Civil Rights in Mississippi* (1994), Adam Fairclough, *Race and Democracy: The Civil Rights Struggle in Louisiana, 1915–1972* (1995) and Charles M. Payne, *I've Got the Light of Freedom: The Organizing Tradition and the Mississippi Freedom Struggle* (1995). We still know too little about the movement and the process of desegregation in the rural South. There are obvious local studies to be done in Atlanta and Nashville; and state studies in Alabama, Georgia, Virginia, and North and South Carolina.

Primary Sources

Abernathy, Ralph D., Sr. *And the Walls Came Tumbling Down: An Autobiography.* New York: Harper and Row, 1989.

Abram, Morris B. *The Day Is Short.* New York: Harcourt Brace Jovanovich, 1982.

Ahmann, Mathew, ed. *The New Negro.* Notre Dame, Indiana: Fides Publishers, 1961.

Allen, Ivan, Jr. *Mayor: Notes on the Sixties.* New York: Simon & Schuster, 1971.

Angelou, Maya. *The Heart of a Woman.* New York: Random House, 1981.

Baldwin, James. *The Fire Next Time.* New York: Dial Press, 1963.

Baraka, Amiri. *The Autobiography of LeRoi Jones/Amiri Baraka.* New York: Freundlich Books, 1984.

―――. *Kawaida Studies: The New Nationalism.* Chicago: Third World Press, 1972.

―――. *The LeRoi Jones/Amiri Baraka Reader.* William J. Harris, editor. New York: Thunder's Mouth Press, 1991.

Barbour, Floyd B., ed. *The Black Power Revolt: A Collection of Essays.* Boston: Porter Sargent, 1968.

Bates, Daisy. *The Long Shadow of Little Rock: A Memoir.* New York: David McKay Co., 1962.

Berry, Mary Frances. *Black Resistance/White Law: A History of Constitutional Racism in America.* New York: Appleton-Century-Crofts, 1971.

―――. *Military Necessity and Civil Rights Policy.* Port Washington, New York: Kennikat Press, 1977.

Bond, Julian. *Black Candidates: Southern Campaign Experiences.* Atlanta: Southern Regional Council, 1969.

Booth, William D. *The Progressive Story: New Baptist Roots.* St. Paul, Minnesota: Braun Press, 1981.

Bracey, John H., Jr., August Meier, and Elliott Rudwick, eds. *Black Nationalism in America.* Indianapolis: Bobbs-Merrill, 1970.

Breitman, George, ed. *By Any Means Necessary.* New York: Pathfinder Press, 1970.

Brown, Elaine. *A Taste of Power: A Black Woman's Story.* New York: Pantheon, 1993.

Brown, H. Rap. *Die, Nigger, Die.* New York: Dial Press, 1969.

Cannon, Poppy. *A Gentle Knight: My Husband, Walter White.* New York: Rinehart, 1956.

Carawan, Guy and Candie. *Freedom Is a Constant Struggle.* New York: Oak Publications, 1968.

Carmichael, Stokely. *Stokely Speaks: Black Power Back to Pan-Africanism.* New York: Random House, 1973.

―――. "Toward Black Liberation." *The Massachusetts Review* 7 (Autumn 1966): 639–51.

―――― and Charles V. Hamilton. *Black Power: The Politics of Liberation in America.* New York: Random House, 1967.

Carson, Clayborne, David J. Garrow, Gerald Gill, Vincent Harding, and Darlene Clark Hine, eds. *The Eyes on the Prize Civil Rights Reader: Documents, Speeches, and Firsthand Accounts from the Black Freedom Struggle, 1954–1990.* Boston: Blackside, Inc., 1991.

Carson, Clayborne, David J. Garrow, Vincent Harding, and Darlene Clark Hine, eds. *Eyes on the Prize: A Reader and Guide.* New York: Penguin, 1991.

Carson, Clayborne. *Malcolm X: The FBI File*. David Gallen, editor. New York: Carroll and Graf, 1991.

————, Ralph E. Luker, et al. *The Papers of Martin Luther King*. Berkeley: University of California Press, 1992– .

Chisholm, Shirley. *The Good Fight*. New York: Harper and Row, 1973.

————. *Unbought and Unbossed*. New York: Harper and Row, 1970.

Clark, James G. *The Jim Clark Story—I Saw Selma Raped*. Birmingham, Alabama: Selma Enterprises, 1966.

Clark, Kenneth B. *The Black Man in American Politics*. Washington, D.C.: Metropolitan Applied Research Center for the Institute for Black Elected Officials, 1969.

————. *The Negro Protest*. Boston: Beacon Press, 1963.

Clark, Septima P. *Echo in My Soul*. New York: E. P. Dutton & Co., 1962.

Cleage, Albert. *Black Christian Nationalism*. New York: Morrow, 1972.

Cleaver, Eldridge. *Eldridge Cleaver: Post-Prison Writings and Speeches*. Robert Scheer, ed. New York: Viking, 1969.

————. *Soul on Fire*. Waco, Texas: Word Books, 1978.

————. *Soul on Ice*. New York: McGraw-Hill, 1968.

Coffin, William Sloane, Jr. *Once to Every Man*. New York: Atheneum, 1977.

Cruse, Harold. *The Crisis of the Negro Intellectual*. New York: Quill, 1967.

Davis, Allison. *Leadership, Love, and Aggression*. New York: Harcourt, Brace, Jovanovich, 1983.

————. *Social-Class Influences upon Learning*. Cambridge, Massachusetts: Harvard University Press, 1948.

Davis, Angela. *Angela Davis: An Autobiography*. New York: Random House, 1974.

————. *If They Come in the Morning: Voices of Resistance*. New York: Third Press, 1971.

————. *Women, Culture and Politics*. New York: Vintage Books, 1990.

————. *Women, Race and Class*. New York: Random House, 1981.

Dees, Morris, with Steve Fiffer. *A Season for Justice: The Life and Times of Civil Rights Lawyer Morris Dees*. New York: Scribner's, 1991.

De Wolf, L. Harold. *A Hard Rain and a Cross*. Nashville, Tennessee: Abingdon Press, 1966.

Durr, Virginia Foster. *Outside the Magic Circle: The Autobiography of Virginia Foster Durr*. University: University of Alabama Press, 1985.

Edwards, Harry. *The Struggle That Must Be: An Autobiography*. New York: Macmillan, 1980.

Evans, Zelia S., with J. T. Alexander, eds. *Dexter Avenue Baptist Church, 1877–1977*. Montgomery, Alabama: Dexter Avenue Baptist Church, 1977.

Evers, Charles. *Evers*. New York: World Publishing Co., 1971.

Evers, Myrlie, with William Peters. *For Us the Living*. Garden City, New York: Doubleday, 1967.

Farmer, James. *Freedom—When?* New York: Random House, 1965.

———. *Lay Bare the Heart: An Autobiography of the Civil Rights Movement*. New York: Arbor House, 1985.

Fields, Uriah J. *The Montgomery Story: The Unhappy Effects of the Montgomery Bus Boycott*. New York: Exposition Press, 1959.

Foner, Philip S., ed. *The Black Panthers Speak*. Philadelphia: Lippincott, 1970.

Forman, James. *The Making of Black Revolutionaries*. New York: Macmillan, 1972.

———. *The Political Thought of James Forman*. Detroit: Black Star Publishing, 1970.

———. *Sammy Younge, Jr.: The First Black College Student to Die in the Black Liberation Movement*. New York: Grove Press, 1968.

Franklin, C. L. *Give Me This Mountain: Life History and Selected Sermons*. Edited by Jeff Todd Titon. Urbana: University of Illinois Press, 1989.

Gallen, David, et al. *Malcolm X: As They Knew Him*. New York: Carroll and Graf, 1992.

Grant, Joanne, ed. *Black Protest: History, Documents, and Analyses, 1619 to the Present*. Greenwich, Connecticut: Fawcett Books, 1968.

Graetz, Robert. *Montgomery—A White Preacher's Memoir*. Minneapolis, Minnesota: Fortress Press, 1991.

Gregory, Dick. *Dick Gregory's Political Primer*. James R. McGraw, editor. New York: Harper and Row, 1972.

———. *From the Back of the Bus*. Bob Orben, editor. New York: Avon Books, 1962.

———. *Nigger: An Autobiography*. New York: Dutton, 1964.

———. *No More Lies: The Myth and Reality of American History*. New York: Harper and Row, 1971.

———. *The Shadow That Scares Me*. James R. McGraw, editor. Garden City, New York: Doubleday, 1968.

———. *Up from Nigger*. New York: Stein and Day, 1976.

Haley, Alex. *Roots: The Saga of an American Family*. Garden City, New York: Doubleday, 1976.

Hampton, Henry, and Steve Fayer, eds. *Voices of Freedom: An Oral History of the Civil Rights Movement from the 1950s through the 1980s.* New York: Bantam Books, 1990.

Hansen, Carl F. *Danger in Washington: The Story of My Twenty Years in the Public Schools of the Nation's Capital.* West Nyack, New York: Parker Publishing Co., 1968.

Harding, Vincent. *Hope and History: Why We Must Share the Story of the Movement.* Maryknoll, New York: Orbis Books, 1990.

————. *The Other American Revolution.* Los Angeles: Center for Afro-American Studies, UCLA, 1980.

Harrington, Michael. *Fragments of the Century: A Social Autobiography.* New York: Saturday Review Press, 1973.

Heath, G. Louis, ed. *The Black Panthers Speak: Huey P. Newton, Bobby Seale, Eldridge Cleaver, and Companions Speak Out.* Metuchen, New Jersey: Scarecrow Press, 1976.

Hilliard, David, with Lewis Cole. *This Side of Glory: The Autobiography of David Hilliard and the Story of the Black Panthers.* New York: Little, Brown, 1993.

Holt, Len. *The Summer That Didn't End.* London: William Heinemann, 1965.

Horton, Myles, with Judith and Herbert Kohl. *The Long Haul: An Autobiography.* New York: Doubleday, 1990.

————, Brenda Bell, John Garenta, and John Marshall Peters. *We Make the Road by Walking: Conversations on Education and Social Change.* Philadelphia: Temple University Press, 1990.

Houser, George, and Bayard Rustin. *We Challenged Jim Crow.* New York: Fellowship of Reconciliation–Congress of Racial Equality, 1947.

Jackson, Jesse. *Keep Hope Alive.* Boston: South End Press, 1987.

————. *Straight from the Heart.* Minneapolis: Fortress Press, 1987.

————. *A Time to Speak: The Autobiography of Jesse Jackson.* New York: Simon and Schuster, 1988.

Jackson, Joseph H. *Unholy Shadows and Freedom's Holy Light.* Nashville, Tennessee: Townsend Press, 1967.

Jordan, Barbara, and Shelby Hearon. *Barbara Jordan: A Self-Portrait.* Garden City, New York: Doubleday, 1979.

Kennedy, Stetson. *Southern Exposure.* Boca Raton: Florida Atlantic University Press, 1991.

King, Coretta Scott. *My Life With Martin Luther King, Jr.* New York: Holt, Rinehart and Winston, 1969.

King, Martin Luther, Jr. *The Measure of a Man.* Philadelphia: Fortress Press, 1959.

————. *Strength to Love.* New York: Harper & Row, 1963.

————. *Stride toward Freedom: The Montgomery Story.* New York: Harper, 1958.

————. *The Trumpet of Conscience.* New York: Harper & Row, 1968.

————. *Where Do We Go From Here: Chaos or Community?* New York: Harper & Row, 1967.

————. *Why We Can't Wait.* New York: Harper & Row, 1964.

King, Martin Luther, Sr. *Daddy King: An Autobiography.* New York: William Morrow, 1980.

King, Mary. *Freedom Song: A Personal Story of the 1960s Civil Rights Movement.* New York: William Morrow, 1987.

Kunstler, William. *Deep in My Heart.* New York: William Morrow, 1966.

————. *Trials and Tribulations.* New York: Grove Press, 1985.

Lester, Julius. *All Is Well: An Autobiography.* New York: William Morrow, 1976.

————. *Falling Pieces of the Broken Sky.* New York: Arcade Publishing, 1968.

————. *Look Out Whitey! Black Power's Gon' Get Your Mamma.* New York: Dial Press, 1968.

————. *Lovesong: On Becoming a Jew.* New York: Henry Holt, 1988.

————. *Revolutionary Notes.* New York: Richard Baron Publishing, 1968.

————. *Search for a New Land: History as Subjective Experience.* New York: Dial Press, 1969.

————. *To Be a Slave.* New York: Dial Press, 1968.

Levy, Peter B., ed. *Documentary History of the Modern Civil Rights Movement.* Westport, Connecticut: Greenwood Press, 1992.

Lomax, Louis E. *The Negro Revolt.* New York: Harper & Brothers, 1962.

————. *To Kill a Black Man.* Los Angeles: Holloway House, 1968.

————. *When the Word Is Given: A Report on Elijah Muhammad, Malcolm X, and the Black Muslim World.* New York: Signet Books, 1963.

Lynd, Staughton, ed. *Nonviolence in America.* Indianapolis: Bobbs-Merrill, 1966.

Lyon, Danny. *Memories of the Southern Civil Rights Movement.* Chapel Hill: University of North Carolina Press, 1992.

Maddox, Lester. *Speaking Out: The Autobiography of Lester Garfield Maddox.* Garden City, New York: Doubleday, 1975.

Malcolm X, and Alex Haley. *The Autobiography of Malcolm X.* New York: Ballantine Books, 1965.

————. *Malcolm X: The Last Speeches.* Bruce Perry, editor. New York: Pathfinder Press, 1989.

————. *Malcolm X: Speeches at Harvard.* Archie Epps, editor. New York: W. Morrow, 1968.

————. *Malcolm X Speaks.* George Breitman, editor. New York: Grove Press, 1965.

Marshall, Burke. *Federalism and Civil Rights.* New York: Columbia University Press, 1964.

Mays, Benjamin E. *Born to Rebel.* New York: Charles Scribner's Sons, 1971.

McKissick, Floyd B. *Three-Fifths of a Man.* New York: Macmillan, 1969.

McLaurin, Melton A. *Separate Pasts: Growing Up White in the Segregated South.* Athens: University of Georgia Press, 1987.

Meier, August, and Elliott Rudwick, eds. *Black Protest in the Sixties.* Chicago: Quadrangle Books, 1970.

Meredith, James. *Three Years in Mississippi.* Bloomington: Indiana University Press, 1966.

Mitchell, Glenford E., and William H. Peace III, eds. *The Angry Black South.* New York: Corinth Books, 1962.

Moody, Anne. *Coming of Age in Mississippi.* New York: Dial Press, 1968.

Morgan, Charles, Jr. *One Man, One Voice.* New York: Holt, Rinehart & Winston, 1979.

Morrow, E. Frederic. *Black Man in the White House.* New York: Coward-McCann, 1963.

Myrdal, Gunnar. *An American Dilemma: The Negro Problem and Modern Democracy.* New York: Harper & Brothers, 1944.

Newfield, Jack. *A Prophetic Minority.* New York: New American Library, 1966.

Newton, Huey P. *Revolutionary Suicide.* New York: Harcourt Brace Jovanovich, 1973.

————. *To Die for the People: The Writings of Huey P. Newton.* New York: Vintage Books, 1972.

Nixon, Richard M. *Six Crises.* Garden City, New York: Doubleday, 1962.

O'Dell, Jack. "The FBI's Southern Strategies." In Bud and Ruth Schultz, eds. *It Did Happen Here: Recollections of Political Repression in America.* Berkeley: University of California Press, 1989: 279–88.

————. "Climbin' Jacob's Ladder: The Life and Times of the Freedom Movement." *Freedomways* 9 (Winter 1969): 7–23.

Parks, Rosa, with Jim Haskins. *Rosa Parks: My Story.* New York: Dial Books, 1992.

Peck, James. *Cracking the Color Line: Nonviolent Direct Action Methods of Eliminating Racial Discrimination.* New York: CORE, 1962.

————. *Freedom Ride.* New York: Simon & Schuster, 1962.

Peters, William. *The Southern Temper.* Garden City, New York: Doubleday, 1959.

Powell, Adam Clayton, Jr. *Adam by Adam: The Autobiography of Adam Clayton Powell, Jr.* New York: Dial Press, 1971.

President's Committee on Civil Rights. *To Secure These Rights.* Washington: U.S. Government Printing Office, 1947.

Raines, Howell, ed. *My Soul Is Rested: The Story of the Civil Rights Movement of the Deep South.* New York: G. P. Putnam's Sons, 1977.

Reddick, Lawrence D. *Crusader without Violence: A Biography of Martin Luther King, Jr.* New York: Harper and Brothers, 1959.

The Report of the National Advisory Commission on Civil Disorders. New York: Bantam Books, 1968.

Robinson, Amelia Boynton. *Bridge across Jordan.* Washington, D.C.: Schiller Institute, 1991.

Robinson, Jackie. *I Never Had It Made.* New York: G. P. Putnam's Sons, 1972.

Robinson, Jo Anne. *Abraham Went Out: A Biography of A. J. Muste.* Philadelphia: Temple University Press, 1981.

———. *The Montgomery Bus Boycott and the Women Who Started It.* Knoxville: University of Tennessee Press, 1987.

Rowan, Carl T. *Go South to Sorrow.* New York: Random House, 1957.

Rustin, Bayard. *Down the Line: The Collected Writings of Bayard Rustin.* Introduction by C. Vann Woodward. Chicago: Quadrangle Books, 1971.

———. *Strategies for Freedom: The Changing Pattern of Black Protest.* New York: Columbia University Press, 1976.

Salter, John R., Jr. *Jackson, Mississippi: An American Chronicle of Struggle and Schism.* Malabar, Florida: Robert E. Krieger Publishing Co., 1987.

Schneider, William J., ed. *The Jon Daniels Story, with His Letters and Papers.* New York: Seabury Press, 1967.

Seale, Bobby. *A Lonely Rage: The Autobiography of Bobby Seale.* New York: Bantam Books, 1978.

———. *Seize the Time: The Story of the Black Panther Party and Huey P. Newton.* New York: Random House, 1968.

Seay, Solomon Snowden, Sr. *I Was There by the Grace of God.* Montgomery, Alabama: The S. S. Seay, Sr. Educational Foundation, 1990.

Sellers, Cleveland, and Robert L. Terrell. *The River of No Return: The Autobiography of a Black Militant and the Life and Death of SNCC.* New York: William Morrow, 1973.

Shakur, Assata. *Assata: An Autobiography.* Westport, Connecticut: Lawrence Hill, 1987.

Smith, Kelly Miller. *Social Crisis Preaching*. Macon, Georgia: Mercer University Press, 1984.

Stokes, Carl B. *Promises of Power: A Political Autobiography*. New York: Simon & Schuster, 1973.

Sutherland, Elizabeth, ed. *Letters from Mississippi*. New York: McGraw-Hill, 1965.

Taylor, Gardner C. *How Shall They Preach*. Elgin, Illinois: Progressive Baptist Publishing House, 1977.

The "Trial" of Bobby Seale. New York: Priam Books, 1970.

Vivian, C. T. *Black Power and the American Myth*. Philadelphia: Fortress Press, 1970.

Vivian, Octavia. *Coretta*. Philadelphia: Fortress Press, 1970.

Walker, Wyatt Tee. *"Somebody's Calling My Name": Black Sacred Music and Social Change*. Valley Forge, Pennsylvania: Judson Press, 1979.

———. *The Soul of Black Worship*. New York: Martin Luther King Fellows Press, 1984.

Warren, Robert Penn. *Who Speaks for the Negro?* New York: Random House, 1965.

Washington, James Melvin, ed. *A Testament of Hope: The Essential Writings of Martin Luther King, Jr.* San Francisco: Harper and Row, 1986.

Webb, Sheyann, and Rachel West Nelson. *Selma, Lord, Selma*. University: University of Alabama Press, 1980.

White, Walter F. *A Man Called White*. New York: Viking Press, 1948.

Wilkins, Roger. *A Man's Life*. New York: Simon & Schuster, 1982.

Wilkins, Roy, with Tom Mathews. *Standing Fast: The Autobiography of Roy Wilkins*. New York: Viking Press, 1982.

———, and Ramsey Clark. *Search and Destroy*. New York: Harper and Row, 1973.

Wofford, Harris. *Of Kennedys and Kings: Making Sense of the Sixties*. New York: Farrar, Straus, and Giroux, 1980.

Wolff, Miles. *Lunch at the Five and Ten: The Greensboro Sit-Ins, A Contemporary History*. New York: Stein & Day, 1970.

Youth of the Rural Organizing and Cultural Center. *Minds Stayed on Freedom: The Civil Rights Struggles in the Rural South, an Oral History*. Boulder, Colorado: Westview Press, 1991.

Zinn, Howard. *SNCC: The New Abolitionists*. 2nd ed. Boston: Beacon Press, 1965.

———. *The Southern Mystique*. New York: Alfred A. Knopf, 1964.

Secondary Sources

Abraham, Henry J. *Freedom and the Court: Civil Rights and Liberties in the United States.* New York: Oxford University Press, 1988.

Acton, Jan, Alan Le Mond, and Parker Hodges. *Mug Shots: Who's Who in the New Earth.* New York: World Publishing Co., 1972.

Albert, Peter J., and Ronald Hoffmann, eds. *We Shall Overcome: Martin Luther King, Jr., and the Black Freedom Struggle.* New York: Pantheon Books, 1990.

Amaker, Norman C. *Civil Rights and the Reagan Administration.* Washington, D.C.: Urban Institute Press, 1988.

Anderson, Alan B., and George W. Pickering. *Confronting the Color Line: The Broken Promise of the Civil Rights Movement in Chicago.* Athens: University of Georgia Press, 1986.

Anderson, Jervis B. *A. Philip Randolph: A Biographical Portrait.* New York: Harcourt Brace Jovanovich, 1973.

Anderson, John W. *Eisenhower, Brownell, and the Congress: The Tangled Origins of the Civil Rights Bill of 1956–1957.* University: University of Alabama Press, 1964.

Ansbro, John J. *Martin Luther King, Jr.: The Making of a Mind.* Maryknoll, New York: Orbis Books, 1982.

Anthony, Earl. *Picking Up the Gun: A Report on the Black Panthers.* New York: Dial Press, 1970.

———. *Spitting in the Wind.* Santa Monica, California: Roundtable Pub., 1989.

Aptheker, Bettina. *The Morning Breaks: The Trial of Angela Davis.* New York: International Publishers, 1975.

Baker, Donald P. *Wilder: Hold Fast to Dreams, A Biography of L. Douglas Wilder.* Cabin John, Maryland: Seven Locks Press, 1989.

Bardolph, Richard, ed. *The Civil Rights Record: Black Americans and the Law, 1849–1970.* New York: Crowell, 1970.

Barkan, Steven E. *Protesters on Trial: Criminal Justice in the Southern Civil Rights and Vietnam War Movements.* New Brunswick, New Jersey: Rutgers University Press, 1985.

Barnes, Catherine A. *Journey from Jim Crow: The Desegregation of Southern Transportation.* New York: Columbia University Press, 1983.

Barrow, Deborah J., and Thomas G. Walker. *A Court Divided: The Fifth Circuit Court of Appeals and the Politics of Judicial Reform.* New Haven, Connecticut: Yale University Press, 1988.

Bartley, Numan V. *The Rise of Massive Resistance: Race and Politics in the South during the 1950s.* Baton Rouge: Louisiana State University Press, 1969.
———. *The New South, 1945–1980.* Baton Rouge: Louisiana State University Press, 1995.

Barton, Betty Lynn. "The Fellowship of Reconciliation: Pacifism, Labor, and Social Welfare, 1915–1960" (Ph.D. diss., Florida State University, 1974).

Bass, Jack. *Unlikely Heroes: The Dramatic Story of the Southern Judges of the Fifth Circuit Who Translated the Supreme Court's Brown Decision into a Revolution for Equality.* New York: Simon and Schuster, 1981.
———, and Jack Nelson. *The Orangeburg Massacre.* 2nd ed. Macon, Georgia: Mercer University Press, 1984.

Bechtel, Judith A., and Robert M. Coughlin. *Building the Beloved Community: Maurice McCrackin's Life for Peace and Civil Rights.* Philadelphia: Temple University Press, 1991.

Belknap, Michael R. *Federal Law and Southern Order: Racial Violence and Constitutional Conflict in the Post-Brown South.* Athens: University of Georgia Press, 1987.

Bell, Derrick A., Jr. *And We Are Not Saved: The Elusive Quest for Racial Justice.* New York: Basic Books, 1987.
———. *Faces at the Bottom of the Well: The Permanence of Racism.* New York: Basic Books, 1992.
———. *Race, Racism and American Law.* Boston: Little, Brown, 1973.

Bell, Inge Powell. *CORE and the Strategy of Nonviolence.* New York: Random House, 1968.

Bennett, Lerone, Jr. *What Manner of Man: A Biography of Martin Luther King, Jr.* Chicago: Johnson Publishing Co., 1968.

Berman, Daniel M. *A Bill Becomes a Law: Congress Enacts Civil Rights Legislation.* 2nd ed. New York: Macmillan, 1962.

Berman, William C. *The Politics of Civil Rights in the Truman Administration.* Columbus: Ohio State University Press, 1970.

Bernick, Michael S. "The Unusual Odyssey of J. Skelly Wright." *Hastings Constitutional Law Quarterly* 7 (1980): 971–99.

Berry, Brian J. L. *The Open Housing Question: Race and Housing in Chicago, 1966–1976.* Cambridge, Massachusetts: Ballinger Publishing Co., 1979.

Bigelow, Barbara Carlisle. *Contemporary Black Biography.* Detroit, Michigan: Gale Research Inc., 1992.

Billington, Monroe. "Freedom to Serve: The President's Committee on Equality of Treatment and Opportunity in the Armed Forces, 1949–1950." *Journal of Negro History* 51 (October 1951): 262–74.

Bloom, Jack M. *Class, Race, and the Civil Rights Movement.* Bloomington: Indiana University Press, 1987.

Blumberg, Rhoda Lois. *Civil Rights: The 1960s Freedom Struggle.* New York: Twayne Publishers, 1984.

Branch, Taylor. *Parting the Waters: America in the King Years, 1954–1963.* New York: Simon and Schuster, 1988.

Brauer, Carl M. *John F. Kennedy and the Second Reconstruction.* New York: Columbia University Press, 1977.

Bray, Rosemary L. "A Black Panther's Long Journey." *New York Times Magazine,* 31 January 1993, pp. 21–23, 26, 68, 76.

Breitman, George, Herman Porter, and Baxter Smith. *The Assassination of Malcolm X.* 3rd edition. New York: Pathfinder Press, 1991.

Brewer, William M. "The Poll Tax and the Poll Taxers." *Journal of Negro History* 29 (July 1944): 260–99.

Brooks, Thomas R. *Walls Come Tumbling Down: A History of the Civil Rights Movement, 1940–1970.* Englewood Cliffs, New Jersey: Prentice-Hall, 1974.

"Building Movements, Educating Citizens: Myles Horton and the Highlander Folk School." *Social Policy* 21 (Winter 1991): 2–79.

Bullard, Sara, ed. *Free at Last: A History of the Civil Rights Movement and Those Who Died in the Struggle.* New York: Oxford University Press, 1989.

Burk, Robert Frederick. *The Eisenhower Administration and Black Civil Rights.* Knoxville: University of Tennessee Press, 1984.

Burke, Joan Martin. *Civil Rights: A Current Guide to the People, Organizations, and Events.* New York: R. R. Bowker Company, 1974.

Burner, Eric R. *And Gently He Shall Lead Them: Robert Parris Moses and Civil Rights in Mississippi.* New York: New York University Press, 1994.

Burstein, Paul. *Discrimination, Jobs, and Politics: The Struggle for Equal Employment Opportunity in the United States since the New Deal.* Chicago: University of Chicago Press, 1985.

Button, James. *Black Violence: Political Impact of the 1960s Riots.* Princeton, New Jersey: Princeton University Press, 1978.

———. *Blacks and Social Change: Impact of the Civil Rights Movement on Southern Communities.* Princeton, New Jersey: Princeton University Press, 1987.

Cagin, Seth, and Philip Dray. *We Are Not Afraid: The Story of Goodman, Schwerner, and Chaney and the Civil Rights Campaign for Mississippi.* New York: Macmillan Publishing Company, 1988.

Carlson, Jody. *George C. Wallace and the Politics of Powerlessness—The Wallace Campaign for the Presidency, 1964–1970.* New Brunswick, New Jersey: Transaction Books, 1981.

Carson, Clayborne. *In Struggle: SNCC and the Black Awakening of the 1960s.* Cambridge, Massachusetts: Harvard University Press, 1981.

————. "Robert Parris Moses." In Bernard K. Johnpoll and Harvey Klehr, eds. *Biographical Dictionary of the American Left.* Westport, Connecticut: Greenwood Press, 1986: 280–281.

————. "Stokely Carmichael." In Bernard K. Johnpoll and Harvey Klehr, eds. *Biographical Dictionary of the American Left.* Westport, Connecticut: Greenwood Press, 1986: 66–67.

Cecelski, David S. *Along Freedom Road: Hyde County, North Carolina, and the Fate of Black Schools in the South.* Chapel Hill: University of North Carolina Press, 1994.

Chafe, William H. *Civilities and Civil Rights: Greensboro, North Carolina and the Black Struggle for Freedom.* New York: Oxford University Press, 1980.

————. *Never Stop Running: Allard Lowenstein and the Struggle to Save American Liberalism.* New York: Basic Books, 1993.

Chait, Richard Paul. "The Desegregation of Higher Education: A Legal History" (Ph.D. diss., University of Wisconsin, 1972).

Chappell, David L. *Inside Agitators: White Southerners in the Civil Rights Movement.* Baltimore: Johns Hopkins University Press, 1994.

Clark, E. Culpepper. *The Schoolhouse Door: Segregation's Last Stand at the University of Alabama.* New York: Oxford University Press, 1993.

Clarke, John Henrik, ed. *Malcolm X: The Man and His Times.* Trenton, New Jersey: Africa World Press, 1969.

Colburn, David R. *Racial Change and Community Crisis: St. Augustine, Florida, 1877–1980.* New York: Columbia University Press, 1985.

Combs, Michael W., and John Gruhl, eds. *Affirmative Action Theories, Analysis and Prospects.* Jefferson, North Carolina: McFarland & Co., 1986.

Cone, James H. *Martin & Malcolm & America: A Dream or a Nightmare.* Maryknoll, New York: Orbis, 1991.

Conot, Robert. *Rivers of Blood, Years of Darkness.* New York: William Morrow, 1968.

Cooper, Algia R. "*Brown v. Board of Education* and Virgil Darnell Hawkins: Twenty-Eight Years and Six Petitions to Justice." *Journal of Negro History* 64 (Winter 1979): 1–20.

Couch, Harvey C. *A History of the Fifth Circuit, 1891–1981.* Washington, D.C.: Bicentennial Committee of the Judicial Conference of the United States, 1981.

Crawford, Vickie L., et al., eds. *Women in the Civil Rights Movement: Trailblazers and Torchbearers, 1941–1965.* Brooklyn, New York: Carlson, 1990.

Dalfiume, Richard M. *Desegregation of the U.S. Armed Forces: Fighting on Two Fronts, 1939–1953.* Columbia: University of Missouri Press, 1969.

Daniel, Pete. *The Shadow of Slavery: Peonage in the South, 1909–1969.* Urbana: University of Illinois Press, 1972.

Davis, Lenwood G., and Marsha L. Moore, eds. *Malcolm X: A Selected Bibliography.* Westport, Connecticut: Greenwood Press, 1984.

Decker, Jeffrey Louis. *The Black Aesthetic Movement.* Detroit: Gale Research, 1991.

DeLeon, David, ed. *Leaders from the 1960s: A Biographical Sourcebook of American Activism.* Westport, Connecticut: Greenwood Publishing Company, 1994.

Dimond, Paul R. *Beyond Busing: Inside the Challenge to Urban Segregation.* Ann Arbor: University of Michigan Press, 1985.

Dionisopoulos, P. Allan. *Rebellion, Racism, and Representation: The Adam Clayton Powell Case and Its Antecedents.* DeKalb: Northern Illinois University Press, 1970.

Dittmer, John. *Local People: The Struggle for Civil Rights in Mississippi.* Urbana: University of Illinois Press, 1994.

Donald, Cleveland, Jr. "Medger Wylie Evers: The Civil Rights Leader as Utopianist." In Dean Faulkner Wells and Hunter Cole, eds. *Mississippi Heroes.* Jackson: University Press of Mississippi, 1971.

Douglas, Davison M. *Reading, Writing, and Race: The Desegregation of Charlotte Schools.* Chapel Hill: University of North Carolina Press, 1995.

Downing, Fred L. *To See the Promised Land: The Faith Pilgrimage of Martin Luther King, Jr.* Macon, Georgia: Mercer University Press, 1986.

Draper, Theodore. *The Rediscovery of Black Nationalism.* New York: Viking Press, 1970.

Duberman, Martin Bauni. *Paul Robeson.* New York: Alfred A. Knopf, 1988.

Dulaney, W. Marvin, and Kathleen Underwood, eds. *Essays on the Civil Rights Movement.* College Station: Texas A & M University Press, 1993.

Dulles, Foster Rhea. *The Civil Rights Commission: 1957–1965.* East Lansing: Michigan State University Press, 1968.

Dunbar, Anthony. *Against the Grain: Southern Radicals and Prophets, 1929–1959.* Charlottesville: University Press of Virginia, 1981.

Dunston, Aingred G. "Black Struggle for Equality in Winston-Salem, North Carolina: 1947–1977" (Ph.D. diss., Duke University, 1981).

Eagles, Charles, ed. *The Civil Rights Movement in America.* Jackson: University Press of Mississippi, 1986.

———. *Outside Agitator: Jon Daniels and the Civil Rights Movement in Alabama.* Chapel Hill: University of North Carolina Press, 1993.

Edds, Margaret. *Claiming the Dream: The Victorious Campaign of Douglas Wilder of Virginia.* Chapel Hill: Algonquin Books, 1990.

Egerton, John. *Speak Now against the Day: The Generation before the Civil Rights Movement in the South.* New York: Alfred A. Knopf, 1994.

Essien-Udom, Essien. *Black Nationalism: A Search for Identity in America.* Chicago: University of Chicago Press, 1962.

Evans, Sara. *Personal Politics.* New York: Alfred A. Knopf, 1979.

Fager, Charles E. *Selma, 1965: The March That Changed the South.* New York: Charles Scribner's Sons, 1974.

————. *Uncertain Resurrection: The Poor People's Washington Campaign.* Grand Rapids, Michigan: William B. Eerdmans, 1969.

————. *White Reflections on Black Power.* Grand Rapids, Michigan: William B. Eerdmans, 1967.

Fairclough, Adam. "Historians and the Civil Rights Movement." *Journal of American Studies* 24 (December 1990): 387–98.

————. *Martin Luther King, Jr.* Athens: University of Georgia Press, 1995.

————. *Race and Democracy: The Civil Rights Struggle in Louisiana, 1915–1972.* Athens: University of Georgia Press, 1995.

————. *To Redeem the Soul of America: The Southern Christian Leadership Conference and Martin Luther King, Jr.* Athens: University of Georgia Press, 1987.

Fender, Stephen, and Michael Heale, eds. "Civil Rights and Student Protest." *Journal of American Studies* 22 (April 1988).

Fendrich, James Max. *Ideal Citizens: The Legacy of the Civil Rights Movement.* Albany: State University of New York Press, 1993.

Findlay, James F., Jr. *Church People in the Struggle: The National Council of Churches and the Black Freedom Movement, 1950–1970.* New York: Oxford University Press, 1993.

Fleming, Cynthia Griggs. "Black Women Activists and the Student Nonviolent Coordinating Committee: The Case of Ruby Doris Smith Robinson." *Journal of Women's History* 4 (Winter 1993): 64–82.

Fogelson, Robert M. *Violence as Protest.* Garden City, New York: Doubleday, 1971.

Franklin, Jimmie Lewis. *Back to Birmingham: Richard Arrington and His Times.* Tuscaloosa: University Press of Alabama, 1989.

Franklin, John Hope, and August Meier, eds. *Black Leaders of the Twentieth Century.* Urbana: University of Illinois Press, 1982.

Freed, Donald. *Agony in New Haven: The Trial of Bobby Seale, Ericka Huggins, and the Black Panther Party.* New York: Simon and Schuster, 1973.

Freyer, Tony. *The Little Rock Crisis: A Constitutional Interpretation.* Westport, Connecticut: Greenwood Press, 1984.

Garfinkel, Herbert. *When Negroes March: The March on Washington Movement in the Organizational Politics for FEPC.* Glencoe, Illinois: Free Press, 1959.

Garrow, David J. "Bayard Rustin." In Bernard K. Johnpoll and Harvey Klehr, eds. *Biographical Dictionary of the American Left.* Westport, Connecticut: Greenwood Press, 1986: 337–39.

―――. *Bearing the Cross: Martin Luther King, Jr., and the Southern Christian Leadership Conference, A Personal Portrait.* New York: William Morrow, 1986.

―――. *The FBI and Martin Luther King, Jr.: From 'Solo' to Memphis.* New York: W. W. Norton, 1981.

―――, ed. *Martin Luther King, Jr., and the Civil Rights Movement.* 18 vols. Brooklyn, New York: Carlson, 1989.

―――. *Protest at Selma: Martin Luther King, Jr., and the Voting Rights Act of 1965.* New Haven, Connecticut: Yale University Press, 1978.

Gentile, Thomas. *March on Washington: August 28, 1963.* Washington, D.C.: New Day Publications, 1983.

Gerber, David. "Haley's *Roots* and Our Own: An Inquiry into the Nature of a Popular Phenomenon." *Journal of Ethnic Studies* 3 (1977): 87–111.

Geschwender, James A., ed. *The Black Revolt.* Englewood Cliffs, New Jersey: Prentice-Hall, 1971.

Giddings, Paula. *When and Where I Enter.* New York: William Morrow, 1984.

Gillon, Steven M. *Politics and Vision: The ADA and American Liberalism, 1947–1985.* New York: Oxford University Press, 1987.

Gilpin, Patrick J. "Charles S. Johnson: An Intellectual Biography." (Ph.D. diss., Vanderbilt University, 1973).

―――. "Charles S. Johnson and the Southern Educational Reporting Service." *Journal of Negro History* 63 (July 1978): 197–208.

―――. "Charles S. Johnson: Scholar and Educator." *Negro History Bulletin* 39 (March 1976): 544–48.

Gitlin, Todd. *The Sixties: Years of Hope, Days of Rage.* New York: Bantam Books, 1987.

Glen, John. *Highlander: No Ordinary School.* Lexington: University Press of Kentucky, 1988.

Goldfield, David R. *Black, White, and Southern: Race Relations and Southern Culture, 1940 to the Present.* Baton Rouge: Louisiana State University Press, 1990.

Goldman, Peter. *The Death and Life of Malcolm X.* Second edition. Urbana: University of Illinois Press, 1979.

Graham, Hugh Davis. *The Civil Rights Era: Origins and Development of National Policy, 1960–1972.* New York: Oxford University Press, 1990.

Greenberg, Jack. *Race Relations and American Law.* New York: Columbia University Press, 1959.

Greene, Kathanne W. *Affirmative Action and Principles of Justice.* New York: Greenwood Press, 1989.

Grossman, Mark. *The ABC-CLIO Companion to the Civil Rights Movement.* Santa Barbara, California: ABC-CLIO, 1993.

Haddad, Yvonne Y., ed. *Muslims of America.* New York: Oxford University Press, 1991.

Haines, Herbert H. *Black Radicals and the Civil Rights Movement, 1954–1970.* Knoxville: University of Tennessee Press, 1988.

Hamilton, Charles V. *Adam Clayton Powell, Jr.: The Political Biography of an American Dilemma.* New York: Macmillan, 1991.

Hardy, Gayle J. *American Women Civil Rights Activists.* Jefferson, North Carolina: McFarland & Company, 1993.

Harris, Fred R., and Roger W. Wilkins, eds. *Quiet Riots: Race and Poverty in the U.S., The Kerner Report Twenty Years Later.* New York: Pantheon Books, 1988.

Harvey, James C. *Black Civil Rights during the Johnson Administration.* Jackson: University and College Press of Mississippi, 1973.

Hauser, Thomas. *Muhammad Ali: His Life and Times.* New York: Simon and Schuster, 1991.

Hawkins, Walter L. *African American Biographies.* Jefferson, North Carolina: McFarland & Co., Inc., 1993.

Haygood, Wil. *King of the Cats: The Life and Times of Adam Clayton Powell, Jr.* Boston: Houghton Mifflin Company, 1993.

Heath, G. Louis. *Off the Pigs! The History and Literature of the Black Panther Party.* Metuchen, New Jersey: Scarecrow Press, 1976.

Hilton, Bruce. *The Delta Ministry.* New York: Macmillan, 1969.

Hine, Darlene Clark. *Black Victory: The Rise and Fall of the White Primary in Texas.* Millwood, New York: KTO Press, 1979.

———, ed. *Black Women in America.* 2 vols. Brooklyn, New York: Carlson Publishing Inc., 1993.

Horne, Gerald. " 'Myth' and the Making of 'Malcolm X'." *American Historical Review* 98 (April 1993): 440–50.

Hughes, C. Alvin. "A New Agenda for the South: The Role and Influence of Highlander Folk School, 1953–1961." *Phylon* 46 (September 1985): 242–50.

Huie, William Bradford. *Three Lives for Mississippi.* New York: WCC Books, 1964.

Inger, Morton. *Politics and Reality in an American City: The New Orleans School Crisis of 1960.* New York: Center for Urban Education, 1969.

Jacoway, Elizabeth, and David R. Colburn, eds. *Southern Businessmen and Desegregation.* Baton Rouge: Louisiana State University Press, 1982.

Jenkins, Betty L., and Susan Phillis, eds. *The Black Separatism Controversy: An Annotated Bibliography.* Westport, Connecticut: Greenwood Press, 1976.

Johnson, Timothy V. *Malcolm X: A Complete Annotated Bibliography.* New York: Garland Publishing, 1986.

Kaufman, Jonathan. *Broken Alliance: The Turbulent Times between Blacks and Jews in America.* New York: Scribner, 1988.

Kelleher, Daniel T. "The Case of Lloyd Lionel Gaines: The Demise of the 'Separate-but-Equal' Doctrine." *Journal of Negro History* 56 (October 1971): 262–71.

Kellogg, Charles F. *NAACP: A History of the National Association for the Advancement of Colored People.* Baltimore: Johns Hopkins University Press, 1967.

Kennedy, Robert F., Jr. *Judge Frank M. Johnson, Jr.* New York: G. P. Putnam's Sons, 1978.

Kirby, John B. *Black Americans in the Roosevelt Era.* Knoxville: University of Tennessee Press, 1980.

Klibaner, Irwin. "The Travail of Southern Radicals: The Southern Conference Educational Fund, 1946–1976." *Journal of Southern History* 49 (May 1983): 179–202.

Kluger, Richard. *Simple Justice: The History of Brown v. Board of Education and Black America's Struggle for Equality.* 2 vols. New York: Alfred A. Knopf, 1975.

Krueger, Thomas A. *And Promises to Keep: The Southern Conference for Human Welfare, 1938–1948.* Nashville: Vanderbilt University Press, 1967.

Lacey, Henry C. *To Raise, Destroy, and Create: The Poetry, Drama, and Fiction of Imamu Amiri Baraka.* Troy, New York: Whitston, 1981.

Lawson, Steven F. *Black Ballots: Voting Rights in the South, 1944–1969.* New York: Columbia University Press, 1976.

———. "Freedom Then, Freedom Now: The Historiography of the Civil Rights Movement." *American Historical Review* 96 (April 1991): 456–71.

———. *In Pursuit of Power: Southern Blacks and Electoral Politics, 1965–1982.* New York: Columbia University Press, 1985.

———. *Running for Freedom: Civil Rights and Black Politics in America since 1941.* Philadelphia: Temple University Press, 1990.

Lefberg, Irving. "Chief Justice Vinson and the Politics of Desegregation." *Emory Law Journal.* 24 (1975): 243–312.

Lerner, Gerda, ed. *Black Women in White America.* New York: Pantheon, 1972.

Levy, Leonard Williams. *Jim Crow in Boston: The Origin of the Separate but Equal Doctrine.* New York: Da Capo Press, 1974.

Lewis, David L. *King: A Critical Biography.* New York: Praeger, 1970.

Lincoln, C. Eric, ed. *Martin Luther King, Jr.: A Profile.* rev. ed. New York: Hill & Wang, 1970.

Lipsitz, George. *A Life in the Struggle: Ivory Perry and the Culture of Opposition.* Philadelphia: Temple University Press, 1988.

Lischer, Richard. *The Preacher King: Martin Luther King, Jr. and the Word that Moved America.* New York: Oxford University Press, 1995.

Logan, Rayford W., and Michael R. Winston, eds. *Dictionary of American Negro Biography.* New York: W. W. Norton, 1982.

Longenecker, Stephen L. *Selma's Peacemaker: Ralph Smeltzer and Civil Rights Mediation.* Philadelphia: Temple University Press, 1987.

Low, Augustus W. *Encyclopedia of Black America.* New York: Da Capo Press, Inc., 1981.

Lowery, Charles D., and John F. Marszalek. *Encyclopedia of African-American Civil Rights: From Emancipation to the Present.* Westport, Connecticut: Greenwood Press, 1992.

Luker, Ralph E. "Martin Luther King, Jr." In Charles H. Lippy, ed. *Twentieth Century Shapers of American Popular Religion.* Westport, Connecticut: Greenwood Press, 1989: 217–25.

———. "Martin Luther King, Jr., and the Modern Civil Rights Movement." In Randall M. Miller and Paul A. Cimbala, eds. *American Reform and Reformers: A Biographical Dictionary.* Westport, Connecticut: Greenwood Press, 1995: 301–15.

———. "Racial Matters: Civil Rights and Civil Wrongs." *American Quarterly* 43 (March 1991): 165–71.

MacGregor, Morris J. *Integration of the Armed Forces, 1940–1965.* Washington, D.C.: Center of Military History, 1981.

Marable, Manning. *Black American Politics: From the Washington Marches to Jesse Jackson.* Revised edition. New York: Routledge, Chapman and Hall, 1991.

———. *From the Grassroots.* Boston: South End Press, 1980.

———. *Race, Reform and Rebellion: The Second Reconstruction in Black America, 1945–1982.* Jackson: University Press of Mississippi, 1984.

Marsh, Clifton E. *From Black Muslims to Muslims: The Transition from Separatism to Islam, 1930–1980.* Metuchen, New Jersey: Scarecrow Press, 1984.

Martin, Robert F. *Howard Kester and the Struggle for Social Justice in the South, 1904–1977.* Charlottesville: University Press of Virginia, 1991.

Mayer, Michael S. "The Eisenhower Administration and the Desegregation of Washington, D.C." *Journal of Policy History* 3 (January 1991): 24–41.

McAdam, Doug. *Freedom Summer.* New York: Oxford University Press, 1988.

———. *Political Process and the Development of Black Insurgency, 1930–1970.* Chicago: University of Chicago Press, 1982.

McCartney, John T. *Black Power Ideologies: An Essay in African-American Political Thought.* Philadelphia: Temple University Press, 1992.

McGuire, Philip. *He, Too, Spoke for Democracy: Judge Hastie, World War II, and the Black Soldier.* New York: Greenwood Press, 1988.

McMillen, Neil R. "Black Enfranchisement in Mississippi: Federal Enforcement and Black Protest in the 1960s." *Journal of Southern History* 43 (August 1977): 351–72.

———. *Citizens' Council: Organized Resistance to the Second Reconstruction, 1954–64.* Urbana: University of Illinois Press, 1971.

———. *Dark Journey: Black Mississippians in the Age of Jim Crow.* Urbana: University of Illinois Press, 1989.

McNeill, Genna Rae. *Groundwork: Charles Hamilton Houston and the Struggle for Civil Rights.* Philadelphia: University of Pennsylvania Press, 1983.

Meier, August, and David Lewis. "History of the Negro Upper Class in Atlanta, Georgia, 1890–1958." *Journal of Negro Education* 28 (Spring 1958): 128–59.

Meier, August, and Elliott Rudwick. *Along the Color Line: Explorations in the Black Experience.* Urbana: University of Illinois Press, 1973.

———. *CORE: A Study in the Civil Rights Movement.* New York: Oxford University Press, 1973.

———. "The First Freedom Ride." *Phylon* 30 (Fall, 1969): 213–22.

Mendelson, Jack. *The Martyrs: Sixteen Who Gave Their Lives for Racial Justice.* New York: Harper & Row, 1966.

Metcalf, George R. *From Little Rock to Boston: The History of School Desegregation.* Westport, Connecticut: Greenwood Press, 1983.

Miller, Arthur Selwyn. *A "Capacity for Outrage": The Judicial Odyssey of J. Skelly Wright.* Westport, Connecticut: Greenwood Press, 1984.

Miller, Keith D. *Voice of Deliverance: The Language of Martin Luther King, Jr. and Its Sources.* New York: Free Press, 1992.

Miller, Loren. *The Petitioners: The Story of the Supreme Court of the United States and the Negro.* New York: Pantheon Books, 1966.

Miller, William R. *Martin Luther King, Jr.* New York: Weybright & Talley, 1968.

Mills, Kay. *This Little Light of Mine: The Life of Fannie Lou Hamer.* New York: Dutton, 1993.

Mills, Nicolaus. *Like a Holy Crusade: Mississippi 1964—The Turning Point of the Civil Rights Movement in America.* Chicago: Ivan R. Dee, 1992.

Moore, Gilbert. *A Special Rage.* New York: Harper and Row, 1971.

Moore, Jesse Thomas, Jr. *A Search for Equality: The National Urban League, 1910–1961.* University Park: Pennsylvania State University Press, 1981.

Morehead, Caroline. *Troublesome People: The Warriors of Pacifism.* Washington, D.C.: Adler and Adler, 1987.

Morris, Aldon. "Black Southern Student Sit-In Movement: An Analysis of Internal Organization." *American Sociological Review* 46 (December, 1981): 744–67.

———. *The Origins of the Civil Rights Movement: Black Communities Organizing for Change.* New York: Free Press, 1984.

Murphy, Paul L. *The Constitution in Crisis Times, 1918–1969.* New York: Harper and Row, 1972.

Murray, Paul T. *The Civil Rights Movement: References and Resources.* Boston: G. K. Hall, 1993.

Muse, Benjamin. *The American Negro Revolution: From Nonviolence to Black Power, 1963–1967.* Bloomington: Indiana University Press, 1968.

Nadelson, Regina. *Who Is Angela Davis? The Biography of a Revolutionary.* New York: P. H. Wyden, 1972.

Navasky, Victor S. *Kennedy Justice.* New York: Atheneum, 1971.

Neary, John. *Julian Bond: Black Rebel.* New York: William Morrow, 1971.

Norrell, Robert J. *Reaping the Whirlwind: The Civil Rights Movement in Tuskegee.* New York: Alfred A. Knopf, 1985.

Nossiter, Adam. *Of Long Memory: Mississippi and the Murder of Medgar Evers.* Reading, Massachusetts: Addison-Wesley, 1994.

Oates, Stephen B. *Let the Trumpet Sound: The Life of Martin Luther King, Jr.* New York: Harper and Row, 1982.

O'Reilly, Kenneth. *"Racial Matters": The FBI's Secret File on Black America, 1960–1972.* New York: Free Press, 1989.

———. "The FBI and the Civil Rights Movement during the Kennedy Years—From the Freedom Rides to Albany." *Journal of Southern History* 54 (May 1988): 201–32.

Padgett, Gregory B. "C. K. Steele and the Tallahassee Bus Boycott" (M.A. thesis, Florida State University, 1977).

Paris, Peter J. *Black Leaders in Conflict.* New York: Pilgrim Press, 1978.

Parker, Frank R. *Black Votes Counts: Political Empowerment in Mississippi after 1965.* Chapel Hill: University of North Carolina Press, 1990.

Parker, J. A. *Angela Davis: The Making of a Revolutionary.* New Rochelle, New York: Arlington House, 1973.

Parris, Guichard, and Lester Brooks. *Blacks in the City: A History of the National Urban League.* Boston: Little, Brown, 1971.

Payne, Charles M. "Ella Baker and Models of Social Change." *Signs* 14 (Summer 1989): 885–99.

———. *I've Got the Light of Freedom: The Organizing Tradition and the Mississippi Freedom Struggle.* Berkeley: University of California Press, 1995.

Peake, Thomas R. *Keeping the Dream Alive: A History of the Southern Christian Leadership Conference from King to the Nineteen-Eighties.* New York: P. Lang, 1987.

Peeks, Edward. *The Long Struggle for Black Power.* New York: Charles Scribner's Sons, 1971.

Peltason, J. W. *Fifty-Eight Lonely Men: Southern Federal Judges and School Desegregation.* Urbana: University of Illinois Press, 1961.

Perry, Bruce. *Malcolm: The Life of a Man Who Changed Black America.* Barry Town, New York: Station Hill Press, Inc., 1991.

Pfeffer, Paula. *A. Philip Randolph: Pioneer of the Civil Rights Movement.* Baton Rouge: Louisiana State University Press, 1990.

Pinkney, Alphonso. *Red, Black, and Green. Black Nationalism in the United States.* New York: Cambridge University Press, 1976.

Porter, Horace A. *Stealing the Fire: The Art and Protest of James Baldwin.* Middletown, Connecticut: Wesleyan University Press, 1989.

Powledge, Fred. *Black Power—White Resistance.* Cleveland, Ohio: World Publishing, 1967.

———. *Free at Last? The Civil Rights Movement and the People Who Made It.* Boston: Little, Brown, 1991.

Pratt, Louis H. *James Baldwin.* Boston: Twayne Publishers, 1978.

Pritchett, C. Herman. *Civil Liberties and the Vinson Court.* Chicago: University of Chicago Press, 1954.

Rabby, Glenda A. "Out of the Past: The Civil Rights Movement in Tallahassee, Florida" (Ph.D. diss., Florida State University, 1984).

Ralph, James R., Jr. *Northern Protest: Martin Luther King, Jr., Chicago, and the Civil Rights Movement.* Cambridge, Massachusetts: Harvard University Press, 1993.

Read, Frank T., and Lucy S. McGough. *Let Them Be Judged: The Judicial Integration of the Deep South.* Metuchen, New Jersey: Scarecrow Press, 1978.

Record, Wilson. *Race and Radicalism: The NAACP and the Communist Party in Conflict.* Ithaca, New York: Cornell University Press, 1964.

Reed, Adolph, Jr. *The Jesse Jackson Phenomenon: Crisis of Purpose in Afro-American Politics.* New Haven: Yale University Press, 1986.

————, ed. *Race, Politics and Culture: Critical Essays on the Radicalism of the 1960s.* Westport, Connecticut: Greenwood Press, 1986.

Reynolds, Barbara A. *Jesse Jackson: The Man, the Movement, the Myth.* Chicago: Nelson-Hall, 1985.

Robinson, Armstead L., and Patricia Sullivan, eds. *New Directions in Civil Rights Studies.* Charlottesville: University Press of Virginia, 1991.

Rogers, Kim Lacy. *Righteous Lives: Narratives of the New Orleans Civil Rights Movement.* New York: New York University Press, 1993.

Rothschild, Mary Aickin. *A Case of Black and White: Northern Volunteers and the Southern Freedom Summers, 1964–1965.* Westport, Connecticut: Greenwood Press, 1982.

Rout, Kathleen. *Eldridge Cleaver.* Boston: Twayne Publishers, 1991.

Ruchames, Louis. *Race, Jobs, & Politics: The Story of FEPC.* New York: Columbia University Press, 1953.

Rustin, Bayard. "A. Philip Randolph." *Yale Review* 76 (Spring 1987): 418–27.

Salem, Dorothy C., ed. *African American Women: A Biographical Dictionary.* New York: Garland Publishing, 1993.

Salley, Columbus. *The Black 100.* New York: Carol Publishing Group, 1993.

Salmond, John A. *Conscience of a Lawyer: Clifford J. Durr and American Civil Liberties, 1899–1975.* Tuscaloosa: University of Alabama Press, 1990.

Schulke, Flip, ed. *Martin Luther King, Jr.: A Documentary—Montgomery to Memphis.* New York: W. W. Norton, 1976.

————, and Penelope McPhee. *King Remembered.* New York: W. W. Norton, 1986.

Shapiro, Herbert. *White Violence and Black Response from Reconstruction to Montgomery.* Amherst: University of Massachusetts Press, 1988.

Sheehey, Gail. *Panthermania: The Clash of Black against Black in One American City.* New York: Harper and Row, 1971.

Sitkoff, Harvard. *The Struggle for Black Equality, 1954–1980.* 2d ed. New York: Hill and Wang, 1981.

————. *A New Deal for Blacks: The Emergence of Civil Rights as a National Issue.* New York: Oxford University Press, 1978.

Smith, Charles U., ed. *The Civil Rights Movement in Florida and the United States.* Tallahassee, Florida: Father and Son Publishing, 1989.

————, and Lewis M. Killian, *The Tallahassee Bus Protest*. New York: Anti-Defamation League of B'nai B'rith, 1958.

Smith, Jessie Carney, ed. *Notable Black American Women*. Detroit, Michigan: Gale Research, 1992.

Smith, Kenneth L., and Ira G. Zepp, Jr. *Search for the Beloved Community: The Thinking of Martin Luther King, Jr.* Valley Forge, Pennsylvania: Judson Press, 1974.

Smith, Robert Collins. *They Closed Their Schools: Prince Edward County, Virginia, 1951–1964*. Chapel Hill: University of North Carolina Press, 1965.

Snow, Melinda. "Martin Luther King's 'Letter from Birmingham Jail' as Pauline Epistle." *Quarterly Journal of Speech* 71 (August 1985): 318–34.

Sollors, Werner. *Amiri Baraka/LeRoi Jones: The Quest for a "Populist Modernism."* New York: Columbia University Press, 1978.

Sosna, Morton. *In Search of the Silent South: Southern Liberals and the Race Issue*. New York: Columbia University Press, 1977.

Southern, David W. *Gunnar Myrdal and Black-White Relations: The Use and Abuse of An American Dilemma, 1944–1969*. Baton Rouge: Louisiana State University Press, 1987.

Stern, Mark. *Calculating Visions: Kennedy, Johnson, and Civil Rights*. New Brunswick, New Jersey: Rutgers University Press, 1992.

Stevenson, Janet. *The Montgomery Bus Boycott*. New York: Franklin Watts, 1971.

Strickland, Arvarh E. *History of the Chicago Urban League*. Urbana: University of Illinois Press, 1966.

Strong, Donald S. *Negroes, Ballots and Judges: National Voting Rights Legislation in the Federal Courts*. University: University of Alabama Press, 1968.

Suggs, Henry Lewis. *P. B. Young Newspaperman: Race, Politics, and Journalism in the New South, 1910–1963*. Charlottesville: University Press of Virginia, 1988.

————. "Black Strategy and Ideology in the Segregation Era; P. B. Young and the *Norfolk Journal and Guide*, 1910–1954." *Virginia Magazine of History and Biography* 91 (April 1983): 161–90.

————. "P. B. Young of the Norfolk Journal and Guide: A Booker T. Washington Militant, 1904–1928." *Journal of Negro History* 64 (Fall 1979): 365–76.

Thernstrom, Abigail M. *Whose Votes Count? Affirmative Action and Minority Voting Rights*. Cambridge, Massachusetts: Harvard University Press, 1987.

Thornton, J. Mills, III. "Challenge and Response in the Montgomery Bus Boycott of 1955–1956." *Alabama Review* 33 (July 1980): 163–235.

Tucker, David M. *Black Pastors and Leaders: Memphis, 1819–1972.* Memphis: Memphis State University Press, 1975.

Tushnet, Mark V. *Making Civil Rights Law: Thurgood Marshall and the Supreme Court, 1936–1961.* New York: Oxford University Press, 1994.

———. *The NAACP's Legal Strategy against Segregated Education, 1925–1950.* Chapel Hill: University of North Carolina Press, 1987.

Urquhart, Brian. *Ralph Bunche: An American Life.* New York: W. W. Norton, 1993.

Van Deburg, William L. *New Day in Babylon: The Black Power Movement and American Culture, 1965–1975.* Chicago: University of Chicago Press, 1992.

Viorst, Milton. *Fire in the Streets: America in the 1960's.* New York: Simon & Schuster, 1979.

Vose, Clement E. *Caucasians Only: The Supreme Court, the NAACP, and the Restrictive Covenant Cases.* Berkeley: University of California Press, 1959.

Wagy, Tom R. *Governor LeRoy Collins of Florida: Spokesman of the New South.* University: University of Alabama Press, 1985.

Waldron, Ann. *Hodding Carter: The Reconstruction of a Racist.* Chapel Hill, North Carolina: Algonquin Books, 1993.

Walker, Jack L. *Sit-Ins in Atlanta.* New York: McGraw-Hill, 1964.

Walters, Ronald. *Black Presidential Politics in America: A Strategic Approach.* Albany: SUNY Press, 1988.

———. *Pan Africanism in the African Diaspora: An Analysis of Modern Afrocentric Political Movements.* Detroit, Michigan: Wayne State University Press, 1992.

Walton, Norman A. "The Walking City, A History of the Montgomery Bus Boycott." *Negro History Bulletin* 20 (October 1956–April 1957): 17–21, 27–33, 102–4, 147–52, 166.

Ware, Gilbert. *William Hastie: Grace under Pressure.* New York: Oxford University Press, 1984.

Waskow, Arthur I. *From Race Riot to Sit-In, 1919 and the 1960s: A Study in the Connections between Conflict and Violence.* Garden City, New York: Doubleday, 1966.

Watters, Pat. *Down to Now: Reflections on the Southern Civil Rights Movement.* New York: Pantheon Books, 1971.

———, and Reese Cleghorn. *Climbing Jacob's Ladder.* New York: Harcourt, Brace & World, 1967.

Weatherby, William J. *James Baldwin: Artist on Fire, A Portrait.* New York: D. I. Fine, 1989.

Weinberg, Jack. "Students and Civil Rights in the 1960s." *History of Education Quarterly* 30 (Summer 1990): 213–24.

Weisbrot, Robert. *Freedom Bound: A History of America's Civil Rights Movement.* New York: W. W. Norton, 1990.

Weiss, Nancy J. *Whitney M. Young, Jr., and the Struggle for Civil Rights.* Princeton, New Jersey: Princeton University Press, 1989.

West, Thomas R., and James W. Mooney, eds. *To Redeem a Nation: A History and Anthology of the Civil Rights Movement.* St. James, New York: Brandywine Press, 1993.

Westin, Alan F., and Barry Mahoney, *The Trial of Martin Luther King.* New York: Thomas Y. Crowell, 1974.

Whalen, Charles and Barbara. *The Longest Debate: A Legislative History of the 1964 Civil Rights Act.* Cabin John, Maryland: Seven Locks Press, 1985.

White, Robert Melvin. "The Tallahassee Sit-Ins and CORE: A Nonviolent Revolutionary Submovement" (Ph.D. diss., Florida State University, 1964).

Whitfield, Stephen J. *A Death in the Delta: The Story of Emmett Till.* New York: Free Press, 1988.

Wilkerson, J. Harvie. *From Brown to Bakke: The Supreme Court and School Integration, 1954–1978.* New York: Oxford University Press, 1979.

Williams, Juan. *Eyes on the Prize: America's Civil Rights Years, 1954–1965.* New York: Viking Press, 1987.

Williams, Roger M. *The Bonds: An American Family.* New York: Atheneum, 1971.

Wilmore, Gayraud S. *Black Religion and Black Radicalism: An Interpretation of the Religious History of Afro-American People.* 2nd. ed. Maryknoll, New York: Orbis Books, 1983.

Wolters, Raymond. *The Burden of Brown: Thirty Years of School Desegregation.* Knoxville: University of Tennessee Press, 1984.

———. *Negroes and the Great Depression.* Westport, Connecticut: Greenwood Publishing Corp., 1970.

Wood, Joe, ed. *Malcolm X: In Our Own Image.* New York: St. Martin's Press, 1992.

Woodward, Comer Vann. *The Strange Career of Jim Crow.* New York: Oxford University Press, 1955.

Worthy, Barbara A. "The Travail and Triumph of a Southern Black Civil Rights Lawyer: The Legal Career of Alexander Pierre Tureaud, 1899–1972" (Ph.D. diss., Tulane University, 1984).

Yancey, Dwayne. *When Hell Froze Over: The Untold Story of Doug Wilder, a Black Politician's Rise to Power in the South.* Dallas, Texas: Taylor Publishing Co., 1988.

Yarbrough, Tinsley E. *John Marshall Harlan: Great Dissenter of the Warren Court.* New York: Oxford University Press, 1992.

————. *Judge Frank Johnson and Human Rights in Alabama.* University: University of Alabama Press, 1981.

————. *A Passion for Justice: J. Waties Waring and Civil Rights.* New York: Oxford University Press, 1987.

Yeakey, Lamont H. "The Montgomery, Alabama, Bus Boycott, 1955–56," (Ph.D. diss., Columbia University, 1979).

Zangrando, Robert L. *The NAACP Crusade against Lynching, 1909–1950.* Philadelphia: Temple University Press, 1980.

About the Author

Ralph E. Luker was born in Louisville, Kentucky, in 1940. He was active in the civil rights movement as an undergraduate at Duke University, where he graduated in 1962. He earned a B.D. at Drew University in 1966 and M.A. and Ph.D. degrees at the University of North Carolina, Chapel Hill, in 1969 and 1973. He has held faculty appointments in history and religion at Allegheny College, Antioch College, Lincoln University, and Virginia Polytechnic Institute. He is currently an adjunct professor of history at Morehouse College.

Luker is the author of *The Social Gospel in Black and White: American Racial Reform, 1885–1912,* which won the Kenneth Scott Latourette Prize and was named an Outstanding Book of 1991 by the Gustavus Myers Center for the Study of Human Rights. His work on Volumes I and II of *The Papers of Martin Luther King* was nominated for the Pulitzer Prize. Luker's articles have appeared in *American Quarterly, Church History,* the *Journal of American History,* the *Journal of Negro History,* the *New England Quarterly, Slavery and Abolition,* the *South Atlantic Quarterly, Southern Studies,* the *Virginia Quarterly Review,* and elsewhere.